Handbook of
# HAWAIIAN FISHES

# Handbook of
# HAWAIIAN FISHES

William A. Gosline and Vernon E. Brock

**THE UNIVERSITY PRESS OF HAWAII**
Honolulu

First printing, 1960
Second printing, 1965
Third printing, 1971
Fourth printing, 1976

Library of Congress Catalog Card Number 58-11692
ISBN 0-87022-302-X
Manufactured in the United States of America

# Contents

# 1. Introduction

It is probable that the Hawaiians of Captain James Cook's time knew more about the fishes of their islands than is known today. Most of this information has now been lost. The first integrated effort to summarize modern knowledge of these fishes was made in 1905. In that year, one volume on Hawaiian deep-water fishes (Gilbert) and another on the shallow-water forms (Jordan and Evermann) appeared.

As the history of work on Hawaiian deep-water fishes is short, it may be dealt with first. Gilbert's 1905 report takes up the 111 species from Hawaiian waters "living at depths of 100 fathoms or more" known up to that time. All, except a few lantern fishes, were taken by a dredge or trawl hauled along the bottom. The report on these fishes has never been superseded. Indeed, no serious deep-water dredging has been done around the Hawaiian Islands since.

Such additions as have subsequently been made to our knowledge of deep-water fishes have come from three sources. First, hand-lining in fairly deep water has procured a few species previously unknown. Second, two of the lava flows that have entered the sea have brought up fish from undetermined, but apparently considerable, depths. Only seven species were collected from the lava flow of 1919 (Jordan, 1922). Far more intensive efforts were made to collect the fishes killed by the 1950 flow (Gosline, Brock, Moore, and Yamaguchi, 1954). The collections obtained however, have been only partially reported (Gosline, 1954; Haig, 1955). The third source of material is that collected by plankton nets and mid-water trawls in connection with the tuna work of the Pacific Oceanic Fishery Investigations. Practically none of this has been worked up as yet. Though these newer sources of Hawaiian deep-water fishes rarely provide additional material for the bottom species all too often described by Gilbert from a single specimen, they do open up the possibility of making Hawaii one of the best-known areas in the world so far as a well-rounded knowledge of deep-water fishes is concerned.

As for the inshore fishes, the first fact to be noted is that any dividing line that can be drawn at present between these and the deep-water forms is purely arbitrary. In general, the depth of Hawaiian waters increases fairly evenly and rapidly away from shore, and there is no bordering shelf the edge of which can be used as a limit for the inshore fishes. What are considered here as inshore fishes are merely those on the shore side of the maximum depth fished by trap and hand-line fishermen; this depth lies well within the 100-fathom boundary.

In 1905 Jordan and Evermann, who in their introduction summarized the scattered previous work on Hawaiian inshore fishes, recognized 441 species. Their material consisted chiefly of forms collected in the market plus the fishes taken on the reefs in 1889 by O. P. Jenkins. Jordan and Evermann had one advantage over later workers in that the number of species entering the markets in their day was far higher than at any period since. Their work, though now both out of date and out of print, remains the one basic reference book on Hawaiian fishes.

Between 1905 and 1948 fish-collecting around Hawaii was carried on in a rather desultory manner. A number of minor papers resulted (e.g., Pietschmann, 1938, etc.); most of these describe a few new species and new or rare records. A few larger works require special notice. Jordan continued his interest in Hawaiian fishes and published two check lists. The earlier (1922) came out with Eric Knight Jordan as coauthor. The later (1926), written with Evermann, lists 547 species of inshore and surface-living Hawaiian fishes.

In 1928 Fowler published his large tome on "The Fishes of Oceania." This is mostly a compilation of bibliographic references to the fishes recorded from "Oceania," including Hawaii, and as such it is very useful. Where Fowler had specimens of the species treated he recorded notes regarding them. Unlike Jordan and Evermann, Fowler gives no keys and very few adequate descriptions. Three supplements to this work (1931, 1934, and 1948) have since been published. Fowler has a different philosophical interpretation concerning the taxonomic status of many Hawaiian fishes than that of Jordan and Evermann. In the slang of taxonomy, Jordan and Evermann tended to be "splitters" whereas Fowler in this instance is very definitely a "lumper"; many of the fishes recognized by Jordan and Evermann as endemic Hawaiian species have been synonymized by Fowler with species described from elsewhere. One cannot avoid the feeling that this difference in interpretation is largely due to the fact that Jordan and Evermann were looking at fishes whereas Fowler was primarily undertaking the very treacherous chore of evaluating literature records. In any event, the names used by Jordan and Evermann and by Fowler for the same Hawaiian fish are very frequently different.

In 1944 Tinker published a guide to Hawaiian fishes. Though it contains no keys and no descriptions it does have a very large number of illustrations. It has proved a very popular and useful little book.

The present handbook deals with 584 species of native Hawaiian fishes, together with some 15 species that are not yet known north of Johnston Island. Another 30 or so have been intentionally introduced to Hawaiian waters. Among the fresh-water introductions many, particularly on Oahu, have been released by aquarists in recent years and several are now thriving.

Of the native species, 136 may be classed, according to the definition given above, as deep-water forms. Many of these described by Gilbert represent forms we have never seen. Our accounts of the deep-water fishes are therefore, generally, carried only to the family level, though references to the individual species may be found in Appendix B.

This leaves 448 inshore or surface-living fishes, all of which are keyed out to species. For each a short account is also given. We have tried to base our information on Hawaiian material, and in this connection collections have been amassed at the University of Hawaii. Even so, we have been forced to base all too many accounts on literature references. Many of the species described by Jordan and Evermann from market material are now unobtainable. Sometimes this is because there is no longer any fishery for these. In other instances, notably in the case of sharks, the species, at least on the high Hawaiian islands, seem to have been fished down to a relatively low level.

In general, our own collections have been based on fishes taken in rotenone poison stations. We have collected in shallow water on most of the islands of the Hawaiian chain (see inset in endpapers). It is probably safe to say that there are very few Hawaiian fishes habitually living in the upper 20 feet of inshore water that remain unrecorded. With the help of aqualung diving gear we have also collected sporadically at depths up to 75 feet. Most of the species added by us to the known Hawaiian fish fauna have come from these deeper-water collections. Much, however, remains to be done even at these depths; though most of the larger species have probably been recorded by now, many smaller forms undoubtedly remain unknown. Below the 100-foot level our knowledge of Hawaiian fishes diminishes rapidly to practically the vanishing point.

Regarding the scientific names, we have followed those of Schultz, *et al.* (1953) wherever possible. Until such time as the Central Pacific fishes can be compared with material from the rest of the tropical Indo-Pacific, no nomenclature used for our fishes can be final. However, it will be many a year before such comparisons can be made; in the meantime the names provided by Schultz, *et al.* are the most up to date we have. It is consequently obvious that whatever scientific nomenclature we use here will eventually become as obsolete as the names in Jordan and Evermann now are. However, our primary concern is not with names but with zoological entities. In the discrimination of these we have had one great advantage over those who have worked in the Central Pacific before us: as inhabitants of the area of which we write, we are not restricted to the information obtainable from the preserved specimens that happen to be at hand. Repeated checking of data obtained from preserved specimens has indicated that perhaps the greatest need in the taxonomy of Central Pacific fishes today is more adequate biological knowledge.

At present it is only rarely possible to identify more than the adult stage of our species. Identification of the juveniles of many is a dubious undertaking, and the basis for determining the larval phases of most of our fishes is almost nonexistent. But even with the adults, repeated observation in the field has shown that all too much of our present species classification is erroneous. In the first place, many of our hitherto recognized species have been based on color differences that merely represent variants of one sort or another (cf., Chapter IV). Though color has been a chief source of ichthyological confusion in the Central Pacific, it is not the only one. Morphological characters sometimes show similar, though usually less conspicuous, variation. The eel *Moringua macrochir* may be cited as an extreme example. The females of this

**3**

species on reaching maturity transform morphologically to such an extent that different phases of maturation have been allocated to four different species; the males of what is almost certainly the same species have been placed in a different genus (see Gosline and Strasburg, 1956). Though a few errors of this sort have now been discovered, more undoubtedly remain uncorrected. Indeed, knowledge of the biology of most Hawaiian fishes remains rudimentary.

## BIBLIOGRAPHY

FOWLER, H. W.

    1928. *The Fishes of Oceania.* Mem. Bishop Mus. Vol. 10. iii + 540 pp., 49 pls., 82 figs.

    1931. *The Fishes of Oceania.* Supplement 1. Mem. Bishop Mus. Vol. 11, No. 5. Pp. 313–381, figs. 1–7.

    1934. *The Fishes of Oceania.* Supplement 2. Mem. Bishop Mus. Vol. 11, No. 6. Pp. 385–466, figs. 1–4.

    1949. *The Fishes of Oceania.* Supplement 3. Mem. Bishop Mus. Vol. 12, No. 2. Pp. 37–186.

GILBERT, C. H.

    1905. *The Aquatic Resources of the Hawaiian Islands. Section II. The Deep-sea Fishes.* Bul. U. S. Fish Comm., 1903. Vol. 23. Pp. i–viii + 577–713, pls. 66–101, figs. 230–276.

GOSLINE, W. A.

    1954. Fishes killed by the 1950 eruption of Mauna Loa. II. Brotulidae. *Pacific Sci.* 8(1): 68–83, figs. 1–3.

GOSLINE, W. A., V. E. BROCK, H. L. MOORE, and Y. YAMAGUCHI.

    1954. Fishes killed by the 1950 eruption of Mauna Loa. I. The origin and nature of the collections. *Pacific Sci.* (8)1: 23–27, figs. 1–3.

GOSLINE, W. A., and D. W. STRASBURG.

    1956. The Hawaiian fishes of the family Moringuidae: another eel problem. *Copeia* 1956: 9–18, figs. 1–3.

HAIG, J.

    1955. Fishes killed by the 1950 eruption of Mauna Loa. III. Sternoptychidae. *Pacific Sci.* 9(3): 318–323.

JORDAN, D. S.

    1922. Description of deep-sea fishes from the coast of Hawaii, killed by a lava flow from Mauna Loa. *U. S. Nat. Mus., Proc.* 59: 643–658, figs. 1–8.

JORDAN, D. S., and B. W. EVERMANN.

    1905. *The Aquatic Resources of the Hawaiian Islands. Part I. The Shore Fishes.* U. S. Bur. Fisheries, Bul. for 1903. Vol. 23. Pp. i–xxviii + 574, 73 col. pls., 65 black and white pls., 229 figs.

    1926. A check list of the fishes of Hawaii. *Jour. Pan-Pacific Research Institute,* 1: 3–15.

JORDAN, D. S., and E. K. JORDAN.

    1922. *A list of fishes of Hawaii, with notes and descriptions of new species.* Mem. Carnegie Mus. Vol. 10, No. 1. Pp. 1–92, pls. 1–4.

PIETSCHMANN, V.

    1938. *Hawaiian Shore Fishes.* Bul. Bishop Mus. 156. Pp. 55, 18 pls., 13 figs.

SCHULTZ, L. P., *et al.*

    1953. *Fishes of the Marshall and Marianas Islands.* Vol. I. U. S. Nat. Mus., Bul. 202. Pp. i–xxxii + 1–685, pls. 1–74, figs. 1–90.

TINKER, S. W.

    1944. *Hawaiian Fishes.* Honolulu: Tongg Publishing Co. Pp. 403, 8 pls., text figs.

# 2. Ecology of Hawaiian Fishes

We are here concerned with the community of fishes in the sea, their inter-relationships, and their relationship to their environment. In discussing these matters, it is convenient to group the fishes by habitat. There are three major subdivisions of the marine habitat considered here, which are, insofar as boundaries are concerned, somewhat arbitrary: open sea (pelagic), bottom (benthic), and inshore or reef. (See Fig. 1.) The open-sea habitat comprises a

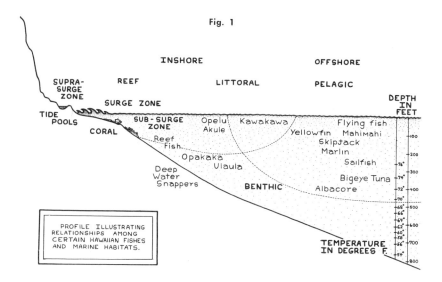

Fig. 1

warm surface isothermal zone (epipelagic) which is ordinarily less than a hundred fathoms deep, and the water below this where the temperature falls rapidly with increasing depth (bathypelagic). The bathypelagic habitat will not be considered in detail here. The discussion of the bottom habitat is restricted to an area of sea floor between 30 and 150 fathoms. Fishes from depths greater than this are grouped into archebenthic and abyssal and are beyond the scope of this book. The inshore or reef habitat is that area of sea floor from the upper surge pools to 30 fathoms. Each of these three

5

habitats supports a characteristic assemblage of fish species, and each can be further divided into subhabitats, the number of such minor divisions which might be considered being perhaps a reflection of the amount of detailed knowledge available concerning these habitats rather than of the variation found within the habitats themselves.

## THE OPEN-SEA HABITAT

The most salient characteristic of this habitat is its seeming uniformity. The upper 100 to 600 feet of water of the open tropical ocean, because of the stirring effect of the trade winds, usually exhibits little variation in temperature or chemical composition. It is difficult to conceive, except in the bathypelagic zone, of a more uniform environment in its physical aspects than that of the epipelagic region of the open tropical ocean. The light intensity does, of course, diminish from the upper to the lower portions of this isothermal layer but less rapidly than for any other geographic area considered here, since Hawaii is a region of maximum clarity of water.

The fish fauna of the open sea has, relative to the other major subdivisions of the marine habitat, few species. These forms are characterized by the ability to live indefinitely in independence of the sea floor or of nearby land masses. All kinds important as food fish are predators (if only on zooplankton), seem to possess keen vision, and are able to swim rapidly for long periods.

Aside from the malolo (flying fish), which attaches its eggs to floating objects such as seabird feathers, the other pelagic species of fish, so far as is known, lay and fertilize numerous small eggs in the sea itself where they drift until hatching. The number of eggs which may be produced by a large tuna or a marlin at a spawning is very great. For example, a 154-pound striped marlin (*Makaira audax*) landed in Honolulu had one ripe ovary weighing 32.2 pounds and filled with loose eggs calculated to number some 13,800,000. The eggs in the other ovary, which weighed only 7.5 pounds, were not ripe.

The newly hatched young of these pelagic species are utterly different from the adult, being as a rule, tiny transparent larvae with conspicuous dark eyes.

Some of the fishes of the pelagic zone are commonly seen and taken in the surface water—all those species which are taken by trolling, for example. Such fishes as malolo (flying fish), mahimahi (dolphin), ahi (yellowfin tuna), aku (skipjack tuna), a'u (marlins), ono (wahoo), and kaku (barracuda) occur at the surface. Other pelagic species such as albacore, bigeye tuna, and broadbill swordfish occur very infrequently in the surface waters but are taken in the Hawaiian area by longline gear which fishes at depths of 20 fathoms or more. Additionally, migrants from even deeper-water layers occur in the surface waters at night. Lantern fishes and squids are commonly found, for example, at the surface of the open ocean during the hours of darkness, but are not in evidence during the day.

Many of the young of reef and inshore fishes are found in the pelagic zone. While in some cases the occurrence of these youthful stages in the waters of the open sea may be the chance effect of current drift sweeping small fish with limited swimming powers away from a normal inshore habitat, the young of some reef fishes such as surgeonfishes, goatfishes, and eels possess certain characteristics which may represent adaptations for an open sea existence. Of course, the abundance of such youthful stages of inshore fishes is greatest near inshore areas from whence they presumably come.

Mention should be made of an inshore pelagic (neritic) zone which may be defined as the upper-water layers where the depth is 100 fathoms or less. This area may contain at times many of the completely pelagic species; additionally, several species are to a major extent restricted to it. The akule, 'opelu, and kawakawa are examples of such species. This zone is of small extent in the Hawaiian Islands; it is of major importance off many continental areas.

## THE BOTTOM (BENTHIC) HABITAT

Compared to both the pelagic and reef habitats, this region is poorly known. Judging from certain characteristics of the fisheries for species which live in this habitat, they are, like those of the reef and unlike those of the open ocean, oriented to a fixed locale, to physical features of the bottom itself. They may, therefore, be subjected rather more than the purely pelagic species to fluctuations in water temperatures, salinities, and thereby fluctuations in food supply. For example, the thickness of the isothermal surface layer of water is strongly influenced by the velocity and duration of the wind. Frequently the trade winds tend to be less vigorous in the fall months and consequently the isothermal layer may be only 100 to 150 feet thick. Water temperatures at a depth of 400 feet during this time may be as low as 68°F. Yet, during periods of heavy trades, the isothermal layer may exceed 400 feet in thickness and water temperatures at this depth may then rise to 78° or 80°F. if such heavy trade winds occur during the latter half of the summer. Additionally, there is some evidence of the existence of internal waves at the thermocline, i.e., at the interface of the warm surface waters and the cooler layers beneath. Some measurements of the magnitude of these waves indicate that they may approach 100 feet in height. Such subsurface waves may, where they impinge on the bottom, send surges of cool water into areas that would otherwise be well above the thermocline. Fishes living at a depth of 400 feet may therefore be subjected to temperature variations of 10° to 12°F. While pelagic species could encounter temperature variations of this magnitude by ranging down from the surface, available evidence regarding the way in which they respond to their environment would indicate that they would not remain at a particular depth or in a given locale if the physical environment became unfavorable. The reef species, while apparently tied to a fixed habitat, are not subjected to temperature fluctuation of this magnitude in the southern part of the Hawaiian chain, since inshore shallow-water temperatures ordinarily range from 75° to 80°F.—a difference of 5°. Of course, fish in tide pools are sometimes subjected to relatively great temperature changes and salinities.

Benthic fish do not live in a reef environment, since that environment seems to disappear at depths of 120 to 180 feet. Where adjacent to a steep slope rising within 80 feet or less of the surface, the bottom may be largely composed of bleached coral fragments. Where the slope is less, coral sand may cover the sea floor, and especially off dry lee areas, such as Kekaha on Kauai or Kaunakakai on Molokai, a thick soft mud bottom occurs. Mud bottoms are not productive of bottom-fish species of commercial importance; such fish seem to be most abundant in areas where a precipitous change in depth occurs, i.e., adjacent to the face of a submarine cliff or in rocky areas generally.

## THE INSHORE OR REEF HABITAT

This region, like the benthic, is limited in extent in the Hawaiian Islands. These islands are the peaks of mountains of sufficient size to reach not only to the surface of an ocean some 12,000 to 18,000 feet in depth, but for Mauna Loa and Mauna Kea on Hawaii, to rise over 13,000 feet above sea level. Since the shallow-water areas are located on the side of these mountainous masses, they are no more than narrow encircling bands. However, should the point where the surface of the sea impinges on the slope remain stable for extended periods of time the effects of wave erosion would create terraces that should, in turn, permit the formation of coral reefs. The geological evidence, according to Stearns (1946), indicates that since the emergences of these volcanic peaks in the Tertiary, there has been a complex series of emergences and submergences, some up to 1200 feet below present sea level. These have been so frequent that little reef was laid down and very little cliffing accomplished. Additionally, there may have been periods when sea-water temperatures were too low for the formation of coral reefs. Air temperatures were less during some periods in the past as indicated by evidence of glaciation on Mauna Kea.

Hence, coral-reef platforms or barriers are not numerous, and shallow-water areas where coral is dominant constituted only about one third of the areas surveyed during the submarine-fish transects by the Hawaiian Fish and Game Division (Brock, 1954b). However, in the areas and depths where reef-building coral can flourish, a characteristic associated fish fauna occurs. Below the depth to which reef-building corals prosper, a fish fauna containing other species occurs; many of the species found in the reef proper also occur here too. Additionally, the dominant coral species and their associated fishes in windward and leeward areas of the same island differ. Insofar as this difference is associated with the occurrence of particular species of fish, the discussion of the matter is covered in the account of that species. However, some of the differences of a general character are properly discussed in this section. We may, therefore discuss zonation on the basis of horizontal distribution—one side of an island as compared to another, and vertical distribution, that is, with depth. There exists some interaction between these general categories, since the vertical and horizontal distributions are meaningful only in that they are in turn associated with the physical and chemical forces that shape the environment. Such forces are the degree of wave action, chemical character of the water flowing on or by reefs, amount of light which ordinarily varies with depth, and nature of the sea floor and of the adjacent land. The effect of land is largely through the volume and character of fresh water that may enter the sea.

8

The abundant Hawaiian coral-reef species are members of certain inshore warm-water families, such as the butterfly fishes (Chaetodontidae), surgeonfishes (Acanthuridae), surmullets (Mullidae), squirrelfishes (Holocentridae), moray eels (Muraenidae), and wrasses (Labridae), to mention a few prominent ones. These families are in general inhabitants of clear water, free of sediment and pollution; in short they are abundant where conditions also favor the growth of coral.

The young of many of the reef species appear to spend more or less time away from the reef or inshore habitat in the early stages of their development. The manini (*Acanthurus sandvicensis*) may be taken as a typical representative of the surgeonfishes and the early life history of this species as worked out by Randall (1955) may serve to illustrate a pattern which is likely true for many of the rest.

The eggs and larvae of this species are pelagic. Larval acanthurids have been taken 140 miles offshore; however, they appear to be more abundant nearer to land, being a common fish in the stomachs of yellowfin tuna, and more abundant in the surface-caught tuna than in those taken at a depth of 100 or more feet. The larval fish feed on zooplankton. The period of pelagic existence is estimated to last for two and one-half months. The spawning period for the manini lasts apparently for about seven months—from December to July. The acronurus stage, which is the last larval pelagic stage, will be found with recently transformed manini in tide pool and inshore habitats between February and October.

The effect of a protracted period of pelagic existence by the younger stages of inshore species of fish is of interest in any consideration of the reproductive efficiency of these fish about an isolated archipelago such as the Hawaiian Islands. Aside from losses from predation by normally pelagic species such as the tunas, the possibility presents itself that variations in the normal pattern of oceanic currents around the islands may sweep a variable number of these young fish with their relatively feeble swimming abilities beyond the point of no return. That the source of the Hawaiian inshore fish fauna is also Hawaiian and that additions are not the result of young swept to these islands from other areas is indicated, at least for the manini and some others, by the fact that the Hawaiian examples of these species are distinguishable from others resident elsewhere in the Tropical Pacific. This argues that the migratory pattern of these fish is uniquely adapted to the prevailing current pattern in a manner to best assure their return to the inshore habitat at the proper time. However, if such an adaptation exists it should be to an average current situation and not to abnormal ones, which may result in major fluctuations in recruitment of young fish independent of the volume of spawning.

## LOCAL DISTRIBUTION OF REEF FISH: HORIZONTAL ZONATION

One peculiar association is the occurrence of melanistic species or phases of species in the South Kona area of Hawaii. Melanistic examples of *Forcipiger longirostris* have been taken and observed in this area as far north as Keahole

Point. *Hemitaurichthys thompsoni,* a melanistic species probably derived from *H. zoster,* is found in this same region, as is *Ctenochaetus hawaiiansis* related to *C. strigosus.* Certain chaetodons rare in Hawaii, such as *C. reticulatus* and *C. ephippium,* have also been observed here.

Well north of Keahole Point on Hawaii, off the Honolulu Harbor entrance on Oahu, and off Waimea on Kauai are regions where the growth of coral is less vigorous than in the region immediately south or east of it. Evidence of the occasional occurrence of muddy water may be detected in the presence of fine sediment in some of the bottom deposits in parts of this region. This is a portion of the area in the lee of the islands and is the northerly or westerly portion of the lee. *Zebrasoma flavescens,* which is an abundant species in the southerly or easterly lee areas, is here absent or rare—as is the case in windward areas as well. Also the paku'iku'i (*Acanthurus achilles*) was not encountered in submarine transects run in the northerly or westerly lee areas on Hawaii, Oahu, or Kauai.

We may recognize, besides the southerly or easterly lee and the northerly or westerly lee, a windward region with characteristic species of coral and fish. These, then, are three broad classes of inshore areas.

## VERTICAL ZONATION

The present section deals only with the vertical zonation of the Hawaiian shore fishes. It is further restricted to typical conditions on the high, eastern islands where the open sea lies within 200 yards of the shore. (See Fig. 2.)

**Fig. 2**

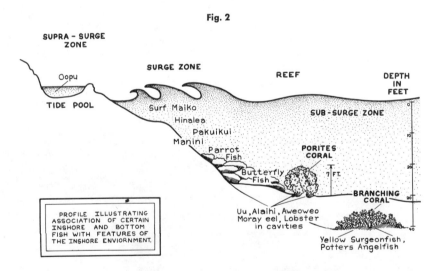

Special conditions, such as those within protected harbors and reef-enclosed bays and lagoons are not discussed. Hawaiian coasts are largely of two types: either an open sand beach or an outer rock face that drops off quite rapidly

**10**

into more than eight feet of water. Rock faces are of two types. The volcanic shore may drop away immediately into the open sea, in which instance the almost constant ocean swell beats directly against the shore; or it may be protected by fringing reef rock, in which case most of the wave force is broken before it reaches the shore. A fringing reef may extend more than a mile out from shore or it may be only a few feet wide. Behind its more or less vertical face there may be channels, crevices, and pockets, or the whole area may be flat and covered with sand. The greatest depth of water that occurs behind a reef face depends to a considerable extent upon how far from shore the reef face is; with a narrow fringing reef the pockets and channels are rarely more than 10 feet deep.

The maximum difference in water level between high and low tides in the eastern Hawaiian Islands is about four feet; this difference is nullified by wave action on open coasts, where the height of swells may vary from nearly zero to more than eight feet. The southwest sides of the islands are on the whole less subject to high swell than the windward north coasts, but on all open coasts in the Hawaiian chain the height reached by the water is probably more dependent on the size of the waves than on the phase of the tide. Consequently, the tide can be practically neglected as a factor in zonation in the areas under discussion, though it may be of considerable importance in enclosed areas.

Indeed, the repeated collecting and observation of Hawaiian shore fishes over a number of years have made it increasingly clear that in shallow water the primary factor governing zonation is wave action.

Four zones may be distinguished above the 50-foot depth, though one of these is rather difficult to delimit and shows many characteristics of a transition or mixed zone. The uppermost may be designated as the supra-surge zone. That below it, including the whole intertidal area and a varying depth of water below, is here called the surge zone. Below that is the area beneath the level of wave action; this zone extends out to the 50-foot depth level and to an unknown distance beyond. How to speak of this zone is something of a problem, particularly since its outer limit is unknown, but it may be called the "sub-surge area." The transition or mixed area is that which lies behind a fringing reef when one is present; it may be called the reef-protected area. (These designations are for convenience in the present connection only; no attempt has been made to correlate them with the nomenclature adopted by ecologists for conditions elsewhere.)

The uppermost level is that made up of pools along the shore that are located so that the water in them will be more or less frequently refreshed by wave action but which are well above the level of maximum wave force. The height of this zone above mean-tide level will generally be higher on windward than on leeward coasts. The zone is often nonexistent or greatly reduced behind fringing reefs, and is, of course, absent from beach areas. The only fishes restricted to this zone are the blenny *Istiblennius zebra* and, probably, the minute, naked goby *Kelloggella oligolepis*. In addition, there are in the Hawaiian Islands several fishes the young of which move up into the higher tide pools

**11**

and then as they mature work back into deeper water. Such species are *Kuhlia sandvicensis*, *Abudefduf sordidus*, *Acanthurus sandvicensis*, and perhaps *Bathygobius fuscus*.

The surge zone is again of varying depth. In some well-protected areas it may extend only a few feet above and below the mean-tide level. At the other extreme are areas such as the coasts of the Molokai Channel (which forms a wind gap between two islands). Here, there is almost always a chop or swell or both. Even in 10 feet of water on one of the calmer days an observer will be carried back and forth over rocks which loom up eerily out of the roiled bottom sand. Above the sea surface this surge will affect a distance about equal to the depth it reaches below sea level.

There seems to be a small number of fishes typical of, resident in, and restricted to this surge area. At the upper limit the blenny *Entomacrodus marmoratus* resides, coming out on the more or less exposed reef rock to "graze." Two fishes that normally do not expose themselves to the air and hence live in the lower levels of the surge zone are the damselfish *Abudefduf imparipennis* and the wrasse *Thalassoma umbrostigma*. Both of these seem to be ubiquitous in surge areas provided there is not too much sand. They may be found along the pock-marked, vertical, outer reef surfaces in the upper 10 feet of water or, again, over rocky bottoms where the surge imparts a primarily horizontal motion to the water. Both species are also common residents of the lower tide pools, and both seem to protect themselves by taking refuge in small holes and cracks, as does *Entomacrodus marmoratus*. There are also two species of surgeonfishes typical of rocky Hawaiian surge zones, namely, *Acanthurus guttatus* and *A. achilles*. These, however, seem to protect themselves from wave action by backing off into open water.

Along sandy beaches fish life is usually relatively scarce, particularly in those long stretches away from rocky areas. There are, however, two species that reside at least near rocks in such sandy areas. The ophichthid eel, *Caecula platyrhyncha*, seems to remain buried at all times and presumably finds its food below the sand surface; the small trichonotid, *Crystallodytes cookei*, apparently lives just above the bottom, but dives into the sand under the slightest provocation. There are also species that habitually enter the surge zone along sandy beaches somewhat as the surgeonfishes do in rocky areas. Such species are *Albula vulpes* and *Polydactylus sexfilis*.

Two species seem to be typical of the surge zone on shores where the volcanic rock is not protected by a fringing reef. These are the small moray *Uropterygius marmoratus* and the pomacentrid *Abudefduf sindonis*.

Beyond the area of wave action is an almost altogether different world. In an area at a depth of 35 feet off Waikiki or off the Kona coast of the Island of Hawaii, both the amount and number of species of corals and of fish are far greater than they ever are in shallower water. For example, 105 species of fishes have been taken in one collection made from 25 to 35 feet of water off Waikiki whereas the best shore collection we have ever made took only 75 species.

Aside from the greater number of species, the composition of the fauna is very different from that found in the zone of wave action. In some cases the difference applies to families. For example, the blennies drop out except for one species, *Exallias brevis*, and the balistids come in. In general, however, the difference is one of replacement of species or genera. For example, in sandy areas the shallow-water burrowing eel *Caecula platyrhyncha* is very largely replaced by the *C. flavicauda*, and *Crystallodytes* is supplanted by *Limnichthys*. *Uropterygius knighti* is never found in the calm water outside the reef, but two other species of *Uropterygius* are. The gobiid genera *Kelloggella* and *Bathygobius* are replaced by others. The inshore damselfishes of the genus *Abudefduf* are largely replaced by other genera, etc.

The distinction between the zone of wave action and that below it is very marked. However, there is a common habitat about Hawaiian shores that is more or less intermediate between the two. This is the habitat made up of holes, cuts, and water pockets between the shore and the reef edge. In such areas there is often some wave action, but the main force of the wave has been broken outside. Within the habitat almost all wave forces can be found from that somewhat below full strength to quiet water. The fishes found here are a mixture of those normally inhabiting the surge zone and those found below it. Some species such as *Muraenichthys cookei, Gymnothorax eurostus, Gymnothorax steindachneri, Conger marginatus, Apogon waikiki,* the adult *Kuhlia sandvicensis, Stethojulis axillaris, Istiblennius gibbifrons, Cirripectus variolosus,* and *Scorpaenopsis gibbosa* seem to concentrate in such areas, but most of these also range outside of them. Many, but by no means all, of the typical surge fishes inhabit such pockets. On the other hand, a good number of the deeper-water forms come in over or through the reef, particularly at night. Though this habitat probably deserves recognition as a zone, it is one with far less clear-cut borders than the other three dealt with.

Within the sub-surge area the assemblage of fish species found will be distributed in certain characteristic patterns. The pattern will depend in part on the species complex and upon their habitat requirements. Swimming near the bottom, both in the shallow and deeper portions of a typically southerly or easterly lee area (a Kona area), will be found surgeonfishes such as the adult manini (*Acanthurus sandvicensis*), palani (*Acanthurus dussumieri*) and the naenae (*Acanthurus olivaceus*) and the yellow tang (*Zebrasoma flavescens*). In the same general habitat will be such chaetodontids as *C. auriga, C. lunula, C. unimaculatus, C. ornatissimus, C. quadrimaculatus, C. fremblii, C. miliaris, C. linolatus,* and *C. multicinctus*. Also in the region immediately off the bottom will be found many small labrids among others, the predominant species being the common hinalea (*Thalassoma duperreyi*). Usually a little higher off the bottom and sometimes well off the bottom will occur the kala (*Naso unicornis*). Other species of *Naso*, such as the 'opelu kala (*N. hexancanthus*) and *N. brevirostris*, are usually in mid-water, at least in depths of 40 to 50 feet. In the upper-water levels will occur fish such as the 'opelu (*Decapterus pinnulatus*), needlefish and halfbeaks, and ranging from the surface to the bottom will be species such as the various uluas or jacks and the barracuda.

Where the bottom is composed of a mass of branching coral full of many holes and cavities, *Centropyge potteri* will be encountered both in lee and windward areas. In the various larger holes and cavities a faunal complex occurs. The u'u (*Myripristis*) and the 'ala'ihi (*Holocentrus*) are abundant members of this fauna, as are the various species of moray eels (*Gymnothorax*), apogonids, lobsters, and a scattering of a variety of other fishes such as pipefishes (*Doryrhamphus*), gobies, and blennies. Many of the species which are found in holes and cavities in the rocks are nocturnal feeders, leaving their place of shelter during the night in order to forage for food. In addition to the species which are almost never found beyond the confines of such shelter, many other species that ordinarily range freely about will be found in such localities, often apparently seeking shelter perhaps from the observer. The majority of the reef-fish species will duck into a hole upon occasion if they feel they are endangered in any way.

In addition to the reef habitats discussed above, there is some evidence that the characteristics of certain areas are such as to provide habitats which resemble those of much deeper water in other areas. For example, off Waikiki in 100 feet of water at one station two uncommon species of fish were found: *Chaetodon corallicola* and *Caesioperca thompsoni*. The bottom here was barren, with coral largely absent. Both species are quite rare in collections. However, in 40 feet of water off Makua Valley on the coast of Waianae, Oahu, both these species were encountered again on a bottom which was as barren as was the deep water off Waikiki. In addition, the area off Waianae was characterized by an abundance of *N. brevirostris*, a surgeonfish that is rarely encountered in Hawaiian waters.

The various species within a genus may occupy similar habitats which are, however, probably not identical in detail. For example, *Holocentrus xantherythrus* is a common species in the Waianae area in cavities in depths to ten or twelve fathoms, below these depths it is apparently replaced by *Holocentrus scythrops*. *Chaetodon corallicola* and *Caesoperca thompsoni* are characteristic of this deeper zone as is *Acanthurus thompsoni*. The last-named species apparently has, for an acanthurid, unusual food habits which may be associated with the lack of suitable algae food at depths of 12 fathoms or more. Stomachs of this species that were examined contained mollusk eggs and copepods, in contrast to the usual content of algae characteristic of the other species of *Acanthurus*.

Also, studies of the local distribution of reef fishes, along the Waianae coast of Oahu for example, have shown that their local abundance is spotty and is associated with good coral growth or with rocky bottom which may provide an abundance of shelter and suitable substrate for the growth of rooted or fixed algae which is probably the primary plant food of the reef fauna.

The causes responsible for these anomalies and discontinuities in the distribution of reef fish may be suggested for only a few species and these seem to relate to food and perhaps to the shelter need of each species. The food available would be determined in the first instance by the chemical and physical characteristics of the water mass and secondarily fixed by the food chain on which the fish species in question feed. In any case, it would seem necessary that we understand these relationships since they have an immediate bearing upon the magnitude of the fish populations which may exist in a given area, and, of course, upon the magnitude of the fish crops which can be harvested. From the point of view of the use man makes of these fishes they may be regarded as the end product of a process which serves to convert the energy of the sun and the chemicals present in the sea into protein which can be utilized for human food.

## PRODUCTIVITY

The appraisal of the fish populations from the point of view of their value as food involves considerations of the quantitative aspects of these populations, aspects that are often considered from the standpoint of population dynamics and of productivity. Very little is known of the population dynamics of marine tropical species; however, life-history studies indicate for some of them both a rapid growth rate and a short life span.

The aku (Brock, 1954a) would seem to mature within a year and live between two and three years in Hawaiian waters, the 'ahi (Moore, 1951) lives perhaps two to three times as long but grows even more rapidly. Species such as 'opelu (Yamaguchi, 1953), akule and nehu (Tester, 1951) are almost an annual crop; however, individuals of these species may live for two years or more. Aholehole (Tester and Takata, 1953) occur in some abundance through the third year of life and beyond; it is possible that kumu and other goatfishes follow a similar pattern. While there exists little if any evidence on the matter, it is suspected that the ulua does not grow nearly as rapidly as some of the other species mentioned earlier, such as the aku. There exists little evidence concerning the growth rate of the surgeonfishes; however, apparently it is slow (Randall, 1955). The pattern of rapid growth and short life span implies that the fish constituting such a population are rapidly replaced; fish populations with these characteristics ordinarily show considerable resilience when subjected to exploitation through fishing.

On the other hand, those species which grow slowly and mature late would seem to lack this resilience, and they are likely less efficient in converting the potential productivity of the sea into a form suitable for man. The food consumed by fish may, in this connection, be divided into two parts. The first is that required to supply the basic metabolic needs, and the second the surplus available for further growth. The slower the growth rates, the greater is the proportion of food utilized merely to maintain the fish. In regard to the efficiency of such conversion, the position a species of fish occupies on a food chain is important. The first step in the transformation of the nutrient salts present in the sea and the energy of the sun involves plants. Some species of fish feed directly on these plants, others feed upon small herbivorous creatures of various kinds or upon other species of fish. Some kinds of fishes may feed upon fish which in turn feed upon other fish which again in turn feed upon small creatures that again may feed upon other smaller creatures which may feed upon plants. The weight of fish produced from a given weight of food is, in such rough estimates as this, taken at one tenth. So for each link in a food chain, the weight carried on is but one tenth of the preceding link. Hence, for

**15**

the example given above, if we began with one million pounds of plant material we would ultimately harvest ten pounds of fish. This could well represent a single fish which required a million pounds of marine plant life for its growth. Therefore, the fewer steps involved in a food chain, the higher the proportion of the total productivity available as harvestable fish. Obviously species of fish which feed directly on plants would be most efficient in this regard. Surgeonfishes such as manini, paku'iku'i, palani, kole and kala are plant feeders. Mullet is another such species.

The various species of ulua feed largely upon other species of fish as does the kaku, or upon marine invertebrates. Hence, the weight of ulua which a reef area can support would ordinarily be much less than the weight of the plant-eating reef fish. In fact, many of the more desirable food and game fish species feed several links up the food chain and thereby constitute the less abundant portions of the fish fauna.

There is also a large group of reef fishes, the smaller damselfishes, the hinaleas or wrasses, most of the chaetodontids or butterfly fishes, some of hawkfish or cirrhitids, and the smaller scorpion fishes, the triggerfishes, filefishes, puffers, moray eels, and sharks which are not directly useful as food. While they may serve as forage for other species, in many instances it is suspected that they are, from the point of view of contributing to eventual human utilization, of very little value. Aside from such large predators as the sharks, the uselessness of the others may be largely due to the lack of a proper predator, which is in turn a good food fish, to consume them.

We have considered some of the internal aspects of productivity on a reef area, some of the factors which influence the efficiency of it as a process of converting the energy of the sun and the fertilizing salts of the sea into food for man. However, the internal efficiency of the process may be of less significance than fluctuations in the supply of energy and raw materials which sustain it. A discussion of the economy of the open tropical sea can best serve to illustrate the nature of the processes involved since the pattern is apparently simpler and has been better investigated than for reef or inshore areas.

The appearance of uniformity of the open tropical sea from one area to another is deceptive; the eye does not measure slight changes in dissolved nutrient salts or water temperatures except, perhaps, indirectly through noting changes in abundance of oceanic fishes and birds, yet the amounts of such nutrient salts as phosphates or nitrates available to the plants determine the abundance of life in the area.

It is only within the region well illuminated by the sun, the photosynthetic zone, that the plants of the open ocean, the diatoms, single-celled algae and other members of the phytoplankton can convert the inorganic salts of the sea into the protoplasm of their cells. Directly or indirectly all other life, from the surface of the ocean to the bottom, which may lie thousands of fathoms below, must depend upon the phytoplankton, confined to the shallow sunlight layers of the surface. The abundance of the animal life is related to the abundance of phytoplankton through various food chains, and as the abundance of phytoplankton is also related to the concentrations of essential nutrient salts such as phosphates and nitrates, through this same chain of relationship, the fishes and other components of the fauna would vary in abundance with variations in nutrient salts.

As the processes of life go on, as small animals feed upon the plants and are in turn fed upon, many of the elements composing their bodies are returned to the water, where again the plants can use them for further growth. However, the death of a creature that is not devoured occurs sooner or later in this gastronomic web, and such a creature may then sink into the region below the photosynthetic zone. The action of bacteria will return to the sea those nutrient salts that were locked in the body, but being in solution now in the dark cold water of the depths, separated by its greater density from the waters of the photosynthetic zone, these nutrients are no longer directly available to plants. So, slowly, the essential nutrient salts are lost from the illuminated upper waters of the ocean where the plants, which may restore them to the cycle of the food chain, can only exist.

Thus, any mechanism of current or water movement which may raise some of the cold, deep, nutrient-rich water to the surface will increase, roughly in proportion, the abundance of life. Vertical movements of water do occur in the tropical ocean, but the difference in density between the warm isothermal surface layers and the cold water below impedes and restricts such movement. Hence, only in such places where the horizontal movement of current has, for some cause, a vertical component of sufficient strength to break across the barrier of a density difference can the nutrient salts find their way back into the photosynthetic zone.

Areas in the tropics where this does occur are not numerous, and where they are of great magnitude they are usually in regions where strong, well-established currents impinge or move away from a continental land mass or shear past another current creating upwellings thereby. The sweep of currents past island masses with a consequent development of leeward eddies may occasion some interchange of surface and deep water.

Very little in the way of estimating productivity has been done generally for warm-water situations and practically none for reef areas. The value of such measurements in relation to the production of those elements in the complex of species which are of value to man may be difficult to demonstrate for reef areas where the food chains are many, and the fraction of the species which are of economic importance is small. The pattern of human utilization, especially concerning such matters as what species and what sizes are acceptable, could profoundly influence the apparent productivity.

A few examples where some estimates of production in terms of human utilization may be of interest. Nelson Marshall (1951) states that during the period from 1923 to 1945 the greatest annual yield of the inshore waters of North Carolina was 6.8 tons per square mile and the poorest 2.6 tons. Clarke (1946) reported yields of 10 to 2.2 tons per square mile for Georges Bank for the same period. Hildebrand and Schroeder (1928) wrote that the catch of fish from Chesapeake Bay was about 11 tons per square mile in 1920 and that of Georges Bank, 3 tons. Galtsoff (1952) gives the production of marine fisheries for a number of areas such as the Sea of Azov with a catch of 22.5 tons per square mile, the Sea of Japan with 8.1 tons, the North Sea with 7.0 tons, the Mediterranean and South China Sea with 4.3 tons, the Atlantic Ocean with 0.2 tons and the Pacific Ocean with 0.17 tons per square mile. Galtsoff's figures suggest an inverse relation between productivity and the extent of the area involved which may imply that the concentration of fishermen influence the figures as well as the concentration of fish. Additionally, Rawson (1955) has indicated an inverse relation between fish catch and mean depth for large Canadian lakes, a situation which may have a marine counterpart.

Wheeler (1955) estimated the inshore- and reef-fish catch for Mauritius, an island in the Indian Ocean, at 12 tons per square mile annually. Mauritius, being fairly remote from continental areas and in tropical waters would seem to resemble Hawaii more than the other places mentioned above. Most of the figures relative to inshore-fish catch taken in Hawaiian waters are difficult to equate with the area from which the catch was obtained since statistical zones for which the catches are reported do not equate with major changes in bottom topography which occur ordinarily within a short distance from shore. Kaneohe Bay, on the windward side of Oahu, is one area where the landings of inshore species can be assigned with fair accuracy. The average annual yield for this bay from 1948 through 1953 was 2.5 tons per square mile, which would seem to be somewhat low as compared to figures of yield for other areas, but even so, it may be high for Hawaiian inshore waters generally since two-thirds of the weight of fish reported was nehu, a prolific species of rapid growth heavily fished as a bait fish for tuna fishing. This estimate does not include the catch of recreational fishermen and is therefore low by an unknown amount.

Any attempt to estimate the unit-area productivity of pelagic fisheries may suffer because the fishing effort varies so greatly over the range of the species concerned. This difficulty is serious where such species as the tunas are concerned. However, without special regard to the problem of the distribution of fishing effort, it may be of interest to consider the yield of a high-seas fishery in an area where it is pursued intensively. The Waianae area off the island of Oahu is considered a productive one for pelagic species. During the fiscal period 1953–1954, 1.6 tons of pelagic fish were taken per square mile of this area.

Any consideration of the productivity to be expected from the sea in terms of man's needs must be made with some awareness of the low efficiency of the process. Estimates by Nelson Marshall for North Carolina waters concerning the percentage of carbon bound up as organic substances by plants from the sea that is finally harvested as fish are from .08 to .06 per cent. In short, less than one tenth of one per cent of the basic productivity in terms of marine plants becomes available as marketable fish. This situation suggests that if we understood the processes involved and related matters, we might be able to increase the efficiency slightly with a resulting major increase in the amount of fish caught.

# BIBLIOGRAPHY

BROCK, VERNON E.
1954a.Some aspects of the biology of the aku, *Katsuwonus pelamis*, in the Hawaiian Islands. *Pacific Sci.* 8(1): 94–104, figs. 1–4.

BROCK, VERNON E.
1954b.A preliminary report on a method of estimating reef fish populations. *Jour. Wildlife Mgt.* 18(3): 297–308, 1 fig.

CLARKE, G. L.
1946. *Dynamics of production in a marine area.* Ecological Monographs, Vol. 16, pp. 321–335.

GALTSOFF, P. S.
1952. *Food Resources of the Ocean in World Production and Future Resources of the Ocean*, Paul K. Hatt, ed. New York: American Book Co. 108–118.

HILDEBRAND, S. F., and W. C. SCHROEDER.
1928. *Fishes of Chesapeake Bay.* U. S. Bur. Fisheries Bul. Vol. 42, Pt. 1, pp. 1–388, figs. 1–211.

MARSHAL, NELSON.
1951. *Hydrography of North Carolina Marine Waters* in *Survey of Marine Fisheries of North Carolina by Harden F. Taylor.* Chapel Hill: University of North Carolina.

MOORE, H. L.
1951. *Estimation of the age and growth of yellowfin tuna (Neothunnus macropterus) in Hawaiian waters.* Fishery Bul. 65, U. S. Fish and Wildlife Service.

RANDALL, J. E.
1955. A contribution to the biology of the Acanthuridae (surgeonfishes). Ph.D. Thesis, University of Hawaii.

RAWSON, D. S.
1955. Morphometry as a dominant factor in the productivity of large lakes. *Int. Assn. Limnology, Proc.* 12:164.

STEARNS, H. T.
1946. *Geology of the Hawaiian Islands.* Hawaii Division of Hydrography, Honolulu, Bul. 8.

TESTER, A. L.
1951. The distribution of eggs and larvae of the anchovy, *Stolephorus purpureus* Fowler, in Kaneohe Bay, Oahu, with a consideration of the sampling problem. *Pacific Sci.* 5(4): 321–346, figs. 1–6.

TESTER, A. L., and M. TAKATA
1953. *Contribution to the biology of the aholehole, a potential bait fish.* I.R.A.C. Grant No. 29, Final Report, Honolulu. Pp. 54, 17 figs.

WHEELER, J. F. G.
1953. Report on the Mauritius: Seychelles Fisheries Survey 1948–1949. *Colonial Office Fishery Publications.* Vol. I, No. 3.

YAMAGUCHI, Y.
1953. The Fishery and Biology of the Hawaiian Opelu *Decapterus pinnalatus* (Ejdoux and Souleyet). M.S. Thesis, University of Hawaii.

# 3. The Nature and Derivation of the Hawaiian Fish Fauna

**GEOGRAPHY**

The Hawaiian Islands form a long narrow chain extending over 1500 miles in an almost straight line from southeast to northwest (see inset in endpapers). They are surrounded by water more than two miles deep. All are volcanic in origin, although at the present time the northwestern islands are reduced to low coral atolls. Though the age of none of the chain is known, it is presumed that these low western islands are older than the high islands to the east. Only on the easternmost is volcanic activity a normal phenomenon today. Within the chain there is no gap between islands more than 200 miles wide.

The nearest island to the Hawaiian group is Johnston, an isolated atoll about 450 miles to the south of the center of the chain (see inset in endpapers). Since the fishes of Johnston are predominantly Hawaiian (Gosline, 1955) they will be included in this book. To the south of Johnston there is a deep-water gap of some 700 miles before the northernmost reef in the Line Island group is reached.

Aside from Johnston, the closest island to the Hawaiian chain is Wake, a northern outlier of the Marshall group. Wake lies about 1200 miles southwest of the western end of the Hawaiian group (see inset in endpapers). Its fishes are almost purely Marshallese.

To the west, north, and east of Hawaii there is no shallow water closer than Japan, the Aleutians, and North America respectively, all 2000 or more miles away. Tokyo is 2500 miles from Midway and Los Angeles is an equal distance from Honolulu.

The whole of the Hawaiian Islands and Johnston lie in the path of the northeast trades with the primary surface current system running from east to west. There is, however, the possibility that in winter at least the westernmost reefs in the chain are bathed by currents flowing in a reverse direction.

The surface-water temperature in July for the full length of the Hawaiian chain is about 79°F. Since the warmest surface temperature south of Hawaii is only about 82°F. there is little difference in summer temperatures between Midway and the equator. The situation in winter is quite different. Winter surface temperatures at the equator south of Hawaii are 79°F., at the island of Hawaii 75°F., and at Midway 64°F., according to available information.

20

Thus in winter there is a far greater difference in surface temperatures between Hawaii and Midway within the Hawaiian chain than between the island of Hawaii and the equator.

## THE HAWAIIAN FISH FAUNA

In dealing with the marine fishes of the Hawaiian Islands it is immediately necessary to distinguish between two groups. One of these contains such truly high-seas forms as the flying fishes, myctophids, etc. The members of this group are only accidental members of the Hawaiian fauna and the only importance the Hawaiian chain may have for them is indirect, i.e., by disrupting the normal configuration of the water masses to which they are restricted or by adding an inshore component, e.g., planktonic larvae, to these masses (see previous chapter). Nothing further will be said here concerning this group.

In contrast, there is a much larger group of fishes that depends upon the proximity of a sea bottom for its food supply or for shelter (or both) during adult life. Though there are deep-water as well as shallow-water bottom species in this category, knowledge of the former is so restricted that the discussion of derivation and differentiation of the Hawaiian fish fauna will be entirely devoted to the inshore forms.

Despite the east-to-west current system, none of the Hawaiian inshore (or reef) fishes have come from the North American coast. Rather, our reef-fish fauna forms an offshoot of that great marine zoogeographic region centered on the East Indies and extending across tropical and subtropical seas from East Africa through the Central Pacific (the crosshatched area on the endpapers). The Hawaiian Islands do, however, represent the most distinctive component of that region.

Turning briefly to Johnston Island, the fish fauna of this island is made up very largely of forms found both to the north and south (Gosline, 1955). A few are Hawaiian "endemics" that go no farther south; about an equal number are tropical Pacific fishes that do not get to Hawaii; and two species have never yet been recorded from anywhere but Johnston.

Within the Hawaiian chain the inshore-fish fauna seems to be approximately uniform. There may be some diminution in the number of species present from east to west, but insufficient collecting has been done in the western end of the chain to more than suggest this. Conversely, only one species—*Gregoryina gygis*—is known from the western end of the chain that has not also been recorded from the high eastern islands. Again, no important differences can at present be established between the species found around the high volcanic islands and those inhabiting the low coralline reefs.

Within species one might expect some differentiation of populations between the eastern and western ends of the chain if only because of the much colder winter temperatures in the west. It is true that the species at the western end appear to grow to a somewhat larger size and to have a spawning period somewhat later in the spring than populations of the same species at the eastern end of the chain. However, in morphological characters the populations from the cooler western waters generally are, if anything, more like their tropical Pacific counterparts than those from the warmer eastern waters. This is the reverse of what one would expect and can apparently be best explained (for those fishes in which the phenomenon occurs, e.g., *Muraenichthys laticaudata* and *Kuhlia sandvicensis*) as the result of some interbreeding between the western (but not the eastern) Hawaiian populations and immigrants (Gosline, 1955).

## ENDEMISM

Unlike the Hawaiian terrestrial endemics, none of the inshore fishes seem to have differentiated very greatly. Among genera, only three are known exclusively from the Hawaiian Islands—*Gregoryina*, *Microbrotula*, and *Pogonemus* —and all of these contain small, rare fishes that may well exist as yet unrecorded elsewhere. At lower levels of differentiation, however, endemics are abundant. Indeed, 34 per cent of the reef fishes recognized in this book have not been taken outside of the Hawaiian chain and Johnston. Not only are endemics abundant, but they are represented with surprising regularity among the various reef-fish families. There is not a single family represented in Hawaii by ten or more species in which there are no endemics; nor is there one such family represented entirely by species restricted to our area.

It is also a striking feature of the Hawaiian reef-fish fauna that many, perhaps the majority, of the abundant and ubiquitous forms are endemics. The two largest families of fishes in the Hawaiian Islands are the Labridae and Muraenidae; in each of these an endemic is probably the commonest member: *Thalassoma duperreyi* and *Gymnothorax eurostus*. Among other large families, *Muraenichthys cookei* or *Caecula platyrhyncha* is probably the most abundant ophichthid, *Scarus perspicillatus* the commonest scarid, and certainly *Acanthurus sandvicensis* the most abundant acanthurid. All are endemics, as are the plentiful *Kuhlia sandvicensis* and *Istiblennius zebra*. One certainly does not get the impression that the Hawaiian endemics are an ill-adapted group that is being displaced by the larger nonendemic portion of the Hawaiian reef-fish fauna. Conversely some of the most successful species in the islands to the south are rare in Hawaii—*Gymnothorax picta*, *Chaetodon ephippium*, etc. Other dominant elements in the tropical fauna to the south, for example the members of the genus *Lutjanus*, all but one species of *Epinephelus*, and all but one *Halichoeres*, fail to reach Hawaii. However, most groups of tropical Central Pacific fishes are represented in Hawaii, and there is nothing like the inequality of representation seen, for example, in the native Hawaiian terrestrial fauna.

## NATURE OF ENDEMIC DIFFERENTIATION

In three characteristics the Hawaiian fishes on the whole appear to differ from those of the more tropical portions of the Central Pacific. First, spawning in the Hawaiian forms tends to be more restricted seasonally than in their counterparts nearer the equator, though the Hawaiian fishes are by no means all summer spawners as might have been expected (Ekman, 1953: 113, but see also Qasim, 1956). Second, the Hawaiian species in general seem to grow

22

to a somewhat larger size than their more southerly counterparts. Third, when there is a difference in fin-ray counts, the Hawaiian form usually has more fin rays than its representative farther south (Strasburg, 1955, and Gosline, 1955). One can perhaps explain these features on the basis of water temperatures in the Hawaiian chain.

There remains a great residue of morphological features characterizing the individual endemics that seem to be of a most haphazard nature. One expected generalization appears to be totally unsupported, namely that since the Hawaiian reefs are relatively dull-colored, the fishes would also be comparatively drab; the Hawaiian fishes are quite as brightly colored as their counterparts to the south. There is, indeed, no pattern of color peculiarities by which the Hawaiian endemic fishes differ from the supposed ancestral, tropical stocks. It would almost seem as if no two Hawaiian endemics have the same or even the same type of color differentiation. This is also true of morphological differences (other than fin-ray numbers). In sum, for those many characters that cannot be directly attributed to the effect of Hawaiian water temperatures (that is, spawning periodicity, individual size, and fin-ray counts), there seems to be no pattern whatever of differentiation among Hawaiian endemics.

In one instance, at least, it is as nearly demonstrable as examples in nature ever are that the most conspicuous peculiarity of one Hawaiian endemic has no selective value. In *Acanthurus sandvicensis* there is a sickle-shaped mark running down from the pectoral base (Fig. 3). Elsewhere in the Indo-Pacific

**Fig. 3**

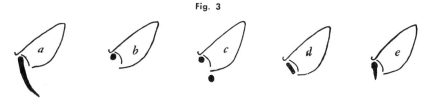

Dark markings at the base of the pectoral fins in various members of the *Acanthurus triostegus* complex: *a,* the sickle-shaped mark found consistently in the Hawaiian form; *b* to *e,* variations occurring in Phoenix and Line Island specimens. (After Schultz.)

there is either a short bar or one or two spots in this same area. In certain areas of the Central Pacific the type of mark present on one side of the fish differs from that on the other in more than one-quarter of the individuals. Such an incidence of asymmetry certainly argues against any strong natural selection pressure for one type of mark or against another. This does not imply that there is no selection for the presence of some clear-cut mark at the pectoral base but merely that the various available types have about equal adaptive values.

If we admit, then, that many of the features characterizing our Hawaiian endemic fishes have, in themselves, almost no selective value, we are forced to the assumption that they have arisen as by-products of some reshuffling in the genetic system. This interpretation does nothing to solve the basic problem of why the genetic system in our Hawaiian endemics has been reshuffled, but it does relieve us of the necessity of looking for an adaptive significance in every taxonomic character.

## TAXONOMIC TREATMENT OF ENDEMICS

Hawaiian endemics show all degrees of differentiation from their tropical counterparts. Some are easily distinguishable, whereas others can be separated only with considerable difficulty. The question then arises as to which of these endemics should be considered as full species, which as subspecies, and which as minor, unnamed variants. This matter has been treated by different workers in very different ways in the past, and no final answer will probably ever be given. Collections have been made at Johnston and Wake, the two islands somewhat intermediate in position between the Hawaiian chain and the island groups to the south (see inset in endpapers), in the hope that the fishes of these two islands might throw some light on the ability or inability of the Hawaiian endemics to interbreed with the tropical forms. If intergrades between the Hawaiian and southern forms had been found at either of these islands, interbreeding could have been postulated and the Hawaiian endemic would have to be considered a subspecies. If both the Hawaiian and the tropical Pacific form had been found living together at either of these islands, then the Hawaiian endemic would have to be recognized as a fully differentiated species. Unfortunately, neither of these things was found at Johnston or Wake: when the Hawaiian form was present at Johnston, there was no sign of intergradation and the tropical Pacific form was absent; conversely when the tropical Pacific form was present at Johnston or Wake there was no obvious intergradation with the Hawaiian form, which was absent. Thus the data from these two islands give no indication regarding the ability or inability of any of the Hawaiian endemics and their tropical Pacific counterparts to interbreed. Evidence from the populations within the Hawaiian chain is again ambiguous. On the one hand, the nature of the populations of certain species at the western end of the chain is such as to indicate some recent interbreeding with their tropical counterparts. On the other, there are certain closely related species pairs that seem to live together in the Hawaiian Islands without interbreeding. One member of each pair would seem to be endemic and the other the parent form which presumably has entered the Hawaiian chain later. Such pairs are *Synodus dermatogenys* and *S. variegatus*, *Apogon snyderi* and *A. menesemus*.

In the absence of proof as to whether the Hawaiian endemics should be recognized as species or assigned infraspecific rank, they are here treated as full species if they are easily and constantly separable. This is, of course, an arbitrary decision, but no other kind seems possible. Three different arbitrary taxonomic interpretations can be postulated for the treatment of Hawaiian endemics. (It should be stressed that the endemics remain endemics whatever interpretation is accepted; it is only the taxonomic level of recognition that is open to differential treatment.) First, as has been done here, the Hawaiian forms that can easily and consistently be differentiated from their tropical counterparts can be recognized as species, with no special taxonomic designation assigned to lower levels of differentiation. Second, the more distinctive Hawaiian forms can be called species, and the less distinctive endemics subspecies. Third, all the Hawaiian endemics with Central Pacific representatives can be called subspecies. Arguments can be advanced in favor of each of these interpretations, and all three have been adopted at one time or another in the past.

Superficially, the second alternative may appear the most attractive; however, it is probably the most difficult to justify on a biological basis. It assumes that level of differentiation is a basis for distinguishing subspecies from species, whereas the generally accepted criterion for separating subspecies from species is intergradation *vs* non-intergradation. As one result of this interpretation, Hawaiian endemics in "difficult" groups would always be subspecies, whereas the endemics in those groups that tend toward plasticity in conspicuous morphological characters would be full species. To systematists, the problems raised here are an old, old story. Suffice it to say that the recognition of both species and subspecies among the Hawaiian endemics (with Central Pacific counterparts) would seem to confuse rather than clarify an understanding of the basic and unresolved problem of whether, biologically, our endemics are full species or not.

In the long view, the third alternative of calling all Hawaiian endemics (with Central Pacific counterparts) subspecies has much more to recommend it. Like that of recognizing these same forms as full species, it is arbitrary and may be incorrect, but it confuses no biological issues. It has the advantage of indicating at a glance the relationships of the Hawaiian forms. Also, in revising groups of fishes with the intent of showing interrelationships it is disadvantageous to consider the Hawaiian forms, which are merely geographic offshoots, at the same level of genetic relationship with fully differentiated species living together (cf., Randall, 1956: 175). Under these circumstances, a logical solution, and one that cannot be proved incorrect, is to lower the Hawaiian endemics to subspecies. Such an interpretation is at odds with that adopted in the present book only insofar as a different arbitrary decision concerning taxonomic levels appears more satisfactory from a different viewpoint.

Here, as already stated, the Hawaiian endemics that are easily and invariably distinguishable will be treated as full species. The arguments in favor of this interpretation are basically two. First, there is no taxonomic or biological reason not to treat them as full species, i.e., they are constantly distinct with no intergrading populations. Second, the Hawaiian endemics are by far the most distinctive offshoots of the whole Indo-West-Pacific fauna (see endpapers); to lower them to subspecies would make it more difficult to deal zoogeographically with the other, relatively minor, areas of endemism within this great area.

### DERIVATION OF THE HAWAIIAN FISH FAUNA

Examination of the Hawaiian reef-fish fauna gives the impression that it has been accumulating over a rather long period. At the one extreme are those Hawaiian fishes that seem to be relicts. For example, the genus *Chlorhinus* is known only from Hawaii, New Britain, and the West Indian region (Böhlke, 1956). The Hawaiian endemic *Holocentrus scythrops* appears to have as its closest relative *H. marianus* of the West Indies. *Caranx cheilio* seems to have been recorded only from Hawaii and Easter Island. *Acanthurus leucopareius* is known only from the Hawaiian Islands, Easter, and Marcus (Randall, 1956: 187). Forms such as these would seem to represent ancient Hawaiian elements. At an intermediate level are the whole host of Hawaiian endemics already discussed, e.g., *Acanthurus sandvicensis*, that represent geographic offshoots of fishes abundant in the Central Pacific. At the other extreme are those tropical fishes that seem to be immigrating constantly at the present time. The single known Hawaiian specimen of *Pomacanthus imperator* (Brock, 1948) is probably an example of a fish arriving under its own impetus. Apparently more numerous are fishes recently introduced intentionally or inadvertently by man. Among the latter are the several species brought into Pearl Harbor among the heavy fouling on the bottom of a barge towed here from Guam (Chapman and Schultz, 1952: 528, and Edmondson, 1951: 183 and 212); *Omobranchus elongatus* may have been introduced with specimens of giant clams (*Tridacna*) brought in from the Samoan Islands (Strasburg, 1956: 257). The intentional introductions will be dealt with in Appendix A.

Regarding immigration routes of Hawaiian fishes, about all that can be said with certainty is that America played a negligible role. Indeed only two possible exceptions are known. A specimen of the American *Myripristis occidentalis* was recorded from Hawaii (under the name *M. sealei*) over 50 years ago, but the species has never been seen since. Second, specimens of *Lobotes* began to appear in Hawaii in 1957; these may have come from Panama. The remainder of the fish fauna is, as already noted, an offshoot from that of the great Indo-West-Pacific faunal region (Ekman, 1953) with its present center in the Indonesian-Philippine area. Nevertheless, the various Hawaiian members of this fauna would seem to have arrived over at least two different routes. *Microcanthus strigatus*, for example, is not known from the Central Pacific and may have come in directly from some such place as Okinawa via the Kuroshio current. On the other hand, several Hawaiian fishes, e.g., *Acanthurus achilles*, are species restricted to the Pacific islands; such forms must have entered from the south via Johnston or Wake, and the very great majority of our fishes probably followed a similar path. Within the Hawaiian chain it is fairly certain that many if not most of the species have arrived at the western end regardless of where they started from (Gosline, 1955). However, in all but a few instances, the actual immigration routes of Hawaiian fishes remain an unsolved and apparently insoluble question.

# BIBLIOGRAPHY

BOHLKE, J.

1956. A synopsis of the eels of the family Xenocongridae (including the Chlopsidae and Chilorhinidae). *Acad. Nat. Sci. Proc. Phila.*, 108: 61–95, pl. 7, figs. 1–8.

BROCK, V. E.

1948. An addition to the fish fauna of the Hawaiian Islands. *Pacific Sci.* 2(2): 298.

CHAPMAN, W. M., and L. P. SCHULTZ.

1952. Review of the fishes of the blennioid genus Ecsenius, with descriptions of five new species. *U. S. Nat. Mus. Proc.* 102: 507–528, figs. 90–96.

EDMONDSON, C. H.

1951. Some Central Pacific crustaceans. *Occ. Pap. Bishop Mus.* 20(13): 183–243, figs. 1–38.

EKMAN, S.

1953. *Zoogeography of the Sea.* London: Sidgwick and Jackson. Pp. xiv + 417, 121 figs.

GOSLINE, W. A.

1955. The inshore fish fauna of Johnston Island, a Central Pacific atoll. *Pacific Sci.* 9(4): 442–480, figs. 1–4.

QASIM, S. Z.

1956. Time and duration of the spawning season in some marine teleosts in relation to their distribution. *Journal du Conseil*, 21: 144–155, fig. 1.

RANDALL, J. E.

1956. A revision of the surgeonfish genus *Acanthurus. Pacific Sci.* 10(2): 159–235, pls. 1–3, figs. 1–23.

STRASBURG, D. W.

1955. North-south differentiation of blenniid fishes in the Central Pacific. *Pacific Sci.* 9(3): 297–303, figs. 1–2.

1956. Notes on the blennioid fishes of Hawaii with descriptions of two new species. *Pacific Sci.*, 10(3): 241–267, figs. 1–4.

# 4. The Identification of Hawaiian Fishes and Keys to Families

A beginner will find it difficult to identify most fishes by sight in the water. This is partly because he does not know what to look for and partly because the water-filtered impression of a fish seen at a distance tends to be inaccurate. It is therefore assumed that the fish to be identified is in hand.

It is also assumed that the fish is in a juvenile or adult stage of development. Many, probably most, of our fishes go through a larval phase that is quite unlike the adult. These larval forms are often unidentifiable, even by the ichthyologist, and no attempt has been made here to provide means for their determination. The question then arises how to tell whether the specimen one wishes to identify is juvenile or adult. It is not correct to assume that a small fish is a larva, for several of our species reach a maximum size of only one inch. It is, however, a safe assumption that anything over six inches long is not larval. In general, the best rule of thumb is that if the fish is transparent and colorless it is in a larval phase, and that otherwise it is not. Unfortunately, at least four of our fishes—*Pseudamiops gracilicauda*, the two species of *Schindleria*, and *Vitraria clarescens*—remain both transparent and colorless throughout life.

## Coloration

Color is the most conspicuous, and to the beginner probably the most treacherous, of all identifying characters for our fishes. First, very similar color and color patterns may occur in quite different fishes, as, for example, in *Echidna polyzona* and *Gymnothorax petelli*. Second, some fishes have the ability to change both color and color pattern, for example, *Antennarius chironectes*. Third, some go through two or even three different color phases and patterns with growth, not including the transparent larval stage; the labrids are the group most notable for this. Fourth, a few seem to have a special spawning coloration. Finally, in a host of Hawaiian fishes the males have a totally different coloration from the females and immatures, e.g., the parrot fishes. Because of these difficulties it is well for the beginner to subordinate color to almost all other taxonomic characters. Only when one has learned by experience what aspects of a color pattern are constant and diagnostic for a species does coloration become a very useful tool in the identification of Hawaiian fishes.

## The Parts of a Fish

A knowledge of at least the principal differentiating features is necessary for the identification of fishes. For many features the figures given below (Figs. 5–9) are self-explanatory. The text deals with only those that are not illustrated or that seem to require further explanation.

**Fig. 4**

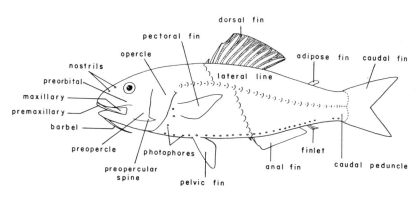

### THE FINS

The fins of bony fishes, except for the adipose fin, are made up of *rays*. These may be either *soft rays* or *spiny rays* (the latter usually referred to simply as *spines*). When spines are present in Hawaiian fishes, they are limited in position to the front of the dorsal and anal fins and to the outside of the pelvics. Normally the spine is an unsegmented, unbranched, stiff unit with a sharp point (e.g., the first two elements in the dorsal of Fig. 4); the soft ray, by contrast, is typically segmented, flexible, and branched (e.g., the posterior elements in the dorsal of Fig. 4). In certain families, however, it is very difficult to determine whether flexible, unsegmented, and unbranched elements are spines or soft rays. The spine in the pelvic fin may also be a small, splintlike structure which is impossible to find without removing flesh.

The *median fins* include all fins that are not paired (Fig. 4), namely, the dorsal and anal and their finlets, the adipose, and the caudal. Some or all of these may be absent in Hawaiian fishes. On the other hand, there may be two or three completely or incompletely separated *dorsal* fins and two *anal* fins. Sometimes the first dorsal or anal fin consists of a single spine or of two or more completely separate spines. *Finlets*, when present, number from one to about eight, and each one consists of a single, free, soft ray; in position finlets follow immediately behind the dorsal or anal (Fig. 4). In contrast, the *adipose* fin, when present, is a single rayless, and often inconspicuous, flap of flesh behind and usually well separated from the dorsal fin (Fig. 4).

**29**

There are never more than two pairs of *paired fins*. When both pairs are present the pectorals (Fig. 4) are placed higher on the body than the pelvics. One or both pairs may be absent; if only one is present, it is the pectoral pair. The *pectorals* are specialized in various ways in different Hawaiian fishes but these specializations need no comment. The variations in the *pelvic* or *ventral fins* must, however, be discussed briefly, for the differences in the pelvics form

Fig. 5

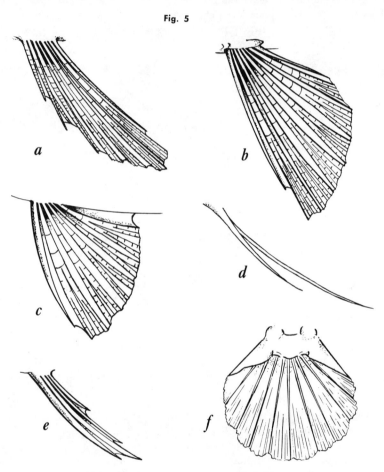

Pelvic or ventral fins: *a* to *e*, lateral views; *f*. bottom view. *a. Synodus variegatus; b. Holocentrus sammara; c. Priacanthus cruentatus; d. Brotula multibarbata; e. Cirripectus alboapicalis; f. Chonophorus stamineus.*

the bases upon which the family subkeys that follow have been constructed. In the lower bony fishes the pelvics, when present, usually have more than five soft rays (Fig. 5a, b, and Subkey A). The pelvic fins of these lower fishes are generally placed well behind the pectorals; indeed any bony fish with the pelvic fins originating behind the tips of the pectoral fins belongs automatically in Subkey A. The higher bony fishes typically have a spine at the outer margin of each pelvic and only five soft rays (Fig. 5c), and these pelvics lie about under the pectorals (Subkey B). There are, however, a number of specializations in pelvic structure among the higher bony fishes. In the gobies the pelvic fins of the two sides are joined along the mid-ventral line to form a single disc-like structure (Fig. 5b). The single pelvic spine is often reduced and difficult to find (as in Fig. 5e). The number of soft rays may be reduced to fewer than five (Fig. 5d, e, and Subkey C). In extreme cases the ventrals may be reduced to filament-like structures (Fig. 5d) far forward of the pectorals; however, unlike the barbels (see Fig. 4) that such pelvics resemble, they are never placed forward of the eye on the chin.

Fig. 6

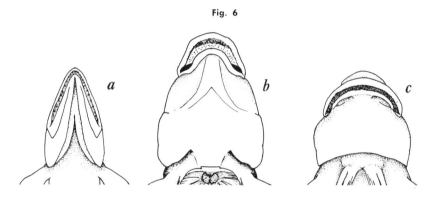

*a. Synodus variegatus*—free.  *b. Awaous guamensis*—broadly attached.
*c. Cirripectus variolosus*—united.

## THE HEAD

There are usually two *nostrils* (Fig. 4) on each side of the snout. However, in the Pomacentridae and certain other Hawaiian families, there is only one nostril on each side. This is an excellent taxonomic character but difficult to make out because a small nostril can easily be confused with a head pore. Generally, nevertheless, pressure applied to the area in which nostrils lie will cause water to exude from them, whereas pressure applied to a pore area will give no result.

Various systematic characters are associated with the *preopercle*. It may have a single enlarged spine, as shown in Figure 4; if so the spine will extend backward from the posteroventral angle of the preopercular border. Above this angle the border may be serrate, that is, may consist of a series of minute, hard projections. The presence of such serrations may best be determined by running the point of a pin along the preopercular border.

Variations in the nature of the *gill openings* again provide good taxonomic characters. In most Hawaiian fishes the *gill covers* or *gill membranes* are *free*

**31**

from one another and from the isthmus of the throat (Fig. 6a). In some the gill openings extend rather far forward on the throat, but in front the gill covers are attached to the isthmus; in this instance the gill membranes are said to be *narrowly attached* to the isthmus. Or the gill covers may be attached to the isthmus rather far back (Fig. 6b), in which case the gill membranes are said to be *broadly attached* to the isthmus. Such attachment naturally limits the gill opening below, and in extreme instances the gill openings become restricted to short slits or even to small round holes. Finally, the gill covers of the two sides may become attached to one another by a membrane and under these circumstances are said to be *united* to one another (Fig. 6c). In this instance the membrane that connects the two gill covers may form either a free fold across the isthmus or be attached to it.

The main portion of the gill cover is made up of the *opercle* (Fig. 4). This bone may bear one or two spines on its posterior border and one to three spines more or less concealed in the flesh forward of the border. The lower portion of the gill cover is made up of two smaller bones and a series of elongate, curved struts called *branchiostegal rays*.

There are four gill-bearing arches in Hawaiian bony fishes. These have *gill filaments* extending from the posterior surface of each arch (Fig. 7). The forwardmost arch often bears on its anterior surface spinelike projections known

**Fig. 7**

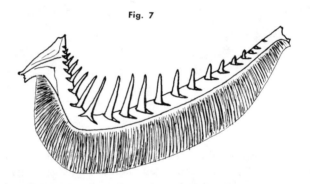

as *gill rakers* (Fig. 7). The posterior gill arches may bear patches of teeth above known as *upper pharyngeal teeth*. Behind the last gill arch are generally a pair of more or less sickle-shaped, tooth-bearing bones, the *lower pharyngeals*. In some groups the two lower pharyngeals are fused into a single bone, and in extreme instances, for example, the parrot fishes, the upper and lower pharyngeals together form a large and powerful crushing apparatus.

On the inside of the gill cover opposite the gill arches there is often another series of gill filaments more or less embedded in the flesh of the gill cover. These when present comprise the *pseudobranch*. The presence or absence of a pseudobranch can be determined only by bending the whole gill cover well away from the head so as to expose its inner surface.

The form and position of the *teeth* are extensively used in identifying fishes. In most forms the teeth are rigid. In some Hawaiian forms, however, for example, the Chaetodontidae, Zanclidae, and some acanthurids and blennies, the teeth are flexible and elastic like the teeth of a comb; if a pin is passed across such teeth, they will bend under it and snap back into position after the pin has passed. Other teeth, said to be *depressible*, may be moved, but in only one direction, namely, backward. The terminology for individual rigid tooth types follows that of mammals; that is, there are canines, incisors, and molars. Many fishes have small, undifferentiated teeth. These may be arranged in *rows* (Fig. 8b) or lines or in *villiform bands* (palatine teeth of Fig. 8a). A villiform band signifies that the whole area of the band is filled with small teeth which show no particular alignment.

Fig. 8

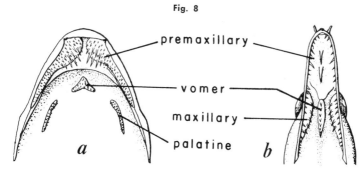

premaxillary

vomer

maxillary

palatine

*a*　　*b*

Teeth-bearing bones. *a. Cephalopholis argus. b. Murenophis pardalis.*

The teeth in the upper jaw are usually present on the *premaxillaries*, but sometimes, in lower bony fishes, they also occur on the *maxillaries* (e.g., Fig. 8b). On the roof of the mouth just behind the upper jaw, teeth may be present on the median vomer and the paired palatines (Fig. 8). The presence of vomerine and palatine teeth can often be established by probing the areas of these bones with a pin.

**THE BODY**

The body character most frequently used in fish identification is probably the *lateral line*. This is a tube running just below the surface along the sides. It is usually marked externally by a series of pores that open out through the scales. Usually there is only a single lateral line on each side of the body, and typically it follows the course indicated for it in Figure 4. It is sometimes difficult to find the lateral line in wet fishes, but if the lateral line area is partially dried by blowing air on it some of the air will usually penetrate the lateral-line tube making it conspicuous. Many variants of the typical lateral line occur. It may, for example, run very low on the sides as in the Belonidae, Hemiramphidae, Exocoetidae, and a few others. The lateral line may be *incomplete*, in which case it stops short of the base of the caudal fin. Again it may be *interrupted*, meaning that it terminates and then recommences after a gap,

**33**

perhaps several scale rows lower down on the body, as in some of the Labridae. Finally, in a fairly large number of families the lateral line is totally *absent*.

## Methods of Counting and Measuring

**COUNTS**

Differences in counts are extremely useful for distinguishing related species of fishes. Unlike measurement features, the countable characters (except in rare instances) do not change with growth. However, a rather high degree of accuracy is usually essential in making counts, and a rough guess may be worse than useless.

If the *spines* are sharp-tipped, the only problem in enumerating them is to make sure that one or more small spines at the front of the fin have not been overlooked. For species in which the spines are not sharp, as in many labrids, some difficulty may be encountered in distinguishing spines from soft rays.

The number of *soft rays* must be determined below the point at which such rays branch. Unless the soft rays are deeply embedded in flesh their number may best be counted either by the use of a microscope with the light directed through the fin from below, or by holding the fin up to the light. The major difficulty with soft rays occurs at the posterior end of the dorsal and anal fins. Here one or more of the rays may be split to the base. Where two (or even three) rays seem to arise from the same base in these areas, they are considered to represent a single ray for enumeration purposes.

If a fin count is given with both Roman and Arabic numerals separated by a comma, the Roman number represents the spinous- and the Arabic number the soft-ray count within a single fin. When a dorsal-fin count is made up of two sections separated by a dash, this means that there are two completely separate dorsal fins.

The *number of lateral-line scales* is counted to the base of the caudal rays but does not include the scales covering the bases of these rays. If no lateral line is present or if the lateral line series is for some reason unrepresentative of a typical longitudinal series, the number of body scales is taken as that along an imaginary line drawn parallel with the usual course of the lateral line series. Sometimes, when there are no scales, as in eels, the number of lateral line pores may still be counted.

Often it is useful to enumerate in some way the number of horizontal scale rows between two points, for example, between the lateral line and the first dorsal spine or between the lateral line and the first anal spine. Because of the way in which scales are placed, it is necessary to make these counts diagonally as indicated in Figure 4. The scale formula for the fish shown in this figure would be written 4/25/8, the count above the lateral line coming first.

To obtain an accurate *gill-raker count*, it is usually necessary to remove carefully the front gill arch, taking care not to lose the anterior gill rakers in the process. However, a reliable count of at least the lower gill rakers can usually be obtained without removing the arch by folding the gill cover well forward and upward.

The gill rakers are divided into an upper and a lower group by the raker

**34**

at the angle of the gill arch which has roots extending both above and below. This is the only raker that has roots extending in both directions (Fig. 7). Some difficulty often arises in deciding which are the terminal gill rakers. Unless otherwise stated, any low knoblike rudiments at the top and the bottom of the arch are excluded from gill-raker counts. The gill-raker formula for the arch shown in Figure 7 would be $7+1+10=18$.

### MEASUREMENT CHARACTERS

Since a fish grows throughout life, the absolute size of any structure, for example the head, will mean nothing unless compared with that of the head of another specimen of the same total size. However, the various parts of a fish grow at approximately the same rates, so that if the head is said to go, for example, 3 times into the standard length, this statement will hold fairly well for individuals in a moderately broad size range. This, then, is the way measurement characters are usually expressed. One feature of these relative lengths should be called to the attention of the beginner. If the depth of the body is contained 3 times in the length for one fish and 5 times in the length for another, the first fish will have the deeper body.

The *total length* of a fish is the straight line distance from the tip of the snout to the tip of the tail. This is the fish length usually used by the layman and is the measurement referred to in this book when reference is made to the length in inches attained by a species. However, the tail is quite subject to injuries of various sorts, and the total lengths of two fishes of the same real size may differ considerably, depending on what may have happened to the tail. For this reason the basic length measurement used in keys and descriptions is the *standard length*. The standard length is the straight line distance from the tip of the snout to the base of the middle caudal rays. Since the caudal rays have their base enclosed in flesh, locating their point of origin may present some difficulty. Usually, if the caudal fin is bent back and forth a crease will form in the caudal peduncle just ahead of the base of the caudal rays. This crease is the terminal point posteriorly for the standard length.

By *depth of body* is meant the greatest depth the body attains. The *head length* is the greatest straight line distance from the snout tip to the posteriormost point on the gill cover. *Snout length* is the straight line distance from the tip of the snout to the anteriormost point of the exposed part of the eye. The *interorbital width* is the straight line distance between the orbits. The *eye diameter* is the horizontal distance across the exposed portion of the eyeball. The *length of a fin base*, except the adipose, is measured from the front of the base of the first ray to the rear of the base of the last. The *depth of the caudal peduncle* is the least depth in that area, and the *length of the caudal peduncle* is the distance from the rear of the base of the last anal ray to the base of the middle caudal ray.

## The Use of Keys

The principle of the key is that each section provides two alternatives. Either the fish to be identified agrees with the first but not the second, or vice

**35**

versa. Having determined the alternative that fits the fish, the reader is referred to a number. This is the number of another section to which he proceeds and which provides a second set of alternatives. By beginning at number 1 and following out successive sets of alternatives in the same fashion the proper determination will, it is hoped, be eventually made. However, the correctness of the identification should be checked by comparing the fish with the species discussion in the text.

An explanation of certain supplementary features of the keys may make them easier to use. Each section consists of two alternative parts but the section number precedes only the first of these. Numbers following the section numbers in parentheses refer to the section from which the reader has just come.

The identification of any individual fish must usually be undertaken in two steps. First, the family to which the fish belongs must be determined by the use of the keys in the next section. This will refer the reader to a key to the Hawaiian species within the family. Since there are 139 families of fishes known from Hawaii but only an average of four species per family, it is the family key that will usually cause the beginner the most difficulty. Certain features have been incorporated in the family keys to aid their use. First, they have been broken up into a preliminary and four subkeys in order to avoid a single unit of unwieldy length. Second, an illustration of a typical member of almost all the salt water families has been included. From a glance at these the user may obtain a quick indication as to whether he has made a correct family determination or not.

### Key to the Families of Fishes
#### As Recorded from the Hawaiian Islands

Those families of fishes chiefly or entirely restricted to deep water are marked with an asterisk (*) and those largely or entirely to fresh water by a dagger (†).

| | | |
|---|---|---|
| 1 | A single gill opening on each side | 12 |
| | Five or 6 external gill slits on each side | 2 |
| 2(1) | Body strongly flattened | 10 |
| | Body more or less cylindrical in cross section | 3 |
| 3(2) | Anal fin present | 4 |
| | Anal fin absent | Fig. 9 and p. 91, SQUALIDAE |

## Fig. 9. SQUALUS FERNANDINUS

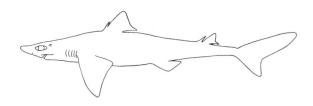

After Bigelow and Schroeder, p. 456, fig. 87e

4(3)   Base of first dorsal fin terminates over or ahead of origin of pelvic fins,
       as in Figs. 11–15.................................................... 6

       Base of first dorsal fin at least partly behind base of pelvic fins, as in
       Fig. 10.......................................................... 5

5(4)   Caudal fin large, lunate, the upper lobe extending almost vertically; size
       large, to over 30 feet...................Fig. 10 and p. 88, RHINCODONTIDAE

## Fig. 10. RHINCODON TYPUS

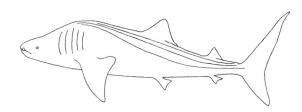

After Bigelow and Schroeder, p. 190, fig. 30

       Caudal fin small, not lunate, the upper lobe extending more or less hori-
       zontally; size small, to about 2 feet.......................SCYLIORHINIDAE*

6(4)   Head of normal shape, not expanded laterally........................ 7

       Head greatly expanded laterally..............Fig. 11 and p. 91, SPHYRNIDAE

## Fig. 11. SPHYRNA LEWINI

A composite figure based on two sources.

7(6)   Caudal fin not lunate, the upper lobe extending far behind the lower, as in Figs. 13–15 . . . . . . . . . . . . . . . . . . . . . . . . . . . . . . . . . . . . . . . . . . . . . . . .   8

Caudal fin lunate, the upper lobe not extending much farther posteriorly than the lower . . . . . . . . . . . . . . . . . . . . . . . . . . . . . . . .Fig. 12 and p. 87, ISURIDAE

### Fig. 12. CARCHARODON CARCHARIAS

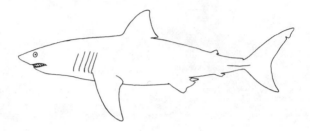

After Bigelow and Schroeder, p. 135, fig. 20

8(7)   Caudal fin much shorter than the body, as in Figs. 14 and 15 . . . . . . . . . . .   9

Caudal fin nearly as long as the body or longer . . . .Fig. 13 and p. 88, ALOPIIDAE

### Fig. 13. ALOPIAS VULPINUS

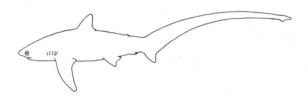

After Bigelow and Welsh, p. 32, fig. 10

9(8)   Teeth low, with 3 or more cusps, and with several series functional simultaneously . . . . . . . . . . . . . . . . . . . . . . . . . . . . . . . . . . .Fig. 14 and p. 88, TRIAKIDAE

### Fig. 14. TRIAENODON OBESUS

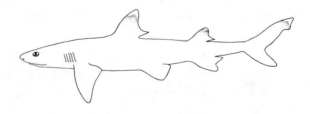

After Fowler, 1928, p. 22, fig. 7

Teeth bladelike, with a single cusp and never with more than 2 series functional simultaneously . . . . . . . . . .Fig. 15 and p. 89, CARCHARHINIDAE

**Fig. 15. EULAMIA PHORCYS**

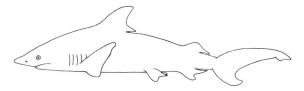

After J. and E., pl. 2

10(2)  Head and eyes ahead of the level of the arc made by the front borders of the pectoral fin, as in Figs. 17 and 18; pectoral wings ending in an acute point laterally............................................................ 11

Head and eyes behind the level of the arc made by the front borders of the pectoral fins; pectorals rounded laterally....Fig. 16 and p. 93, DASYATIDAE

**Fig. 16. DASYATIS HAWAIIENSIS**

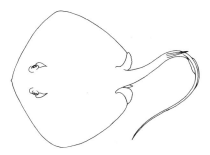

After J. and E., pl. 4

11(10)  No flipper-like folds extending forward from each side of the head
.....................................Fig. 17 and p. 93, MYLIOBATIDAE

**Fig. 17. AETOBATUS NARINARI**

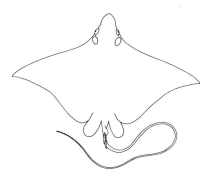

After J. and E., p. 49, fig. 7

**39**

A flipper-like fold extending forward from either side of the head
..............................................Fig. 18 and p. 93, MOBULIDAE

**Fig. 18. MANTA BIROSTRIS**

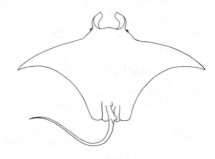

After J. and E., 1900, pl. 18

12(1)    Lateral-line system on front part of head not conspicuous.............. 13

Lateral-line system on front part of head conspicuous; a single strong,
sharp, dorsal spine......................Fig. 19 and p. 94, CHIMAERIDAE*

**Fig. 19. HYDROLAGUS PURPURESCENS**

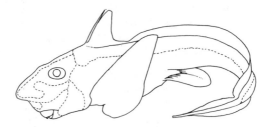

After Gilbert, p. 582, fig. 231

13(12)   One eye on each side of the head................................... 17

Both eyes on the same side of the head............................ 14

14(13)   Pectoral fins present............................................. 15

Pectoral fins absent............................................. 16

15(14)   Eyes on the right side of the fish's head...Fig. 20 and p. 150, PLEURONECTIDAE

### Fig. 20. SAMMARISCUS CORALLINUS

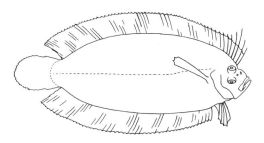

After Norman, p. 410, fig. 298

Eyes on the left side of the fish's head . . . . . . . . . Fig. 21 and p. 147, BOTHIDAE

### Fig. 21. BOTHUS PANTHERINUS, female (left) and male (right)

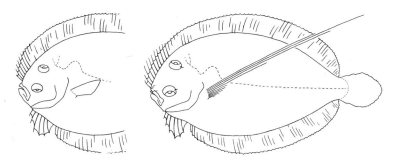

After Norman, p. 234, fig. 177

16(14)    Eyes on the right side of the fish's head . . . . . . . . . . . . . . . . . . . .P. 151, SOLEIDAE

         Eyes on the left side of the fish's head . . . . . Fig. 22 and p. 152, CYNOGLOSSIDAE

### Fig. 22. SYMPHURUS UNDATUS

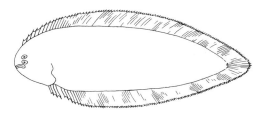

After Gilbert, pl. 98

17(13)    Either the gill openings are in front of the pectoral bases or the pectoral
         fins are absent. . . . . . . . . . . . . . . . . . . . . . . . . . . . . . . . . . . . . . . . . . . . . . .   22

         Gill openings behind the level of the pectoral bases. . . . . . . . . . . . . . . . . .   18

18(17)    Body compressed or rounded, at least as high as wide. . . . . . . . . . . . . . . .   19

         Body depressed, wider than high. . . . . . . . . . . . . . . . . . . . . . . . . . . . . . . . . .   21

19(18)  No stout dorsal spines on the head..................................  20
Two short, blunt, stout dorsal spines on the head.................
...................................Fig. 23 and p. 303, ANTENNARIIDAE

**Fig. 23. ANTENNARIUS CHIRONECTES**

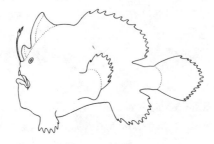

After J. and E., p. 519, fig. 228

20(19)  Gill openings above level of pectoral bases..Fig. 24 and p. 306, CHAUNACIDAE*

**Fig. 24. CHAUNAX UMBRINUS**

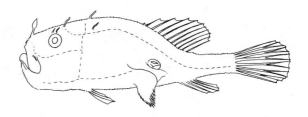

After Gilbert, p. 693, fig. 274

Gill openings below the level of the pectoral bases..................
.......................................Fig. 25 and p. 306, CERATIIDAE*

**Fig. 25. CERATIAS HOLBOELLI**

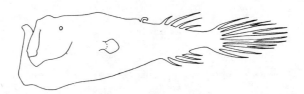

After Gilbert, pl. 99

21(18)  Mouth large, terminal......................Fig. 26 and p. 303, LOPHIIDAE*

**42**

**Fig. 26. LOPHIOMUS MIACANTHUS**

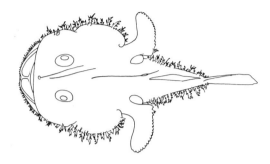

After Gilbert, p. 692, fig. 273

Mouth small, subterminal. . . . . . . . . . . . . .Fig. 27 and p. 306, OGCOCEPHALIDAE*

**Fig. 27. MALTHOPSIS JORDANI**

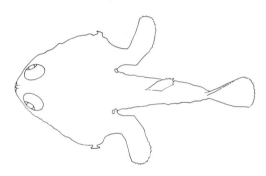

After Gilbert, pl. 100

22(17)  Caudal fin, if present, terminal. . . . . . . . . . . . . . . . . . . . . . . . . . . . . . . . . . . . . . .  23

Caudal fin extending vertically downward from the posteroventral surface of the body, the dorsal fin extending posterior to it along the
horizontal axis of the body. . . . . . . . . . . . . . . .Fig. 28 and p. 133, CENTRISCIDAE

**Fig. 28. CENTRISCUS STRIGATUS**

After Mohr, 1937, p. 25, fig. 15A

23(22)  Pelvic fins present, though sometimes rudimentary or highly modified
(as in Fig. 5d–f). . . . . . . . . . . . . . . . . . . . . . . . . . . . . . . . . . . . . . . . . . . . . . . . . . . . .  24

Pelvic fins totally absent. . . . . . . . . . . . . . . . . . . . . . . . . . . . . . . . . . . . . . . . .SUBKEY D

24(23)   The 2 pelvic fins separate from one another........................ 25

The innermost rays of the 2 pelvic fins attached to one another for their full length by membrane (as in Fig. 5f)..............P. 266, GOBIIDAE

25(24)   Pelvic fins with 5 or fewer soft rays............................... 26

Pelvic fins with more than 5 soft rays...........................SUBKEY A

26(25)   Dorsal fin composed of 2 or more completely separate parts.........SUBKEY B

A single dorsal fin which may be more or less subdivided, but if so the sections connected by at least a basal membrane...................SUBKEY C

## Subkey A

### Pelvic Fins with More Than Five Soft Rays.

1   No stiff, sharp spines at the front of the anal fin...................... 2

One or more stiff, sharp spines at the front of the anal fin.............. 35

2(1)   No adipose fin................................................... 14

Adipose fin present.............................................. 3

3(2)   Snout and mouth without barbels, though a barbel may be present under chin....................................................... 4

Snout and mouth with 6 barbels........................... AMEIURIDAE†

4(3)   Sides of body with photophores.................................... 10

Sides of body without photophores................................. 5

5(4)   Upper rays of pectoral fins not reaching to caudal..................... 6

Upper rays of pectoral fins reaching to or beyond caudal............
..................................Fig. 29 and p. 100, BATHYPTEROIDAE*

### Fig. 29. BATHYPTEROIS ANTENNATUS

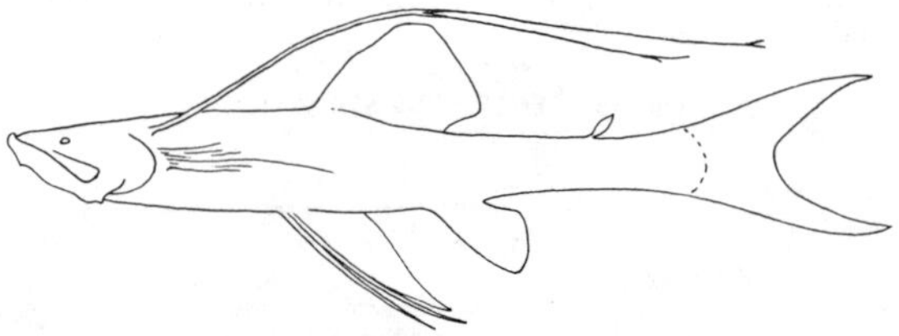

After Gilbert, p. 590, fig. 235

6(5)   Length of dorsal base less than half the body length.................. 7

Length of dorsal base about two-thirds of the body length..........
..................................Fig. 30 and p. 101, ALEPISAURIDAE*

**44**

**Fig. 30. ALEPISAURUS BOREALIS**

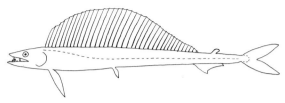

After J. and E., 1900, pl. 96

7(6)    Pectoral fins reaching beyond the level of the base of the pelvic fins . . . . . .    9

Pectoral fins ending far short of the base of the pelvic fins . . . . . . . . . . . . .    8

8(7)    Mouth extending behind eye . . . . . . . . . . . . . . . . . . . . . . . . . . . . . SALMONIDAE†

Mouth not extending behind eye . . . . . . . . Fig. 31 and p. 101, PARALEPIDIDAE*

**Fig. 31. LESTIDIUM NUDUM**

After Gilbert, p. 608, fig. 236

9(7)    Mouth extending well beyond the posterior border of the eye . . . . . . . .
. . . . . . . . . . . . . . . . . . . . . . . . . . . . . . . . . . . . . . . . Fig. 32 and p. 98, SYNODONTIDAE

**Fig. 32. SYNODUS DERMATOGENYS**

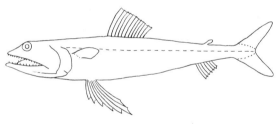

After J. and E., p. 64, fig. 14

Mouth not reaching the posterior border of the eye . . . . . . . . . . . . . . . ..
. . . . . . . . . . . . . . . . . . . . . . . . . . . . . . Fig. 33 and p. 98, CHLOROPHTHALMIDAE*

**Fig. 33. CHLOROPHTHALMUS AGASSIZI**

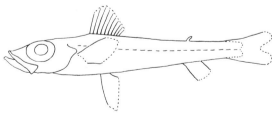

After Gilbert and Cramer, pl. 36

45

10(4)   No barbel below chin.................................................... 11

A large barbel below chin.............. Fig. 34 and p. 97, ASTRONESTHIDAE*

**Fig. 34. ASTRONESTHES LUCIFER**

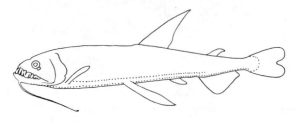

After Gilbert, pl. 71

11(10)   Body not short and deep, the depth contained more than 2 times
in the standard length.................................................... 12

Body short and deep, the depth contained less than 2 times in the
standard length...................... Fig. 35 and p. 97, STERNOPTYCHIDAE*

**Fig. 35. POLYIPNUS NUTTINGI**

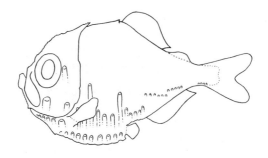

After Gilbert, pl. 73

12(11)   Anal fin commencing about under posterior portion of dorsal fin
...................................... Fig. 36 and p. 100, MYCTOPHIDAE

**Fig. 36. MYCTOPHUM AFFINE**

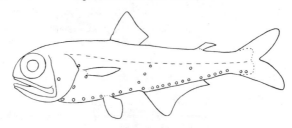

After J. and E., p. 68, fig. 15

Anal fin commencing about under the base of the first dorsal ray
.............................. Fig. 37 and p. 96, in part GONOSTOMATIDAE*

**Fig. 37. CYCLOTHONE ELONGATUM**

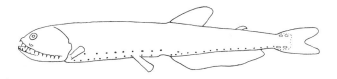

After Gilbert, pl. 71

13(2)   Soft dorsal and anal not followed by finlets.........................   14

Soft dorsal and anal each followed by 5 or more finlets..............
................................Fig. 38 and p. 128, SCOMBERESOCIDAE

**Fig. 38. COLOLABIS SAIRA**

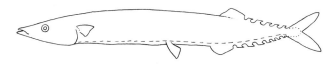

After Tanaka, 1935, pl. 17

14(13)   A separate, well-developed caudal fin...............................   16

No separate, well-developed caudal fin, the body tapering to a point
posteriorly......................................................   15

15(14)   A single, short dorsal fin................Fig. 39 and p. 128, HALOSAURIDAE*

**Fig. 39. HALOSAUROPSIS KAUAIENSIS**

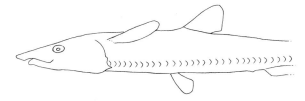

After Gilbert, pl. 74

Two dorsal fins, the second elongate.......Fig. 40 and p. 136, MACROURIDAE*

**Fig. 40. LIONURUS HEBETATUS**

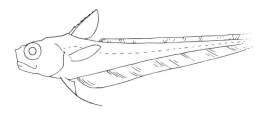

After Gilbert, p. 671, fig. 262

**47**

16(14)  Snout not in the form of an elongate tube with a small mouth at its tip... 18

Snout elongate, tubular, with a small mouth at tip..................... 17

17(16)  Soft dorsal preceded by a series of small, free spines; chin with a barbel; caudal without a median filament.........Fig. 41 and p. 133, AULOSTOMIDAE

### Fig. 41. AULOSTOMUS CHINENSIS

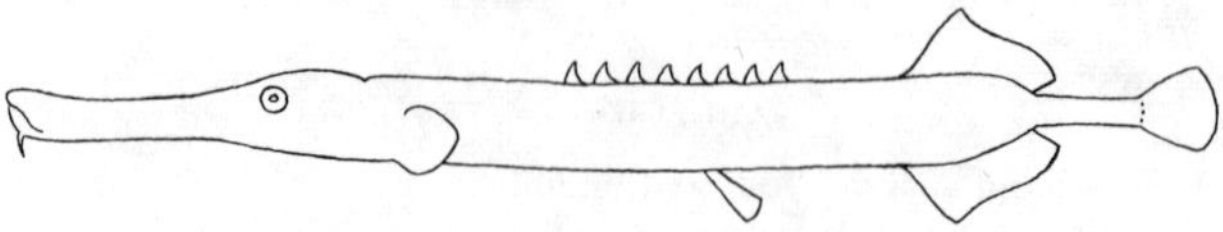

After J. and E., p. 115, fig. 34

No free spines along back; no barbel on chin; caudal with a median filament................................Fig. 42 and p. 132, FISTULARIIDAE

### Fig. 42. FISTULARIA PETIMBA

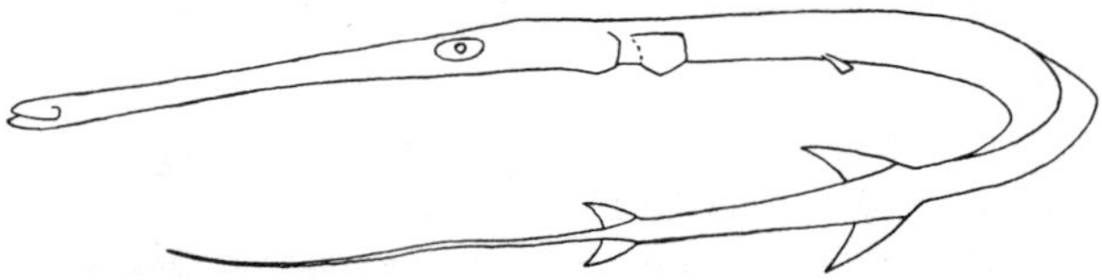

After Weber and de Beaufort, 1922, p. 11

18(16)  Body not ovate, the depth contained more than 2 times in the standard length..................................................... 19

Body ovate, the depth contained less than 2 times in the standard length...................................Fig. 43 and p. 145, LAMPRIDAE

### Fig. 43. LAMPRIS REGIUS

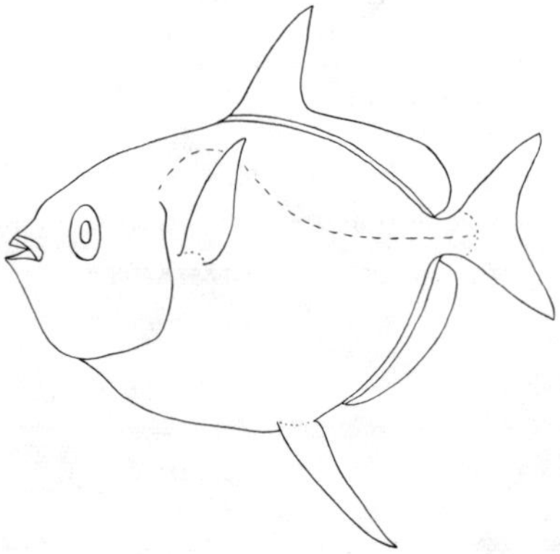

After Fowler, 1928, p. 89, fig. 17

19(18)  No photophores on body........................................... 21

Photophores present along lower sides.............................. 20

48

20(19)  No barbel below chin..........Fig. 44 and p. 96, in part GONOSTOMATIDAE*

**Fig. 44. ARGYRIPNUS EPHIPPIATUS**

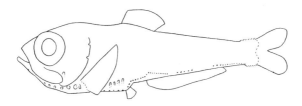

After Gilbert and Cramer, pl. 39

An elongate barbel below chin.............Fig. 45 and p. 97, STOMIATIDAE*

**Fig. 45. LEPTOSTOMIAS MACRONEMA**

After Gilbert, pl. 72

21(19)  Barbels, if present, 4 or fewer ...................................... 23

   A series of 6 or more barbels around mouth .......................... 22

22(21)  Dorsal long, with about 50 rays ........................... CLARIIDAE†

   Dorsal short, with about 9 rays ............................ COBITIDAE†

23(21)  Lateral line, if present, running along the middle of the sides or above.... 26

   Lateral line running very low along sides, commencing below the base
   of the pectoral fin.................................................. 24

24(23)  Pectorals not winglike; one or both jaws produced.................... 25

   Pectorals winglike; neither jaw produced.....Fig. 46 and p. 130, EXOCOETIDAE

**Fig. 46. CYPSELURUS SIMUS**

After J. and E., p. 135, fig. 46

25(24)  Both jaws produced into a long, sharp beak....Fig. 47 and p. 128, BELONIDAE

**49**

**Fig. 47. BELONE PLATYURA**

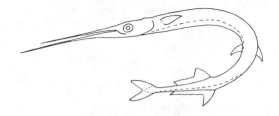

After J. and E., p. 123, fig. 38

Only the lower jaw produced............Fig. 48 and p. 129, HEMIRAMPHIDAE

**Fig. 48. HYPORHAMPHUS PACIFICUS**

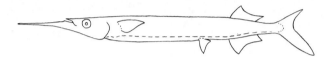

After J. and E., p. 127, fig. 41

26(23)  Pelvic fins inserted well behind pectoral bases........................ 27
Pelvic fins inserted well ahead of pectoral bases...Fig. 49 and p. 136, MORIDAE*

**Fig. 49. ANTIMORA MICROLEPIS**

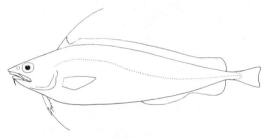

After Günther, 1887, pl. 16

27(26)  Scales smooth; no barbel under the tip of snout...................... 28
Scales rough to the touch; a small, median barbel under the tip of snout
....................................Fig. 50 and p. 98, GONORHYNCHIDAE*

**Fig. 50. GONORHYNCHUS GONORHYNCHUS**

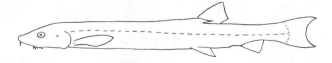

After Kner, 1865, pl. 16

**50**

28(27)    Top of head not scaled to in front of eyes.............................. 30

           Top of head scaled to in front of eyes................................ 29

29(28)    Mouth small, not extending back to the eye.................. POECILIIDAE†

           Mouth large, extending behind eye...................... OPHICEPHALIDAE†

30(28)    Gill membranes not broadly attached to the isthmus.................... 31

           Gill membranes broadly attached to the isthmus............... CYPRINIDAE†

31(30)    Lateral line well developed.......................................... 32

           No lateral line.................................................... 34

32(31)    Mouth small, not extending behind the eye........................... 33

           Mouth large, extending behind the eye........... Fig. 51 and p. 94, ELOPIDAE

### Fig. 51. ELOPS HAWAIENSIS

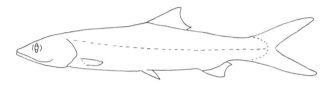

After Weber and de Beaufort, 1913, p. 3, fig. 2

33(32)    Mouth inferior to the overhanging snout........ Fig. 52 and p. 95, ALBULIDAE

### Fig. 52. ALBULA VULPES

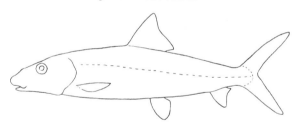

After J. and E., p. 55, fig. 9

           Mouth terminal............................Fig. 53 and p. 97, CHANIDAE

### Fig. 53. CHANOS CHANOS

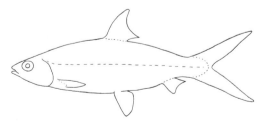

After J. and E., p. 57, fig. 10

**51**

34(31)   Mouth inferior to the overhanging snout......Fig. 54 and p. 96, ENGRAULIDAE

**Fig. 54. STOLEPHORUS PURPUREUS**

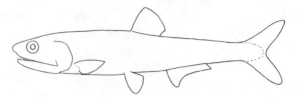

After J. and E., p. 60, fig. 12

Mouth terminal...................... Fig. 55 and p. 95, DUSSUMIERIIDAE

**Fig. 55. SPRATELLOIDES GRACILIS**

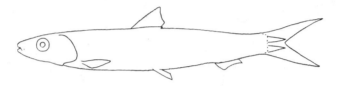

After Weber and de Beaufort, 1913, p. 19, fig. 12

35(1)   No barbels on chin................................................   36

A pair of large barbels on chin...........Fig. 56 and p. 136, POLYMIXIIDAE*

**Fig. 56. POLYMIXIA JAPONICA**

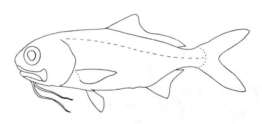

After Gilbert, pl. 78

36(35)   One to 4 spines in the anal fin....................................   37

Seventeen spines in the anal fin.............Fig. 57 and p. 145, VELIFERIDAE

**Fig. 57. VELIFER MULTISPINOSUS**

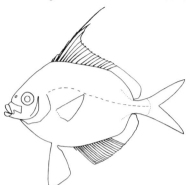

From a Hawaiian specimen

37(36)  Four or more spines in the dorsal fin................................  39
        Two spines at the front of the dorsal fin............................  38

38(37)  Several long, fanglike teeth in the front of the mouth.. P. 136, CAULOLEPIDAE*
        No enlarged teeth......................Fig. 58 and p. 137, MELAMPHAIDAE*

**Fig. 58. MELAMPHAES UNICORNIS**

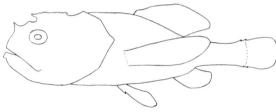

After Gilbert, pl. 77

39(37)  Dorsal fin with 8 or fewer spines, the base of the spinous portion shorter
        than the base of the soft portion, which has more than 20 rays...........  40

        Dorsal fin with 10 or more spines, the base of the spinous portion
        longer than the base of the soft portion, which has 16 or fewer rays...
        ......................................Fig. 59 and p. 137, HOLOCENTRIDAE

**Fig. 59. HOLOCENTRUS LACTEOGUTTATUS**

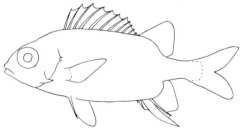

After J. and E., p. 63, fig. 50

**53**

40(39)  Dorsal fin with a distinct notch between the spinous and soft portions,
with more than 5 spines.................................................... 41

Dorsal fin without any notch between the spinous and soft portions,
with only 4 spines...............................................P. 136, BERYCIDAE*

41(40)  No bony bucklers on the abdomen; pelvics not reaching to the middle of
the anal fin............................................................... 42

A series of large, bony bucklers on the abdomen; pelvics reaching to the
middle of the anal fin...........................Fig. 60 and p. 146, ZEIDAE

**Fig. 60. STETHOPRISTES EOS**

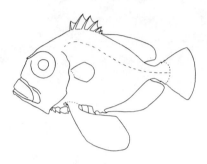

After Gilbert, p. 623, fig. 241

42(41)  Scales in the form of long, vertical, paper-like strips; mouth small, not
reaching the front of eye.............Fig. 61 and p. 147, GRAMMICOLEPIDAE*

**Fig. 61. GRAMMICOLEPIS BRACHIUSCULUS**

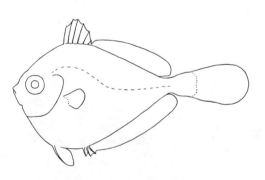

After Jordan, 1922, p. 650, fig. 5

Scales not forming vertically elongate strips; mouth large, reaching
beyond front of eye.......................Fig. 62 and p. 146, CAPROIDAE*

**Fig. 62. CYTTOMIMUS STELGIS**

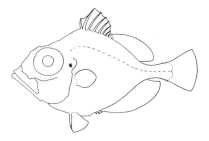

After Gilbert, pl. 80

## Subkey B

**Pelvic Fins Present, with Five or Fewer Soft Rays.**
**Dorsal Fin Composed of Two or More Completely Separate Parts.**

1    First dorsal not composed of a single long ray originating on the top
of head . . . . . . . . . . . . . . . . . . . . . . . . . . . . . . . . . . . . . . . . . . . . . . . . . . . . . . . . . . .    2

First dorsal consisting of a single long ray originating on the top of
head. Pectorals expanded, winglike . . . . . Fig. 63 and p. 290, DACTYLOPTERIDAE

**Fig. 63. DACTYLOPTENA ORIENTALIS**

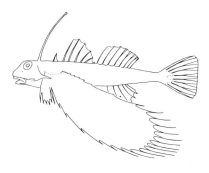

After J. and E., p. 473, fig. 208

2(1)    Upper jaw not projecting as a tapering, bony spear . . . . . . . . . . . . . . . . . . . .    3

Upper jaw projecting as a tapering, bony spear. First dorsal long; size
large . . . . . . . . . . . . . . . . . . . . . . . . . . . . . . . . . . Fig. 64 and p. 261, ISTIOPHORIDAE

**55**

**Fig. 64. ISTIOPHORUS ORIENTALIS**

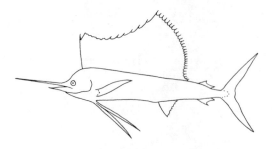

After J. and E., 1926, pl. 15

3(2)  The 2 pelvic fins not fused to one another across the mid-ventral line . . . . .  4

The 2 pelvic fins fused to one another across the mid-ventral line. . . . .
. . . . . . . . . . . . . . . . . . . . . . . . . . . . . . . . . . . . . . . . . Fig. 65 and p. 266, GOBIIDAE

**Fig. 65. ZONOGOBIUS FARCIMEN**

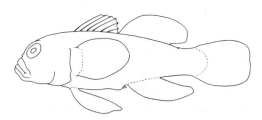

After J. and E., p. 329, fig. 139

4(3)  No spiny ridge running horizontally across cheek to meet the preopercular border; no backwardly projecting spines on top of head behind eye . . . . .  7

A serrate or spiny ridge running horizontally across cheek to meet the
preopercular border; top of head behind eye with backwardly projecting
spines. Anal fin without spines; deep-water families . . . . . . . . . . . . . . . . . . .  5

5(4)  A series of bony plates along sides; lower rays of pectoral fins forming
separate, free, finger-like filaments . . . . . . . . . . . . . . . . . . . . . . . . . . . . . . . .  6

No bony plates; lower pectoral rays normal, not free . . . . . . . . . . . . . . . .
. . . . . . . . . . . . . . . . . . . . . . . . . . . . . . . . Fig. 66 and p. 290, PLATYCEPHALIDAE*

**Fig. 66. BEMBRADIUM ROSEUM**

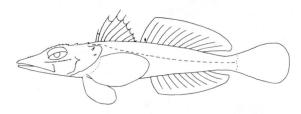

After Gilbert, pl. 82

6(5)    Lower jaw with elongate, fringed barbels...Fig. 67 and p. 289, PERISTEDIIDAE*

### Fig. 67. PERISTEDION HIANS

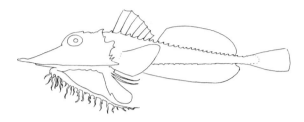

After Gilbert and Cramer, pl. 41, fig. 1

Lower jaw without barbels..............Fig. 68 and p. 290, HOPLICHTHYIDAE*

### Fig. 68. HOPLICHTHYS PLATOPHRYS

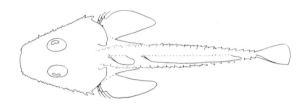

After Gilbert, p. 642, fig. 250

7(4)    Pelvic fins nearer tip of snout than to caudal base.....................    9

        Pelvic fins nearer caudal base than to tip of snout.....................    8

8(7)    Body elongate; first dorsal fin consisting of a number of short, separate
        spines................................Fig. 41 and p. 133, AULOSTOMIDAE

        Body deep and strongly compressed; first dorsal fin high............
        ................................Fig. 69 and p. 133, MACRORHAMPHOSIDAE*

### Fig. 69. MACRORHAMPHOSUS GRACILIS

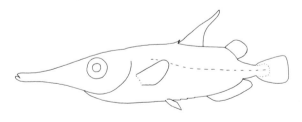

After Gilbert, p. 651, fig. 237

9(7)    Pectoral fin without a separate section below made up of free rays........    10

        Pectoral fin with a separate section below made up of 6 free rays......
        ....................................Fig. 70 and p. 154, POLYNEMIDAE

**Fig. 70. POLYDACTYLUS PLEBEIUS**

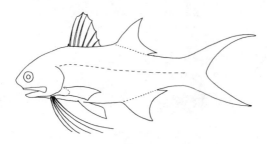

After Smith, 1949, p. 327, fig. 898

10(9)   Soft dorsal fin not followed by finlets.............................. 14

Soft dorsal followed by 1 to several, more or less separate finlets......... 11

11(10)  Anal fin not preceded by 2 free spines.............................. 12

Anal fin preceded by 2 small, sharp spines that are ahead of and free
from the soft portion of the fin.......Fig. 71 and p. 165, in part CARANGIDAE

**Fig. 71. MEGALASPIS CORDYLA**

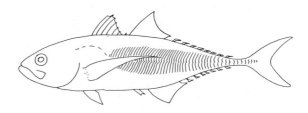

After Weber and de Beaufort, vol. 6, p. 192, fig. 40

12(11)  Soft dorsal followed by 5 or more finlets.............................. 13

Soft dorsal followed by 1 or 2 finlets...Fig. 72 and p. 252, in part GEMPYLIDAE

**Fig. 72. RUVETTUS PRETIOSUS**

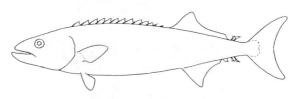

After J. and E., p. 177, fig. 67

13(12)  Lateral line not undulating, entirely on the upper half of the body....
.....................................Fig. 73 and p. 253, SCOMBRIDAE

**Fig. 73. KATSUWONUS PELAMIS**

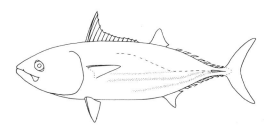

After J. and E., p. 182, fig. 64

Lateral line undulating widely, running well down on to lower half of
the body in places... ............. Fig. 74 and p. 252, in part GEMPYLIDAE

**Fig. 74. LEPIDOCYBIUM FLAVOBRUNNEUM**

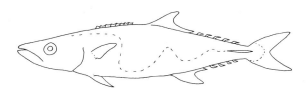

After Munro, pl.1

14(10)  Two dorsal fins. . . . . . . . . . . . . . . . . . . . . . . . . . . . . . . . . . . . . . . . . . . . . . . . . .  15
        Three dorsal fins, the first 2 joined at base. Pelvics with fewer than 5
        rays; size small, to about 2 inches. . . . . . . . .Fig. 75 and p. 276, TRIPTERYGIIDAE

**Fig. 75. TRIPTERYGION ATRICEPS**

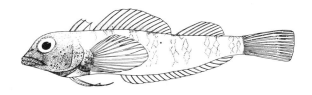

From a Hawaiian specimen

15(14)  Separate first dorsal fin composed of more than 2 rays. . . . . . . . . . . . . . . . . .  16
        Separate first dorsal fin composed of 2 rays on the top of the head.
        Lateral line with a sharp downward jog under the soft dorsal. . . . . . . . . .
        . . . . . . . . . . . . . . . . . . . . . . . . . . . . . . . . . Fig. 76 and p. 213, in part LABRIDAE

**59**

**Fig. 76. INIISTIUS PAVONINUS**

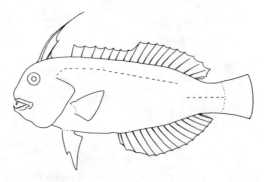

After J. and E., p. 329, fig. 139

16(15)  Body scaled...................................................... 18

Body completely naked.......................................... 17

17(16)  An enlarged preopercular spine; operculum spineless...............
................................................Fig. 77 and p. 271, CALLIONYMIDAE

**Fig. 77. SYNCHIROPUS RUBROVINCTUS**

After Gilbert, p. 651, fig. 252

No preopercular spine; operculum ending in 2 enlarged spines.......
................................................Fig. 78 and p. 273, DRACONETTIDAE*

**Fig. 78. DRACONETTA HAWAIIENSIS**

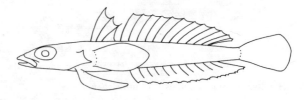

After Gilbert,.pl. 91

18(16)  No pair of barbels on chin....................................... 19

A pair of large barbels under chin.............. Fig. 79 and p. 187, MULLIDAE

**Fig. 79. PARUPENEUS PLEUROSTIGMA**

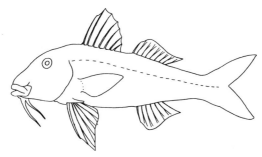

After J. and E., p. 260, fig. 108

19(18) Spinous dorsal base shorter than soft dorsal base...................... 20

Spinous dorsal base longer than soft dorsal base. Scales hard and grooved..........................Fig. 80 and p. 283, TETRAGONURIDAE

**Fig. 80. TETRAGONURUS CUVIERI**

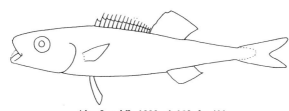

After J. and E., 1900, pl. 152, fig. 411

20(19) Distance between the dorsal fins less than the length of the first dorsal fin base........................................................ 23

Distance between the dorsal fins greater than the length of the first dorsal base. Pelvic fins inserted behind the level of the pectoral bases..... 21

21(20) Lateral line absent; teeth small; scales moderate or large................ 22

Lateral line present; teeth large; scales small...Fig. 81 and p. 91, SPHYRAENIDAE

**Fig. 81. SPHYRAENA BARRACUDA**

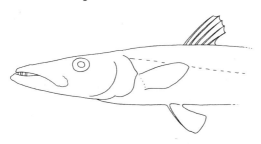

After J. and E., p. 142, fig. 50

22(21) Anal fin with about 17 soft rays; sides with a silvery lateral stripe in life
......................................Fig. 82 and p. 153, ATHERINIDAE

**61**

**Fig. 82. PRANESUS INSULARUM**

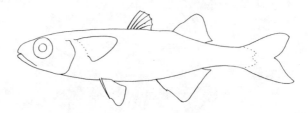

After J. and E., p. 138, fig. 137

Anal fin with 10 or fewer soft rays; sides without a silvery lateral stripe
.............................................Fig. 83 and p. 154, MUGILIDAE

**Fig. 83. MUGIL CEPHALUS**

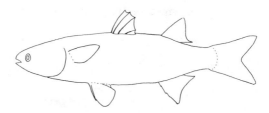

After J. and E., p. 140, fig. 48

23(20)˙ Soft dorsal and anal relatively long, each of 15 or more rays............. 25

Soft dorsal and anal relatively short, each of 12 or fewer soft rays........ 24

24(23) Maxillary exposed and prominent; lateral line usually present, at least
forward...................................Fig. 84 and p. 161, APOGONIDAE

**Fig. 84. APOGON MENESEMUS**

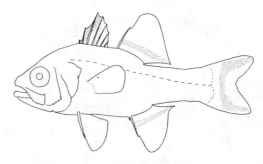

After J. and E., p. 216, fig. 86

Maxillary concealed; lateral line absent........Fig. 85 and p. 265, ELEOTRIDAE

**Fig. 85. EVIOTA EPIPHANES**

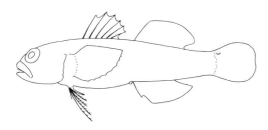

After J. and E., p. 482, fig. 211

25(23)  First dorsal fin with 7 or fewer spines.................................. 26

First dorsal fin with 10 or more spines.........Fig. 86 and p. 281, NOMEIDAE

**Fig. 86. NOMEUS GRONOVII**

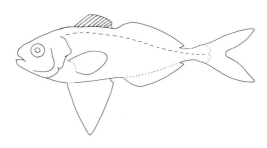

After Goode and Bean, pl. 63, fig. 227

26(25)  Caudal forked or lunate; soft dorsal fin longer than anal................ 27

Caudal rounded; soft dorsal fin somewhat shorter than anal.........
......................................Fig. 87 and p. 240, BEMBROPSIDAE

**Fig. 87. CHRIONEMA SQUAMICEPS**

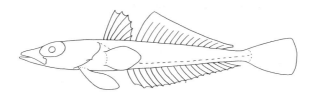

After Gilbert, pl. 86

27(26)  Two lateral lines on body; preopercle with spines...................
...................................Fig. 88 and p. 239, CHAMPSODONTIDAE*

**Fig. 88. CHAMPSODON FIMBRIATUS**

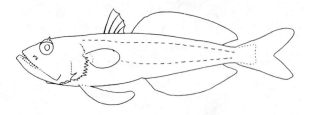

After Gilbert, pl. 88

A single lateral line; preopercle without spines. Posterior portion of lateral line often covered with scutes; anal fin usually preceded by a pair of short, sharp spines that are free from the soft portion of the fin .................................... Fig. 89 and p. 165, in part CARANGIDAE

**Fig. 89. CARANX MELAMPYGUS**

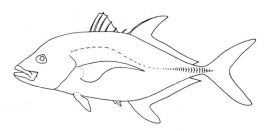

After J. and E., p. 193, fig. 73

## Subkey C

**Pelvic Fins Present, with Five or Fewer Soft Rays.**

**A Single Dorsal Fin Which May Be More or Less Subdivided**

**But if so the Sections Connected by a Basal Membrane.**

| | | |
|---|---|---|
| 1 | Pelvic fins originating ahead of the middle of standard length ........... | 2 |
| | Pelvic fins originating behind the middle of standard length. Body elongate; caudal with a long median filament. . Fig. 42 and p. 132, FISTULARIIDAE | |
| 2(1) | Pelvic fins normal to filamentous, but the longest ray always more than an eye diameter in length .......................................... | 4 |
| | Pelvic fins minute, the longest ray less than an eye diameter in length ..... | 3 |
| 3(2) | Pelvic fins on the ventral surface of the body; body covered with papillae giving it a furry appearance; dorsal commencing behind eye; body short and deep; size small, to about 2 inches. . . . Fig. 90 and p. 289, CARACANTHIDAE | |

**Fig. 90. CARACANTHUS MACULATUS**

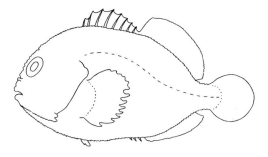

After J. and E., p. 453, fig. 118

Pelvic fins lateral, tucked in just behind the pectoral bases; body without papillae; the long dorsal commencing well forward of eye; body elongate; size to at least 2 feet . . . . . . . . . . . . . . .Fig. 91 and p. 146, LOPHOTIDAE

**Fig. 91. LOPHOTUS CAPELLEI**

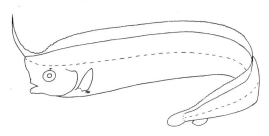

After Goode and Bean, 1895, pl. 115, fig. 390

4(2)    Body not enclosed in bony plates; snout without a bony, knoblike projection . . . . . . . . . . . . . . . . . . . . . . . . . . . . . . . . . . . . . . . . . . . . . . . . . . . . . 5

Body enclosed in bony plates; snout with a bony, knoblike projection. Size small, to about 3 inches . . . . . . . . . . . . . . . .Fig. 92 and p. 290, PEGASIDAE

**Fig. 92. PEGASUS PAPILIO**

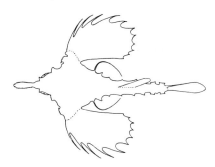

After Gilbert, p. 614, fig. 239

**65**

5(4)   Body scaled, at least along the lateral line.............................  8

       Body completely scaleless............................................  6

6(5)   Gill openings extending far forward on throat........................  7

       Gill openings restricted, not extending far forward on throat.........
       ......................................Fig. 93 and p. 276, BLENNIIDAE

### Fig. 93. ISTIBLENNIUS ZEBRA

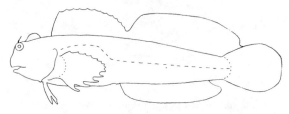

After J. and E., p. 501, fig. 233

7(6)   Lower jaw projecting; pelvic fins normal. Size small, to about 1 inch
       ...................................................P. 271, KRAEMERIIDAE

       Lower jaw included; pelvic fins reduced to a single filament on each
       side...................................Fig. 94 and p. 101, ATELEOPIDAE*

### Fig. 94. ATELEOPUS PLICATELLUS

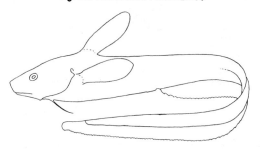

After Gilbert, p. 654, fig. 253

8(5)   Pelvic fins not reduced to 1 or 2 filaments on each side.................  10

       Pelvic fins reduced to 1 or 2 filaments on each side....................  9

9(8)   A single long dorsal fin; dorsal and anal more or less confluent with the
       caudal...................................Fig. 95 and p. 279, BROTULIDAE

### Fig 95  BROTULA MULTIBARBATA

After J. and E., p. 507, fig. 225

Two dorsal fins connected by a low membrane; dorsal and anal completely separate from the caudal..........Fig. 96 and p. 136, in part MORIDAE*

**Fig. 96. LAEMONEMA RHODOCHIR**

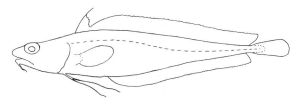

After Gilbert, p. 657, fig. 255

10(8)  Gill openings reaching throat.,...................................  **12**

Gill openings not reaching throat, restricted to the sides of the head......  **11**

11(10)  One or a pair of spines or knobs on the sides of the caudal peduncle; first few dorsal rays not greatly prolonged...Fig. 97 and p. 242, ACANTHURIDAE

**Fig. 97. ACANTHURUS LEUCOPAREIUS**

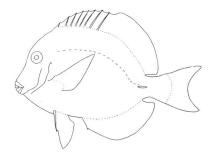

After J. and E., p. 386, fig. 167

No spines or knobs on the sides of the caudal peduncle; first few dorsal spines greatly prolonged....................Fig. 98 and p. 241, ZANCLIDAE

**Fig. 98. ZANCLUS CANESCENS**

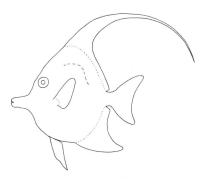

After J. and E., col. pl. 57

**67**

12(10)  Caudal peduncle without a series of platelets; anterior dorsal and anal
rays not forming long, separate streamers............................  13

A series of small platelets along the middle of each side of the caudal
peduncle; anterior dorsal and anal rays prolonged into long, separate
streamers............................Fig. 99 and p. 165, in part CARANGIDAE

### Fig. 99. ALECTIS CILIARIS

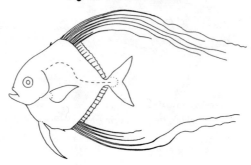

After J. and E., p. 201, fig. 78

13(12)  No spiny ridge running horizontally across cheek below eye; no backwardly projecting spines on top of head behind eyes...................  14

A spiny or at least roughened ridge running across cheek below eye and
joining the preopercle at nearly a right angle; backwardly projecting
spines on top of head behind eyes........Fig. 100 and p. 283, SCORPAENIDAE

### Fig. 100. SCORPAENA CONIORTA

After J. and E., p. 459, fig. 200

14(13)  No sucking disc on top of head....................................  15

A sucking disc on top of head.............Fig. 101 and p. 291, ECHENEIDAE

### Fig. 101. REMORA REMORA

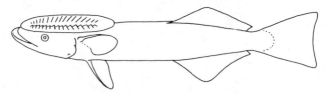

After Smith, 1949, p. 341, fig. 947

**68**

15(14)  Lateral line nowhere running below middle of body; jaws about equal
or the lower projecting............................................ 16

Lateral line descending posteriorly to just above the posterior portion
of the anal base; snout extending considerably in front of lower jaw.
................................Fig. 102 and p. 240, TRICHONOTIDAE

#### Fig. 102. CRYSTALLODYTES COOKEI

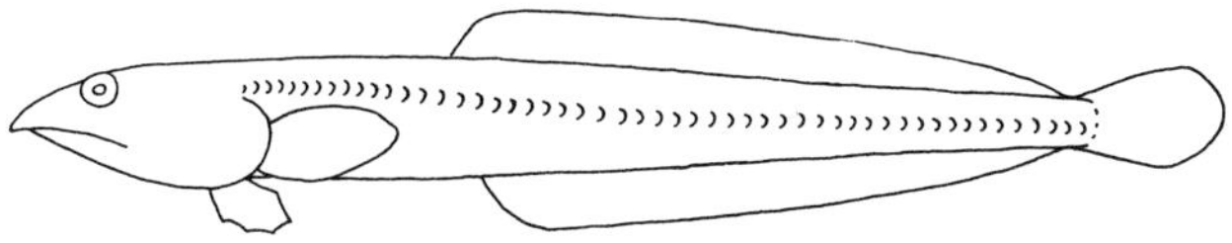

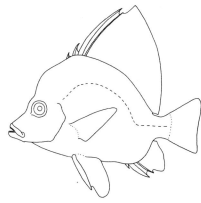

After Fowler, p. 426, fig. 69

16(15)  No barbels on chin................................................ 17

A dense cluster of small barbels on chin. Body with broad black and
white vertical bars....................Fig. 103 and p. 202, HISTIOPTERIDAE

#### Fig. 103. HISTIOPTERUS TYPUS

After Temminck and Schlegel, pl. 45

17(16)  Body longer than deep........................................... 18

Body about as deep as long. Color plain red..Fig. 104 and p. 146, ANTIGONIIDAE

**Fig. 104. ANTIGONIA EOS**

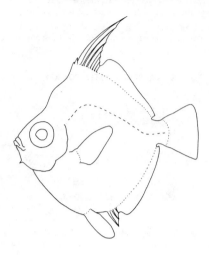

After Gilbert, pl. 80

18(17)  Anterior nostril without a small, fringed tentacle...................... 20

Anterior nostril with a small, fringed tentacle. Lower pectoral rays unbranched and somewhat swollen, their tips projecting well beyond the
interradial membranes............................................. 19

19(18)  Soft dorsal long, of about 29 rays; color pattern of alternating black and
white bands.......................Fig. 105 and p. 202, CHEILODACTYLIDAE

**Fig. 105. CHEILODACTYLUS VITTATUS**

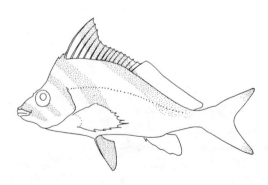

After J. and E., pl.54

Soft dorsal short, of 14 or fewer rays; color pattern not of alternating
black and white bands....................Fig. 106 and p. 203, CIRRHITIDAE

**70**

**Fig. 106. CIRRHITUS ALTERNATUS**

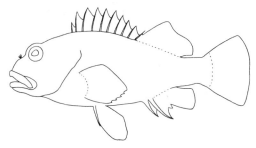

After J. and E., col. pl. 70

20(18)  Anal spines, if present, not separated from the soft portion of the fin; no short, partly concealed spine at the upper end of the preopercular border.................................................................... 21

Anal spines connected with the soft portion of the fin by a low membrane, if at all; a short, partly concealed spine at the upper end of the preopercular border................Fig. 107 and p. 158, PSEUDOCHROMIDAE

**Fig. 107. APOROPS BILINEARIS**

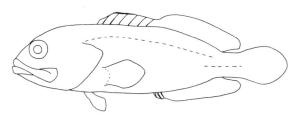

After Schultz, 1943, fig. 9

21(20)  Lateral line present, at least forward................................. 22

Lateral line absent. Scales prickly; anal fin with at least 30 rays........
.......................................Fig. 108 and p. 180, BRAMIDAE

**Fig. 108. COLLYBUS DRACHME**

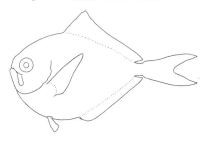

After J. and E., pl. 34

**71**

22(21)  No single, sharp, more or less conical spine on the opercle............ 24

A single, sharp, more or less conical spine on the opercle. Anal without spines and with 18 or more soft rays................................ 23

23(22)  Caudal fin with a pair of prominent, longitudinal, black bars; anal fin with about 50 rays....................Fig. 109 and p. 165, MALACANTHIDAE

### Fig. 109. MALACANTHUS PARVIPINNIS

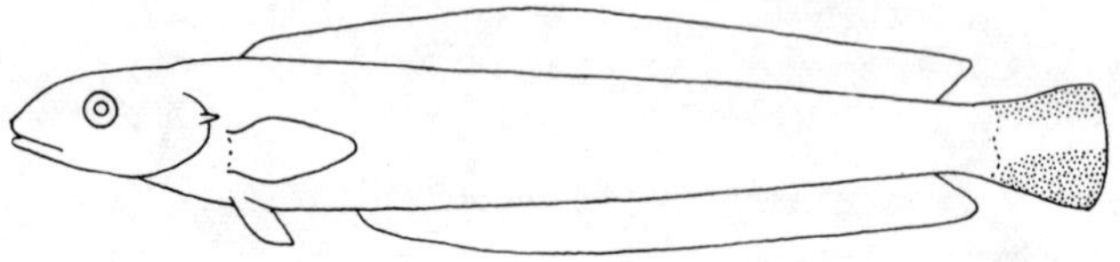

After J. and E., p. 276, fig. 118

Caudal fin without prominent longitudinal bars; anal with about 20 rays.............................Fig. 110 and p. 239, in part PARAPERCIDAE

### Fig. 110. NEOPERCIS ROSEOVIRIDIS

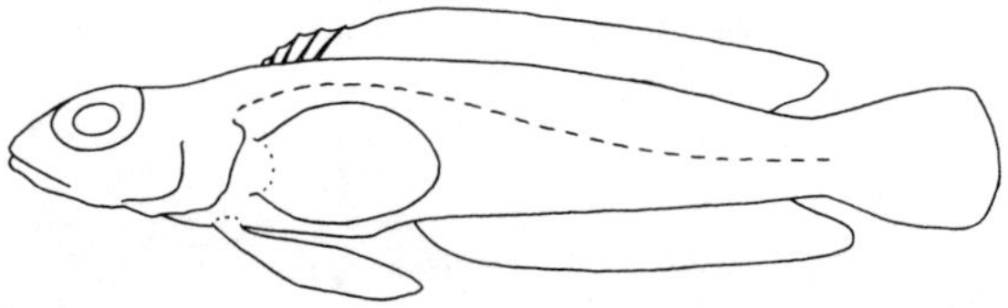

After Gilbert, pl. 83

24(22)  Dorsal fin with fewer than 25 soft rays......................... 25

Dorsal fin with more than 50 rays........Fig. 111 and p. 181, CORYPHAENIDAE

### Fig. 111. CORYPHAENA HIPPURUS

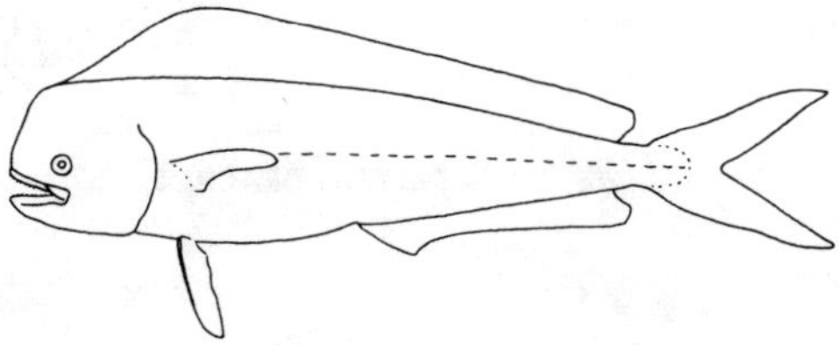

After J. and E., p. 204, fig. 79

25(24)  Branched caudal rays about 15; gill covers attached to the isthmus far forward or entirely free from it. Two or more sharp anal spines.......... 27

Branched caudal rays 11 or 12; gill covers broadly attached to the isthmus or to one another by a membrane across the isthmus. Scales cycloid; caudal often lunate but never forked................................ 26

26(25)  Jaws with a single series of separate teeth in front...................
.............................................Fig. 112 and p. 213, LABRIDAE

**72**

**Fig. 112. THALASSOMA LUTESCENS**

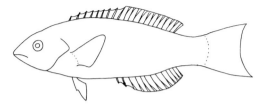

After J. and E., pl. 41

Jaw teeth either fused into a beaklike structure or with 2 to several series
of overlapping incisors in front..............Fig. 113 and p. 234, SCARIDAE

**Fig. 113. SCARUS DUBIUS**

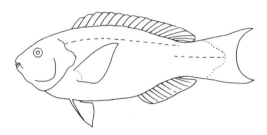

After J. and E., p. 350, fig. 151

27(25) Teeth not fused into a beaklike structure ........................... 28

Teeth fused into a beaklike structure ...Fig. 114 and p. 202, HOPLEGNATHIDAE

**Fig. 114. HOPLEGNATHUS FASCIATUS**

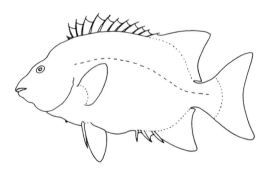

After Temminck and Schlegel, pl. 46

28(27) Anal fin with 3 or more spines.................................... 29

Anal fin with 2 spines. Lateral line ending under the soft dorsal fin; a
single nostril on each side of the head...Fig. 115 and p. 205, POMACENTRIDAE

**73**

### Fig. 115. ABUDEFDUF SORDIDUS

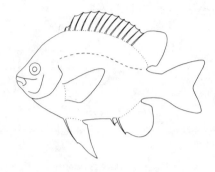

After J. and E., p. 274, fig. 117

29(28)  Sides never plain silvery.............................................  31

Sides plain silvery, darker above..................................  30

30(29)  Chest keeled; maxillary not reaching front of eye; anal soft rays 7.....
.................................................P. 159, GREGORYINIDAE

Chest rounded; maxillary reaching beyond front border of eye; anal
soft rays 11..............................Fig. 116 and p. 158, KUHLIIDAE

### Fig. 116. KUHLIA TAENIURA

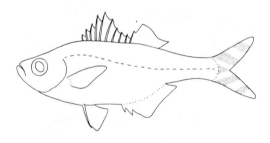

After J. and E., p. 209, fig. 81

31(29)  Mouth moderate or large, the maxillary reaching to behind the level of
the anterior nostril; teeth firm. Lateral line reaching caudal base..........  33

Mouth small, not reaching the level of the anterior nostril; teeth more
or less flexible, like the teeth of a comb. Body deep and strongly
compressed.......................................................  32

32(31)  Dorsal with 12 or more spines.........Fig. 117 and p. 194, CHAETODONTIDAE

### Fig. 117. CHAETODON UNIMACULATUS

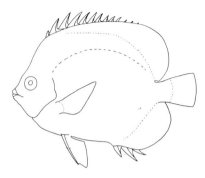

After J. and E., p. 369, fig. 161

Dorsal with 11 spines. Color pattern of about 6 black, nearly horizontal bands on a plain greenish ground; lateral line reaching caudal base....
................................................Fig. 118 and p. 193, SCORPIDIDAE

### Fig. 118. MICROCANTHUS STRIGATUS

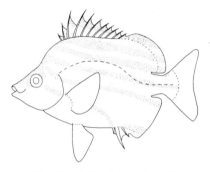

After Temminck and Schlegel, pl. 41

33(31)  Dorsal spines 11 or fewer......................................... 35

        Dorsal spines 12 or more......................................... 34

34(33)  Preopercle serrate; 2 nostrils on each side of the head..............
................................................Fig. 210 and p. 187, LOBOTIDAE

        Preopercle smooth; a single nostril on each side of the head......CICHLIDAE†

35(33)  Soft dorsal and anal not covered by a sheath of scales.................. 37

        Soft dorsal and anal covered by a sheath of scales. Largest dorsal spines longer than longest soft dorsal rays; pelvics inserted entirely behind pectoral bases; preopercular border smooth.......................... 36

36(35)  Spinous and soft portions of dorsal fin continuous; teeth incisiform; nostrils in a shallow groove that extends forward from about the middle of the anterior border of the orbit; color in life usually green or bluish
................................................Fig. 119 and p. 194, KYPHOSIDAE

**75**

### Fig. 119. KYPHOSUS ELEGANS

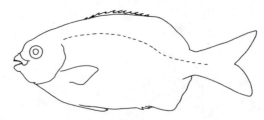

After Meek and Hildebrand, pl. 64

Dorsal fin divided nearly to the base between spinous and soft portions; teeth minute or absent; nostrils not in a groove, nearly on a level with the top of eye; color in life plain orange. Fig. 120 and p. 182, EMMELICHTHYIDAE

### Fig. 120. ERYTHRICHTHYS SCHLEGELI

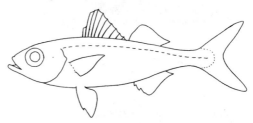

After J. and E., col. pl. 19

37(35)   Anal soft rays 12 or fewer . . . . . . . . . . . . . . . . . . . . . . . . . . . . . . . . . . . . . . . . . . . . . 38

Anal soft rays 14 or more. Pelvic fins attached to the abdomen by a broad membrane; color primarily or entirely red; scales small and very rough, more than 80 in a longitudinal series . . . . . Fig. 121 and p. 159, PRIACANTHIDAE

### Fig. 121. PRIACANTHUS CRUENTATUS

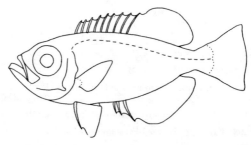

After J. and E., p. 230, fig. 94

38(37)   Color pattern not composed of vertical white bars with blackish areas in between . . . . . . . . . . . . . . . . . . . . . . . . . . . . . . . . . . . . . . . . . . . . . . . . . . . . . . . . 39

Color pattern of about 4 vertical white bars with blackish areas in between. Maxillary completely concealed under the cheek when the mouth is closed . . . . . . . . . . . . . . . . . . . . . . . . . . . . . Fig. 122 and p. 193, SPARIDAE

**76**

**Fig. 122. MONOTAXIS GRANDOCULIS**

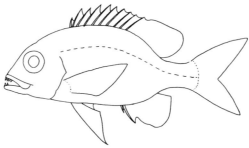

After J. and E., p. 243, fig. 101

39(38)  Anal with 9 or fewer soft rays...................................... 40

Anal with 10 to 12 soft rays............................CENTRARCHIDAE†

40(39)  Dorsal fin with 11 or fewer soft rays; depth of caudal peduncle contained about twice in the distance from the base of the last dorsal ray to the base of the middle caudal ray. All of the teeth rigidly attached to the jaw bones; maxillary never heavily scaled.....Fig. 123 and p. 182, LUTJANIDAE

**Fig. 123. BOWERSIA VIOLESCENS**

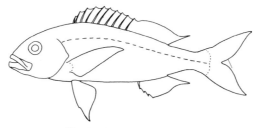

After J. and E., p. 237, fig. 97

Dorsal fin with 14 or more soft rays; depth of caudal peduncle about equal to the distance from the base of the last dorsal ray to the base of the middle caudal ray. Top of head between and behind the eyes completely scaled; no enlarged, pointed scale along the side of the pelvic base; posterior end of maxillary completely exposed when the mouth is closed.................................Fig. 124 and p. 155, SERRANIDAE

**Fig. 124. CEPHALOPHOLIS ARGUS**

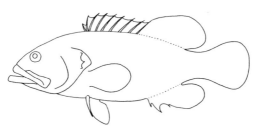

After J. and E., p. 222, fig. 88

**77**

## Subkey D

### Pelvic Fins Totally Absent.

1       No separate caudal fin at the end of a constricted caudal peduncle........    2

A separate caudal fin at the end of a constricted caudal peduncle as is usual in fishes..................................................................   16

2(1)    Body not enclosed in bony plates....................................   3

Body completely enclosed in bony plates...........................
.............................Fig. 125 and p. 134, in part SYNGNATHIDAE

**Fig. 125. HIPPOCAMPUS KUDA**

After J. and E., p. 120, fig. 36

3(2)    Body elongate eel-like.............................................   4

Body deep and compressed....................Fig. 126 and p. 303, MOLIDAE

**Fig. 126. RANZANIA LAEVIS**

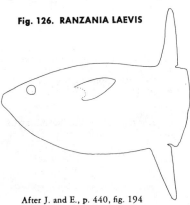

After J. and E., p. 440, fig. 194

4(3)    Dorsal and anal continuous around the tip of tail.....................   5

Body terminating posteriorly in a sharp, hard, finless point...........
.............................................P. 121, in part OPHICHTHIDAE

5(4)    Gill openings of the 2 sides of the head well separated, not extending
down on to the ventral surface of the body.............................. 10

Gill openings of the 2 sides of the head meeting or very nearly meeting
on the mid-ventral line. ........................................... 6

6(5)    Jaws short and blunt, the snout length considerably shorter than the
distance from the eye to the gill opening........................... 8

Jaws long and tapering, the snout length equal to or greater than the
distance from the eye to the gill opening........................... 7

7(6)    Dorsal fin commencing on head; snout much longer than distance from
eye to gill opening....................Fig. 127 and p. 119, NEMICHTHYIDAE*

### Fig. 127. NEMATOPRORA POLYGONIFERA

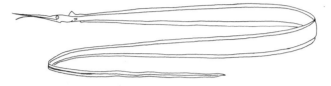

After Gilbert, p. 587, fig. 234

Dorsal fin commencing well behind head; snout about equal to the distance from the eye to the gill opening. Fig. 128 and p. 118, SERRIVOMERIDAE*

### Fig. 128. SERRIVOMER BEANII

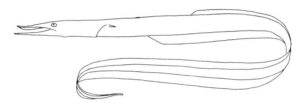

After Goode and Bean, pl. 47

8(6)    Anus ahead of center of body; pectoral fins well developed.............. 9

Anus behind center of body; pectoral fins absent........... SYMBRANCHIDAE†

9(8)    Anus and anal origin below or in front of pectoral fins; gill openings
extending up in front of pectoral bases........Fig. 129 and p. 280, CARAPIDAE

### Fig. 129. CARAPUS HOMEI

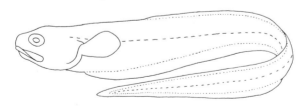

After Gilbert, p. 656, fig. 254

**79**

Anus and anal origin behind pectoral fins; gill openings restricted to the
ventral surface of the body........Fig. 130 and p. 127, SYNAPHOBRANCHIDAE*

**Fig. 130. SYNAPHOBRANCHUS BRACHYSOMUS**

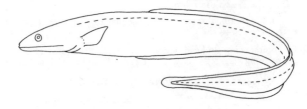

After Gilbert, p. 583, fig. 232

10(5)   Lower jaw on either side without a reverted lip that has a free edge below ...   12

Lower jaw on either side with a reverted lip that has a free edge below.
No fanglike teeth in mouth . . . . . . . . . . . . . . . . . . . . . . . . . . . . . . . . . . . . . . . . .   11

11(10)   Pectoral fin well developed, reaching the dorsal surface of the body
when bent upward; posterior nostril in front of or above the eye. . . . . . .
. . . . . . . . . . . . . . . . . . . . . . . . . . . . . . . . . . . . . . .Fig. 131 and p. 119, CONGRIDAE

**Fig. 131. ARIOSOMA BOWERSI**

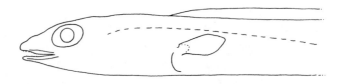

After J. and E., p. 77, fig. 16

Pectoral fin small or absent, not reaching the dorsal surface of the body
when bent upward; posterior nostril in the upper lip. Body plain brown;
fins with light borders; maximum size about 8 inches. . . . . . . . . . . . . . .
. . . . . . . . . . . . . . . . . . . . . . . . . . . . . . . . . . . . Fig. 132 and p. 117, XENOCONGRIDAE

**Fig. 132. KAUPICHTHYS DIODONTUS**

After Schultz, 1943, pl. 6

12(10)   Posterior nostril not an elongate slit that extends behind the eye on the
top of head. . . . . . . . . . . . . . . . . . . . . . . . . . . . . . . . . . . . . . . . . . . . . . . . . . . . . .   13

Posterior nostril an elongate slit that extends behind the eye on the top
of head. . . . . . . . . . . . . . . . . . . . . . . . . . . . . . . . . . .Fig. 133 and p. 119, NETTASTOMIDAE*

**Fig. 133. METOPOMYCTER DENTICULATUS**

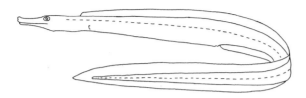

After Gilbert, p. 585, fig. 233

13(12)  Jaws subequal in length or the lower included within the tip of the upper...  14

Lower jaw distinctly protruding. Anus well behind the middle of the body, which is long and worm-like........Fig. 134 and p. 118, MORINGUIDAE

**Fig. 134. MORINGUA MACROCHIR**

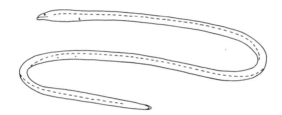

After J. an E., pl. 8

14(13)  Pectorals absent; no thornlike projections extending laterally from the sides of the upper jaw...........................................  15

Pectorals well developed; 3 thornlike projections extending laterally from each side of the upper jaw.................P. 119, MURAENESOCIDAE*

15(14)  Fins enclosed in heavy layers of flesh forming ridges that are not sharply demarcated from the body; posterior nostril above the level of the eye...............................Fig. 135 and p. 102, MURAENIDAE

**Fig. 135. GYMNOTHORAX EUROSTUS**

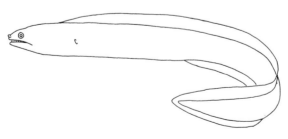

After J. and E., p. 95, fig. 24

**81**

Fins low, but not enclosed in flesh, sharply demarcated from the body;
posterior nostril in the upper lip below eye. Wormlike eels of plain
yellowish coloration, not attaining a length of more than 15 inches
...............................Fig. 136 and p. 121, in part OPHICHTHIDAE

**Fig. 136. MURAENICHTHYS COOKEI**

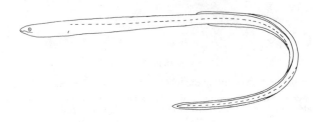

After Fowler, p. 41, fig. 9

16(1)   Body not transparent in the adult...................................  17

Body highly transparent. Pelagic fishes never attaining a length of more
than 1.5 inches......................Fig. 137 and p. 273, SCHINDLERIIDAE

**Fig. 137. SCHINDLERIA PRAEMATURUS**

After Bruun, 1940, p. 7, fig. 1

17(16)  Body not contained in a series of bony rings........................  18

Body contained in a series of bony rings. Snout tubular with a small
mouth at tip; size small, to about 8 inches........................
................. ...............Fig. 138 and p. 134, in part SYNGNATHIDAE

**Fig. 138. DORYRHAMPHUS MELANOPLEURA**

After J. and E., p. 121, fig. 37

18(17)  Gill covers broadly united to the isthmus, restricting the gill openings
to short slits.....................................................  19

Gill covers completely free from the isthmus.........................  24

19(18)  A single dorsal fin composed entirely of soft rays.....................  21

Two, well-separated dorsal fins, the first composed of one or more
strong, rough spines...............................................  20

20(19)  Sides somewhat prickly or furry to the touch, the individual scales not
visible; anterior dorsal spine inserted over eye......................
.....................................Fig. 139 and p. 295, MONACANTHIDAE

**Fig. 139. PERVAGOR SPILOSOMA**

After J. and E., pl. 48

Sides covered by hard, plate-like scales; anterior dorsal spine inserted
slightly behind eye ....................... Fig. 140 and p. 291, BALISTIDAE

**Fig. 140. BALISTES NYCTERIS**

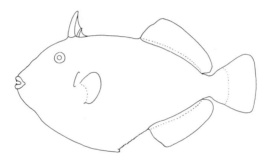

After J. and E., p. 408, fig. 179

21(19)  Body not enclosed in a bony box; abdomen inflatable................. 22

Head and body enclosed in a bony box; abdomen not inflatable......
.....................................Fig. 141 and p. 297, OSTRACIONTIDAE

**Fig. 141. OSTRACION LENTIGINOSUS**

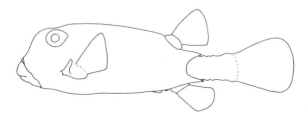

After J. and E., p. 442, fig. 195

**83**

22(21)   Body not covered with sharp spines................................... 23

Body covered with sharp spines............Fig. 142 and p. 302, DIODONTIDAE

### Fig. 142. DIODON HYSTRIX

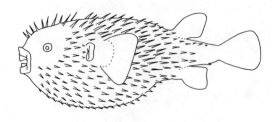

After J. and E., p. 437, fig. 192

23(22)   Body about as wide as deep; gill opening extending more than half way down the pectoral base; a well-developed narial flap or tube..........
....................................Fig. 143 and p. 298, TETRAODONTIDAE

### Fig. 143. AROTHRON HISPIDUS

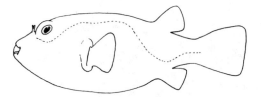

Body somewhat compressed; gill openings extending less than half way down the pectoral bases; nostrils inconspicuous....................
....................................Fig. 144 and p. 300, CANTHIGASTERIDAE

### Fig. 144. CANTHIGASTER AMBOINENSIS

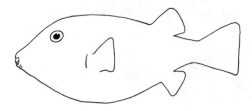

24(18)   Snout not swordlike ............................................... 25

Snout projecting in a swordlike fashion ........Fig. 145 and p. 264, XIPHIIDAE

**Fig. 145. XIPHIAS GLADIUS**

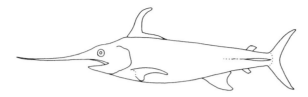

After J. and E., p. 168, fig. 70

25(24)  A separate finlet behind both the dorsal and the anal . P. 252, in part GEMPYLIDAE\*

No separate finlets behind the dorsal or anal. Size small, to about 4 inches...........................................Fig. 239, AMMODYTIDAE

**Fig. 146. BLEEKERIA GILLI**

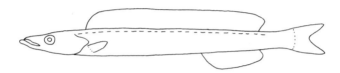

After Fowler, p. 426, fig. 80

# 5. Accounts of Families and Species of Hawaiian Fishes

## SHARKS

The sharks, together with their relatives the rays and chimaeras, constitute one of the two major fish groups found in Hawaii. This group, which has been separated from the bony-fish stock for some 400 million years, is characterized by many features, of which the absence of internal bony structures is probably the most striking.

The sharks as a group are easily recognized. They may be distinguished from all other fishes by the five or more gill slits on each side that extend, at least in part, above the bases of the pectoral fins (the skates and rays have the gill slits restricted to the ventral surface of the body).

Though they include the largest of all fishes, a few of the species of sharks never reach a length of more than a foot. Some sharks lay eggs, but many others are viviparous, and it is not uncommon for a female shark brought aboard a boat to give birth to living young on deck. All sharks live on animal food, and unfortunately a few of them occasionally experiment with human beings as an item of diet. In Hawaii, eight shark attacks, three of which were fatal, have occurred in the last ten years. Geographically, many, probably most, sharks are wide-ranging. Several of the species recorded from Hawaii occur in tropical and subtropical waters around the world. Other widely distributed species not yet recorded from Hawaii can be expected to turn up here sooner or later. Most sharks keep to the offshore side of reefs, although the nehu fishermen often take young hammerheads in the shallow waters of Kaneohe Bay. Some species do not seem to stray far from land; others are high-seas forms; and still others are restricted to deep water.

In the high Hawaiian islands sharks seem to have been fished down to a marked extent, though they are by no means rare, particularly in deeper and offshore waters. In any event the shark concentration around such low, leeward reefs as French Frigate Shoals, Laysan, Lisianski, etc., seems to be far higher than that around the windward islands.

Taxonomically, the families and genera of sharks are well worked out and, in general, well agreed upon. They have recently been excellently reviewed on a world-wide basis by Bigelow and Schroeder in "Fishes of the Western North

Atlantic" Vol. I (1948). The species of tropical Pacific sharks, however, are in about as great a state of confusion as any group of fishes in that area. When a thorough review of Pacific sharks (similar to that on the Western North Atlantic sharks) is made, it seems probable that many of the specific names used in the account that follows will have to be changed.

The impression is widely held that a species of shark can be identified from its teeth alone. Some sharks do have a very distinctive dentition, but most do not. The teeth of the majority of sharks in Hawaiian waters can be misidentified as those of the man-eater with little difficulty. Such determinations are more likely to be impressive than correct. For the problems of shark-tooth identification the reader is referred to the excellent illustrations in the work of Bigelow and Schroeder mentioned above.

## Family ISURIDAE

This is one of the two families of sharks in which the upper lobe of the caudal fin stands erect (see Fig. 12) and extends very little farther posteriorly than the lower lobe. The other family with this character is represented by the whale shark, which can be at once distinguished from the Isuridae by the white spotting on the head and back.

The isurids are all wide-ranging, pelagic sharks attaining a large size, and one of them is probably responsible for the majority of the attacks on human swimmers in our area.

Key to the Hawaiian species of the family Isuridae:

Teeth rough-edged; anterior 2 teeth in both jaws similar in shape to the others............................*Carcharodon carcharias*

Teeth smooth-edged; anterior 2 teeth in both jaws noticeably more slender than the others........................*Isurus glaucus*

### CARCHARODON CARCHARIAS (Niuhi, man-eater)

This shark is readily recognized by the combination of nearly erect tail and large serrate teeth (see Fig. 12). An Australian specimen was 36½ feet in length. Any Hawaiian sharks over about 12 feet long probably belong to this species. It is not a common shark about Hawaii, nor does it seem to be extremely rare.

The species feeds on large marine animals, such as tuna and probably seals and turtles. Humans are at times attacked, but are more often avoided. The reaction of a man-eater shark to a human swimmer probably depends partly on the shark, particularly on how hungry he is, and partly on the actions of the swimmer. Though this or any Hawaiian species of shark should be treated with respect, one is far safer from sharks in Hawaiian waters than from his fellow human beings in automobiles on land.

### ISURUS GLAUCUS

This high-tailed Hawaiian shark can be at once distinguished from the man-eater by the smooth-edged teeth. Unlike most sharks, it is in life a blue gray or steel blue above and white beneath. Though the generic identification of *Isurus* is beyond doubt, the applicability of the specific name *glaucus* to the Hawaiian form is questionable.

Attains a length of some 12 feet.

### Family ALOPIIDAE (Thresher Sharks)

This family includes only one genus, unique among sharks in having the tail practically as long as the body. Several species are recorded from the Pacific but only one, and that perhaps misidentified, from Hawaii. It may also be that two or more species are included in the Hawaiian records, or at least occur in Hawaii.

#### ALOPIAS VULPINUS (Thresher shark)

If only one species of thresher shark occurs in Hawaii, it is sufficiently characterized by the elongate tail noted above (see Fig. 13).

Attains a length of 20 feet or more, although half of this length would be tail. Encountered occasionally in Hawaiian waters, where it is sometimes taken on a hook.

### Family RHINCODONTIDAE (Whale Sharks)

The family Rhincodontidae contains a single species, *Rhincodon typus*, the largest of all fishes. It reaches a measured length of 45 feet and a weight of over 10 tons, but according to sight records the whale shark grows much larger. The huge beast can be distinguished from true whales by the high, vertical caudal fin. Despite its great size the whale shark appears to be harmless, feeding on small plankton organisms.

It is circumtropical in distribution and is included here only on the basis of one sight record.

### Family SCYLIORHINIDAE

A family of small, primarily deep-water sharks. The only Hawaiian species, *Apristurus spongiceps*, is known from a single mature female 2 feet long, taken in 313 to 800 fathoms of water. Any small, deep-water sharks taken in Hawaiian waters either belong to this family or, if they lack an anal fin, to the Squalidae.

### Family TRIAKIDAE

This is the only Hawaiian family of sharks in which there are numerous rows of small 3- or 5-cusped teeth in the jaws. Only one species recorded.

#### TRIAENODON OBESUS

In addition to the many-rowed teeth in the jaws, this is one of the two known Hawaiian sharks in which the dorsals and the caudal are white-tipped (see Fig. 14). The other Hawaiian white-tipped shark is *Pterolamiops*, with sharp-edged, bladelike teeth.

The only recorded Hawaiian specimen appears to have been 5 feet long.

## Family CARCHARHINIDAE

This family includes a number of generalized sharks with no particular distinguishing features. In fact, it can be best identified by the absence of the peculiarities found in each of the other shark families. It is also the largest shark family, and the classification of the many Pacific species of the *Carcharhinus-Eulamia* complex is utterly hopeless at the present time. Far more intensive and extensive work on a world-wide basis will have to be done before this situation is rectified.

The family includes both inshore and offshore forms. In the leeward Hawaiian Islands members of the family commonly work into water of very few feet of depth and occur in considerable numbers, but such inshore forms seem to be rare about the high windward islands. Other species seem to be high-seas forms and constitute a considerable nuisance to long-line tuna fishermen.

Provisional key to the Hawaiian species of the family Carcharhinidae:

| | | |
|---|---|---|
| 1 | Mid-point of base of first dorsal fin considerably nearer to axil of pectoral than to origin of pelvics.......................... | 2 |
| | Mid-point of base of first dorsal fin nearer to origin of pelvics than to pectoral axil..............................*Prionace glauca* | |
| 2(1) | Length of furrow extending forward from corner of mouth, if present, shorter than the distance from the front of mouth to the tip of snout; body without dark spots or blotches............ | 3 |
| | Length of furrow extending forward from corner of mouth greater than the distance from the front of mouth to the tip of snout; body with brown spots or blotches...........*Galeocerdo cuvieri* | |
| 3(2) | A cross furrow on the upper surface of body just ahead of base of tail; no spiracle (or pore) just behind eye.................... | 4 |
| | No cross furrow on the upper surface of the body just ahead of base of tail; a small spiracle (or pore) just behind eye. *Galeorhinus zyopterus* | |
| 4(3) | First dorsal and pectorals sharp-tipped........................ | 5 |
| | First dorsal and pectorals bluntly rounded. Tips of fins light or light-spotted; a blunt-nosed (when viewed from above) offshore species...................................*Pterolamiops longimanus* | |
| 5(4) | First dorsal and lower caudal lobe plain or dusky................ | 6 |
| | First dorsal and lower caudal lobe abruptly black-tipped. A small, blunt-nosed, inshore form............*Carcharhinus melanopterus* | |
| 6(5) | Pelvic origins nearer to end of snout than to tip of caudal; length of pectoral contained about 5 times in the total length; no high, rounded anterior lobe on the second dorsal.................... | 7 |
| | Pelvic origins nearer to tip of caudal than to end of snout; length of pectoral contained about 4 times in the total length; a distinct, raised, rounded anterior lobe on the second dorsal.. *Carcharhinus nesiotes* | |
| 7(6) | Body rather chunky, the greatest depth contained about 6.5 times in the total length...........................*Eulamia phorcys* | |
| | Body relatively long and low, the greatest depth contained nearly 8 times in the total length.................*Eulamia floridanus* | |

### PRIONACE GLAUCA (Great blue shark)

This tends to be an offshore species reaching a length of at least 12 feet. It is frequently hooked on tuna long lines.

### GALEOCERDO CUVIERI (Tiger shark)

This is our only shark with prominent dark stripes and spots. It appears to be a nocturnal species. Said to reach a length of 30 feet.

### GALEORHINUS ZYOPTERUS

A single specimen of this species, 5 feet in length, was recorded from Laysan over 50 years ago.

### PTEROLAMIOPS LONGIMANUS (Whitetip shark)

This pelagic species ranges widely in both the Atlantic and the Pacific. Around Hawaii and to the south it is one of the two species that give the greatest trouble to tuna long-line fishermen, taking the bait and biting great chunks out of the hooked tuna.

The species is said to attain a length of 12 or 13 feet.

### CARCHARHINUS MELANOPTERUS (Blacktip shark)

Though several of our sharks have the fins becoming gradually darker toward the tips, this is the only one with abruptly black fin tips.

In the areas to the south the same species is commonly seen swimming in over the reef in shallow water, but in the high Hawaiian islands, at least, it appears to be rare today. Apparently the blacktip reaches only about 4 feet in length.

### CARCHARHINUS NESIOTES

This is apparently another of our inshore sharks rare about the high eastern islands today. We have not examined it. The original description was based on several specimens the largest of which was just under 6 feet long.

### EULAMIA PHORCYS

This species has been inadequately described on the basis of several small specimens (see Fig. 15). We have not seen it.

### EULAMIA FLORIDANUS (Silky shark)

The common name of this shark stems from the relatively smooth skin: most sharks are definitely prickly-skinned but the dermal denticles of this one are so small as to leave the skin almost smooth to the touch.

This is the other of the two sharks that do so much damage to the tunas caught on long lines off shore. In general, it appears to stay at somewhat greater depths than its fellow predator, the whitetip. As might be guessed from its offshore existence, the silky shark is wide ranging, occurring in both the Atlantic and Pacific. Attains a length of at least 10 feet.

## Family SPHYRNIDAE (Hammerhead Sharks)

The hammerhead and bonnethead sharks that comprise the family Sphyrnidae can always be readily distinguished by their having the eyes on the edges of flattish lateral expansions of the head. The species within the family are still rather confused. Though there may be several closely related species in Hawaiian waters, only one can at present be identified with certainty.

### SPHYRNA LEWINI (Hammerhead, Mano kihikihi)

All of the Hawaiian hammerheads we have seen appear to belong to this species, which has a slight indentation of the anterior profile of the head at the mid-line (see Fig. 11). Other species with or without this indentation may, however, be present.

*Sphyrna lewini* occurs frequently in Kaneohe Bay, and the young of the species is frequently taken in the nehu seines of tuna-bait fishermen there.

Reaches a length of over 7 feet. Indeed, much larger hammerheads have been sighted, but whether they belong to this or some other species of *Sphyrna* is not known.


## Family SQUALIDAE (Spiny Dogfishes)

The Squalidae is the only Hawaiian family of sharks lacking an anal fin. Only one of the six species in our area attains a length of over 3 feet, and all of them are found either in or over fairly deep water.

Key to the Hawaiian species of the family Squalidae:

| | | |
|---|---|---|
| 1 | Both dorsal fins preceded by a well-developed spine; first dorsal fin in front of the middle of total length...................... | 4 |
| | No spines at front of dorsal fins; first dorsal fin behind the middle of the total length................................... | 2 |
| 2(1) | Pelvic fins originating behind the front of the first dorsal fin; upper lobe of caudal fin bluntly rounded; posteriormost gill slit short, not extending below pectoral base.................... | 3 |
| | Pelvic fins originating in front of the first dorsal fin; upper lobe of the caudal fin tapering to a point; posteriormost gill slit extending well below the pectoral base.............. *Echinorhinus brucus* | |
| 3(2) | Second dorsal fin about twice as long as the first; teeth of lower jaw strongly bent outward................... *Euprotomicrus bispinatus* | |
| | The 2 dorsal fins of similar size; teeth of lower jaw erect...... .......................................... *Isistius brasiliensis* | |
| 4(1) | The 2 dorsal fins of approximately similar size or the second larger; no fleshy ridges running along the sides of the caudal peduncle........................................... | 5 |
| | First dorsal fin considerably larger than the second; a fleshy ridge running along either side of the caudal peduncle. *Squalus fernandinus* | |
| 5(4) | Teeth in the upper and lower jaws similar, tricuspid; several series of teeth in each jaw functioning at the same time....... .......................................... *Centroscyllium nigrum* | |

Upper teeth tricuspid, lower with a single cusp that points laterally; many series in the upper jaw functioning simultaneously, but only a single functional row in the lower jaw. *Etmopterus villosus*

### ECHINORHINUS BRUCUS

The Hawaiian record of this species is based on a single specimen about 6 feet long taken southeast of Kauai.

### EUPROTOMICRUS BISPINATUS

Specimens of this small shark, which seems to reach a maximum length of less than a foot, have been netted at a night light well out to sea in the Hawaiian area.

#### Fig. 147. ISISTIUS BRASILIENSIS

After Bigelow and Schroeder, p. 509, fig. 98

### ISISTIUS BRASILIENSIS

Two specimens of this species, both less than a foot long, were found in the Honolulu market more than 20 years ago.

### SQUALUS FERNANDINUS (Mano)

This is the only species of Squalidae known from Hawaiian inshore waters. Attains a length of about 3 feet and is said to have once been common off Kailua, Hawaii. We have a single specimen.

### CENTROSCYLLIUM NIGRUM

A single specimen 9 inches long, taken in half a mile of water off Kauai, was reported from our area over 50 years ago.

### ETMOPTERUS VILLOSUS

Described from a single 7-inch specimen taken from about half a mile of water off Molokai.

## SKATES AND RAYS

The body shape (see Figs. 16–18) of the skates and rays is unique among Hawaiian fishes. Though rays are sometimes sufficiently numerous to be a nuisance to surf casters, they do not appear to get into shallow waters where bathers are likely to step on them. We know of no record of stingray injury in Hawaii.

## Family DASYATIDAE (Stingrays)

The characteristic spine or spines on the tail of these forms should always be treated circumspectly, for the fish can cause severe wounds with them. We have not seen adult specimens of either of the two species known from Hawaii.
Key to the Hawaiian species of the family Dasyatidae:

> Tail with a fleshy fold both above and below......*Dasyatis hawaiiensis*
>
> Tail with a fleshy keel below only.....................*Dasyatis lata*

### DASYATIS HAWAIIENSIS

Specimens of this species with a disc measuring 4 feet across have come into the Honolulu market in the past (see Fig. 16).

### DASYATIS LATA

Judging from known records this species does not reach so large a size as the former.

## Family MYLIOBATIDAE

The members of this family also have one or more spines on the tail but these originate far forward, between the tips of the pelvic fins, rather than farther back as in the Dasyatidae.

### AETOBATUS NARINARI (Hihimanu, Eagle ray)

The numerous round, white spots on the dark back of this ray will distinguish it immediately (see Fig. 17). Attains a width of at least 3 feet.

## Family MOBULIDAE (Manta Rays)

Mantas have twice been recorded in the literature from Hawaii, but insufficient material of either specimen has been preserved to make any certain species identification. The flaplike appendages extending forward on each side of the mouth (see Fig. 18) are an immediate recognition character for all members of the family. Mantas reach a tremendous size—to over 20 feet in width and more than 3000 pounds in weight.

The two species somewhat dubiously determined from Hawaii are *Mobula japonica* and what is probably *Manta alfredi*. The Hawaiian name apparently applied to members of this family is halalua.
Key to presumed species of Hawaiian Mobulidae:

> Mouth on lower surface of the head; teeth in both jaws; tail about twice as long as body, with a basal spine........*Mobula japonica*
>
> Mouth terminal, extending across front of head; teeth in lower jaw only; tail about equal to the body length, without a basal spine...................................................*Manta alfredi*

**93**

#### MOBULA JAPONICA

Judging from existing descriptions, the two recorded Hawaiian manta rays should be easy to separate on deck, but we can find no character that would seem to be very useful for separating them in the water.

What is apparently this species is represented by a cast in the Bishop Museum. The fish reaches at least 8 feet in width.

#### MANTA ALFREDI

The closely related *Manta birostris* (see Fig. 18) reaches a width of at least 30 feet. The only Hawaiian record of *Manta alfredi* is of a specimen 8 feet across.

## THE CHIMAERAS

### Family CHIMAERIDAE

The chimaeras are amongst the strangest of fishes (see Fig. 19). The only record of the group from Hawaiian waters is over 50 years old. The single specimen, 3 feet long, was caught off Kauai at about 1 mile in depth.

## THE HERRING-LIKE FISHES

The term herring-like fishes is here broadly interpreted to include the two orders of fishes known to ichthyologists as the isospondylous and iniomous fishes. There is no doubt that these two orders are closely related, and the difficulty is to find an adequate reason for separating them. In any event they comprise the oldest of Hawaiian bony fishes. Primitive features include the absence of spines in the fins, the many-rayed pelvic fins far back along the abdomen, and a number of internal features. That the herring-like fishes are primitive does not mean that they are a dwindling group. Indeed, from the viewpoint of numbers of individuals they are probably the most successful vertebrates living today.

Ecologically there are two major types of herring-like fishes: the silvery, inshore forms like the awa, 'o'io, piha, and nehu; and the black forms, often with light organs, living at mid-depths in the open sea. The second category, though seldom seen, is much better represented in the Hawaiian region.

### Family ELOPIDAE (Ladyfishes)

The Elopidae is a family of few species but wide distribution in tropical waters. One species is known from Hawaii.

#### ELOPS HAWAIENSIS (Awa'aua, Awaawa)

The awa'aua is one of several large, silvery, herring-like fishes from Hawaii. It can be identified by the following combination of characters: mouth extending back behind the eye; pelvic fin set far back, almost under the middle of the body, and with about 15 rays; lateral line present; coloration silvery (see Fig. 51).

The young of this species goes through a leptocephalus larval stage which is flat and transparent, resembling the adult in no way. This larval form resembles that of the 'o'io (*Albula vulpes*) and of eels. From the latter it can be distinguished by the presence of a forked caudal and from the former by the presence of a larger number of body segments (Hildebrand, 1943, p. 93).

The species occurs off sandy shores and is a frequent inhabitant of fishponds. In this latter habitat it feeds on small fish and crustacea (Hiatt, 1947, p. 255). It attains a length of perhaps 2 feet.

## Family ALBULIDAE (Bonefishes)

Another family of few species but wide distribution in the tropics. The single Hawaiian species is at present considered to be the same as that known as the bonefish in Florida.

### ALBULA VULPES ('O'io)

The 'o'io may be recognized by the following combination of characters: snout projecting well in front of mouth; pelvic fins about under middle of body; lateral line present (see Fig. 52).

This fish occurs along open, sandy shores where it is sometimes taken by surf fishermen. Formerly, it was brought into the markets in some abundance. The maximum length attained is about 3 feet.

## Family DUSSUMIERIIDAE

The fishes of this family are close relatives of the herrings. The Hawaiian dussumieriids have the pelvic fins far back, below or behind the dorsal fin, a small, normal mouth, no lateral line, and the coloration predominantly silvery. The two Hawaiian species seem to be very seasonal in occurrence, but are found in schools when they do occur.

Key to the Hawaiian species of the family Dussumieriidae:

Eye completely covered with adipose tissue so that there is no free border to the orbit; pelvic fins inserted somewhat behind the base of the last dorsal ray . . . . . . . . . . . . . . . . . . . . . . . . *Etrumeus micropus*

Eye not covered by adipose tissue, the orbit with a free border; pelvic fins inserted somewhat ahead of base of last dorsal ray . . . . . . . . . . . . . . . . . . . . . . . . . . . . . . . . . . . . . . . . . . *Spratelloides delicatulus*

### ETRUMEUS MICROPUS (Makiawa)

This species occurs around Honolulu from time to time in some numbers. It reaches a length of at least 10 inches.

### SPRATELLOIDES DELICATULUS (Piha)

The piha is a small, silvery fish occurring at certain seasons in great numbers (for a figure of a closely related form, see Fig. 55). At such times it is used as tuna bait by the fishermen.

The maximum length attained by the species is probably not over 3 inches.

The Engraulidae is represented in Hawaii by one well-known representative, the nehu. This is another silvery fish with the pelvic fins set far back but

## Family ENGRAULIDAE

it may be distinguished from others by the lack of a lateral line and by the very characteristic head shape: the snout projects well ahead of the upper jaw but the mouth is large, extending well behind the eye.

(Since this book went to press a second species, apparently fairly abundant offshore, has been discovered.)

### STOLEPHORUS PURPUREUS (Nehu)

The nehu is the most important tuna-bait fish in the Hawaiian Islands (see Fig. 54). Inasmuch as the unavailability of nehu is one of the chief bottlenecks of the aku fishery, it has been the subject of considerable biological investigation. Indeed, it can be said that the nehu is the Hawaiian fish for which the life history is most completely known.

The nehu occurs chiefly in certain brackish, turbid inshore waters. Thus the greatest concentrations of nehu around Oahu are to be found in Kaneohe Bay, Pearl Harbor, and the Ala Wai canal. The species also enters fishponds, though never in great number (Hiatt, 1947, p. 271). It is evident that the nehu can and does live under a variety of salinities. That no particular salt concentration is favored is indicated by a detailed investigation of egg concentrations in Kaneohe Bay; in this investigation no correlation could be established between salinity and egg number (Tester, 1951, p. 338).

Spawning of the nehu occurs throughout the year (Tester, *op. cit.*). The eggs develop suspended in the water near the surface. The hatched larvae develop rapidly and directly, transforming into the adult form at somewhat less than 2 inches in total length. It appears that growth is rapid and that the adult fish may be only a few weeks old (Tester, *op. cit.*, p. 341). If so, there may be several generations per year.

The food of the nehu consists very largely of planktonic crustacean larvae (Hiatt, 1951). It is known that the nehu populations of various localized areas differ from one another in such features as the size attained and vertebral number (Tester and Hiatt, 1952). The maximum size for the species is probably around 4 inches.

## Family GONOSTOMATIDAE

Among the fishes related to the herrings are a rather large number of families restricted to the lightless zones of the open sea. The fishes in these families are all black, gray, or silvery. Characteristically, but by no means invariably, they are small, have one or two lines of photophores or light organs along the lower sides, and an adipose fin. These families have wide distributions, and it seems very probable that when the zones in which they live are more thoroughly investigated most of them will prove to be represented in Hawaiian waters. At the present time, however, our knowledge of them is extremely fragmentary. Under the circumstances, it does not seem worth while giving a species-by-species account of them in the text, though references to the literature of the forms recorded from Hawaii may be found in the Appendix.

The gonostomatids are among the most generalized of deep-water fishes and have no marked peculiarities by which they can be distinguished from other families inhabiting the same zone. Four species have been recorded from Hawaii; they are dealt with in detail by Gilbert (1905). Two of these fishes are figured in the family keys (Figs. 37 and 44).

### Family STERNOPTYCHIDAE

The Sternoptychidae, or hatchet fishes, are small, deep-bodied, silvery fishes with large light organs on the lower sides (see Fig. 35). They appear to be rather common below the lighted zone of the open sea around Hawaii. The five Hawaiian species have recently been reviewed by Haig (1955).

### Family ASTRONESTHIDAE

This deep-water family is known in Hawaii from one species, *Astronesthes lucifer* (Fig. 34), of which two specimens have been recorded.

### Family STOMIATIDAE

This family is known in Hawaii from only a single specimen (Fig. 45), 3 inches long, taken in about 2000 feet of water.

### Family CHANIDAE

The Chanidae is represented throughout a large portion of the tropical Pacific by a single shallow-water species of considerable commercial importance. This species may be recognized by the following combination of characters: coloration silvery; pelvic fins far back, under the dorsal; mouth small, terminal; lateral line present. Technically, the Chanidae is separated from the herring-like fishes by the fact that the number of branchiostegal rays is reduced to four on each side.

#### CHANOS CHANOS (Awa, Milkfish)

The awa seems to be best represented in lagoons and brackish water areas (see Fig. 53). It is one of the dominant elements in fishponds and occurs frequently in the markets. Nevertheless, the fishpond culture for the awa in Hawaii has never reached anything like the level of technical development that it has throughout Southeast Asia. In the Philippines, for example, the transparent and needle-like fry are caught along sandy shores, transferred to specially prepared nursery ponds, and retransferred as fingerlings to rearing ponds (Mane, Villaluz, and Rabanal, 1953).

In Hawaii, as in the Philippines, the food of the awa consists of plant material. The type of plants eaten, however, changes somewhat with growth (Hiatt, 1947).

The awa attains a length of at least 3 feet—the largest for any Hawaiian herring-like fish.

## Family GONORHYNCHIDAE

The family Gonorhynchidae is made up of a single genus of pelagic fishes. It is an extremely peculiar genus, with rough scales and the pelvic fins set far back, behind the middle of the body; the mouth is on the lower surface of the head, below the eye, with the snout projecting far forward.

### GONORHYNCHUS GONORYNCHUS

This species is recorded in the Hawaiian Islands from time to time (see Fig. 50). So far as can be determined from the few available records it is an offshore form. The largest Hawaiian specimen is about 6 inches long.

## Family CHLOROPHTHALMIDAE

The Chlorophthalmidae is a family of deep-water fishes known from Hawaii by only one species (Fig. 33). This species has been reported from a number of "Albatross" dredging stations in water of over 100 fathoms.

## Family SYNODONTIDAE

The synodontids (exemplified by Fig. 32) are the only Hawaiian inshore fishes with an adipose fin (see Fig. 5). They may be distinguished from Hawaiian deep-water and fresh-water families with an adipose fin by the presence of well-developed teeth on the tongue.

Members of the family are found most commonly in sandy areas. Here they frequently bury themselves up to the eyes, making short dashes to escape or to capture prey. One species, however, has been taken down to a depth of 178 fathoms, and another frequently enters brackish water.

All the species are highly carnivorous and at times apparently cannibalistic. The maximum size attained by any Hawaiian synodontid is about 18 inches.

Six species are known from Hawaiian waters, and all of them have essentially the same prehistoric, lizard-like appearance (see Fig. 32).

Key to the Hawaiian species of the family Synodontidae:

1      Anal fin relatively short, with 9 to 11 rays, the anus closer to the caudal base than to the pelvic origin; snout, measured to anterior border of orbit, contained less than 3 times (stepped) in upper jaw length and less than 6 times in head length............ 2

Anal fin relatively long, with 15 or 16 rays, the anus closer to the pelvic origin than to the caudal base; eye far forward on head, the snout contained more than 3 times in upper jaw length and more than 6 times in head length...........*Trachinocephalus myops*

2(1)   Only a single row of widely spaced teeth showing outside the edge of the lips; at least 2 longitudinal series of teeth on the tongue, more or less separated by a median furrow; inner rays of pelvic fins at least twice as long as outermost rays............ 3

Three or more tiers of closely spaced teeth showing outside the edge of the lips; a single longitudinal series of teeth on the tongue arising from a raised median ridge; inner rays of pelvic fins less than twice as long as outermost rays..........*Saurida gracilis*

3(2) Chin a hard fleshy point that extends forward of the anterior-most premaxillary teeth....................................... 4

"The narrow tip of the mandible soft and flexible, fitting behind the premaxillary teeth"............................*Synodus kaianus*

4(3) Four and a half to 6 scale rows between lateral line and base of first dorsal ray; 59 or more scales in lateral line; no black spot on tip of snout; pectoral axil not darker than surrounding area........ 5

Three and a half or 4 scale rows between lateral line and base of first dorsal ray; 54 to 57 scales in the lateral line; a black spot on tip of snout; pectoral axil dusky................*Synodus binotatus*

5(4) Thirteen or 14 dorsal rays in all (counting the last split ray as one); 63 or more lateral-line scales (not counting the 2 or 3 scales on the caudal base)....................*Synodus dermatogenys*

Eleven or 12 dorsal rays; 59 to 62 lateral-line scales..*Synodus variegatus*

## TRACHINOCEPHALUS MYOPS

The most distinctive member of the family, readily separable from other Hawaiian synodontids in general appearance and by means of the characters given in the key.

Not uncommon, though less abundant in Hawaii than several other species of the family. Apparently does not reach a length of more than about 9 inches.

## SAURIDA GRACILIS

In appearance quite similar to the species of *Synodus*, from which it can be separated by the characters given in the key and by the presence of a dou-ble series of teeth on each side of the palate.

It often occurs in sandy areas together with *Synodus dermatogenys* and *Synodus variegatus*, but unlike these species frequently enters brackish waters over muddy bottoms. The brackish-water specimens differ quite significantly, though apparently not consistently, from the marine form. *Saurida gracilis* also occurs in deeper water, as evidenced by Gilbert's records of the species down to 73 fathoms.

Attains a length of more than a foot.

## SYNODUS KAIANUS

The only Hawaiian record of this species consists of nine specimens taken over 50 years ago between the depths of 122 and 178 fathoms. There are no other Hawaiian records of any synodontids from depths of over 100 fathoms.

## SYNODUS BINOTATUS

There are certain differences in color pattern by which this species can be differentiated from *Saurida* and other shallow-water species of *Synodus*. The single median dark spot on the tip of the snout of *Synodus binotatus* is not found in other species. Furthermore, the dark markings on the body tend to

**99**

be oriented longitudinally rather than vertically. The tongue of *S. binotatus* is much narrower than that of *S. dermatogenys* or *S. variegatus* and has only two longitudinal series of teeth, whereas in the latter two species the tongue is broad and club-shaped with a broad patch of teeth.

This species seems to inhabit water of 15 to 50 feet in depth. It has not been hitherto recorded from Hawaii, but it would appear to be the commonest fish at the depths listed. It is not known to reach a length of more than 5 inches.

### SYNODUS DERMATOGENYS

This species and *Synodus variegatus* are very similar (see Fig. 32). Both species are often found together. The safest way to distinguish them is to count the scales and fin rays (see key). In addition, there are a number of minor and less reliable differences. For example, *S. dermatogenys*, though apparently growing to the larger size, seems to be a lean and cadaverous looking fish, whereas by contrast *S. variegatus* is round and chubby. Again, *S. dermatogenys* appears to lose its juvenile coloration at a somewhat larger size than *S. variegatus*. For example, a five-inch specimen of *S. variegatus* will have narrow, sharply defined bars on the dorsal and about 7 similar bars on each caudal lobe; *S. dermatogenys* at the same size has rather diffuse, broad bars on the dorsal and caudal, 4 or 5 on each caudal lobe. However, a ten-inch specimen of *S. dermatogenys* will have essentially the same coloration as a five-inch *S. variegatus*.

*Synodus dermatogenys* reaches a length of at least 16 inches. One small specimen dredged from about 20 fathoms is tentatively identified as this species, but the normal habitat of the species seems to be far shallower. *S. dermatogenys*, *S. variegatus*, and *Saurida gracilis* appear to be the commonest synodontids in the Hawaiian Islands.

### SYNODUS VARIEGATUS

The difficulty of distinguishing this species from *Synodus dermatogenys* has already been discussed under the account of the latter.

So far as is known, *S. variegatus* does not reach a length of more than about 10 inches in Hawaii.

## Family BATHYPTEROIDAE

Another deep-water family with a single species (Fig. 29) recorded from Hawaiian waters.

## Family MYCTOPHIDAE

The Myctophidae is one of the best-known of oceanic fish families. One member or another (Fig. 36) of this family can be caught almost anywhere over deep water around Hawaii by simply putting a light in the water at night and picking up in a dip net what comes along. The first little steel-blue fish with light organs that comes in will be a myctophid.

Apparently myctophids migrate into deeper layers of water during the day, at which time the greatest number of species in the family probably occur below the level of light penetration. Only a few of the species come all the way to the surface at night, and some live at considerable depth. It has been held with sound reason that the fish species with the most numerous individuals in the world is probably some form of myctophid or gonostomatid.

Fourteen species of Myctophidae have been recognized from Hawaii to date.

### Family PARALEPIDIDAE

A family of oceanic, large-toothed, elongate, silvery fishes (Fig. 31), of which two have been recorded from Hawaii to date.

### Family ALEPISAURIDAE

The alepisaurids are large, oceanic fishes with tremendous teeth and a long, high dorsal fin.

#### ALEPISAURUS BOREALIS

An account of this species is given here because it is not infrequently taken by the long-line tuna fishermen around the Hawaiian Islands. Nevertheless, it does not seem to have been previously recorded here.

The species apparently reaches a length of about 4 feet, but since the fish is made up to a large extent of dorsal fin and teeth it attains no great weight (see Fig. 30).

### Family ATELEOPIDAE

One deep-water species (Fig. 94) of this family is known from Hawaii. In appearance it somewhat resembles a chimaerid but differs immediately in lacking a dorsal spine. The combination of the pelvic filament under the throat with a short dorsal and long anal is diagnostic for the family.

The one species has been described by Gilbert (1905) from specimens taken in over 250 fathoms of water.

## THE EELS

The eels, though highly specialized, indicate their derivation from some primitive bony-fish stock by the presence of teeth on the maxillary, and other characteristics.

Eels come in many sizes but only one shape. An eel-like form is not, however, restricted to the eels, but also occurs, among Hawaiian fishes, in the unrelated carapids and the introduced fresh-water symbranchids. Despite high specialization, eels have adapted themselves to several habitats. In our area they are probably best represented in cracks and holes in the coral. However, a number of especially wormlike forms burrow in the sand, where they may completely disappear or lie with only the front part of the body protruding. An altogether different, open-water environment is occupied by the larval stages of all eels and by the adults of some of our deep-water species.

## Family MURAENIDAE (Moray Eels or Puhis)

The Muraenidae is the largest and most abundant eel family in Hawaii. Indeed, after the Labridae, it is the largest family of Hawaiian fishes.

The puhis are in many respects the most specialized of the eels. They have lost all trace of paired fins and the dorsal and anal are never represented by more than fleshy ridges. The gill openings are reduced to small holes. The anterior nostrils are in a tube and the posterior nostrils lie high on the head, either in front of or over the eye. Typically the mouth contains enlarged, depressible, needle-like teeth.

Most of the morays appear to be fish-eaters. Apparently the prey is sought out chiefly by scent. The large, fanglike teeth allow them to hold relatively large fishes, which are swallowed whole or broken into two pieces. The distensible jaws, throat, and stomach, and the accessory pharyngeal jaws also appear to be adaptations to feeding on large prey. One meal apparently suffices for a considerable length of time, for the stomachs of puhis are usually empty. One genus, *Echidna*, has aberrant food habits in that it is said to eat mollusks, which are crushed by pebble-like teeth.

The casual observer will generally underestimate the abundance of morays, for they usually remain far back in holes and crevices. Some species push their way under rocks and must actively burrow. Judging from the absence of morays in areas of pure sand, they keep fairly close to rocks and coral heads.

A few species of this family appear in the Honolulu market in small numbers, but, beyond that, their chief importance seems to be as predators on other fishes. Morays appear to be at the end of the food chain in Hawaii, but what kills them off is difficult to say. One possible factor in this respect is a parasitic isopod which very frequently settles in one of the gill cavities, but whether this is eventually fatal has yet to be determined.

In size, the Hawaiian morays do not reach more than 5 or 6 feet, though they grow to a considerably larger size in Johnston. After the sharks, they are the most dangerous of Hawaiian fishes, though no deaths seem to have been attributed to Hawaiian morays. That they will bite people is beyond doubt, as a month's sojourn in the hospital by one of the authors of this book will testify. It is, therefore, perhaps fortunate that the majority of the Hawaiian muraenids attain a maximum length of less than 2 feet.

The identification of many of the species within the Muraenidae presents considerable difficulty to one not familiar with them. Indeed, the species of the largest genus, *Gymnothorax*, have been hopelessly confused by such earlier authors as Jordan and Evermann (1905). The primary morphological characters used for identification are the degree of fin development (for genera), the teeth, and the nature and position of the posterior nostril. Since the fins are enclosed in a heavy layer of flesh, their point of origin can easily be misinterpreted. To examine the teeth it is often necessary to break the lower jaw in order to open the mouth. The tooth pattern may change somewhat with growth; indeed in *Echidna polyzona* the dentition alters so markedly (Fig. 148 c and d) that several of the growth stages have been described as separate species. Furthermore, certain specimens, particularly very old individuals, lack many teeth. With practice, one other character, color pattern, is very useful. Again, however, some species, notably *Gymnothorax eurostus*, the commonest puhi in Hawaii, are quite variable both in color and color pattern.

**Fig. 148**

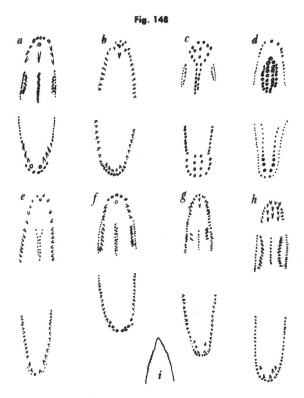

Diagrams of tooth patterns of certain morays, viewed as if the jaws had been opened back until the upper and lower are in line with one another; above, upper jaw; below, lower jaw. In morays, as in other eels, the two premaxillaries and the vomer, together with the ethmoid, are fused into a single bone, and the premaxillary and vomerine teeth sometimes form a continuous series. Nevertheless, the group at the front of the upper jaw (*b*) are considered premaxillary teeth, whereas the series running back along the center of the mouth roof are considered vomerine. Vomerine teeth may be uniserial (as in *g*), biserial (as in *f*), or form a broad plate of pebble-like, crushing teeth (as in *d*). The maxillary teeth are in one (*b*) or two (*b*) rows on either side and may be continuous forward with the premaxillary group (*b*) or well separated (*a*). *a, Rabula fuscomaculata; b, Uropterygius inornatus; c, Echidna polyzona* at 5 inches; *d*, same species 20 inches long; *e, Gymnothorax pictus; f, G. melatremus; g, G. hilonis; h, G. eurostus; i,* a lower lateral tooth of *G. moluccensis.*

**103**

## Key to the Hawaiian eels of the family Muraenidae:

1      Dorsal fin developed as a fleshy ridge at least as far forward as gill openings. Posterior nostril ahead of center of eye ............ 13

         Dorsal fin, if present, commencing well behind gill opening ...... 2

2(1)     Anal fin, if present, restricted to the tail region ................. 3

         Anal fin extending forward as a low, fleshy fold nearly to the middle of the body, stopping just short of the anus. . *Rabula fuscomaculata*

3(2)     Anus about at or ahead of the middle of body; posterior nostril above or behind the middle of the eye ........................ 6

         Anus well behind the middle of the body; posterior nostril ahead of the middle of the eye ............................. 4

4(3)     Body without numerous, narrow, white encircling rings; all of the teeth sharp ................................................ 5

         Body with about 30 narrow, white, encircling rings; teeth blunt and pebble-like ............................. p. 111, *Echidna zebra*

5(4)     Body plain brown in coloration; posterior nostril somewhat ahead of eye ................................... *Uropterygius sealei*

         Body with distinct oval or roundish black spots on a lighter background; posterior nostril over front of eye ...... *Uropterygius tigrinus*

6(3)     Body without distinct oval or roundish black spots on a light background ................................................ 7

         Body with distinct oval or roundish black spots on a light background ................................... *Uropterygius polyspilus*

7(6)     Posterior nostril with a large lateral-line pore within an eye diameter of it, sometimes separated from it only by a narrow fleshy partition (Fig. 149) .................................... 11

         Posterior nostril without a lateral-line pore within an eye diameter of it ............................................. 8

8(7)     Gill openings above the middle of sides; ground color basically brownish ................................................ 9

         Gill openings below the middle of sides; ground color basically blackish ................................... *Uropterygius knighti*

9(8)     Teeth in 3 or more series on either side of both jaws; snout shorter than the distance from the eye to the corner of the mouth; body spotted or mottled at least posteriorly ....................... 10

         Teeth in jaws primarily uniserial (Fig. 148b); snout longer than the distance from the eye to the corner of the mouth; body plain brown ................................... *Uropterygius inornatus*

10(9)    Chin and fore part of body plain, spotted and often mottled posteriorly, the markings becoming gradually more prominent toward the tail; size small, to about 10 inches .... *Uropterygius fuscoguttatus*

         Chin and head mottled in the same manner as the rest of the body; size larger, to about 18 inches .......... *Uropterygius supraforatus*

11(7)    A lateral-line pore slightly ahead of and median to each posterior nostril, not enclosed in a white area (Fig. 149b) ................ 12

         An enlarged lateral-line pore just behind and median to each posterior nostril, enclosed in the same white area with the nostril (Fig. 149a) ................................... *Anarchias leucurus*

**Fig. 149**

 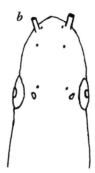

Top of head to show relation of posterior nostril to lateral-line pore in a, *Anarchias leucurus; b. A. cantonensis.*

12(11)  Head and sides of lower jaw with distinct dark markings......
.............................................*Anarchias cantonensis*

Head and chin plain brown except for the light lateral-line
pores..............................................*Anarchias allardicei*

13(1)   Posterior nostril not enclosed by an elongate flap that is longer
than the anterior nostril; no bright red on the body in life........  14

Posterior nostril enclosed in an elongate flap that is longer than
the anterior nostril (Fig. 150) and is usually bright red in life;
body in life with red and black markings...........*Muraena pardalis*

14(13)  Anterior nostril in a tube that extends forward from the snout tip...  15

Anterior nostril on top of snout and nearly an eye diameter from
snout tip, usually with a leaflike projection that extends upward
(Fig. 151). Posterior nostril in a large trough that lies almost entirely ahead of eye; a plain brown eel that attains at least 5 feet
in length......................................*Enchelynassa canina*

15(14)  Teeth on sides of lower jaw sharply pointed...................  18

Teeth on sides of lower jaw rounded and pebble-like...........  16

16(15)  Sides of body either plain or with dark crossbands..............  17

Sides of body with 2 rows of irregular dark blotches with
round light centers...............................*Echidna nebulosa*

17(16)  Edges of fins and areas around head pores abruptly light. Not
known north of Johnston......................*Echidna leucotaenia*

Edges of fins and areas around head pores not lighter than ad-
joining regions. Body with dark crossbands in the young, these
becoming progressively less distinct with age........*Echidna polyzona*

18(15)  Anus at or ahead of the middle of the length..................  19

Anus well behind the middle of the length. Body color plain;
fins plain, but with white borders..............*Gymnothorax hepaticus*

19(18)  Head, body, and fins not a plain, uniform dark brown; none of
the teeth with rough, serrate edges...........................  20

**105**

Head, body, and fins a plain, uniform, dark brown; the larger teeth in both jaws with rough, serrate edges (Fig. 148i). A small eel, reaching a length of about a foot, apparently rare in Hawaii ..........................................*Gymnothorax moluccensis*

20(19)  Vomerine teeth, if present, uniserial; corner of mouth at least one eye diameter behind eye.............................  22

Vomerine teeth at least partly biserial (Fig. 148 e and f); corner of mouth less than one eye diameter behind eye. None of the teeth long and needle-like; rim of posterior nostril with a low fringe; ground color gray, yellow, or orange...................  21

21(20)  Color pattern in adult consisting solely of innumerable black specklings on a gray ground; maxillary teeth uniserial (Fig. 148e)........................................*Gymnothorax pictus*

Posterior portion bright orange or yellow in life, often with darker mottling; maxillary teeth biserial (Fig. 148f). Gill opening often in a dark area; size to about a foot; a common species at a depth of 50 feet .......................*Gymnothorax melatremus*

22(20)  No narrow green band in life around the edges of the fins posteriorly........................................................  23

A narrow light green band around the edges of the fins posteriorly in life (this fading quickly in preservative). Body dark brown with blackish spotting, gill opening in a blackish area (Fig. 152)................................*Gymnothorax flavimarginatus*

23(22)  A single continuous row of teeth on each maxillary, though 1 to 4 long, needle-like teeth may occur to form an incomplete inner row; 3 longitudinal rows of teeth in the front of the upper jaw (Fig. 148g)........................................  26

Two almost equally long rows of teeth on each maxillary, an outer row of small teeth and an inner row of 8 or more larger ones; 5 longitudinal rows of teeth in the front of the upper jaw (Fig. 148h). Tip of tail white...........................  24

24(23)  Color pattern consisting entirely of round white spots on a black background; gill opening in an especially black area (Fig. 153) ........................................*Gymnothorax meleagris*

Color pattern of various mottling often including white spots, but never consisting solely of round white spots on a plain black background; gill opening not in an especially dark area.........  25

25(24)  Chin and throat marked in the same manner as the rest of the head; jaws not completely closing for their full length. Color extremely variable; our commonest inshore eel.....*Gymnothorax eurostus*

Chin and throat region plain; jaws completely closing........ ........................................*Gymnothorax buroensis*

26(23)  Borders of gill opening of the same color as the surrounding area....  28

Borders of gill opening definitely darker than the surrounding area......................................................  27

27(26)  Body yellowish-brown with distinct but irregular darker brown markings; creases at and below corner of mouth dark (Fig. 155)................................*Gymnothorax steindachneri*

Body with broad light patches separated by narrower dark areas; creases at and below corner of mouth not darker than the surrounding region...........................*Gymnothorax berndti*

28(26) Body with spotting, mottling, or irregular, ill-defined vertical banding. . . . . . . . . . . . . . . . . . . . . . . . . . . . . . . . . . . . . . . . . . . . . . . 29

About 20 regular, sharply delimited dark crossbars (Fig. 156), which are approximately equal in width to the light areas between them (the light ground color becomes darker with age so that the dark barring is less obvious in large specimens). . . . . . .
. . . . . . . . . . . . . . . . . . . . . . . . . . . . . . . . . . . . . . . . . . . *Gymnothorax petelli*

29(28) Jaws long, the distance from the tip of the snout to the corner of the mouth contained about 2½ times in the head length (measured to gill opening); lateral-line pores on head not surrounded by conspicuous light areas. . . . . . . . . . . . . . . . . . . . . . . . . . . . . . . . 30

Jaws short, the distance from the tip of the snout to the corner of the mouth contained about 2¾ times in the head length; head pores on upper jaw and chin surrounded by conspicuous light areas. Fins without prominent light borders. . . . *Gymnothorax hilonis*

30(29) Body brown with indefinite darker vertical patches; anal with a light border for its full length. . . . . . . . . . . . . . . . . . . . . . . . . . . . . 31

Body nearly black, with narrow, white, wavy lines especially prominent posteriorly; anal with the white border, if present, best developed posteriorly. . . . . . . . . . . . . . . . . . . *Gymnothorax undulatus*

31(30) Dorsal with a light border for almost its full length; a dark bar extending across top of head above the corner of the mouth; maximum size about 10 inches. . . . . . . . . . . . . . *Gymnothorax gracilicaudus*

Dorsal without a light border; no dark bar running across top of head at the level of the corner of the mouth; size of only known specimen about 30 inches. . . . . . . . . . . . . . . . . . . . . . *Gymnothorax mucifer*

### Genus RABULA

In all other Hawaiian muraenids, the fleshy dorsal ridge either extends forward to over the gill region or is restricted to the tail area; *Rabula* is intermediate, having a low dorsal ridge running forward to a point roughly above the anus. Unfortunately, the ridge tapers to nothing anteriorly so that its point of origin can be only approximately determined.

One known Hawaiian species.

### RABULA FUSCOMACULATA

At first sight a rather nondescript, mottled brown eel with a blunt snout (for tooth pattern, see Fig. 148a). The dorsal fin character will separate it from all others. In addition, the nostrils and head pores are in white areas and the posterior nostril lies behind the middle of the eye.

The genus (and species) is apparently rare in Hawaii, for it has been taken only once (among dead coral near Diamond Head in about 10 feet of water). The largest specimen obtained was 8 inches long.

### Genus UROPTERYGIUS

*Uropterygius* and the related *Anarchias* represent the ultimate point in snakelike or wormlike development among the morays. The only trace of fins is to be found in the flattened tail region, and, forward of the tail, many of the species are almost round in cross section. The basic difference between *Uropterygius* and *Anarchias* lies in the presence of a lateral-line pore close to the posterior nostril in the latter genus. Unfortunately, all of the species of *Anarchias* are small, so that it requires magnification to determine whether the pore is present or not.

Though there are 10 species of *Uropterygius* and *Anarchias* known from Hawaii, only one, *Uropterygius knighti*, is common along shore, and this is very abundant on rocky coasts. Indeed, the chances are excellent that any small, blackish, finless moray taken from among the rocks in the surge zone will prove to be *U. knighti*.

### UROPTERYGIUS SEALEI

There are a number of plain brown eels in Hawaii, but this is the only one with the anus two-thirds of the way back along the body.

Very few specimens of this species have ever been taken in Hawaii. It apparently reaches a length of about 3 feet.

### UROPTERYGIUS TIGRINUS

The location of the anus far back on the body plus the distinct roundish dark spots will distinguish this species from all other morays. The total absence of fins will differentiate it from the somewhat similarly spotted ophichthid eel *Myrichthys maculosus*.

*Uropterygius tigrinus* appears to be relatively uncommon in Hawaii. It grows to be at least 4 feet long, at which length the greatest depth of the body is not much more than 1 inch.

### UROPTERYGIUS POLYSPILUS

This species looks very much like the young of *U. tigrinus*, but the anus is in its normal forward position. In the young, the tip of the snout is abruptly light.

The species has not hitherto been recorded from Hawaii. We have a single specimen, 17 inches long.

### UROPTERYGIUS KNIGHTI

The posterior part of the body of this fish is black or very dark gray upon which are superimposed lighter gray, snowflake-shaped markings; the throat and abdomen are considerably lighter. This is the only species of *Uropterygius* with a gray-and-black coloration. In addition, the gill openings are well below the middle of the sides, and the teeth are in two rows on each side of the jaw, with those of the inner row fewer, larger, erect, and needle-like.

The species is very common along rocky shores, where it apparently lives just below the low-tide level in areas of heavy wave action. It is the only *Uropterygius* inhabiting such areas, and in turn does not seem to be present in water more than 10 feet deep where other species of the genus are encountered.

Attains a length of about 14 inches.

### UROPTERYGIUS INORNATUS

A small, nondescript, plain brown eel sometimes taken in 15 or more feet of water. One would suspect it of being the young of *Uropterygius sealei* except that it has the anus forward (in the normal position). From the rather similar *Anarchias allardicei* it differs in lacking the pore near the posterior nostril. Indeed, the only distinctive thing about the fish seems to be the uniserial teeth on the sides of both jaws and the complete lack of teeth on the vomer. (see Fig. 148b).

No Hawaiian specimens longer than 8 inches have been taken.

### UROPTERYGIUS FUSCOGUTTATUS

This seems to be the commonest *Uropterygius* below the zone of wave action. The rear of the body is speckled with brown but the head region is a plain brown. The head pores are large and surrounded by narrow light rings, beyond which there is a concentration of dark pigment; the result is that the head pores stand out rather prominently. The teeth are in three rows on either side of each jaw; they are all erect and needle-like and are graduated in size from the outer to the inner row.

Attains a length of about 12 inches, the individuals apparently becoming somewhat darker in coloration as they get larger.

### UROPTERYGIUS SUPRAFORATUS

Similar to *U. fuscoguttatus* except that the dark mottling is continued forward onto the head and lower jaw, and that the teeth are in about 5 rows on each side of either jaw.

Known from Johnston and from one specimen 18 inches long from Oahu.

### Genus ANARCHIAS

As already mentioned, *Anarchias* differs from *Uropterygius* chiefly in having a lateral-line pore near the posterior nostril (see Fig. 149). In addition, the Hawaiian species of *Anarchias* all have the teeth on either side of both jaws in two rows: the outer small, close-set, and pointing backward; the inner larger, more widely spaced, erect, and needle-like.

The genus is made up of small eels, none of them reaching a foot in length and none of them occurring in less than 10 feet of water.

### ANARCHIAS LEUCURUS

Unlike the two other species of the genus, *Anarchias leucurus* has the pore near the posterior nostril slightly behind the nostril and in the same white area with it (see Fig. 149a). In color pattern it is very similar to *A. cantonensis*, with the head and sides of the lower jaw mottled; it differs however in that the inner series of large, needle-like teeth in the upper jaw does not extend behind the eye.

Apparently the commonest species of *Anarchias* in Hawaii. Reaches a length of about 10 inches.

### ANARCHIAS CANTONENSIS

Differs from *Anarchias allardicei* in the mottled coloration and from *A. leucurus* in having the inner row of teeth in the upper jaw extending the full length of the jaw, as well as in the position of the pore near the posterior nostril (see Fig. 149b).

Only two specimens of *A. cantonensis*, each about 8 inches long, are known from Hawaii.

### ANARCHIAS ALLARDICEI

A small, plain, light brown eel greatly resembling *Uropterygius inornatus*. From this it differs in having a pore near the posterior nostril and a distinct inner row of enlarged needle-like teeth.

Known from Hawaii and Johnston on the basis of a few specimens less than 7 inches long.

### Genus MURAENA

The elongate, erect, red tube enclosing the posterior nostril is diagnostic for our species of *Muraena*. This tube is about equal to an eye diameter in length, and thus much longer than the low collar surrounding the posterior nostril of numerous other muraenids.

**Fig. 150. MURAENA PARDALIS**

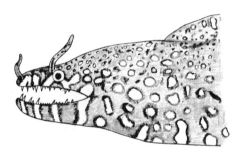

After J. and E., pl. 11

### MURAENA PARDALIS (Puhi-oa, Puhi-kauhila)

This is probably the most brilliantly colored of Hawaiian eels, with a color pattern made up of white and red spots and blotches on a dark ground. This together with the large teeth in the hooked jaws give this eel a rather vicious and even poisonous appearance. It has been seen to extend the head and fore part of the body from a hole and snap at anything going by.

Not uncommon in certain rocky areas. Appears to reach a size of 2 or 3 feet.

### Genus ENCHELYNASSA

*Enchelynassa* differs from *Muraena* in having a flaplike appendage on the anterior rather than on the posterior nostril, the latter in *Enchelynassa* being a large, broad-rimmed opening. Though the form of the nostrils is the diagnostic feature by which the genus is recognized, the single Hawaiian species may be identified easily by general appearance alone.

**110**

Fig. 151. ENCHELYNASSA CANINA

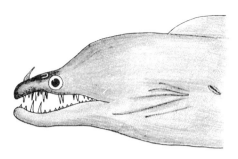

## ENCHELYNASSA CANINA

This species is probably the most dangerous of Hawaiian eels. It has numerous long fanglike teeth and hooked jaws that leave a wide gap between them when the tips are closed. The color is a plain dark brown without any markings.

*Enchelynassa canina* may be the largest of Hawaiian eels, attaining a length of at least 5 feet. Apparently it grows to a considerably larger size at Johnston. Its relatively heavy body and strong jaws can make it a dangerous antagonist, but in our area, at least, it has never been known to attack without provocation. It seems to be neither common nor particularly rare. Specimens smaller than 2 feet in length have never been taken in Hawaii.

### Genus ECHIDNA

Some of the species of *Echidna* look superficially like *Gymnothorax*. When species of the two genera are compared the specimens of *Echidna* usually have the blunter head; none of them has the long jaws that fail to close found in *Muraena, Enchelynassa,* and several species of *Gymnothorax*. The technical feature that separates *Echidna* from *Gymnothorax* is the presence of pebble-like teeth in two or more rows on the vomer; it is frequently or usually necessary to break the lower jaw to observe these. In the young of at least *Echidna nebulosa,* the vomerine teeth are biserial in front, uniserial posteriorly, but the vomerine series always extends farther back than the jaw teeth. In the adult the vomerine teeth may spread out laterally to form a broad, somewhat raised plate covering most of the roof of the mouth (Fig. 148d). These teeth are said to be used for crushing mollusk shells.

## ECHIDNA ZEBRA

The specific name of this fish is indicative of its color pattern. It is the only black eel with numerous narrow white bands encircling the body. Dorsal and anal fin ridges are not developed except near the tail area, and the anus is far back on the tail portion of the body. This combination of features makes *Echidna zebra* the easiest of all eels to recognize.

It is not particularly common as compared with certain other Hawaiian eels, nor is it a rarity. Reaches perhaps 3 feet in length.

**111**

### ECHIDNA NEBULOSA

This is the only Hawaiian eel with round light centers in each of the large, dark, amoeba-shaped blotches on the sides.

Uncommon. It seems to inhabit rocky coasts and young specimens have been taken in tide pools. Apparently does not reach 2 feet in length.

### ECHIDNA LEUCOTAENIA

A brown eel fairly frequent at Johnston but not yet taken in Hawaii. The white spots surrounding the head pores will distinguish it from other species of the genus. Attains a known length of 21 inches.

### ECHIDNA POLYZONA

The prominent, broad, black vertical bars in the young of this species are only duplicated in *Gymnothorax petelli* among Hawaiian morays (for tooth pattern, see Fig. 148 c and d). The sharp teeth of *G. petelli* will immediately differentiate that species. In both black-barred forms the barring becomes less marked with age, fading out more or less completely in large specimens. Indeed, in the Hawaiian Islands, any almost plain, very dark colored moray over 15 inches long with a broad patch of pebble-like vomerine teeth will be this species.

*Echidna polyzona* is quite common in certain areas. We have seen it nosing about in perhaps a foot of water off the Honolulu yacht harbor breakwater. It probably attains a length of about 2 feet.

### Genus GYMNOTHORAX

The genus *Gymnothorax* contains all of the puhis that are ordinarily seen in the water or in the market. The species of this large genus are among the most difficult of Hawaiian fishes to identify. A few can be recognized by additional characters, but in general the identification of species within the genus depends upon two features: color and teeth. Unfortunately, both of these are variable within species. In *Gymnothorax eurostus*, for example, different individuals vary from light tan to almost black. Consequently it is necessary to restrict the use of color as an identifying character to certain features of pattern that appear to be relatively constant. The tooth pattern for any one species seems to be fairly constant, but a number of individual teeth may be missing in any particular specimen; this is particularly true of old individuals, which may have fewer teeth. The fact that it is often necessary to break the lower jaw in order to examine the dentition is a further discouraging feature connected with identification in *Gymnothorax*. Because of these difficulties the classification of the Hawaiian species of the genus has been until recently badly confused, and even now much remains to be done.

### GYMNOTHORAX HEPATICUS

The position of the anus in the posterior half of the body immediately sets *Gymnothorax hepaticus* apart from other members of the genus. The plain coloration with light fin borders and the tapering tail are other features by which the species may be recognized.

The species appears to be decidedly rare in Hawaii and indeed is known only from three specimens, all more than 3 feet long.

### GYMNOTHORAX MOLUCCENSIS

This is the only plain brown *Gymnothorax* in Hawaii that does not have light borders to the fins, at least posteriorly (see Fig. 148i). A more secure diagnostic character is the serrations along the borders of the teeth, but these, unfortunately, are difficult to see without a microscope. Still another distinguishing character is the presence of only a single enlarged, needle-like tooth in the middle of the front of the upper jaw.

Not common. Apparently does not reach a length of over 18 inches.

### GYMNOTHORAX PICTUS

The innumerable small, well-defined dark specklings on a light ground will immediately distinguish this species from all other Hawaiian members of *Gymnothorax* (see Fig. 148e). Additional peculiarities are that the vomerine teeth are distinctly two-rowed anteriorly and that there are no depressible, needle-like teeth in the mouth.

The species is one of the commonest forms of *Gymnothorax* in the islands of the Central Pacific but appears to be rather rare in Hawaii. It reaches a length of about 2 feet.

### GYMNOTHORAX MELATREMUS

Any small, bright yellow or orange eel taken in more than 20 feet of water is likely to be this species (see Fig. 148f). In markings it is quite variable. Some are perfectly plain; others have dark reticulations posteriorly, and the majority have a dark patch around the gill openings. The teeth are diagnostic in that there are two short rows on each maxillary that end about under the posterior border of the eye.

Attains a length of perhaps a foot.

**Fig. 152. GYMNOTHORAX FLAVIMARGINATUS**

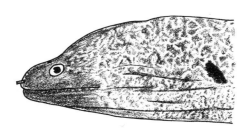

113

**GYMNOTHORAX FLAVIMARGINATUS (Puhi-paka)**

This species can always be identified in life by the narrow, bright green border to the fins posteriorly, but this fades rapidly in preservative leaving a narrow, inconspicuous light border. The general body color is brown, usually with darker brown spotting. Often the fish is so dark that the black rim around the gill opening becomes indistinct. This is a snub-nosed *Gymnothorax*, with the distance from the front of the eye to the corner of the mouth much greater than the snout length.

One of the commonest, if not the commonest, of our larger eels. Attains a length of perhaps 4 feet.

**Fig. 153. GYMNOTHORAX MELEAGRIS**

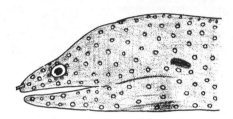

**GYMNOTHORAX MELEAGRIS**

This is the only moray in which small, roundish white spots constitute the only markings on the body in the adult. The additional character of a blackish area immediately around the gill openings should be sufficient to distinguish the species from other species of *Gymnothorax*, the young of which may be white-spotted up to a length of perhaps 7 inches.

The species is rather common at a depth of 30 feet or more and attains a length of at least 3 feet.

**Fig. 154. GYMNOTHORAX EUROSTUS**

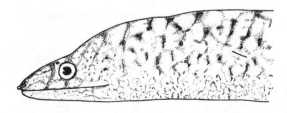

**GYMNOTHORAX EUROSTUS**

This is without much doubt the commonest eel in the Hawaiian Islands. However, it is very variable in color, different individuals running from a light

**114**

gray through brown to black, with light spotting in the young. Indeed, it is impossible to identify this species with any certainty from color alone. Fortunately, the dentition is very characteristic (see also Fig. 148h). It is only necessary to open the mouth sufficiently far to see whether there are two or more long rows of teeth on each side of the upper jaw in the area below the eye. Any mottled fish with such rows belongs to this species. There are other morays that have an inner row of as many as five teeth on the maxillary, but *Gymnothorax eurostus* always (along with *G. buroensis* and often *G. meleagris*) has nine or more. The mottling on the head, throat, and body, in addition to the white spots when these are present, will serve to distinguish *G. eurostus* from both *G. meleagris* and *G. buroensis*.

*G. eurostus* is abundant everywhere along rocky shores in water less than 40 feet deep. It spawns in May around Oahu. Many specimens, as high as 70 percent in some populations, have isopod parasites in one gill cavity or the other. Whether or not they eventually kill the fish remains unknown. The species reaches a maximum length of perhaps 2 feet.

#### GYMNOTHORAX BUROENSIS

This species is known from one specimen that was taken from the heavy fouling on the bottom of a barge brought in from Guam. As the barge was in Pearl Harbor some time before being dry-docked, it is possible that *Gymnothorax buroensis* has become established there.

The species is very like *G. eurostus* except for the characters given in the key and the fact that it does not reach so large a size. The maximum length attained in its home area to the south is about 14 inches.

**Fig. 155. GYMNOTHORAX STEINDACHNERI**

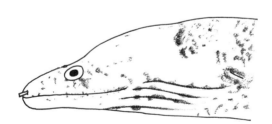

#### GYMNOTHORAX STEINDACHNERI

A yellowish-brown fish with distinct dark markings. The dark areas running back along the furrows behind the lower jaw are especially diagnostic. As compared with *Gymnothorax flavimarginatus*, this is a long-snouted species, with the snout length about equal to the distance from the front of the eye to the corner of the mouth.

Quite common in some shallow waters. Attains a length of perhaps 2 feet.

### GYMNOTHORAX BERNDTI

The extensive light patches separated by narrow, dark interspaces seem to be characteristic of this species. It is known only from a few large specimens (about 3 feet long) collected in the Honolulu market long ago.

**Fig. 156. GYMNOTHORAX PETELLI**

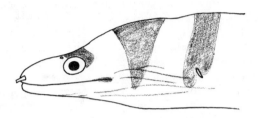

### GYMNOTHORAX PETELLI

In the broad, regular, vertical bands separated by interspaces of about equal width this species could be confused only with *Echidna polyzona*. In both these fishes the barring becomes less prominent with growth, practically disappearing in very large specimens, which in both species are an almost uniform dark gray. Aside from tooth characters, *Gymnothorax petelli* may be distinguished from *Echidna polyzona* by the fact that the posterior nostril lies in a whitish area, and by the very long jaws: the lower jaw, measured to the corner of the mouth, goes into the head length to gill opening about 2½ times in *Gymnothorax petelli*, about 3 times in *Echidna polyzona*.

*Gymnothorax petelli* is quite common, and large examples frequently appear in the market. It reaches a length of about 3 feet.

### GYMNOTHORAX HILONIS

This species was described from a single very dark specimen taken 50 years ago. We somewhat doubtfully identify with it a number of light brown specimens taken in Kaneohe Bay. These resemble the original example in the very short jaws, the small teeth, the tooth pattern, (see Fig. 148g) and the presence of light areas around the lateral-line pores on the jaws.

The largest specimen is about a foot long.

**Fig. 157. GYMNOTHORAX UNDULATUS**

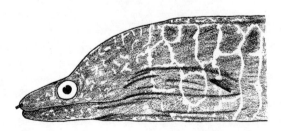

### GYMNOTHORAX UNDULATUS (Puhi-laumilo)

The narrow, white, wavy lines on a blackish ground of this fish are duplicated only in *Gymnothorax hilonis*, a short-jawed, small-toothed species known from only one specimen.

*Gymnothorax undulatus* is fairly common and reaches a length of at least 3 feet.

**Fig. 158. GYMNOTHORAX GRACILICAUDUS**

### GYMNOTHORAX GRACILICAUDUS

*Gymnothorax gracilicaudus* is a small eel that apparently does not reach a foot in length. It is very slender-bodied for a puhi and has as its most diagnostic feature a white area extending down the middle of the snout from in back of the eye. This white area is sometimes encroached upon by brown spotting.

Rather common in about 20 feet of water.

### GYMNOTHORAX MUCIFER

This species is known from one specimen about 30 inches long collected over 50 years ago. In color it is said to be a "rich dark brown with flakes of white." Some of the front teeth are exceedingly long and needlelike with slight bulbous expansions just below their tips.

## Family XENOCONGRIDAE

The Xenocongridae is represented in Hawaii by two small eels with the body plain brown and the fins light-bordered. Though they have no striking peculiarity which will at once distinguish them from all other eels, they do have a number of characters by which, taken together, they may be easily recognized. The gill opening is a small hole (as in the Muraenidae); the posterior nostril opens into the mouth from the inside of the upper lip (as in the Ophichthidae); the lower lip has a reverted flap on either side (as in the Congridae); and the vomerine teeth are in two, well-separated rows.

Key to the Hawaiian species of the family Xenocongridae:

Pectoral fins present, well developed; distance from tip of snout to anus contained about twice in the distance from the anus to tip of tail......................................*Kaupichthys diodontus*

Pectoral fins absent; distance from tip of snout to anus about equal to the distance from the anus to the tip of tail.........
............................................*Chilorhinus platyrhynchus*

**117**

**KAUPICHTHYS DIODONTUS**

This small brown eel differs from other Hawaiian eels in having a well-developed pectoral fin above a round gill opening, in the slight knobs all over the surface of the snout, and in the extremely long tail region (see Fig. 132).

It is not common and apparently reaches a maximum length of about 8 inches.

**Fig. 159. CHILORHINUS PLATYRHYNCHUS**

**CHILORHINUS PLATYRHYNCHUS**

*Chilorhinus platyrhynchus* is the only eel in the Hawaiian Islands in which the snout length is less than the distance between the eyes: it has an exceedingly short, flat snout with a very broad, shallow mouth.

Not uncommon in certain areas, reaching perhaps 7 inches in length.

## Family MORINGUIDAE

The family Moringuidae is represented in Hawaii by a single species. This elongate, wormlike form can always be distinguished by a combination of the following two features: the anus is located far back, on the posterior third of the body, and the chin protrudes well beyond the upper jaw.

**MORINGUA MACROCHIR**

The commonest form of this eel is a long yellowish creature with rudimentary eyes and fins; it lives buried in the sand (see Fig. 134). In this respect it resembles the ophichthid eels of the genus *Caecula*, from which it differs in the posterior anal position and projecting chin. Upon reaching sexual maturity, however, *Moringua macrochir* becomes black above and silvery below, and the eyes and fins develop. In this phase it is sometimes collected at a night light on the surface.

Attains a length of perhaps 18 inches.

## Family SERRIVOMERIDAE

This is one (see Fig. 128) of the several eel families that has taken up a deep-water existence. The snout is long and tapers to a sharp point, as in the Nemichthyidae. The two families may be easily separated, however, by the characters given in the family key.

Two species of this family have been recorded from Hawaiian waters by Gilbert (1905).

## Family NEMICHTHYIDAE

A most peculiar family of oceanic midwater eels with extremely long tapering bodies and jaws.

One species (see Fig. 127) is known from Hawaiian offshore waters, recorded from a single specimen by Gilbert (1905).

## Family MURAENESOCIDAE

The only Hawaiian record for this family is based on a single dried specimen killed and brought to the surface by the lava flow of 1919. Whether this fish is really a muraenesocid seems questionable.

## Family NETTASTOMIDAE

Another family of deep-water eels so far recorded from Hawaii on the basis of a single specimen. It seems to be unique among Hawaiian eels in having the elongate posterior nostrils extending behind the eye on the top of the head.

The one specimen (see Fig. 133) is recorded by Gilbert (1905).

## Family CONGRIDAE (Conger or White Eels)

The Congridae is represented by both shallow-water and deep-water forms. Among the shallow-water species the white eel, or puhi-uha, is among the best-known of our Hawaiian eels. All of the members of the family have a well-developed pectoral fin, and the shallow-water representatives, at least, can be distinguished from all other Hawaiian eels by their plain white or silvery coloration and by a deep furrow running from the anterior nostril to the end of the jaw separating the upper lip from the side of the head.

Six species are known from Hawaii at present, but other deep-water forms will undoubtedly turn up.

Key to the Hawaiian species of the family Congridae:

| | | |
|---|---|---|
| 1 | Teeth present on jaws and vomer.......................... | 2 |
| | No teeth on jaws and vomer.................... *Veternio verrens* | |
| 2(1) | Snout reaching less than an eye diameter in front of tip of lower jaw.................................................. | 3 |
| | Snout reaching more than an eye diameter in front of tip of lower jaw................................ *Promyllantor alcocki* | |
| 3(2) | Teeth on the sides of the lower jaw in a single row forming a cutting edge................................................ | 4 |
| | Teeth on the sides of the lower jaw in about 3 rows, not forming a cutting edge........................ *Congrellus aequoreus* | |
| 4(3) | Length of gill opening less than half the distance between gill openings; the distance from the tip of snout to the anus contained 1⅔ or more times in the distance from the anus to the tip of tail................................................ | 5 |

**119**

Length of gill opening nearly equal to the distance between the gill openings; the distance from tip of snout to the anus going 1½ or fewer times into the distance from the anus to the tip of tail. . . . . . . . . . . . . . . . . . . . . . . . . . . . . . . . . . . . . . . . . . . . . . . . . . . . . . . . *Ariosoma bowersi*

5(4)  Dorsal commencing about over pectoral bases; in half-grown and adults there is a black band extending backward and downward from above upper lip. . . . . . . . . . . . . . . . . . . . . . . *Conger marginatus*

Dorsal commencing about over tip of depressed pectorals; no black band extending back from above upper lip. . . . . . . . *Conger wilsoni*

### VETERNIO VERRENS

The total absence of teeth will immediately distinguish this fish from all other congrid eels.

Apparently only two specimens of this species are known. One of these found in the Honolulu market was over 20 inches long.

### PROMYLLANTOR ALCOCKI

Aside from the characteristic projecting snout, this species could be distinguished by having a combination of 4 or 5 well-defined series of teeth along the sides of the jaws and the dorsal fin commencing about over the tips of the pectoral fins.

The only known specimens, 7 to 10 inches long, were dredged in about 300 fathoms of water.

### CONGRELLUS AEQUOREUS

This deep-water fish looks very much like *Conger marginatus* but differs in having the teeth on the sides of the jaws in a narrow band instead of in a single row and in the much larger pores above the upper lip and on the lower jaw.

Apparently rather common in depths of from 100 to 400 fathoms. Reaches a length of perhaps 2 feet.

### ARIOSOMA BOWERSI

A small silvery species that burrows in the sand (see Fig. 131). It has a larger eye than any other Hawaiian congrid but the eye is covered by a heavy layer of transparent flesh. In addition to the characters given in the key, *Ariosoma* may be separated from the two Hawaiian species of the genus *Conger* by the fact that the posterior nostril of *Ariosoma* is at least as close to the upper lip as to the eye; in *Conger* the posterior nostril opens immediately in front of the eye.

Quite common in certain shallow-water, sandy areas. Attains a length of perhaps 16 inches.

### CONGER MARGINATUS (White eel, Puhi-uha)

This is a well-known and abundant species in Hawaiian shallow waters. It can be distinguished at a glance by the dark mark extending along above the posterior portion of the mouth. This mark does not develop, however, until the fish reaches a length of some 8 inches.

The species reaches a length of at least 3 feet and probably more.

## CONGER WILSONI

Much like *Conger marginatus* but differing in the more posterior dorsal origin and in lacking the dark mark above the mouth.

This species is known to reach 5 feet in length. It appears to be considerably less common than *Conger marginatus*.

### Family OPHICHTHIDAE

Any eel with the tip of the tail formed by a sharp, fleshy point that protrudes behind the dorsal and anal fin is a member of this family. However, there are also fin-tailed ophichthids, and these are more easily confused with other eel families. If fin-tailed eels have the following two characters, they are ophichthids: posterior nostril opening into the mouth from the inside of the upper lip and dorsal fin commencing at least a head length behind the gill openings. A sure means of identifying members of this family is the branchiostegal ray structure, but it is usually necessary to peel back the skin of the throat region to observe this character. In the Ophichthidae and no other eel family the branchiostegal rays from the two sides of the head overlap on the mid-ventral line.

The Ophichthidae is one of the largest and most variable of eel families. On sandy bottoms within and around reefs, individuals are sometimes abundant, but they usually spend the daylight hours, at least, largely or completely buried. Ophichthids rarely take a hook and are so slim-bodied that they can pass through the mesh of a fish trap. The front end of one of these eels may sometimes be noted sticking out of the sand, and an occasional specimen will swim into a night light, but, in general, ophichthids escape notice.

Key to the Hawaiian species of the family Ophichthidae:

| | | |
|---|---|---|
| 1 | Tip of the tail consists of a hard, fleshy point that protrudes beyond the posteriormost dorsal and anal fin rays.............. | 6 |
| | Tip of tail completely enclosed in a series of short fin rays. Pectorals absent; coloration plain, without spots or bars; wormlike eels, all of very similar appearance, which never reach a length of more than about a foot.............................. | 2 |
| 2(1) | The low or rudimentary dorsal fin commences ahead of anus or less than a head length behind it; teeth present on premaxillary and vomer........................................ | 3 |
| | Dorsal fin commencing more than the length of the fish's head (measured to the gill opening) behind the anus; teeth lacking on the premaxillary and vomer...............*Schultzidia johnstonensis* | |
| 3(2) | Base of the tube of the anterior nostril above or behind the tip of the lower jaw, which extends forward much more than half-way from the front of the eye to the tip of snout.............. | 4 |
| | Tubular anterior nostrils entirely in front of the tip of the short lower jaw, which extends only about halfway from the front of the eye to the tip of snout. Not known north of Johnston..... .......................................................*Leptenchelys labialis* | |

4(3)  The cleft of the mouth extends less than an eye diameter behind the eye.............................................................. 5

The cleft of the mouth extends relatively far back, so that about half the length of the lower jaw lies behind the center of the eye. Not known north of Johnston................*Muraenichthys schultzei*

5(4)  Dorsal fin originating over or ahead of the anus; head relatively broad, its width at eyes greater than the snout length..*Muraenichthys cookei*

Dorsal fin originating behind the anus; head long and narrow, width at eyes less than the snout length. Not known north of Johnston...............................................*Muraenichthys gymnotus*

6(1)  Dorsal and anal fin present, though sometimes low and inconspicuous; gill openings lateral.............................. 8

Body without traces of fins anywhere; gill openings on the ventral surface of the body...................................... 7

7(6)  Posterior nostril opening on the inside of upper lip; head contained about 10 times in the body length.........*Caecula platyrhyncha*

Posterior nostril opening on the outside of upper lip; head contained 15 to 20 times in the body length............*Caecula flavicauda*

8(6)  Dorsal commencing approximately over or behind gill openings... 12

Dorsal commencing well ahead of gill openings............... 9

9(8)  Pectorals present; tail longer than trunk...................... 10

Pectorals absent; tail (measured from the anus) shorter than trunk (measured from gill openings to anus).........*Callechelys luteus*

10(9)  Pectoral short and rounded, the length of its rays shorter than the width of its base; upper lip not fringed.................... 11

Pectoral considerably longer than broad; edge of upper lip fringed...............................................*Cirrhimuraena macgregori*

11(10)  Color pattern consisting of large, round, dark spots..*Myrichthys maculosus*

Color pattern consisting of about 29 dark saddles, which extend across the back and down on to the sides. Not known north of Johnston.....................................*Myrichthys bleekeri*

12(8)  Lower jaw weak and inferior, without enlarged teeth; cleft of mouth extending little behind eye.......................... 13

Lower jaw strong, little if at all inferior, with some enlarged teeth; cleft of mouth extending at least as far behind as before eye.................................................... 14

13(12)  Color plain greenish; anterior nostril with a large, leaflike flap ..........................................*Phyllophichthus xenodontus*

Head and back with a series of sharply marked dark saddles; anterior nostril without a large, leaflike flap........*Leiuranus semicinctus*

14(12)  Dorsal commencing well behind tip of pectoral fin; lower jaw projecting....................................................... 15

Dorsal commencing approximately over gill opening; jaws subequal.............................*Ophichthus polyophthalmus*

15(14)  Dorsal fin plain, pale; snout contained about 15 times in head length. Not known north of Johnston.........*Brachysomophis sauropsis*

Dorsal fin black with a white border; snout contained about 10 times in head length....................*Brachysomophis henshawi*

### SCHULTZIDIA JOHNSTONENSIS

This fish differs in general appearance from representatives of the related genera *Leptenchelys* and *Muraenichthys* in being strongly compressed throughout and in having the body coloration dark above, light below. By contrast, the species of *Leptenchelys* and *Muraenichthys* have the fore part of the body round or elliptical in cross section and are plain yellowish or whitish in coloration. The most diagnostic feature of *Schultzidia*, however, is the tooth pattern noted in the key.

Rare in the Hawaiian chain and at Johnston, inhabiting patches of sand among rocks and coral. Reaches about a foot in length.

### LEPTENCHELYS LABIALIS

The low dorsal fin of this species extends farther forward than in any Hawaiian fin-tailed ophichthid, commencing about a head length behind the gill opening. *L. labialis* may also be identified immediately by the long, deep median cleft running forward between the nostrils on the lower surface of the snout.

Known in our area from only three specimens less than 6 inches long taken at Johnston.

### MURAENICHTHYS SCHULTZEI

The posterior position of the corner of the mouth, which lies about two eye diameters behind the eye, will distinguish this form from other Hawaiian species of *Muraenichthys* and from *Schultzidia*. The double row of vomerine teeth is also diagnostic. The dorsal fin of *M. schultzei* commences somewhat behind the anus.

Known only from Johnston Island in the Hawaiian area, from a number of specimens less than 5 inches long.

#### Fig. 160. MURAENICHTHYS COOKEI

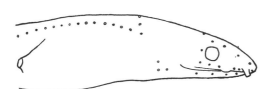

### MURAENICHTHYS COOKEI

*Muraenichthys cookei* is the only yellow ophichthid in Hawaii (there are others at Johnston). It frequently turns up in poison stations run in shallow water over sandy patches among rocks and coral. These areas it shares with another wormlike eel, *Moringua*, and sometimes with the silvery or transparent *Ariosoma*. *Muraenichthys cookei* can always be distinguished from *Moringua* by its inferior lower jaw and by having the anus under the forward portion of the body.

Despite its frequency, this species never seems to occur in abundance. It reaches a size of perhaps 10 inches. A ripe female 7 inches in length was taken at Johnston in February.

## MURAENICHTHYS GYMNOTUS

The posterior origin of the almost rudimentary dorsal fin, which commences somewhat behind the anus, will distinguish this species from other forms of *Muraenichthys* except *M. schultzei*, and the more anterior mouth will separate it from that.

The only specimens from our area are three less than 5 inches long from Johnston.

### Fig. 161. CAECULA PLATYRHYNCHA

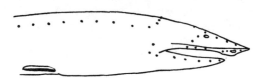

## CAECULA PLATYRHYNCHA

The two species of *Caecula* are the only Hawaiian eels with the fins totally lacking. *C. platyrhyncha* is a much stockier fish than *C. flavicauda*. In addition, the eye is smaller, the snout is more or less triangular in cross section, and the borders of the two gill openings run almost parallel to one another (Fig. 161b).

*C. platyrhyncha* occurs in abundance below low-tide mark along some of the beaches near rock outcrops. However, the individuals lie totally buried in the sand, through which they burrow either forward or backward with great rapidity. As a result of this mode of life, the species was not even known until large numbers of individuals were brought to the surface by the use of rotenone.

The usual length of specimens obtained is about 14 inches.

### Fig. 162. CAECULA FLAVICAUDA

## CAECULA FLAVICAUDA

By contrast with *Caecula platyrhyncha*, this eel is extremely elongate, its eye is larger, and the borders of its gill openings (Fig. 162) extend outward and backward.

Whereas *C. platyrhyncha* is common in depths of 3 to 8 feet, *C. flavicauda* seems to remain in deeper water. The known depth range of this latter species is 10 to 350 feet for the ten or so specimens known.

The maximum length is at least 18 inches.

**Fig. 163. CALLECHELYS LUTEUS**

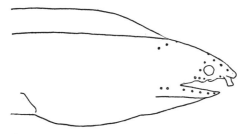

## CALLECHELYS LUTEUS

The characters given in the key will readily distinguish this species from other ophichthids. In addition, the relatively high dorsal fin extends farther forward (to almost over the corner of the mouth) than in any other member of the family.

Only a half-dozen specimens of this eel are known, and two of these are individuals that swam into a night light. *Callechelys luteus* attains a length of over 3 feet, but its body is so slim and wiry that a 3-foot specimen is hardly more than an inch in greatest diameter.

**Fig. 164. CIRRHIMURAENA MACGREGORI**

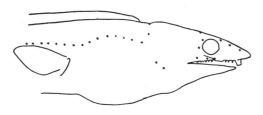

## CIRRHIMURAENA MACGREGORI

This is the only Hawaiian ophichthid with the dorsal fin extending well forward of the gill openings that has normal, elongate, fishlike pectorals. In its plain coloration, low dorsal fin, and wormlike body, *C. macgregori* has the general appearance of *Muraenichthys* and *Moringua*.

Only some half-dozen specimens of this species are known. The largest of these is 10.5 inches long.

## MYRICHTHYS MACULOSUS

This is the only Hawaiian eel with large, dark greenish spots. These spots are of different sizes, but the largest are about 5 eye diameters in width.

Fig. 165. MYRICHTHYS MACULOSUS

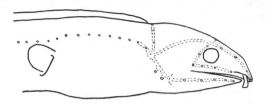

This eel is not rare in some areas. At Johnston it appears at night and makes a nuisance of itself around the pier by taking the hooks that happen to be lowered too near the bottom. *M. maculosus* attains a length of about 3 feet.

### MYRICHTHYS BLEEKERI

This species and *Leiuranus semicinctus* are our two ophichthids with well-defined dark saddles. However, the dorsal fin of *M. bleekeri* extends well forward of the gill opening; that of *Leiuranus* does not.

Known in the Hawaiian area only from some dozen Johnston Island specimens which average about 14 inches long.

Fig. 166. PHYLLOPHICHTHUS XENODONTUS

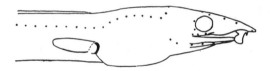

### PHYLLOPHICHTHUS XENODONTUS

This is the only Hawaiian ophichthid with a leaflike appendage on the anterior nostril.

It is known from only three specimens, two Hawaiian and one Marshallese. The largest is 10 inches long.

Fig. 167. LEIURANUS SEMICINCTUS

### LEIURANUS SEMICINCTUS

Within the Hawaiian chain itself this is the only ophichthid with prominent black saddles running across the back and down on to the sides.

**126**

The species turns up occasionally in our poison station collections, but we have never taken more than a very few individuals from any one area. Reaches a length of perhaps 2 feet.

### OPHICHTHUS POLYOPHTHALMUS

Unlike the ophichthids dealt with up to this point, the remaining species seem to be voracious forms with enlarged teeth presumably similar to the morays in feeding habits. *Ophichthus polyophthalmus* can be distinguished from the other Hawaiian species in this category by its relatively normal head shape and more forward dorsal origin.

We have never taken this species. Most of the known specimens were collected more than 20 years ago in the market, and the only one we have seen was taken by a fisherman.

### BRACHYSOMOPHIS SAUROPSIS

*Brachysomophis*, with its eye far forward on the snout (Fig. 168), has a unique appearance among Hawaiian eels.

The present species is represented from the Hawaiian area by a single small Johnston Island specimen 14 inches long. When first sighted, this individual had only the head and a small portion of the body projecting above the surface of the sand in typical ophichthid posture.

**Fig. 168. BRACHYSOMOPHIS HENSHAWI**

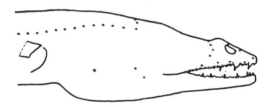

### BRACHYSOMOPHIS HENSHAWI

This is the only *Brachysomophis* so far recorded from the Hawaiian chain itself, and is known from only two specimens. The larger of these is 2.5 feet long.

## *Family* SYNAPHOBRANCHIDAE

In addition to the peculiarities mentioned in the family key, the synaphobranchids may be distinguished from all other Hawaiian eels by the presence of scales on the body. These are highly specialized, narrow, and arranged in such a fashion that those in one row lie at right angles to those above.

One deep-water species (see Fig. 130) described by Gilbert (1905).

# THE HALOSAUROID FISHES

## Family HALOSAURIDAE

A family of peculiar, elongate, deep-water fishes. As in the Ateleopidae, the dorsal is short and the anal long, but in our members of the Halosauridae the pelvic fins are abdominal in position and 9-rayed. The pectoral is inserted high on the sides and the lateral line runs low and consists of enlarged scales in the known Hawaiian forms.

Three species have been described by Gilbert (1905), all taken in over 300 fathoms of water.


# THE NEEDLEFISHES, FLYING FISHES, AND THEIR ALLIES

Both taxonomically and ecologically this is a well-marked group. In structure, its members can be readily distinguished by the fact that the lateral line runs very low on the body, practically on the abdomen, a feature found elsewhere only in the deep-water halosaurids. Ecologically, these are all silvery fishes of the surface waters and they have the proclivity for jumping, skittering, or gliding over the surface.

## Family SCOMBERESOCIDAE

This is the only family with the pelvics under the middle of the body that has a number of small separate finlets behind the dorsal and anal (see Fig. 39). All of the members of the family seem to live in the surface waters of the high seas.

Only one species is known about the Hawaiian Islands.

### COLOLABIS ADOCETUS

This species has not been previously recorded from Hawaii, but is represented by four specimens, about 2 inches in total length, taken at a night light off Kauai. The largest specimen known is only slightly longer.

Another member of the same genus, *Cololabis saira*, has been reported from the waters peripheral to the Hawaiian chain and may occur here. It may be differentiated from *C. adocetus* as follows: pectoral rays 13 or more (9 or 10 in *C. adocetus*) and gill rakers on the lower limb of the first arch 35 or more (17 to 20 in *C. adocetus*). *C. saira* also grows to a considerably larger size, and any *Cololabis* more than 5 inches long may be presumed to be of that species.

## Family BELONIDAE (Needlefishes)

The needlefishes are the only Hawaiian fishes in which both jaws are extended forward into a long, sharp beak; in addition, the pelvic fins are many-rayed and located near the middle of the body, and the lateral line runs very low along the sides.

The needlefishes are all silvery fishes living in the surface layers of the ocean. A few of them are sometimes found far from land.

Key to the Hawaiian species of the family Belonidae:

1    Caudal peduncle deeper than broad; gill rakers absent or rudimentary. . . . . . . . . . . . . . . . . . . . . . . . . . . . . . . . . . . . . . . . . . . . . . . . . . .   2

    Caudal peduncle broader than deep; gill rakers developed. .*Belone platyura*

2(1)  Body greatly compressed, its greatest width less than half the depth. . . . . . . . . . . . . . . . . . . . . . . . . . . . . . . . . . . . . . . . . . .*Ablennes hians*

    Body more or less cigar-shaped in cross section, the greatest width more than half the greatest depth. . . . . . . . . . . .*Strongylura gigantea*

### BELONE PLATYURA

This fish can be easily distinguished from other needlefishes by the greatly flattened caudal peduncle, the least depth of which is only about half its width (see Fig. 47).

Attains a length of about 15 inches.

### ABLENNES HIANS ('Aha'aha)

A much thinner, deeper fish than any of the other needlefishes, and apparently a more offshore species. It reaches a length of at least 40 inches.

### STRONGYLURA GIGANTEA ('Aha'aha, Auau)

Though the caudal peduncle of this species is not depressed as in *Belone platyura*, the lateral line does form a rough keel along the peduncle somewhat as in the uluas. This character is sufficient to distinguish *Strongylura gigantea* from other Hawaiian needlefishes.

Attains a length of at least 40 inches.

## Family HEMIRAMPHIDAE (Halfbeaks)

The halfbeaks have received their common name from the fact that whereas the lower jaw projects into a long point the upper is short. All members of the family are elongate, silvery fishes that appear to move in small schools. A few of them seem to be fishes of the open sea, but the majority are generally found close to shore.

Three species have been recorded from Hawaii.

Key to the Hawaiian species of the family Hemiramphidae:

1    Pectoral fin moderate, about equal to or shorter than the length of the head without the beak; anal fin short, its base less than the length of the lower caudal lobe; usually inshore fishes. . . . . . . . .   2

    Pectoral fin long, about twice the length of the head without the beak; anal fin base considerably longer than the lower caudal lobe. A high-seas fish. . . . . . . . . . . . . . . . .*Euleptorhamphus viridis*

2(1)  Dorsal commencing about over, and containing fewer rays than, the anal; pelvics not reaching the level of the dorsal origin . . . . . . . . . . . . . . . . . . . . . . . . . . . . . . . . . . . . . . . . . .*Hyporhamphus pacificus*

    Dorsal commencing well anterior to, and containing more rays than, the anal; pelvics reaching the level of the dorsal origin . . . . . . . . . . . . . . . . . . . . . . . . . . . . . . . . . . . . . . . . . .*Hemiramphus depauperatus*

#### EULEPTORHAMPHUS VIRIDIS (Iheihe)

Though this is a halfbeak, its long pectoral fins are used, as in the flying fishes, to glide above the surface of the water.

Reaches a length of about 18 inches.

#### HYPORHAMPHUS PACIFICUS

Compared with the next species, this is a relatively elongate, cigar-shaped fish; the length of the anal base is considerably greater than the maximum depth of the body (see Fig. 48). The relationship between *Hyporhamphus pacificus* and *H. acutus*, the Central Pacific species occurring to the south of Hawaii, remains to be determined.

Attains a length of about 10 inches.

#### HEMIRAMPHUS DEPAUPERATUS (Me'eme'e, Iheihe)

A relatively deep halfbeak, with the maximum depth of the body considerably greater than the length of the anal base.

Grows to more than 15 inches.

## Family EXOCOETIDAE (Flying Fishes)

The flying fishes are among the most pelagic of fishes, occurring everywhere in the high seas of tropical and subtropical waters. Despite the fact that members of the group are seen in great abundance, they are difficult to capture, and collections of flying fish depend largely on the few specimens that happen to have flown aboard ships. They do this not infrequently at night, at which time they seem to fly much higher above the water surface than in daytime, judging from specimens found in the morning on decks 20 feet or more above sea level. Despite such specimens, the classification of the species of Pacific flying fishes is hopelessly confused, and the account of the species found in Hawaiian waters provided below is necessarily inadequate.

Provisional key to the Exocoetidae of Hawaiian Waters:

| | | |
|---|---|---|
| 1 | Pectoral fins very long, reaching beyond the middle of the dorsal base.............................................................. | 4 |
| | Pectoral fins moderate, not reaching beyond the middle of the dorsal base.............................................................. | 2 |
| 2(1) | Pectorals reaching beyond the ventral bases; longest dorsal rays reaching at least to the caudal base............................ | 3 |
| | Pectorals not reaching beyond the ventral bases; longest dorsal rays not reaching the caudal base............*Oxyporhamphus micropterus* | |
| 3(2) | Snout considerably longer than the eye diameter; dorsal rays 9; anal rays 10......................................*Fodiator rostratus* | |
| | Snout considerably shorter than the eye diameter; dorsal rays 12 or 13; anal rays 13 or 14....................*Parexocoetus brachypterus* | |
| 4(1) | Pelvic fins long, reaching well beyond the anal origin............. | 5 |
| | Pelvic fins ending far short of the anal origin.........*Exocoetus volitans* | |

| 5(4) | Second ray from the top of the pectoral fin branched like the rays below it.................................................. 6 |
| | Top 2 rays of the pectoral fin simple, unbranched..*Prognichthys gilberti* |
| 6(5) | No light band across the middle of the lower pectoral rays; anal rays 8 to 11; pectoral rays 13 to 16........................... 7 |
| | A light band across the middle of the lower pectoral rays; anal rays 11 to 13; pectoral rays 17 to 19...............*Cypselurus speculiger* |
| 7(6) | Pectoral rays 13 or 14; anal rays 9 to 11....................... 8 |
| | Pectoral rays 16; anal rays 8 or 9...................*Cypselurus simus* |
| 8(7) | Pectoral fin with small dark spots or bands on the membranes; 33 or more predorsal scales................................. 9 |
| | Pectoral fin without dark spots or bands; 29 to 32 predorsal scales.....................................*Cypselurus spilonotopterus* |
| 9(8) | A large black blotch on the dorsal fin..............*Cypselurus atrisignis* |
| | No dark blotch on the dorsal fin................*Cypselurus spilopterus* |

### OXYPORHAMPHUS MICROPTERUS (Malolo)

The pectoral fins of this species are far shorter than those of any other Hawaiian flying fish. It is one of the smaller members of the family, apparently reaching a length of about 8 inches.

### FODIATOR ROSTRATUS

Probably this species may best be distinguished from *Parexocoetus brachypterus* by the much longer snout. It is still known from only a single specimen taken about a century ago, and it is perhaps permissible to wonder whether it was really taken in the Hawaiian Islands. The specimen is 6.5 inches long.

### PAREXOCOETUS BRACHYPTERUS (Malolo, Puhiki'i)

Most of the small flying fishes seen about the Islands undoubtedly belong to this species. Unlike the larger species, the pectorals are relatively short and the posterior half of the dorsal fin is elongate, so that the longest dorsal rays are nearly half the length of the pectoral.

The maximum size appears to be about 7 inches.

### EXOCOETUS VOLITANS

*Exocoetus volitans* has the long pectorals of the larger Hawaiian flying fishes, but unlike them the pelvics are very short. The species appears to be rather rare about Hawaii. The known specimens are between 6 and 10 inches long.

### PROGNICHTHYS GILBERTI

This species has a higher number of pectoral rays (17 or 18) than any of our flying fishes except *Cypselurus speculiger*. From the other large species it can be most readily separated by the fact that the second pectoral ray is unbranched and considerably shorter than those below it.

The three known specimens are all from well offshore and are all about 1 foot long. To the south the species grades into or is replaced by *Prognichthys albimaculatus*.

### CYPSELURUS SPECULIGER

The light wedge running into the lower border of the pectoral seems to be an excellent diagnostic character for this species.

Apparently uncommon; the usual size seems to be around 15 inches.

### CYPSELURUS SIMUS (Malolo)

From existing descriptions, this species, which we have never seen, appears to be most easily differentiable on the basis of the counts given in the key (see Fig. 46). The color of the species is either quite variable or else two or more species have been confused in the available descriptions.

Said to reach 14 inches.

### CYPSELURUS SPILONOTOPTERUS

Appears to be sufficiently distinguishable, among Hawaiian species of *Cypselurus*, by the plain dark pectorals and the black blotch in the dorsal.

A rather common species, reaching perhaps 16 inches in length.

### CYPSELURUS ATRISIGNIS

Combines a series of scattered dark flecks on the pectoral membranes with a dark spot or blotch on the dorsal.

Another large species, to about 14 inches.

### CYPSELURUS SPILOPTERUS

Has the dark spots on the pectoral, but the dorsal appears to be plain. The counts given for the species, which we have never seen, are close to those of *C. atrisignis*.

The species seems to have been recorded only twice from the Hawaiian Islands.

## THE CORNET FISHES, PIPEFISHES, AND THEIR ALLIES

The members of this group are varied in shape, but they all have in common a tubular mouth which functions as a sort of pipette, i.e., they place the small mouth close to the object they are after and then suck it in with a certain amount of surrounding water. None of the members of the group are active swimmers, perhaps because their method of feeding calls for more accuracy of aim than activity.

### Family FISTULARIIDAE

The cornet fishes are extremely elongate, with a small mouth at the tip of a protruding snout and a long filament extending from the middle of the tail. About the only fishes they might be confused with are the pipefishes and the trumpet fishes, and neither of these groups has a tail filament.

Two species are recorded from the Hawaiian Islands.

Key to the Hawaiian species of the family Fistulariidae:

No row of keels down the middle of the back before and behind
dorsal fin.........................................*Fistularia petimba*

A row of keels down the middle of the back, both before and
behind dorsal fin...............................*Fistularia villosa*

### FISTULARIA PETIMBA (Cornet fish)

This long, greenish sticklike fish may be rather frequently seen in the
water (see Fig. 42). Despite its small mouth it manages to engulf rather large
organisms (shrimps, etc.), and it is sometimes caught on a hook and line.

Attains a length of perhaps 4 feet.

### FISTULARIA VILLOSA

This species has been recorded only once from Hawaiian waters.

## Family AULOSTOMIDAE

The trumpet fishes resemble the cornet fishes in the elongate body and
snout but differ in having a barbel on the chin, in the several small, separate
spines along the back, and in lacking a caudal filament.

One species in Hawaii.

### AULOSTOMUS CHINENSIS (Trumpet fish, Stick fish, Nunu)

The trumpet fish can be readily distinguished from all other Hawaiian
fishes by the combination of two characters: the pelvic fins behind the middle
of the body and the series of small, separate spines along the back (see Fig.
41). It occurs in several color phases: green, brown, and orange.

Quite common and frequently seen as it rests, straight and motionless,
near the bottom. Apparently reaches a length of about 2 feet.

## Family MACRORHAMPHOSIDAE

This family is closely related to the Centriscidae, but the extreme peculiarities of that family are lacking. The single known Hawaiian species may,
however, be easily identified by the combination of pelvic fins situated nearer
the tip of tail than the tip of snout, and the short high spinous dorsal fin.

### MACRORHAMPHOSUS GRACILIS

Only two specimens of this species, from 1 to 2 inches long, have ever
been recorded from the Hawaiian Islands (see Fig. 69). These were taken in
over 350 feet of water off Laysan.

## Family CENTRISCIDAE

The members of the family Centriscidae are certainly among the oddest of
fishes. The whole body is covered with thin, bony plates which form a sharp
keel along the mid-ventral line. In the adult, the dorsal projects behind the
caudal fin, which extends downward from the posteroventral surface of
the body.

One species known from Hawaii.

This species may be sufficiently distinguished from all other Hawaiian fishes by the family characters noted above. It is known from our waters only on the basis of four specimens, 3 to 4 inches long, taken in Honolulu some 30 years ago (see Fig. 28).

## Family SYNGNATHIDAE (Pipefishes and Sea Horses)

The family Syngnathidae includes the pipefishes and sea horses: small, highly specialized fishes with the body completely enclosed in rings of bony armor. Seven species are known from around Hawaii. None of them appear to be common and none reach a length of more than 8 inches. Most of the syngnathids are inshore forms, but one of the sea horses is often taken well out at sea in such areas as the Molokai Channel.

Key to Hawaiian syngnathids (prepared by E. S. Herald):

| | | |
|---|---|---|
| 1 | Caudal fin present; head not directed forward at approximately right angles to the body...................................... | 3 |
| | Caudal fin absent, tail prehensile and ending in a point; head directed at approximately right angles to the body............... | 2 |
| 2(1) | Pale dots, more or less whitish, on body; head with whitish streaks; tubercles on body spiny in adult...........*Hippocampus histrix* | |
| | No pale dots present on body, which may sometimes show small dark spots and be variously colored with orange, golden, or red in life; tubercles on body not spiny...............*Hippocampus kuda* | |
| 3(1) | Lateral trunk ridge continuous with inferior tail ridge............ | 4 |
| | Lateral trunk ridge subcontinuous about at the anus with lateral tail ridge, which continues dorsally on the side of the tail to become confluent with the superior tail ridge at about the end of the dorsal fin.......................................*Syngnathus balli* | |
| 4(3) | Superior trunk ridge discontinuous with superior tail ridge, with the break occurring at approximately the end of the dorsal fin..... | 5 |
| | Superior trunk ridge continuous with superior tail ridge, without a break at approximately the end of the dorsal fin........ ........................................*Ichthyocampus erythraeus* | |
| 5(4) | Brood pouch under tail of male; tail rings at least 1.5 times the number of trunk rings........................................ | 6 |
| | Brood pouch under belly of male; trunk and tail rings approximately equal in number.................*Doryrhamphus melanopleura* | |
| 6(5) | Trunk rings 21 to 23; anterior supraorbital crests confluent with nasal crest...........................*Micrognathus brachyrhinus* | |
| | Trunk rings 17 or 18; anterior supraorbital crests not confluent with median nasal crest....................*Micrognathus edmondsoni* | |

### HIPPOCAMPUS HISTRIX

The only Hawaiian record of this species is that of Fowler (1928), based on one specimen, 3 inches long, in poor preservation, from Maui. The species appears to be separable from *Hippocampus kuda* not only in having white spotting, but also in having the tubercles ending in a sharp point.

### HIPPOCAMPUS KUDA

The body rings of *Hippocampus kuda* give off, in the adult, a number of knobs of various shapes, but always blunt (see Fig. 125).

This appears to be the common sea horse of the Hawaiian Islands. It has apparently been taken in such areas as Pearl Harbor, but our specimens, all about 3 to 4 inches long and including males with brood pouches, were taken well offshore. The species has also been taken in dredge hauls at 30 fathoms.

### SYNGNATHUS BALLI

*Syngnathus balli* is a very small pipefish, attaining a maximum known length of about 4 inches. In this feature it resembles *Doryrhamphus melanopleura*, from which, aside from the key characters, it can immediately be distinguished by the minute tail; in *D. melanopleura* the tail is longer than the snout length, but in *Syngnathus balli* it is about half the snout length.

A not uncommon inshore species.

### ICHTHYOCAMPUS ERYTHRAEUS

This species seems to be known only from a single specimen, 2 inches long, taken in about 150 feet of water off the south coast of Molokai.

### DORYRHAMPHUS MELANOPLEURA

A small, rather stubby pipefish attaining a length of perhaps 4 inches (see Fig. 138). It can be distinguished immediately from all other Hawaiian forms by the large, fan-shaped tail, which is longer than the snout length.

Appears to be the commonest pipefish in the Hawaiian Islands.

### MICROGNATHUS BRACHYRHINUS

Another pipefish known in Hawaii from only one small specimen, a little over 1 inch long, taken in deep water, this time off the south coast of Oahu.

### MICROGNATHUS EDMONDSONI

A relatively elongate species, reaching a length of at least 7 inches, which makes it the largest pipefish recorded from the Islands. The few specimens that have been taken have come from shallow water, one of them from a rocky tide pool.


## THE CODLIKE FISHES

The cods and their allies are notable for, among other peculiarities, the absence of a true caudal skeleton, the tail when present apparently having been developed from the dorsal and anal.

In northern seas the cods are among the most important of "bank" fishes, but the only relatives of this group in the Hawaiian area are black, deep-water forms.

## Family MACROURIDAE

The rattails or grenadiers form a prominent component of the deep-sea-bottom fish fauna. They have never been recorded from depths of less than 1000 feet around Hawaii (see Fig. 40).

The species known from our region are listed in the Appendix.

## Family MORIDAE

This family (see Figs. 49 and 96) contains a few black, deep-water forms related to the cods of northern seas. Once in a while a specimen of this family turns up in the market, but in general they live out of range of fishermen and scientists alike.

For the species recorded from Hawaiian waters, see the Appendix.

## THE SQUIRRELFISHES AND THEIR ALLIES

From the point of view of fish evolution, this group falls only slightly below the perchlike fishes. It has the typical spinous fins of the latter group, but retains the many-rayed pelvic fins and a primitive head bone of forms lower in the evolutionary scale.

The whole group is basically an oceanic one, with the squirrelfishes (Holocentridae) about the only inshore members. That the squirrelfishes are allied to deeper-water forms is indicated by their large eyes, nocturnal activity, and predominantly red coloration.

## Family BERYCIDAE

A high-seas family of fishes that presumably lives at moderate depths, judging from the bright red coloration. The one recorded Hawaiian species, *Beryx decadactylus*, may be sufficiently distinguished by the characters given in the family key.

## Family POLYMIXIIDAE

Another family represented by a single species from rather deep water. *Polymixia japonica* (Fig. 56) combines the barbels of the goatfishes with the high pelvic fin count (7 rays) of the lower fish orders.

## Family CAULOLEPIDAE

The members of this family belong to the great assemblage of large-headed, long-fanged, black, deep-sea fishes. The single species recorded from off Hawaii, *Caulolepis longidens*, has been taken twice at a depth of over two miles.

## Family MELAMPHAIDAE

Deep-sea fishes with large, rough heads and small teeth. The single Hawaiian species, *Melamphaes unicornis* (Fig. 58), is known from a single specimen a little more than an inch long taken at a depth of more than a mile.

## Family HOLOCENTRIDAE (Squirrelfishes)

The holocentrids, generally called squirrelfishes, include the ala'ihis and mempachis or 'u'us. The members of this family can be distinguished from all other Hawaiian fishes by the combination of seven soft rays in the pelvics and 11 or 12 well-developed spines in the dorsal. With one exception the basic color of all Hawaiian squirrelfishes is red, and the head and scales of all the species are extremely rough and spiny. Many of the species in the family look very much alike, the mempachis of the genus *Myripristis* being especially difficult to separate. Fortunately, the species often differ diagnostically in counts, which are therefore given for each species as an aid to identification.

All of the squirrelfishes appear to be nocturnal, retreating into holes in the day time. Only one of the Hawaiian forms, *Holocentrus lacteoguttatus*, occurs regularly in less than 10 feet of water. Though the ala'ihis are not much used for food, the mempachis are highly esteemed and command a high price in the Honolulu market.

Key to the Hawaiian species of the family Holocentridae:

1        No enlarged spine at the lower angle of the preopercle (Figs. 175 and 176); longest dorsal spine longer than longest anal spine...    10

          A conspicuous spine extending backward from the lower angle of the preopercle (Figs. 59, 169–174); longest dorsal spine equal to or shorter than longest anal spine.......................    2

2(1)    Body primarily reddish; depth contained 3 or fewer times in the standard length; soft anal rays 9 or 10.......................    3

          Body silvery with brown markings; a relatively elongate fish, the depth contained about 3.5 times in the standard length; soft anal rays 8. Prominent brown spots on cheek, as well as on body; outer caudal rays dark........................*Holocentrus sammara*

3(2)    Upper profile of head more or less convex; greatest depth of body contained 2.6 to 3 times in standard length; interorbital width contained fewer than 1.3 times in the snout length (not including the upper lip); longest dorsal spine somewhat or considerably shorter than the longest anal spine..................    4

          Upper profile of head straight in the young (see Fig. 170), more or less concave in the adult; depth of body contained about 2.5 times in the standard length; interorbital very narrow, its width contained more than 1.3 times in the snout length; longest dorsal and anal spines subequal..................*Holocentrus spinifer*

4(3)    More than 1 opercular spine usually enlarged; highest section of spinous dorsal fin part way back, the 3rd or 4th spine the longest; 3 (4 in *H. scythrops*) scale rows between the lateral-line series and the bases of the middle dorsal spines; size small or medium, to less than 1 foot.................................    5

A single greatly enlarged opercular spine (see Fig. 171); spinous dorsal highest in front, the 2nd spine the longest; 4(3½) scale rows between the lateral line and the bases of the middle dorsal spines; size relatively large, to more than 1 foot . . . . . . *Holocentrus ensifer*

5(4)    Interorbital width less than or equal to the length of the median groove that runs up the snout to between the eyes; no dark speckling or smudging on chest . . . . . . . . . . . . . . . . . . . . . . . . . . . . .  6

Interorbital broad, greater than the median groove in the snout and greater than the snout length; chest silvery, usually with dark speckling or smudging. Two opercular spines of nearly equal size; longest anal spine, when depressed, falling short of caudal base; a shallow-water species reaching a length of about 5 inches . . . . . . . . . . . . . . . . . . . . . . . . . . . . . *Holocentrus lacteoguttatus*

6(5)    In life, the sides with well-marked stripes along the scale rows and a prominent silvery bar running backward and downward across cheek; one of the opercular spines usually distinctly larger than the others and of approximately the same size as the preopercular spine; maxillary falling short of center of eye; size small, to about 6 inches . . . . . . . . . . . . . . . . . . . . . . . . . . . . . . . . . . . . . . . . .  8

In life, the sides with faint stripes or plain; no prominent silvery bar on cheek; opercle with 2 subequally enlarged spines, neither of them projecting half as much as the preopercular spine; maxillary about reaching center of eye; size moderate, to at least 10 inches . . . . . . . . . . . . . . . . . . . . . . . . . . . . . . . . . . . . . .  7

7(6)    In the adult, dorsal spines all low, shorter than the longest soft dorsal rays; largest anal spine, when depressed, not reaching tips of longest soft rays and not reaching caudal base; last dorsal spine about equidistant from preceding spine and first soft ray . . . . . . . . . . . . . . . . . . . . . . . . . . . . . . . . . . . . . . . . . . *Holocentrus tiere*

Dorsal spines relatively high, longer than the highest soft rays; largest anal spine extending farther back than the longest soft rays and about reaching caudal base; last dorsal spine considerably nearer first soft ray than to preceding spine . . . . . *Holocentrus scythrops*

8(6)    Spinous dorsal mostly red; the last spine connected by membrane to the back just ahead of the soft dorsal but not to the first soft ray, when depressed hardly reaching the base of the first soft ray . . . . . . . . . . . . . . . . . . . . . . . . . . . . . . . . . . . . . . . . .  9

Spinous dorsal mostly black or dark brown, but with a light, irregular band running part way up the fin membranes (Fig. 173); the last dorsal spine, when depressed, overlapping the lower portion of the first soft ray and connected to it by a membrane . . . . . . . . . . . . . . . . . . . . . . . . . . . . . *Holocentrus diadema*

9(8)    Longest anal spine, when depressed, reaching caudal base; interorbital width about equal to the length of the median nasal groove; no dark blotch in pectoral axil . . . . . . . . . *Holocentrus microstomus*

Longest anal spine, when depressed, falling short of caudal base; interorbital width less than length of median nasal groove; a dark blotch in pectoral axil, at least in preserved material . . . . . . . . . . . . . . . . . . . . . . . . . . . . . . . . . . . . . . . . . . . . *Holocentrus xantherythrus*

10(1)    Eye very large, its diameter usually greater than the postorbital head length; distance from base of last anal ray to the tip of the tail greater than the head length; last dorsal spine considerably longer than the preceding spine, forming a part of the second dorsal fin; developed gill rakers on the first arch, more than 30 . . .  12

**138**

Eye medium, its diameter about equal to or less than the post-orbital head length; distance from base of last anal ray to the tip of the tail less than the head length; last dorsal spine somewhat smaller than the preceding one, not forming a component of the second dorsal fin; developed gill rakers on the first arch, fewer than 20 . . . . . . . . . . . . . . . . . . . . . . . . . . . . . . . . . . . . . . . . . . . . . . . . . . .    11

11(10)   Scales relatively large, 2½ scale rows between the lateral-line series and the base of the middle dorsal spines; size to at least a foot. . . . . . . . . . . . . . . . . . . . . . . . . . . . . . . . . . . . . . . . . .*Ostichthys japonicus*

Scales relatively small, 4½ scale rows between the lateral-line series and the base of the middle dorsal spines; size to about 7 inches. . . . . . . . . . . . . . . . . . . . . . . . . . . . . . . . . . . . . . . . .*Holotrachys lima*

12(10)   Fins mostly red in life; 3rd anal spine shorter than the 4th and less than the length of the caudal peduncle. . . . . . . . . . . . . . . . . . . . .    13

Fins mostly yellow in life; 3rd anal spine extending farther back than the 4th and about equal to the length of the caudal peduncle. . . . . . . . . . . . . . . . . . . . . . . . . . . . . . . . . . . . . .*Myripristis chryseres*

13(12)   Anal soft rays 14 or fewer; lateral-line scales (counted to but not including the small scales on the base of the caudal fin) fewer than 40; a dark area restricted to the gill cover and not continued downward across body to the dark mark under the pectoral base. . . . . . . . . . . . . . . . . . . . . . . . . . . . . . . . . . . . . . . . . . . . . . . .    14

Anal soft rays 15 or 16; lateral-line scales 40 or more; the dark mark on opercle continued down as a dark bar to the inner base of the pectoral fin. . . . . . . . . . . . . . . . . . . . . . . . .*Myripristis multiradiatus*

14(13)   Width of the bony interorbital over middle of eye contained more than 4½ times in the head length (to the tip of the opercular spine); the dark mark on the inner face of the pectoral base usually abruptly restricted to the upper half of the pectoral axil . . . . . . . . . . . . . . . . . . . . . . . . . . . . . . . . . . . . . . . . . . . . . . .*Myripristis berndti*

Width of the bony interorbital over middle of eye contained fewer than 4 times in the head length; the dark mark on the inner face of the pectoral base more or less continuous across the whole pectoral axil. . . . . . . . . . . . . . . . . . . . . . .*Myripristis argyromus*

### Fig. 169. HOLOCENTRUS SAMMARA

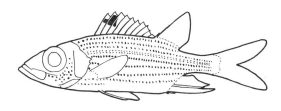

### HOLOCENTRUS SAMMARA

Counts on four Hawaiian specimens are as follows: soft dorsal rays (with the last double ray considered as 1), 12; soft anal rays (with the last double ray considered as 1), 8; total pectoral rays (including the short ray at the top as 1), 14; lateral-line scales, i.e., those bearing the lateral-line tube and not including the several tubeless scales on the caudal base (the lateral-line tube in holocentrids is difficult to see in wet specimens but becomes prominent

**139**

with slight drying), 39–41; scales between lateral-line series and middle dorsal spines (counting the modified scale row along dorsal base as 1), 3; and scale rows around the abdomen between the lateral-line series on either side (counted just behind the pelvic tips, and not including the lateral-line series), 15.

There should be no trouble separating this brown-spotted species from the other holocentrids, all of which are red. It is also the only Hawaiian *Holocentrus* with only 8 soft anal rays. The closely related brown-spotted form which lacks the black blotch on the spinous dorsal, *Holocentrus laevis*, apparently does not occur in Hawaiian waters.

Moderately common, reaching a length of perhaps a foot.

**Fig. 170. HOLOCENTRUS SPINIFER**

### HOLOCENTRUS SPINIFER

Counts on one Hawaiian specimen (made as noted under *H. sammara*): soft dorsal rays, 15; soft anal rays, 10; total pectoral rays, 15; tubed lateral-line scales, 44; scale rows between lateral line and middle dorsal spines, 4; and scale rows around abdomen between lateral-line series, 17.

This is the most deep-bodied and compressed of the Hawaiian holocentrids. The spinous dorsal is relatively high with the longest spine about equal in length to the longest anal spine. The concave upper profile of the head is distinctive in specimens over 7 inches long. This is also the only Hawaiian species with 8½ scale rows between the lateral line and the abdominal mid-line.

*Holocentrus spinifer* is one of the most ubiquitous of holocentrids at Johnston and to the south, where it attains probably the largest size of any member of the family (about 2 feet). In Hawaii, the species appears to be relatively rare.

### HOLOCENTRUS ENSIFER

Counts on three Hawaiian specimens (made as noted under *H. sammara*): soft dorsal rays, 14; soft anal rays, 10; total pectoral rays, 15; tubed lateral-line scales, 44–45; scale rows between lateral line and middle dorsal spines, 4; and scale rows around abdomen between lateral-line series, 15.

This species is characterized by the single, large opercular spine. Most other holocentrids have two opercular spines on each side, though some specimens of *Holocentrus xantherythrus* have only the one. *H. ensifer* is said to have yellow longitudinal bands in life, unlike the white bands of other forms.

Fig. 171. HOLOCENTRUS ENSIFER

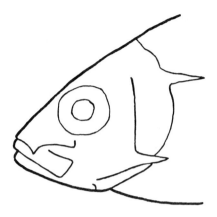

*H. ensifer* appears to be a rather deep-water form. It reaches a larger size than most species of the genus.

### HOLOCENTRUS LACTEOGUTTATUS (Ala-'ihi)

Counts on six Hawaiian specimens (made as noted under *H. sammara*): soft dorsal rays, 13; soft anal rays, 9; total pectoral rays, 15; tubed lateral-line scales, 43–47; scale rows between lateral line and middle dorsal spines, 3; and scale rows around abdomen between lateral-line series, 15 (see Fig. 59).

Any small inshore *Holocentrus* with the two opercular spines almost of equal size and with sootlike marks on the chest is undoubtedly this species. Indeed, *H. lacteoguttatus* is almost the only holocentrid to come in over the reef, and any individual found in less than 6 feet of water is probably this species.

Abundant, to about 5 inches.

Fig. 172. HOLOCENTRUS TIERE

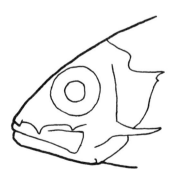

141

### HOLOCENTRUS TIERE

Counts on two Hawaiian specimens (made as noted under *H. sammara*): soft dorsal rays, 14–15; soft anal rays, 9–10; total pectoral rays, 14; tubed lateral-line scales, 47–49; scale rows between lateral line and middle dorsal spines, 3; scale rows around abdomen between lateral-line series, 13.

In life, this species is distinctive in having a pale spot on each membrane between the dorsal spines. It has one fewer scale row (6½) between the lateral line and the abdominal mid-line than any other Hawaiian *Holocentrus*.

Restricted to water over 20 feet deep. To perhaps 10 inches.

### HOLOCENTRUS SCYTHROPS

Counts on six Hawaiian specimens (made as noted under *H. sammara*): soft dorsal rays, 13–14; soft anal rays, 9; total pectoral rays, 13–14; tubed lateral-line scales, 44–45; scale rows between lateral line and middle dorsal spines, 4; and scale rows around abdomen between lateral-line series, 15.

This is a large-jawed form, with the maxillary extending back to the middle of the eye. The combination of this feature together with the fact that the longest anal spine reaches well behind the longest soft ray will distinguish it from any other red Hawaiian *Holocentrus*.

Apparently restricted to rather deep water. Attains a length of 10 inches.

**Fig. 173. HOLOCENTRUS DIADEMA**

### HOLOCENTRUS DIADEMA

Counts on six Hawaiian specimens (made as noted under *H. sammara*): soft dorsal rays, 13–14; soft anal rays, 9–10; total pectoral rays, 14; tubed lateral-line scales, 46–49; scale rows between lateral line and middle dorsal spines, 3; and scale rows around abdomen between lateral-line series, 15.

The very largely black, not red, dorsal fin will distinguish this fish from any other Hawaiian member of the family. In addition, there is a distinctive black mark on the membranes between the last 2 anal spines in most specimens.

A small, not uncommon species, to about 6 inches.

### HOLOCENTRUS MICROSTOMUS

Counts on three Canton Island specimens (made as noted under *H. sammara*): soft dorsal rays, 13; soft anal rays, 9; total pectoral rays, 15; tubed lateral-line scales, 49–52; scale rows between lateral line and middle dorsal spines, 3; and scale rows around abdomen between lateral-line series, 15.

**Fig. 174. HOLOCENTRUS MICROSTOMUS**

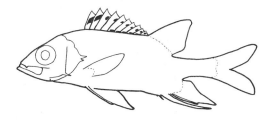

Like *H. diadema*, this is one of the small holocentrids with a greatly projecting anal spine.

We have not seen the species in Hawaii.

### HOLOCENTRUS XANTHERYTHRUS

Counts on five Hawaiian specimens are exactly the same as those given for *H. microstomus* except that the tubed lateral-line scales number 45–48.

The alternating bars on the scale rows of this species are almost pink, thus giving it a somewhat lighter general appearance than the other barred species.

*H. xantherythrus* is perhaps the most abundant *Holocentrus* in waters from 20 to 50 feet deep and seems to be restricted to the outer side of the reefs. It does not reach more than 7 inches in length.

### OSTICHTHYS JAPONICUS

Counts on one Hawaiian specimen (made as noted under *Holocentrus sammara*): soft dorsal rays, 14; soft anal rays, 11; total pectoral rays, 15; tubed lateral-line scales, 30; scale rows between lateral line and middle dorsal spines, 3; and scale rows around abdomen between lateral-line series, 13.

Aside from the larger scales, *Ostichthys* can immediately be distinguished by the fact that there is a broadly triangular trough at the front of the skull under which the upper jawbones slide.

This is probably the deepest-water species of all the holocentrids. It reaches at least a foot in length.

### Fig. 175. HOLOTRACHYS LIMA

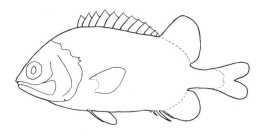

**143**

## HOLOTRACHYS LIMA

Counts on one Hawaiian specimen (made as noted under *Holocentrus sammara*): soft dorsal rays, 16; soft anal rays, 12; total pectoral rays, 18; tubed lateral-line scales, 39; scale rows between lateral line and middle dorsal spines, 5; and scale rows around abdomen between lateral-line series, 19.

The prickliest of a prickly family. The absence of a preopercular spine will immediately distinguish it from *Holocentrus*, and the small eye indicates it is no mempachi. From *Ostichthys* it can immediately be distinguished by the smaller scales and by the fact that the front of the upper jaw slides up under a narrow opening between the sides of the skull.

This curious, prehistoric-looking fish is not uncommon. It attains a length of some 7 inches.

## MYRIPRISTIS CHRYSERES (Pa'u'u)

Certain counts on three Hawaiian specimens (made as noted under *Holocentrus sammara*): soft dorsal rays, 14; soft anal rays, 12; and tubed lateral-line scales, 33–35.

Whereas the fins of the other mempachi are primarily red, those of this species are yellow in life. This species is also the most elongate of the mempachis, the length of the third anal spine going into the depth measured at the base of this spine 2 or fewer times; in the other species of *Myripristis* the length of the third spine would go into the depth at this point more than 2.5 times.

Apparently it is the rarest of the group, though it appears in the market at times. Recorded specimens are less than 10 inches in length, but it may reach a larger size.

## MYRIPRISTIS MULTIRADIATUS

Certain counts on six Hawaiian specimens (made as noted under *Holocentrus sammara*): soft dorsal rays, 16–17; soft anal rays, 15–16; and tubed lateral-line scales, 38–43.

A small menpachi that is more ovate than the others. In addition to the key characters, it may be noted that whereas in other species of *Myripristis* the dark mark on the gill cover is restricted to the opercular membrane, the dark pigment in *M. multiradiatus* extends forward onto the opercular bone itself.

Apparently does not reach more than 7 inches in length.

## MYRIPRISTIS BERNDTI ('U'u, Menpachi)

Certain counts on four Hawaiian specimens (made as noted under *Holocentrus sammara*): soft dorsal rays, 14–15; soft anal rays, 12–13; and tubed lateral-line scales, 29–30.

This and *Myripristis argyromus* are the two species most commonly speared and most abundant in the market. They are also the most difficult to separate. Our experience has been that though most specimens can be separated by color, the interorbital width is the only certain means of distinguishing all specimens. In addition to the characters given in the key, *M. berndti* usually has white on the front of the soft dorsal and anal fins; *M. argyromus* does not.

144

A secondary check on the identification of these two species is provided by the differences in tubed lateral-line scale counts.

In water of 20 to 50 feet *M. argyromus* appears to be the more abundant of the two species. Both reach a maximum length of perhaps 14 inches.

**Fig. 176. MYRIPRISTIS ARGYROMUS**

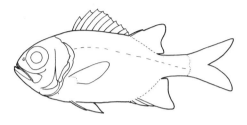

**MYRIPRISTIS ARGYROMUS ('U'u, Menpachi)**

Certain counts on five Hawaiian specimens (made as noted under *Holocentrus sammara*): soft dorsal rays, 15–16; soft anal rays, 13–14; and tubed lateral-line scales, 33–36.

The front of the soft dorsal and anal fins of this species may be tipped with black, but the first rays are rarely, if ever, white (as they generally are in the very similar *M. berndti*).

The commonest of the menpachis in 20 feet of water; to about 14 inches.

## THE LAMPRIDIFORM FISHES

This is another open-sea group rarely seen. The members come in all shapes and sizes and are united chiefly in the peculiar, protrusible mouth.

### Family LAMPRIDAE

This family is made up of a single large, deep-bodied, wide-ranging, oceanic species, *Lampris regius* (Fig. 43). In appearance it most closely resembles the ocean sunfishes (Molidae), but unlike them it has a well-developed caudal fin. There appear to be only two records of *Lampris regius* from Hawaii, both based on specimens more than 3 feet long.

### Family VELIFERIDAE

Another oceanic family. A single Hawaiian species is known from two specimens of *Velifer multispinosus* (Fig. 57) about 8 inches long, taken in deep-water fish traps. The 17 sharp spines in the anal fin will immediately distinguish the species from all other Hawaiian fishes.

**145**

## Family LOPHOTIDAE

A family of elongate, greatly compressed, high-seas fishes. The dorsal fin commences over or ahead of the upper jaw and extends all the way to the tail. *Lophotus capellei* (Fig. 91), the only species recorded from Hawaii, is known from a single specimen 18 inches long.

## THE JOHN DORIES AND THEIR ALLIES

The zeiform fishes, of which the John Dory of Europe is the only species well enough known to have acquired a common name, form another spiny-rayed group that falls just short of the percoid level of fish evolution, as indicated by the frequently many-rayed pelvic fins. All of the members of this group are deep-bodied, silvery or red, open-sea forms.

## Family ZEIDAE

This is another oceanic family for which only a single Hawaiian species, *Stethopristes eos* (Fig. 60), has been recorded. This fish is peculiar in the bony plates along the abdomen and in having the pelvics about three times as long as the pectorals. Several specimens about 5 inches long have been taken at depths over half a mile.

## Family CAPROIDAE

Related to the Zeidae, but without the abdominal plates. Represented only by *Cyttomimus stelgis* (Fig. 62), a species known only from a single specimen less than 4 inches long, taken about half a mile down.

## Family ANTIGONIIDAE

The Antigoniidae are plain red fishes in which the depth of the body is at least as great as the standard length.

Key to the Hawaiian species of the family Antigoniidae:

Dorsal spines 8; anal spines and soft rays completely separated
. . . . . . . . . . . . . . . . . . . . . . . . . . . . . . . . . . . . . . . . . . . . . *Antigonia steindachneri*

Dorsal spines 9; anal spines and soft rays joined by a membrane
. . . . . . . . . . . . . . . . . . . . . . . . . . . . . . . . . . . . . . . . . . . . . . . . *Antigonia eos*

### ANTIGONIA STEINDACHNERI

The complete separation of the three anal spines from the soft portion of the fin is almost enough to distinguish *Antigonia steindachneri* from all other Hawaiian fishes.

Specimens some 7 inches long appear not infrequently in the Honolulu market. The only specimen for which a depth of capture seems to be known is a single small individual taken in 1000 feet of water. The market specimens are doubtless taken nearer the surface.

Said to differ from *Antigonia steindachneri* in the characters given in the key (see Fig. 104). Unlike that species, *A. eos* has never been found in the market, despite the fact that it was the commoner of the two species in dredge hauls made at depths of 300 to 700 feet.

The maximum size of the dredged and only known specimens is not given, but the type is a little over 3 inches long.

## Family GRAMMICOLEPIDAE

Another family recorded from Hawaii on the basis of a single specimen, this one brought to the surface by the lava flow of 1919. Like other grammicolepids, *Vesposus egregius* (Fig. 61) has unique scales formed of vertically elongate, paper-like strips. The scales of larval acanthurids are somewhat similar, but these fishes do not have the nearly separate spinous dorsal of *Vesposus*. The one specimen is 13.5 inches long.

## THE FLATFISHES

As indicated by skeletal features, the flatfishes are percoid derivatives that have regressed towards the more primitive fishes in that they sometimes have more than five soft rays in the pelvics. On the other hand, the flatfishes have become uniquely specialized in the development of asymmetry. This asymmetry develops within the life of the individual, for the larval stages have the eyes in the normal position and swim in an upright manner as other fishes do.

In temperate-zone waters flatfishes comprise an important element of the commercial catch. In our waters they have no importance whatever. Nevertheless, Hawaii has a fair representation of species, some in shallow water and others recorded only from considerable depths. All flatfishes live on the bottom, and our inshore species, at least, cover themselves with sand, which they resemble in coloration. As a result they usually pass unobserved except when making short dashes from one point to another.

## Family BOTHIDAE

Of the four families of flatfishes recorded from Hawaii the family Bothidae is the only one that is at all well known. The bothids can be distinguished from the Soleidae and Cynoglossidae by the well-defined preopercular border, and from the Pleuronectidae by the fact that they are "left-handed," that is to say, the eyes are on the left side of the head when the fish is placed ventral surface downward.

Only two species of bothids are commonly taken: *Bothus mancus* and *B. pantherinus*. These are frequently found in shallow water over sandy patches among coral. Nevertheless, the number of other species dredged on the offshore "banks" indicates that the family is well represented in Hawaiian waters even if its members are infrequently captured. All the Hawaiian bothids are light brown in coloration often with darker and lighter blotches and rings. The coloration is almost useless in separating the species of bothids.

The members of the family range in length from a few inches to about 18 inches. The inshore members, at least, spend much of their time buried in the sand and are very difficult to find.

Key to the Hawaiian species of the family Bothidae (adapted from Norman):

1 Pelvic fin of the blind side short-based; that of the ocular side elongate, its anterior ray well in advance of the first ray of the pelvic fin on the blind side.................................... 2

    Pelvic fins about equal in size and symmetrical in position. Lateral line absent on the blind side; mouth small, the maxillary less than ⅓ of the head length; anterior rays of the anal, as well as those of dorsal, prolonged as filaments.......... *Taeniopsetta radula*

2(1) Mouth of small or moderate size, the length of the upper jaw (from tip of snout to posterior end of maxillary) less than half the head length.................................................... 4

    Mouth very large, the upper jaw more than half the head length. Lower jaw projecting; body elongate.......................... 3

3(2) Lower jaw greatly projecting, its length greater than the head length (from tip of snout); upper eye farther forward than the lower.................................. *Pelecanichthys crumenalis*

    Lower jaw only slightly projecting, its length less than the head length; upper eye somewhat behind the lower... *Chascanopsetta prorigera*

4(2) Pelvic base of the eyed side not reaching forward to below the middle of the upper eye; depth of body contained more than 2 times in the standard length................................. 7

    Pelvic base of the eyed side about reaching to below the front of the upper eye; depth of body contained 2 or less than 2 times in the standard length..........................:................. 5

5(4) Anal rays 62 to 73; 5 to 8 gill rakers (including rudiments) on the lower limb of the first gill arch; lower eye partially below upper eye.................................................................. 6

    Anal rays 74 to 80; 9 to 11 gill rakers on the lower limb of the first gill arch; lower eye completely in advance of the upper eye in specimens over 6 inches long...................... *Bothus mancus*

6(5) All of the scales of the ocular side ctenoid in specimens over 3 inches long; interorbital width about equal to or less than the horizontal diameter of the eye.................... *Bothus pantherinus*

    Scales of the ocular side cycloid except at the bases of the fins; interorbital width nearly twice the horizontal eye diameter.... ...................................................*Bothus bleekeri*

7(4) Fifty or fewer scales in a longitudinal series..................... 10

    Eighty or more scales in a longitudinal series.................. 8

8(7) Scales on the ocular side ctenoid; interorbital forming a concave trough; body with blotches and ocelli........................ 9

    Scales all cycloid; interorbital a narrow bony ridge; body without blotches or ocelli................................*Arnoglossus debilis*

9(8) Depth about 2⅓ in the standard length; interorbital width equal to or greater than the diameter of the pupil...... *Parabothus chlorospilus*

**148**

Depth about $2\frac{3}{5}$ in the standard length; interorbital width
much less than the diameter of the pupil..........*Parabothus coarctatus*

10(7)　Eye small, contained more than 3 times in the head length; lips
with a fringe of well-developed fleshy projections; anal with 58 or
fewer rays.............................*Engyprosopon hawaiiensis*

Eye large, contained about $2\frac{2}{3}$ times in the head; lips without
any fleshy fringe; anal with more than 61 rays....*Engyprosopon xenandrus*

### TAENIOPSETTA RADULA

This fish is sufficiently characterized in the key. Judging from dredging
operations, it is abundant at depths of 500 to 1000 feet. It seems to reach a
length of about 6 inches.

### PELECANICHTHYS CRUMENALIS

A strange, long-jawed fish for which the generic name is descriptive.
Dredged at a number of stations in the Pailolo Channel at depths from 1200
to 2000 feet. Seven to 10 inches in length.

### CHASCANOPSETTA PRORIGERA

A modified *Pelecanichthys*. Known from only one specimen 9 inches long
taken at about 1000 feet.

### BOTHUS MANCUS (Paku, 'Ui'ui)

There are three species of *Bothus* recorded from Hawaiian waters. Of these,
*B. mancus* and *B. pantherinus* are rather common over sandy patches in shallow
water; *B. bleekeri*, by contrast, is known only from a single specimen. In
coloration the three species are almost identical, and in morphological characters there is a greater difference between the sexes of a single species than
between species: the adult males have the eyes more widely separated and
sometimes fringed, the snout with bony tubercles, and the upper pectoral
rays greatly elongate (see Fig. 21).

In addition to the characters given in the key, *B. mancus* usually differs
from *B. pantherinus* in lacking the small tentacle on the eyeball, in having 11
rather than 10 pectoral rays, and in having the snout of large specimens rather
deeply indented.

*B. mancus* attains a length of about 14 inches.

### BOTHUS PANTHERINUS (Paku, 'Ui'ui)

For the difficulties encountered in separating *B. pantherinus* from *B. mancus*,
see the account of the latter species (see Fig. 21).

*B. pantherinus* also reaches somewhat over a foot in length.

### BOTHUS BLEEKERI

Known only from one Hawaiian specimen about 5 inches long. The species apparently has the widely separated eyes of the adult *B. mancus* but the
counts of *B. pantherinus*.

### ARNOGLOSSUS DEBILIS

An offshore species, dredged at several stations from 800 to 1000 feet. We have not seen it. The type specimen is 7 inches long.

### PARABOTHUS CHLOROSPILUS

Known from several specimens about 7 inches long taken in 400 to 1000 feet of water.

### PARABOTHUS COARCTATUS

Very similar to and taken at approximately the same depths with *Parabothus chlorospilus*.

### ENGYPROSOPON HAWAIIENSIS

A much smaller-eyed, more inshore species than *E. xenandrus*. Actually two species of *Engyprosopon* have been described from, and may be present in, the inshore area but our own specimens suggest that only one is valid.

Not known to attain over 4 inches in size.

### ENGYPROSOPON XENANDRUS

This species and *Engyprosopon hawaiiensis* are the only large-scaled flatfishes known from Hawaii. They are also the smallest flounders we have. *E. xenandrus* is said to be abundant at depths of 250 to 600 feet. Reaches perhaps 4 inches in length.

## Family *PLEURONECTIDAE*

The pleuronectids are the "right-handed" flounders, i.e., they have the eyes on the right side of the head. The family is represented in Hawaii by only three species, none of which appear to reach a length of more than 5 inches.

Key to the Hawaiian species of the family Pleuronectidae:

| | | |
|---|---|---|
| 1 | Body rather elongate, its depth contained about 3 times in the standard length; right pectoral narrow-based, with only 4 rays; left pectoral absent; lateral line straight...................... | 2 |
| | Body ovate, its depth contained about 2 times in the standard length; right pectoral with 10 rays; left pectoral present; lateral line arched over pectoral....................*Poecilopsetta hawaiiensis* | |
| 2(1) | Three prominent black ocelli along the lateral line; anal with about 55 rays; about 77 scales in the lateral line...*Samariscus triocellatus* | |
| | No ocelli along the lateral line though there are 2 on the posterior third of body just below the fin bases; anal with about 65 rays; about 98 scales in the lateral line...........*Samariscus corallinus* | |

### POECILOPSETTA HAWAIIENSIS

This is the only one of our Hawaiian flatfishes with the general appearance of the bothids but with the eyes on the right side. It is known from nine specimens taken in 800 to 1300 feet of water. To 5 inches.

### SAMARISCUS TRIOCELLATUS

A rather common inshore form with three prominent lifesaver-like dark circles along the lateral line (actually the posteriormost one is mostly below the lateral line). Though some specimens are light and others dark, the three ocelli seem to be constantly present. The species can be recognized by this color pattern alone, though other species of flounders, notably those of the very differently shaped *Bothus*, do have ocelli.

Attains a length of perhaps 5 inches.

### SAMARISCUS CORALLINUS

Like *Samariscus triocellatus*, but the ocelli differently placed (see Fig. 20). The genus *Samariscus* can immediately be distinguished from all other Hawaiian flatfishes by the peculiarities of the pectoral fins (4-rayed on the right, absent on the left).

Known only from a few specimens about 5 inches long taken in 250 feet of water.

## Family SOLEIDAE

The soleid so far recorded from Hawaii may at once be distinguished from other "right-handed" flatfishes by the complete absence of pectoral fins on both sides of the body. One small species of this family has recently been found in our inshore collecting.

**Fig. 177. ASERAGGODES KOBENSIS**

### ASERAGGODES KOBENSIS

A number of specimens, very provisionally identified here as *Aseraggodes kobensis*, have recently been taken in 30 to 75 feet of water. The very characteristic head resembles that of the cynoglossids, but the latter have the eyes on the left side of the head and have no separate caudal fin.

Our largest specimen is about 4 inches long.

## Family CYNOGLOSSIDAE

The members of this family, the so-called tongue soles (see Fig. 22), are separable from other flatfishes by the fact that the caudal fin is continuous with the dorsal and anal. Up to the present time the family is recorded from Hawaii on the basis of two small species dredged in over 500 feet of water.

## THE PERCHLIKE FISHES

The fishes assigned to the order Perciformes (or Percomorphi) by systematists form by far the largest single group in Hawaii or, for that matter, in any other tropical marine inshore environment. Indeed, nearly half of the fishes in the Hawaiian Islands belong to this order, and anyone asked to name a typical fish would certainly cite a member of the group. In view of the vastness of the order, there are few characters that apply to all the members. About all that can be said is that the pelvics are usually present, are under the anterior third of the body, and have five or fewer soft rays; and that there are usually spines at the front of the dorsal and anal.

Because of the size of the order Perciformes, the various major divisions within it will each be allotted its own group heading.

## THE MULLETS, SILVERSIDES, BARRACUDAS, AND THREADFINS

The members of this group make up the suborders Mugiloidei and Polynemoidei of the order Perciformes. They differ from the typical perchlike fishes in that the pelvic fins are set some way behind the pectoral fins, so that the pelvic girdle does not articulate directly with the pectoral girdle. All members of this group also have a small spinous dorsal well separated from the soft portion of the fin; all of them lack a true lateral line; and all are gray or silvery. So far as habits are concerned, it is difficult to think of fishes more different than the barracuda and the gray mullet.

### Family SPHYRAENIDAE (Barracudas)

The barracudas are too well known to need much description. They are the only long-jawed, large-toothed Hawaiian fishes with an anterior spinous dorsal well separated from the soft dorsal. Though the larger of our two barracudas reaches a length of 6 feet and is the same species so much feared in the West Indies, it does not have an evil reputation in Hawaii; in fact no record of barracuda attack in the Hawaiian Islands is known to us.

Key to the Hawaiian species of the family Sphyraenidae:

Pectorals reaching beyond the pelvic bases; lateral-line scales about 85.....................................*Sphyraena barracuda*

Pectorals not nearly reaching the pelvic bases; lateral-line scales about 135.........................................*Sphyraena helleri*

**SPHYRAENA BARRACUDA (Kaku)**

This species, the larger of our two barracudas, is cosmopolitan in tropical waters (see Fig. 81). It is also found in a wide range of habitats. The young occur frequently in brackish waters such as Kaneohe Bay. They enter drainage ditches and fishponds; in the latter they are said to grow to a large size and to be very destructive to other fishes. On the other hand, large individuals are sometimes caught far out at sea.

Specimens up to 6 feet in length have been seen in the Honolulu market.

**SPHYRAENA HELLERI (Kawalea)**

A much smaller fish than *Sphyraena barracuda*, reaching a length of only 2 feet. It is said to be an inshore species entering mullet ponds, but none of our pondfish barracudas are this species.

## Family ATHERINIDAE (Silversides)

The silversides are so named because of the rather broad silver stripe along the sides; in the restriction of this silver area to the middle of the sides they differ from many of the herring-like fishes that are silvery all over. The small, separate, spinous dorsal can also be used for separating the atherinids from similar fishes, though unfortunately the spinous dorsal is not conspicuous.

Key to the Hawaiian species of the family Atherinidae:

Abdomen rounded in cross section; head length greater than body depth; tips of caudal lobes dusky............*Pranesus insularum*

Abdomen deep, keeled in specimens over 1½ inches; head length less than body depth; caudal lobes light...............*Iso hawaiiensis*

**PRANESUS INSULARUM ('Iao)**

The 'iao is a small, schooling fish that is often used for tuna bait (see Fig. 82). Its importance in this respect is second only to that of the nehu. Unfortunately, the supply of 'iao seems to be highly unreliable. Like the nehu it is usually taken close to shore.

Attains a length of 4 inches.

**Fig. 178. ISO HAWAIIENSIS**

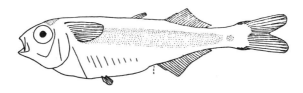

**ISO HAWAIIENSIS**

A small fish that appears to be limited to areas close to the surf zone. In this respect it frequently inhabits the same general area as the piha, another small fish for which *Iso* could most easily be mistaken.

To only about 2 inches.

## Family MUGILIDAE (Gray Mullets)

The mullets have a very characteristic look. The lower jaw is either flat or folded downward on either side of the mid-ventral line and the minute teeth are set in the lips rather than on the jaws.

Key to the Hawaiian species of the family Mugilidae:

> Teeth of the lower jaw easily visible, projecting outward and downward from the edge of the jaw; no adipose tissue covering the anterior and posterior borders of eye............*Neomyxus chaptalii*
>
> Teeth of lower jaw minute, not projecting downward from the edge of the jaw; eye in the half-grown and adult to a large extent covered by adipose tissue.........................*Mugil cephalus*

### NEOMYXUS CHAPTALII (Uouoa)

This is the mullet of open sandy shores and tide pools. The young, at least, seem to be common everywhere about the islands, and the adults are often seen in the Honolulu market.

The species appears to attain a length of about 18 inches.

### MUGIL CEPHALUS ('Ama'ama)

*Mugil cephalus* does occur along open coasts, but it seems to prefer brackish-water areas (see Fig. 83). It is the form occurring in the mullet ponds. The food of this fish in Hawaii consists of diatoms and other small plants which it dredges and filters from the surface of the bottom. The young are silvery pelagic fishes that may be taken at a night light well offshore in spring.

The species reaches a length of perhaps 18 inches.

## Family POLYNEMIDAE

The threadfins are characterized by the divided pectoral with the upper and lower portions entirely different. The overhanging snout, rather like that of the nehu, is also distinctive.

Apparently only one species in Hawaiian waters.

### POLYDACTYLUS SEXFILIS (Moi, Moi-li'i)

The moi is one of the most characteristic and sought-after fish of the sandy shores (see Fig. 70). Here it can be expected along with the awa and 'o'io.

It appears to reach 18 inches or so.

## THE SEA BASSES AND THEIR ALLIES

This group constitutes the suborder Percoidei of the order Perciformes. It is both the most generalized and the largest suborder in the order, and as such it can be characterized only by saying that it lacks the specializations found in the other suborders. In Hawaii the group is represented by 29 families, including the largest of all our families—the Labridae. Almost all conceivable environments except the deep sea are inhabited by one or another

154

member of these families, from the sand-diving trichonotids to the high-seas mahimahis; the coral reef swarms with representatives, and the lutjanids of the offshore banks form an important market staple.

## Family SERRANIDAE (Groupers)

The serranids are a large and varied family without peculiarities that permit immediate recognition. Indeed, there is no agreement among ichthyologists as to exactly which fishes should be included in, and which excluded from, the Serranidae. The following characters may be helpful for recognizing the Hawaiian members of the family: pelvic fins with a well-developed spine and 5 soft rays but without an enlarged, pointed axillary scale at the outside of each pelvic base; spinous and soft dorsals connected by at least a low membrane, the latter with 13 to 21 soft rays; anal with 3 spines; posterior portion of maxillary never slipping below the cheekbones when the mouth is closed.

The classification of the Hawaiian species of Serranidae is also badly confused. The deep-water forms need to be critically compared with those described from Japan and elsewhere and the limits of the genera to which they belong more carefully defined. The Hawaiian records for the species of *Epinephelus* present a special difficulty. Five species have been recorded, but four of the five only once. All five certainly do not occur here, but how many of these records are valid is impossible to say. Only two species of *Epinephelus* are here recognized, and the others are placed in a tentative synonymy of these (see Appendix B). Again, *Serranus myriastes* ( = *Cephalopholis argus*) was recorded from Hawaii over 100 years ago, but this well-known species has never been found in Hawaii since; it seems best to regard this record as an error of some sort, perhaps due to an erroneous locality label, and to omit *Cephalopholis argus* from the list of native Hawaiian fishes. The species has, however, been recently introduced (see Appendix A).

Unlike the condition in the atolls to the south, there are no truly shallow-water Hawaiian serranids. However, the deeper-water forms are abundantly represented. They vary not only in structure but tremendously in size: two of our Hawaiian species reach a maximum of about 3 inches; another gets to be at least 6 feet long. Most of the larger species appear sparingly in the market from time to time.

One deep-water species, *Grammatonotus laysanus*, is here included in the Serranidae following Gilbert. It probably belongs elsewhere, but just where is impossible to say at the present time.

Key to the Hawaiian species of the family Serranidae:

1      No distinct dark spots on the posterior part of the caudal peduncle; size moderate or large. . . . . . . . . . . . . . . . . . . . . . . . . . . . . . . . . 3

        Two or more distinct dark spots on the posterior part of the caudal peduncle; maximum size about 3 inches. . . . . . . . . . . . . . . . . 2

2(1)   Maxillary reaching beyond eye; dorsal with 13 soft rays, the spinous and soft portions of this fin nearly separate. *Pteranthias longimanus*

        Maxillary not reaching middle of eye; dorsal with 8 soft rays, the spinous and soft portions of this fin not divided. . *Grammatonotus laysanus*

**155**

3(1) Pectoral rounded or the upper rays longest, the fin equal to or shorter than the head length; dorsal soft rays 17 or fewer.......... 4

   The middle pectoral rays extended well beyond the others; dorsal soft rays 19 to 21..............................*Caprodon schlegelii*

4(3) Caudal fin lunate, trilobate, or forked; scales 65 or fewer in a longitudinal series.................................................... 6

   Caudal fin rounded; scales more than 100 in a longitudinal series.... 5

5(4) Color nearly black, often with light spots; maxillary about reaching posterior border of orbit; soft dorsal, anal, and caudal with pale borders....................................*Epinephelus quernus*

   Color brown, often with dark spots; maxillary reaching beyond eye; soft dorsal, anal, and caudal without pale borders........ ................................................*Epinephelus tauvina*

6(4) Dorsal spines 9 to 11; pectoral rounded, the middle rays the longest..................................................... 7

   Dorsal spines 8; upper pectoral rays the longest. Body red, with yellow longitudinal lines on head, dorsal, anal, and caudal..*Pikea aurora*

7(6) Lateral line considerably arched, reaching to within 3 scales of, and to less than an eye diameter from, the dorsal base; fewer than 50 scales in a longitudinal series............................. 8

   Lateral line gently arched, always separated from the dorsal base by more than 4 scales and more than 1 eye diameter; about 60 scales in a longitudinal series..................*Caesioperca thompsoni*

8(7) Dorsal originating about over preopercular border; last dorsal spine little shorter than preceding spine; pelvics reaching beyond pectorals..................................................... 9

   Dorsal originating slightly behind head; last dorsal spine considerably shorter than the preceding spine; pectorals reaching beyond pelvics.............................*Pseudanthias kelloggi*

9(8) Third dorsal spine about a third longer than the others; none of the soft fin rays filamentous; no white bar across caudal peduncle ........................................*Odontanthias fuscipinnis*

   Third dorsal spine only slightly longer than fourth; third (and usually fourth) soft dorsal ray prolonged into a filament; a white bar across caudal peduncle..................*Odontanthias elizabethae*

### PTERANTHIAS LONGIMANUS

A very small species having the general appearance of a cirrhitid (hawk-fish), except that the lower pectoral rays are not particularly swollen. There are 2 round black spots at the base of the tail on each side, 1 above and 1 below, and 2 more at the base of the soft anal and soft dorsal, respectively. The scales are large, with about 25 in the lateral line, and the pectorals reach well beyond the anal base.

The species is here recorded from three specimens some 2 inches long taken in about 30 feet of water off Waikiki. It has not been found elsewhere outside of the East Indies.

### GRAMMATONOTUS LAYSANUS

In this species there are a number of minute but distinct punctulations scattered across the base of the tail. Known from a single specimen about 1½ inches long taken in over 500 feet of water.

### CAPRODON SCHLEGELII

A rather large red-and-yellow species taken from time to time by hook and line fishermen in about 500 feet of water. The dorsal and anal fins are low and heavily scaled.

Recorded specimens are about 17 inches long.

### EPINEPHELUS QUERNUS (Hapu'upu'u)

This is about the only typical member we have of the tremendous genus *Epinephelus* that occurs throughout tropical seas. This particular species is very dark, usually with light spots and fin edges. It is not infrequently taken by fishermen in fairly deep water and appears to attain a length of about 3 feet.

### EPINEPHELUS TAUVINA

There is at least one tremendous species of serranid occurring in Hawaiian waters. Just what species it is and whether there is more than one remain unknown. Furthermore, it seems likely that the young of the species has been recorded under different names than the adult, for it is well verified that these tremendous serranids lose their enlarged teeth and with growth change greatly in proportional characters and in coloration. Under the circumstances, it seems best to provisionally recognize only one species from Hawaii and to call it *Epinephelus tauvina*, the oldest name under which it has been recorded.

Reaches a length of at least 8 feet and may attain a length of 12 feet.

### PIKEA AURORA

This brilliantly colored red-and-yellow fish has been collected in the market from time to time even though it has a maximum recorded length of less than 8 inches. It is the only Hawaiian serranid with 8 dorsal spines.

### CAESIOPERCA THOMPSONI

A small, rather nondescript, pinkish fish rather abundant in certain areas in depths of about 100 feet. One or two of the posterior soft dorsal rays and the outer caudal rays are usually produced as filaments.

Reaches perhaps 7 inches in length.

### PSEUDANTHIAS KELLOGGI

A red-and-white fish in life. The scales are rather large for a serranid, there being only about 36 in the lateral line.

Known specimens have been obtained by hook and line in rather deep water. The largest is 8½ inches in length.

### ODONTANTHIAS FUSCIPINNIS

A yellow species with a deeply forked caudal and the third dorsal spine projecting considerably beyond the others. Attains a length of at least 9 inches and has been found from time to time in the Honolulu market.

### ODONTANTHIAS ELIZABETHAE

Differs from the preceding most notably in the white bar on the caudal peduncle and in the elongation of one or more of the soft dorsal rays.

Known only from several specimens some 7 inches long obtained in the Honolulu market.

## Family PSEUDOCHROMIDAE

The pseudochromids are closely related to the Serranidae. Like that family they have the maxillary completely exposed on the side of the cheek, and the rounded pectorals recall *Epinephelus*. However, the pseudochromids differ from the serranids in having the lateral line either incomplete or discontinuous; in having a sturdy, more or less concealed spine at the upper end of the pre-opercular border; in the low dorsal spine count; and in having the third anal spine so low and inconspicuous that the anterior 2 spines when raised form almost a separate fin.

Two species known from Hawaii, both small.

Key to the Hawaiian species of the family Pseudochromidae:

> A dark earlike mark on the gill cover; anterior nostril a simple tube; spine at upper end of preopercular border projecting downward.............................*Pseudogramma polyacantha*
>
> No dark earlike mark on the gill cover; anterior nostril in a tube surrounded by a projecting rosette-like border; spine at upper end of preopercular border projecting backward.......*Aporops bilinearis*

### PSEUDOGRAMMA POLYACANTHA

A small brown fish rather common about holes in reef rock at depths of 6 to 30 feet. The general appearance of this fish is sufficient to distinguish it from all other species except *Aporops bilinearis*.

Reaches about 6 inches.

### APOROPS BILINEARIS

Very much like *Pseudogramma* in appearance and general coloration (see Fig. 107). The characters given in the key should serve to distinguish it.

Apparently a much rarer fish than *Pseudogramma*. Also reaches about 6 inches.

## Family KUHLIIDAE (Aholeholes)

The Kuhliidae are large-eyed, silvery, inshore fishes with a rather deep indentation in the outline of the dorsal fin between the spinous and soft portions, and with an oblique mouth and exposed maxillary (Fig. 116). They are almost our only silvery inshore fishes with a single dorsal fin.

Despite the recognition of as many as four species from the Hawaiian Islands and Johnston, there seems to be only one form present.

### KUHLIA SANDVICENSIS (Aholehole)

*Kuhlia sandvicensis* lacks the black crossbars on the tail shown in Fig. 116 but is otherwise very similar. It is a highly esteemed table fish, attaining a length of perhaps a foot.

The adults may be found during the daytime in holes in the reef rock and in sunken ships at depths from 5 to perhaps 50 feet of water. They seem to be primarily nocturnal in their activity, judging from the fact that they are most easily taken on hook and line at night.

From the fact that the young are found all during the year it appears that the aholehole spawn at all seasons. The young seem to work their way into shallow water and are abundant inhabitants of tide pools. Indeed, they will go into pure fresh water where this is available. The half-grown of from 4 to 8 inches form schools that cruise close to shore. Whether they, like the adults, are primarily nocturnal remains unknown, but it is certain that they can be taken in large numbers with throw nets during the daytime in the leeward Hawaiian Islands.

The aholehole is very adaptable, and there is little that it does not feed on. The stomachs of the young are often full of algae, and the best bait for adults seems to be bread. In fresh water the fish appears to like ants and will come to the surface of a tide pool to snap at any insect that has fallen in.

## Family GREGORYINIDAE

The family Gregoryinidae is based on, and known only from, a single specimen a little over 2 inches long "obtained at Laysan Island, where it was brought to a nest by a white tern." The specimen has a keeled chest and abdomen. In addition, the fin-ray counts seem to be highly distinctive: dorsal XV,24; anal III,7. Under the circumstances there seems nothing to do but to provisionally recognize the family and hope that some day more specimens will be forthcoming.

### GREGORYINA GYGIS

Further characters that may be useful in distinguishing this species are as follows: mouth oblique; maxillary completely exposed posteriorly; fourth and fifth dorsal spines the longest, the last two very low; a sheath of scales along the dorsal and anal bases.

## Family PRIACANTHIDAE ('Aweoweos)

The 'aweoweos are large-eyed, reddish fishes with small, rough scales. Unlike the other red fishes with which they might be confused, they have the inner ray of the pelvic fins joined to the abdomen by a broad membrane.

Only one genus, *Priacanthus*, seems to be represented in Hawaii, but the local species of this genus, aside from *P. boops*, are quite similar in appearance and badly confused taxonomically.

Though several species are said to appear in the market from time to time, only one, *P. cruentatus*, is common in less than 50 feet of water. This species, like *Kuhlia* and the holocentrids, seems to be most active at night, retiring into holes and crevices in the daytime.

Key to the Hawaiian fishes of the family Priacanthidae:

1      Neither the pelvic nor the soft dorsal rays as long as the head......  2

Both the pelvic and the longest soft dorsal rays longer than the head..........................................*Priacanthus boops*

2(1)    Scales on cheek extending almost to the border of the preopercle; spine at angle of preopercle, if present, not reaching to edge of gill cover; dorsal soft rays 14...............................  3

Preopercle with a broad scaleless border and with a flat spine that reaches the edge of the gill cover; dorsal soft rays 13.....
..........................................*Priacanthus cruentatus*

3(2)    Scales in a longitudinal series 85 to 90............*Priacanthus alalaua*

Scales in a longitudinal series more than 100.........*Priacanthus meeki*

### PRIACANTHUS BOOPS

This long-finned form seems to be the only distinctive Hawaiian *Priacanthus*. Aside from the fin peculiarities, *P. boops* differs in having the nasal organ at the bottom of a broad, open trough.

Only a few specimens, 8 to 14 inches long, are known from Hawaii. Probably this is a relatively deep-water species.

### PRIACANTHUS CRUENTATUS ('Aweoweo)

The posterior nostril of *P. cruentatus* is a long slit, but does not have the membrane across the rear portion found in *P. meeki* and apparently in *P. alalaua* (see Fig. 121). The color is quite variable, ranging from plain red to mottled red to silvery. There are often black specks on the fins, and the caudal usually has a rather narrow black border.

This is the inshore *Priacanthus;* indeed it may be found in as little as 6 feet of water. One finds large isopods fastened to the fins of this fish more often perhaps than is the case with any other species. Reaches about a foot in length.

### PRIACANTHUS ALALAUA ('Alalaua)

Very difficult to distinguish from *Priacanthus meeki* except on the basis of the larger scales. *P. alalaua* may be a synonym of *P. hamrur* from the tropical Pacific but seems to have a somewhat larger number of gill rakers and deeper body.

This species has been said to come into the market frequently, but we have not noted it. Reaches 14 inches in length.

In large specimens of this species the preopercular spine is completely wanting, though it is probably present in the young.

Reaches about a foot in length.

## Family APOGONIDAE (Cardinal fishes or 'Upapalus)

The apogonids or cardinal fishes, of which the 'upapalu is perhaps the best known in Hawaii, are small- to moderate-size fishes with 2 completely separate dorsal fins, the second with 10 or fewer soft rays, and with only 2 anal spines. The mouth is large and the males incubate the eggs in the mouth. The members of the family have a rather wide depth range. Most are found inshore, but two of the Hawaiian forms have never been taken in less than 1000 feet of water.

Key to the Hawaiian species of the family Apogonidae:

| | | |
|---|---|---|
| 1 | Body relatively short and deep, the length of the caudal peduncle (measured from the base of the last anal ray to the base of the middle caudal ray) less than the body depth; anus almost in front of the anal fin........................................ | 3 |
| | Body elongate, the length of the caudal peduncle greater than the body depth; anus separated from the anal fin by at least half an eye diameter............................................. | 2 |
| 2(1) | Caudal rounded; maxillary reaching past eye. Inshore, transparent fishes with a maximum length of 2 inches..*Pseudamiops gracilicauda* | |
| | Caudal forked; maxillary not reaching middle of eye. Offshore, pelagic fishes.............................*Epigonus atherinoides* | |
| 3(1) | Spines in first dorsal fin 6 to 8; no enlarged teeth............... | 4 |
| | Spines in first dorsal fin 9; some of the teeth enlarged. A deep-water species..................................*Synagrops argyrea* | |
| 4(3) | Scales in the lateral line of the same size as those above and below it, fewer than 30 in a longitudinal series; shallow-water species..... | 5 |
| | Scales in the lateral line much larger than those above and below it, more than 50 in a longitudinal series below the lateral line; a deep-water species.............................*Apogon evermanni* | |
| 5(4) | Lateral line complete........................................ | 6 |
| | Lateral line ending under the soft dorsal. Body and fins without distinct markings; size to about 3 inches........*Apogon brachygrammus* | |
| 6(5) | Caudal forked; preopercle serrate............................ | 7 |
| | Caudal rounded; preopercle smooth..................*Apogon waikiki* | |
| 7(6) | Head, body, and fins with some dark bars in life; spines in first dorsal 7 or 8; size to at least 4 inches......................... | 8 |
| | Head, body, and fins a transparent red in life; spines in first dorsal 6; size to about 3 inches....................*Apogon erythrinus* | |
| 8(7) | No dark spot on the center of each scale of the upper part of body; preopercle with 2 rows of serrations.................... | 9 |
| | A dark spot on the center of each scale on the upper part of body, these forming about 8 longitudinal rows; only the posterior border of the preopercle serrate..................*Apogon maculiferus* | |

9(8)　　No black on any of the caudal rays except the outermost; total gill rakers on lower limb of first arch (including rudiments but not including the raker at the angle) 12 to 14..........*Apogon snyderi*

A black area extending across the caudal fin near the base of the rays; total gill rakers on the lower limb of the first arch 16 or 17 ..............................................*Apogon menesemus*

**Fig. 179. PSEUDAMIOPS GRACILICAUDA**

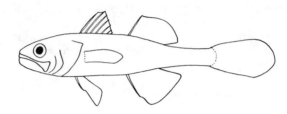

### PSEUDAMIOPS GRACILICAUDA

This small apogonid, described recently from the Marshalls, has also been taken in the Hawaiian Islands and Johnston. Whether the fish is rare or whether it has simply not been collected because it is almost impossible to see in the water remains unknown.

Known specimens are less than 2 inches long.

### EPIGONUS ATHERINOIDES

A large-eyed, deep-water form differing from all our other apogonids in that the small mouth does not even reach as far back as the pupil of the eye. All except one of the known Hawaiian specimens have been disgorged by larger fishes.

Reaches at least 7 inches.

### SYNAGROPS ARGYREA

A deep-water form taken in several dredge hauls in more than 1000 feet of water. *Synagrops argyrea* and *Pseudamiops gracilicauda* are the only known Hawaiian apogonids with enlarged canine teeth.

To about 6 inches.

### APOGON EVERMANNI

This apparently deep-water species is known from only a single specimen found in the market over 50 years ago. The scales, except for the enlarged ones in the lateral line, are the smallest found among Hawaiian apogonids.

The type specimen is 5.6 inches long.

### APOGON BRACHYGRAMMUS

This nondescript little apogonid seems to live in great numbers in dead coral. We have taken as many as 1000 from a small area in Kaneohe Bay by

Fig. 180. APOGON BRACHYGRAMMUS

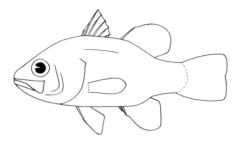

the use of rotenone. The fact that the lateral line of this fish ends below the soft dorsal is distinctive.

To about 3 inches.

Fig. 181. APOGON WAIKIKI

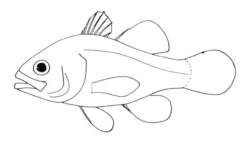

### APOGON WAIKIKI

A rather pretty little fish with all of the soft fins with rounded outlines and dark brown in coloration, except for the narrow gray borders.

To about 4 inches.

Fig. 182. APOGON ERYTHRINUS

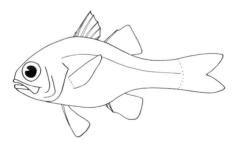

**APOGON ERYTHRINUS**

Bright red in life. The 6 dorsal spines will also serve to distinguish this species from any other Hawaiian apogonid.

Seems to occur over a wide range of shallow-water habitats but nowhere abundant. To about 3 inches.

**Fig. 183. APOGON MACULIFERUS**

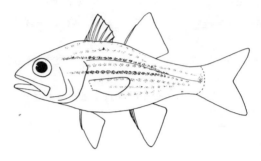

**APOGON MACULIFERUS**

No other Hawaiian apogonid has dark spotting on the sides nearly as conspicuous as in this species.

To about 6 inches.

**Fig. 184. APOGON SNYDERI**

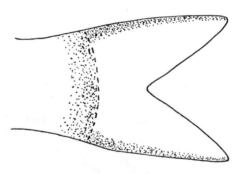

**APOGON SNYDERI ('Upapalu)**

This species and the very similar *Apogon menesemus* are the most abundant and largest apogonids in the Hawaiian Islands. Probably the most certain method of separating these two species is the gill-raker count, though the caudal marking is easier to use. In addition to the absence of black on the middle caudal rays, the dark longitudinal bands on the outer caudal rays of *A. snyderi* are either absent or very narrow. The young of *A. snyderi* have black bands on the dorsal and anal just as in the adult *A. menesemus*, but in specimens 3 inches long these begin to fade out in *A. snyderi*, that on the dorsal disappearing completely in the adult. Thus, large specimens, but not the young, of *A. snyderi* can also be separated from *A. menesemus* on the basis of the soft dorsal marking.

Both of these species seem to occur together in about equal numbers. Both reach about 9 inches.

Fig. 185. APOGON MENESEMUS

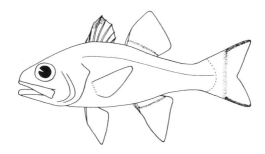

### APOGON MENESEMUS ('Upapalu)

Though the center of the caudal fin of this species, unlike that of *Apogon snyderi*, is very dark, the black pigment is actually concentrated on the inter-radial membranes. This black ends abruptly forward at the edge of the scalation that extends on to the fin, but fades out gradually to the rear. The black longitudinal bars on the outer caudal rays are much broader than in *A. snyderi*.

## Family *MALACANTHIDAE*

The Malacanthidae seems to be represented in Hawaii by only one species, the maka-'a. This elongate fish, with a single sharp opercular spine and the caudal black except for the middle rays, is very distinctive.

### MALACANTHUS HOEDTII (Maka-'a)

Sufficiently recognizable by the characters given in the family diagnosis (see Fig. 109). Not uncommon in the market. Reaches about a foot in length.

## Family *CARANGIDAE*

### (By Yoshio Yamaguchi)

The fishes of the ulua, pompano, or jack crevally family are characterized by having 2 free spines preceding the anal and 4 to 8 generally weak spines in the first dorsal (in some adults the spines disappear with age). Except for the kahala, lae, pilot fish, and rainbow runner, Hawaiian representatives of the family have the straight portion of the lateral line armed with scutes; indeed, any Hawaiian fish with a single row of numerous scutes along the posterior part of the lateral line is a carangid. Young individuals (less than 4 inches long) of most species have 4 to 5 dark vertical bars over the sides of the body.

As far as is known, the eggs of carangids are planktonic or free-floating. All members of the family are carnivorous. They are considered good food fishes, supporting a valuable commercial and sport fishery.

The number of *scutes* in the posterior portion of the lateral line is used extensively in determining species. Some confusion frequently arises as to what is a scute. In our identification, a scale along the posterior straight portion of the lateral line may be considered as modified into a scute when it has a definite point on the hind margin and a keel or ridge on its outer surface. The keel or ridge in some instances is not definite; in such cases the modified scale is counted as a scute when there is a definite point on the hind margin.

The number of *gill rakers* on the first gill arch have also been used in the key; rudimentary rakers have been included in these counts.

Key to the Hawaiian species of the family Carangidae:

| | | |
|---|---|---|
| 1 | Lateral line armed with scutes or plates...................... | 6 |
| | Lateral line not armed with scutes or plates................... | 2 |
| 2(1) | Dorsal and anal fins of equal length; posterior half of soft dorsal fin with rays developed into finlets.............*Scomberoides sancti-petri* | |
| | Anal fin less than ⅔ of the length of the second dorsal, with or without a single detached finlet.............................. | 3 |
| 3(2) | No detached finlet behind dorsal or anal fins.................. | 4 |
| | A 2-rayed, detached finlet behind dorsal and anal fins...... .............................................*Elagatis bipinnulatus* | |
| 4(3) | Body without 6 or 7 dark crossbands; rays in second dorsal fin more than 30; membranes present between spines of first dorsal fin...................................................... | 5 |
| | Body with 6 or 7 dark crossbands; rays in second dorsal fin 28 or fewer; no membranes present between the spines of the first dorsal fin in the adult............................*Naucrates ductor* | |
| 5(4) | Gill rakers (including rudiments) on lower portion of first gill arch 15 or fewer; not over 33 rays in second dorsal fin...*Seriola dumerili* | |
| | Gill rakers on lower portion of first arch about 22; over 34 rays in second dorsal fin.............................*Seriola aureovittata* | |
| 6(1) | No detached finlets behind soft dorsal or anal fins.............. | 9 |
| | One or more detached finlets behind soft dorsal and anal fins..... | 7 |
| 7(6) | A single detached finlet behind soft dorsal and anal fins......... | 8 |
| | Six to 10 finlets behind soft dorsal and anal fins. Scutes in lateral line 53–58, extending forward to under base of dorsal spines... .............................................*Megalaspis cordyla* | |
| 8(7) | Lateral line with 20–27 scutes; depth contained more than 5 times in standard length...........................*Decapterus pinnulatus* | |
| | Lateral line with 32–37 scutes; depth contained fewer than 5 times in standard length......................*Decapterus maruadsi* | |
| 9(6) | Portion of shoulder girdle that forms posterior margin of gill opening without a deep furrow............................ | 10 |
| | Portion of shoulder girdle that forms posterior margin of gill opening with a deep furrow (Fig. 186).....*Trachurops crumenophthalmus* | |

**Fig. 186**

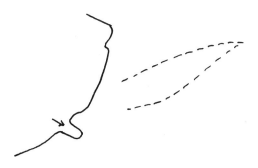

10(9)    Teeth in jaws............................................... 11

       Jaws with a hard bony plate but without teeth. Body slightly yellow in color with 8 to 12 vertical blackish bands in small, fresh specimens; 12–22 weakly developed scutes along posterior portion of lateral line........................... *Gnathanodon speciosus*

11(10)  Depth of body contained more than 2 times in the standard length; scutes strongly developed, numbering more than 20; anterior rays of second dorsal and anal fins not produced into filaments................................................ 13

       Body deep and compressed, the depth going less than twice in the standard length; scutes weakly developed, numbering fewer than 18 (though there may be numerous small plates); anterior rays of second dorsal and anal produced into long filaments in specimens less than 25 inches long........................... 12

**Fig. 187**

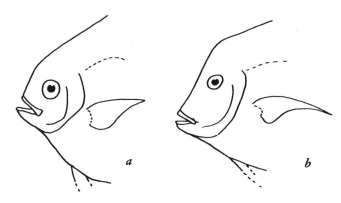

12(11)  Depth of preorbital not greater than diameter of eye (Fig. 187a); gill rakers long and slender........................... *Alectis ciliaris*

       Depth of preorbital nearly twice the diameter of eye (Fig. 187b); gill rakers short and stout........................... *Alectis indica*

Body silvery, without transverse bands; scales and scutes in straight portion of lateral line about 56 (10 scales +46 scutes); gill rakers 45, about 16 above..........................*Caranx kalla*

**Fig. 188. SCOMBEROIDES SANCTI-PETRI**

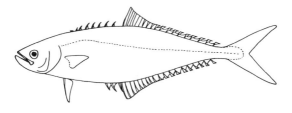

After Smith, 1948, p. 224, fig. 544

### SCOMBEROIDES SANCTI-PETRI (Lae, Leatherback, Runner)

The lae is easily distinguished from other members of the ulua family by the leathery skin imbedded with tiny, needle-like scales, the non protractile premaxillaries, and the equal length of dorsal and anal. The last 6 or 7 rays of each of these fins are detached into semi finlets. The slightly arched lateral line, unlike that of most other members of the family, is not armed with scutes. Though three species of *Scomberoides* have been recorded from Hawaii, only *S. sancti-petri* seems to be represented by the material available.

The young of 1 to 4 inches in length are frequently found in shallow water, especially in brackish-water areas, preying on schools of nehu. The adults live in the coastal area. They are carnivorous mid-water or surface feeders. The lae is a good game fish but is locally considered of poor quality as food. Its leathery, silver skin is frequently used in making trolling lures. The maximum observed size is about 25 inches, but most of those caught measure 12 to 15 inches.

**Fig. 189. ELAGATIS BIPINNULATUS**

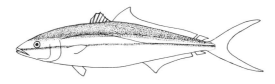

After Günther, 1876, pl. 90

### ELAGATIS BIPINNULATUS (Rainbow runner, Kamanu, Hawaiian salmon)

The rainbow runner derives its name from its color, which is bluish on the upper half of the body and paler below with a yellowish tinge. There are two conspicuous longitudinal bluish bands on the sides of the body, the upper

**169**

beginning at the hind margin of the eye and passing to the dorsal margin of the caudal peduncle, whereas the lower band begins at the snout and passes below the eye, across the opercle, and above the pectoral fins to the tail. The lateral line is not armed with scutes but forms a low fleshy keel near the tail. There is a two-rayed detached finlet behind the dorsal and anal fins.

This fish inhabits essentially the same areas of the open sea as the kawa-kawa. It is not a schooling fish in Hawaiian waters; rather, an occasional individual is caught trolling or on a long line. It is an excellent food fish.

Attains a size of about 3 feet.

### Fig. 190.  NAUCRATES DUCTOR

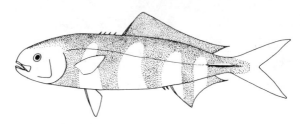

After J. and E., p. 182, fig. 68

**NAUCRATES DUCTOR (Pilot fish)**

The pilot fish is easily identified by the 5 to 7 broad dark vertical bands over the side of the body extending on to the fins. The lateral line is not armed with scutes but on the caudal peduncle there is a low lateral keel. The head profile shows a slight hump above the nostrils.

The young are frequently found far out at sea around floating logs or other objects. The adults are sometimes seen with schools of large tunas and sharks, appearing to lead the larger fishes—hence the name pilot fish. The species is of no commercial significance and is only occasionally caught by hand line. It reaches a length of about 2 feet.

### Fig. 191.  SERIOLA DUMERILII

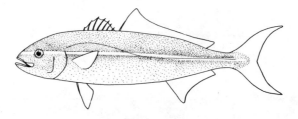

After Temminck and Schlegel, pl. 62

**SERIOLA DUMERILII (Kahala, Amberjack, Yellowtail)**

The kahala is one of the two species of *Seriola* reported from Hawaiian waters. The fishes of this genus can be differentiated from other Carangidae by

**170**

the light, metallic brown color with a purplish tinge, together with the lack of any scutes along the lateral line and the absence of detached finlets behind the dorsal and anal. The kahala has a light lemon-yellow horizontal band extending from the head to the base of the tail; this band becomes lighter and nearly disappears after the fish is caught. Young of *Seriola dumerilii* less than 4 inches long have 5 or 6 dark crossbands over the body.

A very important commercial species and an excellent food fish taken in the deeper coastal waters, at 40 to 100 fathoms, by hand line. It lives on or just off the bottom and is not a mid-water or surface fish. The species is only rarely taken in shallow, inshore reef areas. The young are frequently found around floating logs or other objects far out at sea. The species grows to almost 4 feet.

### SERIOLA AUREOVITTATA (Kahala 'opio)

The kahala 'opio is very similar to the kahala in appearance. In addition to the characters given in the key, another distinguishing feature is the dense patch of scales on the upper portion of the opercle (the kahala has a scaleless opercle).

We have not seen this species. It was first recorded from Hawaii as a new species, and Jordan and Evermann stated in 1905 that it was seen in the Waikiki aquarium.

### MEGALASPIS CORDYLA

This is the only species in the entire family that has several (7 or 8) completely detached finlets behind the dorsal and anal fins (see Fig. 71).

A fish of the open sea, very rare in Hawaii, and not seen by us. It is reported to grow to a length of 5 feet.

**Fig. 192. DECAPTERUS PINNULATUS**

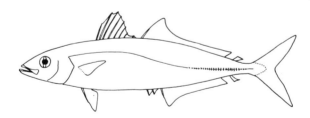

After J. and E., pl. 30

### DECAPTERUS PINNULATUS ('Opelu, Mackerel scad, 'Opelu-mama)

The 'opelu is one of the two species of the genus *Decapterus* in Hawaii. The fishes belonging to this genus are readily distinguished from all other Hawaiian carangids by the almost perfectly fusiform (cigar-shaped) body. They have a single finlet behind the dorsal and anal fins and scutes along the posterior portion of the lateral line. The two species may be distinguished by the characters given in the key. The color of *D. pinnulatus* in life is usually

**171**

bluish on the upper third of the body and silvery white below; however, some individuals are a greenish yellow above and whitish below. There is a dark spot on the gill cover.

In Hawaii, the adult 'opelu inhabits the coastal waters of all the islands. It is found mostly in schools on the surface and in mid-water and has never been seen within 5 feet of the bottom. The young of less than 5 inches school far out at sea and are frequently preyed upon at the surface by schools of aku and flocks of birds (which the tuna fishermen use to locate good fishing grounds).

The 'opelu feeds on plankton, with the crustacean elements (such as amphipods and larval crabs), arrowworms, and fish larvae comprising the major portion of its food. Known predators on the adult 'opelu are tuna, ono, mahimahi, marlin, and the rainbow runner.

It is an excellent food fish and supports two valuable commercial fisheries —hand line at night during the dark of the moon and hoop nets during the day. The 'opelu is used as bait in the Hawaiian long-line fishery for large tunas and marlins.

The 'opelu grows to about 9 inches in a year and to about 12 inches in 2 years. In Hawaiian waters the spawning season is from March to the middle of August, with most of the spawning occurring during May, June, and July. The young fish matures in one year and the mature fish spawns only once during the spawning season. A fish of 9 inches has about 82,000 eggs in its ovary. The planktonic eggs are spawned in the coastal inshore waters in depths ranging from 10 to 50 fathoms. The juveniles move well offshore, but at about 5 inches return toward land. The 'opelu reaches a maximum size of 20 inches but is usually caught at less than 10 inches.

### DECAPTERUS MARUADSI ('Opelu)

This species is very similar to the common 'opelu, *Decapterus pinnulatus*. In addition to those given in the key, a distinguishing character is the presence of vomerine teeth (*D. pinnulatus* does not have vomerine teeth). It can further be separated by the yellow color of the fins in life and the white border on the soft dorsal fin.

It is not a common species in Hawaii but is occasionally caught with *D. pinnulatus* in the hoop-net fishery during the day. Attains a length of about 12 inches.

### Fig. 193. TRACHUROPS CRUMENOPHTHALMUS

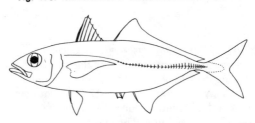

After J. and E., p. 187, fig. 71

**172**

**TRACHUROPS CRUMENOPHTHALMUS (Akule, Hahalalu [young], Aji, Bigeye scad)**

The akule may be easily identified by its large eyes, the diameter of which goes about 3 times into the length of the head. Its most diagnostic feature, however, is the deep notch in the bone that forms the hind border of the gill opening (see Fig. 186). The body shape is typically mackerel-like and the color in life is bluish silvery on the upper third of the body and silvery white below.

The akule is one of our commonest carangids and is an important commercial species in Hawaii. It is a schooling fish inhabiting the coastal waters around all the islands. It feeds on minute plankton in the middle and surface waters. During the spawning season, which extends from February through August, the fish forms large schools in shallow, sandy- or flat-bottomed areas less than 12 fathoms in depth and is very vulnerable to seine fishing. The eggs are free-floating.

The young fish of 4 to 7 inches appear in large schools in shallow waters from July to December and are called hahalalu. Frequently these schools of young fish are herded by ulua or kawakawa. In 12 months the akule grows to about 9 inches and is ready to spawn; in two years it grows to about 12 inches in length. In Hawaii the adult fish are taken by hand line at night, as well as with beach seines. The maximum size is about 15 inches.

**Fig. 194. GNATHANODON SPECIOSUS**

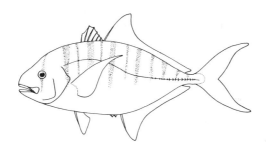

After J. and E., col. pl. 12

**GNATHANODON SPECIOSUS (Pa'opa'o, Pa'apa'a ulua, Yellow ulua)**

The yellowish tinge to the silvery color of this fish and the 8 to 12 alternating dark and light vertical bands over the side of the body make this species easy to distinguish from other carangids. One vertical band goes through the eye. The scutes are small and weak and there is a toothless, bony plate in each jaw.

The species is valued as a food and game fish. Attains a length of 3 feet.

**ALECTIS CILIARIS (Ulua kihikihi, Kagami ulua)**

The ulua kihikihi is one of the most beautiful fishes in our inshore waters (see Figs. 99 and 187a). The first 4 or 5 rays of the dorsal and anal fins are

**173**

produced into long, trailing streamers extending about 2 times the length of the body. As the fish grows larger the streamers diminish in length. The spines of the dorsal and anal also grow shorter with age and in some adults the spines disappear completely. The scutes in the posterior portion of the lateral line are weak, and in small specimens (5 inches or less) the scutes are merely enlarged scales without keel or point. *Alectis ciliaris* can be distinguished from the other representative of the genus, *A. indica*, by the deeper body shape, the depth going about 1.9 times into the standard length (in *A. indica* the depth is contained about 2.3 times in the length).

This species is found in bays and in shallow waters where it is common in Hawaiian waters. It attains a length of about 15 inches.

### ALECTIS INDICA (Kagami ulua)

In *Alectis indica* the streamers, not as long as in *A. ciliaris*, extend only to about the end of the tail (see Fig. 187b). As the fish grows these streamers become shorter. The scutes on the straight portion of the lateral line do not develop the usual keels and ridges until the fish is about 12 inches long.

The recorded length of Hawaiian specimens is 2 feet, but the species is said to reach 5 feet in length in Indian waters.

### CARANGOIDES GYMNOSTETHOIDES (Ulua)

This species is very similar in appearance to *Carangoides ferdau*. Both species have a scaleless area at the base of the pelvic fins, but that of *C. gymnostethoides* widens out more broadly forward: the width of this scaleless section in front is nearly 3 times its width in front of the pelvics. The lateral line is not strongly arched but has slight undulations. The soft dorsal and anal are not produced into falcate lobes and the margin of the dorsal fin is dusky. The pectoral fins are long, reaching to above the 14th or 15th anal fin ray. The head is scaleless except for 5 scales on the cheek and temporal region.

Reaches a length of over 2 feet. One Bishop Museum specimen examined.

**Fig. 195. CARANGOIDES FERDAU**

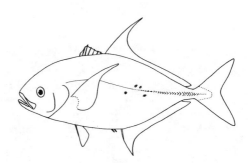

After J. and E., p. 198, fig. 77

**174**

### CARANGOIDES FERDAU (Ulua)

Several lemon-colored spots with dusky centers, clustered above and below the lateral line near the beginning of its straight portion, make this species easy to identify. The spots vary in position and number (usually 2 or 3), and in specimens larger than 15 inches they tend to disappear. This is a rather heavy-bodied fish with the depth going about 2.5 times in the standard length. The anterior rays of the dorsal and anal are elongate, forming falcate lobes, the length of the longest ray being slightly longer than the length of the head. The scutes and scales on the straight portion of the lateral line number 66 to 70, of which 26 to 30 are scutes. The breast is scaleless.

This species is fairly common in inshore waters, particularly in rocky coves and just beyond the outer reef. It is not a schooling fish. Attains a length of about 2 feet.

**Fig. 196. CARANGOIDES AJAX**

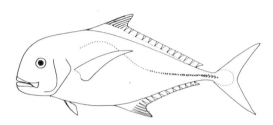

After J. and E., pl. 33

### CARANGOIDES AJAX (White ulua)

The white ulua derives its name from the almost dead-white color of the lower half of the body. The upper half in small specimens (less than 20 inches) is also white; however, larger specimens have a dusky color along the back. It may be distinguished from related species by the fewer anal rays, these numbering about 16. The snout and frontal region are elevated somewhat as in the bull mahimahi. The spinous dorsal and the two anal spines grow shorter with age, and in adults over two feet in length the spines of the dorsal and anal fins may disappear.

This fish, known only from the Hawaiian Islands, inhabits the coastal waters beyond the outer reef and is frequently caught by the trap and hand-line fishermen. Attains 3½ feet in length.

### CARANGOIDES EQUULA (Ulua)

This ulua is one of the four Hawaiian representatives of the genus *Carangoides*. The fishes of this genus can be distinguished from other uluas by the tiny teeth in villiform bands in the mouth (instead of sharp conical teeth). Also, the lateral line is only slightly arched, and the pectoral fins are long and falcate. *Carangoides equula* can be distinguished from the other three members of the genus by the scutes, which are small but well developed, numbering about 21, and are present along the whole length of the posterior straight

**175**

portion of the lateral line. Other differences between the four species of *Carangoides* are tabulated below:

|  | Scutes | Dorsal Rays | Anal Rays | Gill Rakers |
|---|---|---|---|---|
| *C. equula* | 21–26 | 23 | 21 | 30 |
| *C. gymnostethoides* | 23–25 | 33–36 | 28 | 25–27 |
| *C. ajax* | 32 | 19 | 16 | 20 |
| *C. ferdau* | 25 | 29–32 | 20 | 30 |

**URASPIS REVERSA**

Whereas the scutes along the posterior straight portion of the lateral line are directed posteriorly in other carangids, each of the 26 scutes of this species has a blunt spine directed forward. Otherwise, it is quite similar to *Caranx helvolus*.

Known only from Hawaii. Not seen by us.

**Fig. 197. CARANX HELVOLUS**

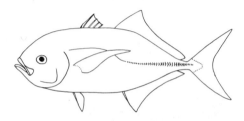

After J. and E., pl. 32

**CARANX HELVOLUS (Black ulua, Papio [young])**

The dead-white color of the tongue and the roof of the mouth and the distinct blue-black of the inner-mouth surface make this species unmistakable. The inner surface of the gill opening and pharynx is also blue-black. The mouth opens nearly at the level of the eye and the cleft is at a sharp downward angle giving the fish a rather pugnacious look. The color is generally dusky.

It attains a size of 2½ feet.

**CARANX IGNOBILIS (Pa'u'u, Ulua, Papio [young])**

The pa'u'u is one of the commonest of the uluas found in Hawaiian waters, and a large proportion of the papio caught by shoreside anglers belong to this species. The pa'u'u is easily distinguished from other carangids by the scaleless breast except for a small median patch (of about 10 scales) in front of the pelvic fins. The scutes along the posterior portion of the lateral line number from 30 to 33 and start immediately where the curving lateral line straightens out. This characteristic is found in only two other species: *Caranx sexfasciatus* and *Caranx lugubris;* these species, however, have completely scaled breasts.

**176**

### Fig. 198. CARANX IGNOBILIS

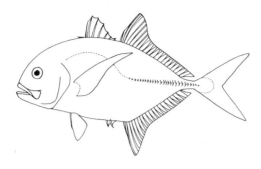

After J. and E., p. 189, fig. 72

The adult fish is frequently found within the reef close to shore. It feeds to a large extent on crabs and other crustaceans, also on small fish. Young (less than 4 inches) are found in protected bays and in brackish-water areas and are frequently caught in tuna-bait nets along with nehu. The species attains a length of about 3 feet.

### Fig. 199. CARANX CHEILIO

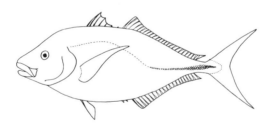

After J. and E., pl. 33

**CARANX CHEILIO (Thick-lipped ulua, Pig ulua, Butaguchi, Buta ulua)**

The conical, pointed snout and the slight concave depression in the profile above the eyes make this ulua easy to identify. Another distinguishing characteristic is the gilded yellow horizontal streak along the side of the body from the base of the tail through the eye; the streak is especially pronounced in specimens less than 12 inches in length.

This ulua is a highly valued food fish of commercial importance. A fish of bays and coastal waters, it is not now common around the main Hawaiian Islands but is abundant from French Frigate Shoals to Midway.

Attains a length of about 3 feet.

**177**

Fig. 200. CARANX MELAMPYGUS

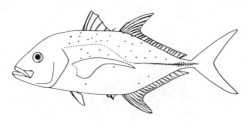

After J. and E., p. 193, fig. 73

### CARANX MELAMPYGUS ('Omilu, 'Omilumilu, Hoshi ulua, Blue crevally)

The 'omilu is one of the most frequently caught of our many uluas. Another local name, hoshi ulua—"hoshi" meaning "star" in Japanese—quite aptly describes the most distinctive characteristic of this species: that of having the entire body covered with scattered blue-black spots. The color is usually brownish blue above and silvery tan below with the spots all over the body. However, this color is highly variable, and often the fish appears almost black, with bluish reflections on the upper half and silvery below, with infrequent spotting. The breast is completely scaled and the posterior straight portion of the lateral line starts with 4 or 5 scales not modified into scutes.

The young frequently school and are found in shallow bays and estuarine waters. Fish 6 to 20 inches long are often caught by anglers on the reef areas, and the larger fish are taken on trolling gear just outside the reefs. An excellent game fish, also a highly valued commercial species. Attains a length of 3 feet.

### Fig. 201. CARANX LUGUBRIS

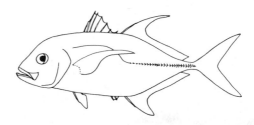

After Wakiya, 1924

### CARANX LUGUBRIS (Ulua, Papio [young])

This ulua is very similar in appearance to *Caranx sexfasciatus*. It may be distinguished from the latter by the darker color of the body and the almost black head. In addition, the mouth of *C. lugubris* opens at a level about one eye diameter below the eye, whereas in *C. sexfasciatus* the mouth opens only slightly below the level of the eye. (For other differences see the key and the account of *C. sexfasciatus*.)

A fish of the outer reef channels, it is said to grow to 3 or 4 feet in length. Not seen by us.

178

**Fig. 202. CARANX SEXFASCIATUS**

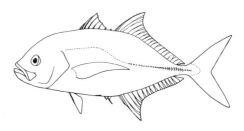

After Wakiya, 1924, pl. 25

### CARANX SEXFASCIATUS (Ulua, Pake ulua, Mempachi ulua, Papio [young])

*Caranx sexfasciatus* and *C. lugubris* may be distinguished from other uluas by the scaly breast and the scutes along the lateral line, which number 27 to 34 and start immediately at the straight portion of the lateral line. *C. sexfasciatus* can be distinguished from *C. lugubris* by the teeth: the former has 2 rows of teeth in the upper jaw with the outer row canine-like and widely spaced, the inner a narrow band of teeth; *C. lugubris* has a single row of teeth in the upper jaw. *C. sexfasciatus* is also characterized by the relatively large eyes, the diameter of which goes approximately 3.5 times in the head length.

This is one of the commoner uluas. The papio (juvenile fish) range from tide pools and brackish-water areas to deeper coastal waters. Large ulua caught by surf casting and spearing usually are this species. Attains a length of about 5 feet.

**Fig. 203. CARANX MATE**

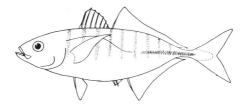

After J. and E., p. 195, fig. 76, modified

### CARANX MATE ('Omaka)

The most distinctive features of the 'omaka are the 9 or 10 dark vertical bars on the body and the greenish-yellow tinge over the silvery-colored side. The last dorsal and anal rays are finlet-like and a little separated from the rest of the fin. The body shape is similar to the akule, with the greatest depth going about 3.5 times in the standard length.

The habitat of the 'omaka is the mid-waters of protected bays, estuaries, and harbors such as Pearl Harbor and Kaneohe Bay. It is a rather voracious plankton feeder. Young less than an inch long are frequently taken under jellyfishes. The species is not found in open coastal waters. A common and excellent food fish. Attains a length of about 12 inches.

### CARANX KALLA

A slender fish, with the body shape of the 'omaka and the akule. It is very similar to the 'omaka but does not have the vertical bars, and the black opercular spot is confined to the opercle and not expanded onto the shoulder girdle as in the 'omaka and akule. The pectoral fin extends well beyond the beginning of the straight portion of the lateral line.

Unlike the 'omaka, this species inhabits the open coastal waters. It is rare in Hawaii and has not been seen by us. Attains a length of 13 to 15 inches.

## Family BRAMIDAE

The Bramidae is entirely made up of high-seas fishes that are rarely seen. All are scaled forward to the snout and on the maxillaries. The ventral profile is at least as steep as the dorsal profile, and there is a single long dorsal fin.

Four species are recorded from our area, but none of them is known from more than a few specimens.

Key to the Hawaiian species of the family Bramidae:

| | | |
|---|---|---|
| 1 | Dorsal and anal fins normal, the dorsal commencing behind the eyes........................................................ | 2 |
| | Dorsal and anal fins high and sail-like, the dorsal commencing on the head in front of the eyes......................*Pteraclis velifer* | |
| 2(1) | Pectoral fin length less than the greatest depth of body, going 1.5 or more times into the greatest body depth................. | 3 |
| | Pectoral fin length approximately equal to greatest body depth ..............................................*Taractes longipinnis* | |
| 3(2) | Dorsal rays 34; anal rays 30 or 31; known specimens all less than 8 inches long.....................................*Collybus drachme* | |
| | Dorsal rays 31; anal rays 22; known only from specimens about 2 feet long.......................................*Eumegistus illustris* | |

### PTERACLIS VELIFER

The long, high, sail-like fins are highly characteristic of this species. The anal fin extends forward to nearly below the eye.

Known in Hawaii from a single specimen about 4 inches long in poor condition taken from the stomach of an aku off Hilo. The genus is here recorded from Hawaiian waters for the first time.

### TARACTES LONGIPINNIS

Recorded from Hawaii on the basis of a single specimen about 2 feet long.

### COLLYBUS DRACHME

Apparently the most abundant and smallest species of Bramidae in Hawaii (see Fig. 108). Young examples are sometimes taken when hauling nets for offshore plankton.

**EUMEGISTUS ILLUSTRIS**

This genus (and species) is known only from the original description, which was based on partly cut-up market material. Further specimens are therefore badly needed in order to ascertain the validity of the species.

Two feet in length.

## Family CORYPHAENIDAE (Mahimahis)

There are two species in this circumtropical family, one of which is taken much more frequently than the other.

Key to the species of the family Coryphaenidae:

> Fifty-five to 65 rays in the dorsal fin; tongue narrow, rounded in front, not filling floor of mouth; greatest depth of body forward of center; pectoral fins more than half head length. Mahimahi . . . . . . . . . . . . . . . . . . . . . . . . . . . . . . . . . . . . . . . . . . . . *Coryphaena hippurus*
>
> Fifty-one to 55 rays in the dorsal fin; tongue broad, square-cut in front, filling the floor of the mouth; greatest body depth at about the center; pectoral fins about one-half head length. Little mahimahi . . . . . . . . . . . . . . . . . . . . . . . . . . . . . . . . . . . . . *Coryphaena equisetis*

**CORYPHAENA HIPPURUS (Mahimahi, Dolphin)**

The body is flat-sided, the dorsal fin long and continuous (see Fig. 111). Males have an almost vertical anterior profile. Large males approach 70 pounds in weight; females are much smaller. The average size of fish taken commercially is about 17 pounds. The mahimahi is essentially a fish of the warm seas, straying into northern waters during the summer months. Mahimahi have been taken off Astoria, Oregon, on a few occasions; however, this is certainly well beyond the normal range. It occurs in the Atlantic, Pacific, and Indian oceans. The mainland name for the mahimahi is dolphin, which by derivation and by usage refers properly to a porpoise.

This is a common sport fish in Hawaii, being one of the most abundant species taken by trolling. It is one of the best-known local table fishes in eating establishments and as such is frequently a visitor's first acquaintance with the excellent quality of many Hawaiian table fishes. This is in contrast to opinions regarding the edibility of this species elsewhere (Pacific Coast of Mexico) where, according to Walford, the flesh is considered coarse and dry.

The mahimahi feeds largely on flying fish and other fish of similar size and squid in the upper water layers. The mahimahi will follow a flying fish by swimming swiftly below it, ready to seize it when it drops back into the sea. Often a mahimahi will be observed to charge a trolled lure, leaving a wake across the surface of the water, from a hundred feet or more away. This may be indicative of the keen vision of this species.

Mahimahi are often found in the vicinity of a floating log or box to which they may be attracted by various small pelagic species that seek shelter beneath floating objects. This is such a frequent habit that experienced fishermen will always troll a lure around a floating object. Also, often when a mahimahi is hooked and fought near the stern of the boat, others will follow and may be induced to bite if the first fish is not landed immediately.

**181**

Occasionally, porpoise have been observed to pursue mahimahi, the fish leaping out of the water presumably to escape. Once the captain and crew of the *Makua*, research vessel of the Division of Fish and Game, Territory of Hawaii, observed a mahimahi impaled on the spear of a marlin off Kona, Hawaii.

Fish with well-developed gonads filled with loose transparent eggs have been taken in Hawaiian waters in February, March, and May. Fish taken in late fall and early winter months had small ovaries.

Young mahimahi, 2 to 4 inches in length, have been taken in September under a light at night off Kona, Hawaii.

The commercial catch of this species in Hawaiian waters was 235,800 pounds in 1954, 265,500 pounds in 1955, and 183,600 pounds in 1956.

### CORYPHAENA EQUISETIS (Little mahimahi, Little dolphin)

This is very much like the common mahimahi in appearance, but is smaller, reaching a length of about 30 inches. It is also much less common; however, its apparent rarity may be due in part to this species being confused with the common mahimahi by fishermen. From what little is known, it appears that its range and habits are much like those of the common mahimahi.

## Family EMMELICHTHYIDAE

The single Hawaiian species of this family most closely resembles the lutjanids ('opakapakas and 'ula'ulas) in general appearance but differs from them in a number of minor features. The top of the head is scaled forward nearly to the tip of snout; there are no enlarged, sharp teeth; the maxillary is almost completely exposed on the surface of the cheek; and the soft dorsal and anal have a heavy basal scaly sheath.

### ERYTHROCLUS SCHLEGELII

*Erythroclus schlegelii* is a reddish-yellow fish in life (see Fig. 120). The small mouth with minute teeth is very protrusible and the longitudinal struts of the upper jawbones pass well up the front of the skull to between the eyes. The two dorsal fins are only very slightly connected.

The species attains a length of about 15 inches and is brought into the market from time to time along with 'ula'ulas.

## Family LUTJANIDAE ('Opakapakas or Snappers)

The lutjanids form one of the most important groups of Hawaiian market fishes, including such well-known forms as the onaga, kalikali, and 'opakapaka. Most of our species are taken by hook and line over the offshore "banks." As with the serranids, the shallow-water lutjanids so plentiful farther south are not native to Hawaii, though one of them has been recently introduced (see Appendix A).

Lutjanids are lacking in outstanding peculiarities. With the exception of the yellow-striped *Rooseveltia brighami* all of our species are plain in coloration, tending toward a red or steel blue. Perhaps the families with which they are most likely to be confused are the Serranidae and the Emmelichthyidae. However, in the serranids there are 3 flat spines on the opercle, the maxillary never slips under the cheekbone (preorbital), and there are 15 or more rays in the soft dorsal fin; by contrast our lutjanids have only 1 or 2 flat spines on the opercle, the maxillary is partly concealed under the cheekbone when the mouth is closed, and there are only 9 to 11 soft rays in the dorsal. Our single emmelichthyid may be distinguished from lutjanids by the practically toothless mouth, the heavy sheath of scales on the soft dorsal and anal, and the almost complete separation of the dorsal into two parts.

Key to the Hawaiian species of the family Lutjanidae:

1 Scales on top of head not extending forward to the eyes; no knobs projecting forward from the front of the lower jaw; anal soft rays 8 . . . . . . . . . . . . . . . . . . . . . . . . . . . . . . . . . . . . . . . . . . . . . . . . . . . 2

Scales completely covering top of head forward to the nostrils; a pair of tooth-bearing knobs projecting forward from the front of the lower jaw on either side of the midline; anal soft rays 7 . . . . . . . . . . . . . . . . . . . . . . . . . . . . . . . . . . . . . . . . . . . . . . . . *Symphysanodon typus*

2(1) Color in life without alternating red and yellow transverse bands . . . . 3

Color in life with alternating red and yellow transverse bands on the upper sides . . . . . . . . . . . . . . . . . . . . . . . . . . . . . . . . . *Rooseveltia brighami*

3(2) Gill openings not extending forward of the eyes; some of the jaw teeth of moderate or large size; maxillary not extending behind middle of eye . . . . . . . . . . . . . . . . . . . . . . . . . . . . . . . . . . . . . . . . . . . . . 5

Gill openings extending forward of the front of the eye; all of the teeth minute, of similar size; maxillary extending back to below posterior border of pupil . . . . . . . . . . . . . . . . . . . . . . . . . . . . . . . . . . . . . . . . 4

4(3) Color steel blue; about 16 gill rakers on the lower limb of the first arch; to about 15 pounds . . . . . . . . . . . . . . . . . . . . . *Aphareus furcatus*

Color dull red; about 34 gill rakers on the lower limb of the first arch; to about 35 pounds . . . . . . . . . . . . . . . . . . . . . . . . *Aphareus rutilans*

5(3) A deep indentation in the outline of the dorsal fin between the spinous and the soft portions, the last spine being less than half the length of the first soft ray . . . . . . . . . . . . . . . . . . . . . . . . . . . . . . . . . . 8

No deep indentation in the outline of the dorsal fin, the last spines and first soft rays being of approximately equal size . . . . . . . . 6

6(5) Pectorals relatively long, about as long as head; no longitudinal groove along the side of the snout slightly below the nostrils . . . . . . 7

Pectorals short, about half the length of the head; a longitudinal groove along each side of the snout slightly below the nostrils . . . . . . . . . . . . . . . . . . . . . . . . . . . . . . . . . . . . . . . . . . . . . . . . . . . . *Aprion virescens*

7(6) Front of upper jaw about on a level with the middle of the eye (see Fig. 207); vomerine teeth in an elongate diamond-shaped patch, with the blunt end of the diamond facing forward (Fig. 204a); about 20 gill rakers on the lower limb of the first arch . . . . . . . . . . . . . . . . . . . . . . . . . . . . . . . . . . . . . . . . . . . . . *Pristipomoides sieboldii*

Front of upper jaw on a level with the lower border of the eye; vomerine teeth in a V-shaped patch with the point of the V facing forward (Fig. 204b); 12 to 15 gill rakers on the lower portion of the first arch . . . . . . . . . . . . . . . . . . . . . . . . . . . . . . . *Pristipomoides microlepis*

Fig. 204

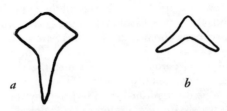

*a*                                         *b*

8(5)     Upper caudal lobe produced, longer than head; about 15 gill rakers on the lower limb of the first arch. . . . . . . . . . . . .*Etelis carbunculus*

Upper caudal lobe not produced, shorter than the head; 12 or fewer gill rakers on the lower limb of the first arch. . . . . . . .*Etelis marshi*

### SYMPHYSANODON TYPUS

This is a plain, greenish fish that apparently lives well offshore. Specimens more than 6 inches long may be immediately recognized by the pair of sharp knobs protruding from the front of the lower jaw. In addition, the border of the lower jaw has a sharp upward jog about two-thirds of the way back along its length.

The fish has never been seen in the market and has been recorded from Hawaii only on the basis of specimens killed by lava flows. We have such specimens, the largest of which is about a foot long.

### ROOSEVELTIA BRIGHAMI

The alternating red and yellow vertical bars in life will immediately distinguish this species from the other Hawaiian lutjanids. It also has a deeper body (depth about 3 times into the standard length) than any of our other species.

The fish is brought into the market from time to time along with catches of other species of the family. The largest specimen we have seen is about 14 inches long.

### Fig. 205. APHAREUS FURCATUS

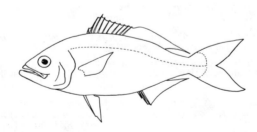

### APHAREUS FURCATUS (Gurutsu)

The genus *Aphareus* can be separated from our other lutjanids in a number of ways: when the mouth is open the gill rakers can be easily seen between the sides of the lower jaw; there are no enlarged jaw teeth and no vomerine or palatine teeth whatever; the lower jaw has deep sides and is strongly projecting and bulldog-like; and the length of the upper jaw is considerably greater than the postorbital head length.

Of the two Hawaiian species of *Aphareus* that occasionally enter the market with catches of onaga, *A. furcatus* appears to be much the smaller. The species is said to reach a length of 2 feet but we have never seen specimens much more than a foot in length.

### APHAREUS RUTILANS

This is the larger of our two species of *Aphareus*. It can be readily distinguished from *A. furcatus* by the brick-red coloration and the gill-raker count.

To at least 3 feet in length.

**Fig. 206. APRION VIRESCENS**

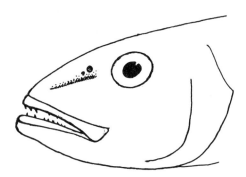

### APRION VIRESCENS (Uku)

This is the most cylindrical of our lutjanids, with a long head in which the snout is as long as the postorbital head length. It is also our only lutjanid in which the short pectoral is not falcate and in which there is a prominent groove along either side of the snout. The fish is gray-blue in color.

Attains a length of at least 2 feet.

**Fig. 207. PRISTIPOMOIDES SIEBOLDII**

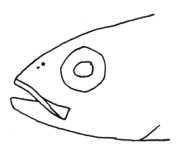

**185**

### PRISTIPOMOIDES SIEBOLDII (Kalikali)

The genus *Pristipomoides* is represented in Hawaiian waters by two species: the kalikali and the 'opakapaka. (A third species, *P. typus,* said to have alternating yellow and violet stripes on the head, is perhaps to be expected.) The kalikali is our only lutjanid with a median series of teeth projecting back along the roof of the mouth from the main vomerine series (see Fig. 204a). In the kalikali the mouth is both smaller and more oblique than in the 'opakapaka. Also, the 'opakapaka has 55 to 65 pored scales in the lateral line whereas the kalikali has about 75.

To about 2 feet in length. An important commercial species.

### PRISTIPOMOIDES MICROLEPIS ('Opakapaka)

The relationship with the kalikali is discussed under that species (see Fig. 204b).

A very important market species, attaining a length of at least 3 feet.

**Fig. 208.  ETELIS CARBUNCULUS**

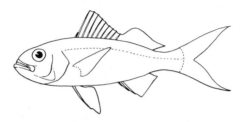

### ETELIS CARBUNCULUS (Onaga)

The two Hawaiian species of *Etelis* are rather similar in appearance, and both of them come into the Honolulu market together. In addition to the tapering caudal lobes (the upper of which is the more elongate), the following characters will help to distinguish the onaga: the two enlarged teeth at the front of each jaw are followed by a regular row of more than 20 subequal teeth, none of them especially enlarged; the inside of the mouth is pink or red in life; and there is no yellow band along the middle of the sides in life.

The onaga is one of the most important of our commercial fishes. To perhaps 3 feet.

**Fig. 209.  ETELIS MARSHI**

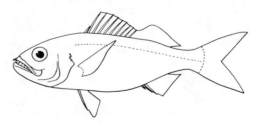

**ETELIS MARSHI ('Ula'ula)**

This fish differs from the quite similar onaga in lacking the elongate outer caudal rays; in having about 5 widely spaced, enlarged, needle-like teeth on each side of both jaws; in lacking the red coloration inside the mouth; and usually in possessing a yellowish band along the middle of the sides.

Taken with the onaga but said to reach a slightly smaller size (2 feet).

## Family LOBOTIDAE (Tripletails)

The single Hawaiian representative of this family is one of the few plain black fish in our waters. It differs from the smaller *Chromis verater* in having a distinctly serrate preopercle; from *Epinephelus quernus*, and incidentally also from the blackish chaetodontids and acanthurids, in having an outer row of firmly set conical teeth, all of about equal size, in both jaws. The body scales are rather large, 42–44 in the lateral-line series.

**Fig. 210. LOBOTES SURINAMENSIS**

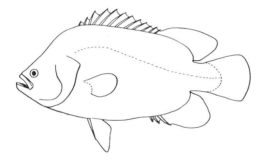

**LOBOTES SURINAMENSIS (Tripletail)**

The tripletail, well known in American and East Indian waters, was taken in Hawaii for the first time in 1957. At almost the same time specimens were collected in Tahiti. (The affinities of the Hawaiian *Lobotes* appear to be with the Pacific American form rather than with the West and East Indian species, but until the taxonomy of the genus is more completely worked out we call our fish *L. surinamensis*.) As it is a large and conspicuous inshore fish that would not easily have been missed, the suspicion arises that it has somehow been recently introduced. Hawaiian individuals have now been caught in Nawiliwili Harbor, Kauai, and Kaneohe Bay, Oahu, so the species is presumably well established.

The specimens we have seen are about 18 inches long, but in the East Indies it is said to reach a length of 40 inches. A good food fish.

## Family MULLIDAE (Goatfishes)

The goatfishes are among the most highly esteemed table fishes in the Hawaiian Islands, containing such well-known forms as the wekes and kumu.

Members of this family can be readily recognized by the pair of large barbels originating directly under the chin. Only one other Hawaiian family, the deep-water Polymixiidae, has a pair of barbels similarly situated. The only failure to recognize the goatfishes immediately will occur when, particularly in the young, the barbels are tucked away under the sides of the lower jaw.

Adult wekes occur in large schools, but otherwise the goatfishes appear to be solitary. Several species seem to come in over the reef at night to sleep in shallow water. In feeding, the goatfishes move over the bottom with the barbels extended forward nervously probing everything. Young goatfishes of several species, at least, appear in shallow water in the spring. At first they are silvery in color and much more elongate than the adults. These have apparently come in from a pelagic existence, for young goatfishes are often found in tuna stomachs. All of the species seem to be carnivorous throughout life.

Goatfishes reach a length of at least 9 inches, and some go on up to 2 feet or more.

Key to the Hawaiian species of the family Mullidae:

1     Lobes of the caudal fin without a series of well-marked black crossbands. . . . . . . . . . . . . . . . . . . . . . . . . . . . . . . . . . . . . . . . . . . 2

      Each lobe of the caudal fin with 4 or 5 well-marked black cross-bands. . . . . . . . . . . . . . . . . . . . . . . . . . . . . . . . . . . . . *Upeneus arge*

2(1)   Base of the second dorsal fin contained fewer than 2 times in the distance from the base of the last dorsal ray to the base of the central caudal ray; about 30 scales in the lateral line and 2½ scales between the lateral line and the middle of the back between the dorsal fins. . . . . . . . . . . . . . . . . . . . . . . . . . . . . . . . . . . . . . . . . 5

      Base of the second dorsal fin contained more than 2 times in the distance from the base of the last dorsal ray to the base of the middle caudal ray; about 37 scales in the lateral line and 3½ scales between the lateral line and the middle of the back between the dorsal fins. . . . . . . . . . . . . . . . . . . . . . . . . . . . . . . . . . . . . . . . . . 3

3(2)   Body reddish in life, without a blackish spot under the tips of the pectorals. . . . . . . . . . . . . . . . . . . . . . . . . . . . . . . . . . . . . . . . 4

      Body silvery in life, with a longitudinal yellow band (which fades rapidly in preservative) running its whole length; usually a blackish spot part way along the band under the tip of the pectorals. Lining of the body cavity dark-colored; gill rakers on the lower limb of the first arch 18 or 19. . . . . . . . . . . . *Mulloidichthys samoensis*

4(3)   Membrane lining the walls of the abdominal cavity dark; eye large, its diameter almost equal to the snout length and contained less than 4 times in the head length. . . . *Mulloidichthys auriflamma*

      Membrane lining the abdominal cavity light; eye relatively small, its diameter contained about twice in the snout length and 4 or more times in the head length. . . . . . . . . . . . . . . . . . *Mulloidichthys pflugeri*

5(2)   No single, well-marked spot on the sides below the last dorsal spine; total pectoral rays 15 or 16. . . . . . . . . . . . . . . . . . . . . . . . . . 6

      A single, well-marked spot on the sides below the last dorsal spine; total pectoral rays 17. About 22 gill rakers on the lower limb of the outer arch (including rudiments but not the raker at the angle). . . . . . . . . . . . . . . . . . . . . . . . . . . . . . . . . . . . *Parupeneus pleurostigma*

6(5)    Body red, greenish, or blackish without a bright yellow saddle just behind the soft dorsal fin in life; barbels contained 1.2 or more times in the head length; more than 20 gill rakers on the lower limb of the first arch....................................... 7

Body purplish with a bright yellow saddle just behind the soft dorsal fin in life; barbels very long, about equal to the head length; about 20 gill rakers on the lower limb of the first arch
.............................................. *Parupeneus chryserydros*

7(6)    Anal fin partly or entirely green or black; body with 2 or more black blotches running down from the back below the dorsal fins; gill rakers on lower limb of the outer arch about 29.......... 9

Anal fin red, yellow, or white; no dark vertical bands but often a dark longitudinal bar running upward and backward from eye; gill rakers on the lower limb of the outer arch about 24........... 8

8(7)    Barbels short, about reaching the level of the preopercular border; longest dorsal spines, when depressed, falling well short of the second dorsal origin; depth of body contained about 3 times in the standard length; color usually greenish, but sometimes reddish in deeper water....................... *Parupeneus porphyreus*

Barbels long, reaching to within 2 scales of the pelvic bases; longest dorsal spines, when depressed, about reaching the origin of the second dorsal fin; depth contained about 3.4 times in the standard length; body reddish................. *Parupeneus chrysonemus*

9(7)    Body not particularly deep, the greatest depth contained about 3.5 in the standard length; barbels light in color and relatively long, reaching to within 2 scales of the pelvic fin bases.......
.......................................... *Parupeneus multifasciatus*

Body relatively short and high, the greatest depth contained about 3 times in the standard length; barbels dark and short, reaching about to the level of the preopercular border........
............................................. *Parupeneus bifasciatus*

**Fig. 211. UPENEUS ARGE**

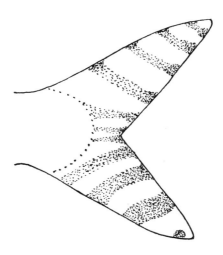

### UPENEUS ARGE (Weke pueo, Weke pahula)

The black crossbands on the tail of this species (Fig. 211) will immediately distinguish it from all other goatfishes. It is also the only species with teeth on the vomer and palatines.

The weke pueo seems to prefer turbid waters with mud bottoms. It does not appear too frequently in the market at the present time.

**Fig. 212. MULLOIDICHTHYS SAMOENSIS**

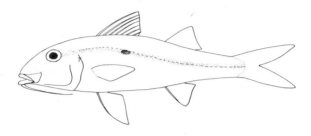

### MULLOIDICHTHYS SAMOENSIS (Weke, Weke-'a'a)

*Mulloidichthys samoensis* is the most elongate of our goatfishes (aside from *Upeneus arge*), the depth going about 4 times in the standard length. As compared with *Mulloidichthys auriflamma* the snout is longer, almost half the head length, and the gill rakers less numerous, with 18 or 19 on the lower limb of the outer arch (including rudiments). The black spot under the pectoral tip, when present, will distinguish this species immediately from other species of *Mulloidichthys*, as will the black blotch on the inside of the gill cover.

*Mulloidichthys samoensis* is undoubtedly the commonest of our shallow-water goatfishes. Schools of from 10 to more than a hundred can frequently be observed resting or swimming over sandy patches between the coral. The elongate, silvery young appear in great numbers in the spring.

Attains a length of perhaps 18 inches.

### MULLOIDICHTHYS AURIFLAMMA (Weke-'ula)

There are three similar-looking red goatfishes in Hawaiian waters (a fourth, *Parupeneus porphyreus*, frequently occurs in a red phase). Of the three, *Parupeneus chrysonemus* can be distinguished from the other two by the characters given for separating *Mulloidichthys* from *Parupeneus* in the key (section 2); it can further be separated by the fact that the anterior nostril is slightly nearer to the tip of the snout than to the eye (in the other two it is much nearer the eye). *Mulloidichthys auriflamma* (also *M. samoensis*) is immediately distinguishable from *M. pflugeri*, the third red goatfish in this series, by the black membrane lining the abdominal cavity. Furthermore, in life *M. auriflamma* usually has a yellow horizontal band along the upper sides and other yellowish markings, whereas *M. pflugeri* does not.

There seems to be a rather clear, only slightly overlapping, vertical zonation of the three species of *Mulloidichthys* in Hawaii, with *M. samoensis* in the shallowest water and *M. pflugeri* in the deepest. *M. auriflamma* occurs in between, at depths from 20 to 100 feet. It forms large schools during the day, at which time individuals do not feed but are frequently taken by net. These schools seem rather permanent, judging by one off Waianae in 80 feet of water that has been observed within 20 feet of the same place at 6 month intervals. At night the schools apparently break up and the individuals roam for food.

Reaches about 16 inches in length, and is frequently seen in the market, though perhaps in smaller number than the larger *M. pflugeri*.

### MULLOIDICHTHYS PFLUGERI

For distinguishing characters, see the previous account. Probably all of the large, red goatfishes that appear in the market belong to this species. It is a deeper-water form than the other *Mulloidichthys*.

Recorded as reaching 2 feet in length.

#### Fig. 213. PARUPENEUS PLEUROSTIGMA

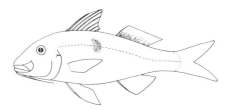

### PARUPENEUS PLEUROSTIGMA (Malu)

In the light coloration and the single black spot on the sides this species most closely resembles *Mulloidichthys samoensis*. However, the form of the body is quite different, with a much shorter caudal peduncle. Also, unlike *M. samoensis*, the base of the soft dorsal fin is very dark, and the black blotch on the sides is deeper than long.

Quite common, reaching perhaps 16 inches in length.

### PARUPENEUS CHRYSERYDROS (Moano kea)

The purplish coloration and bright yellow saddle on the caudal peduncle will immediately distinguish this species. The extremely long snout, small eye, and long barbels are also distinctive.

Not uncommon, reaching at least 2 feet in length.

### PARUPENEUS PORPHYREUS (Kumu)

This fish is usually greenish, but sometimes reddish, in coloration. In either color phase there is a prominent white saddle just behind the dorsal fin. There is also usually a dark stripe running through the eye and on up to below the spinous dorsal. In the reddish color phase the kumu can be most easily confused with the young of the following species, but the latter does not have the white saddle behind the soft dorsal.

**Fig. 214. PARUPENEUS PORPHYREUS**

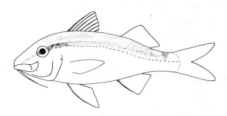

Probably the commonest of the inshore species of *Parupeneus*. The young, about 40 mm. in standard length, appear in shallow water in March. By August they have doubled in size. Adults appear never to grow very large, reaching perhaps 16 inches in total length.

### PARUPENEUS CHRYSONEMUS

This is one of the more poorly known of our goatfishes. It is described as a bright red fish with yellow barbels. We have seen small brick red individuals with a bar extending from the eye back to below the first dorsal fin, which we take to be the same species. (See account of *Mulloidichthys auriflamma*.)

Certainly not common. Reaches 9 inches in length so far as is known.

**Fig. 215. PARUPENEUS MULTIFASCIATUS**

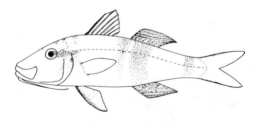

### PARUPENEUS MULTIFASCIATUS (Moano)

This and *Parupeneus bifasciatus* are our two goatfishes with black stripes extending across the sides. At first sight they are quite similar, but *P. multifasciatus* has a black bar extending down from between the dorsal fins, whereas *P. bifasciatus* does not. The two can also be distinguished by the characters given in the key.

Common. Apparently does not reach more than a foot in length.

Fig. 216. PARUPENEUS BIFASCIATUS

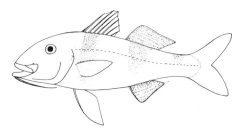

**PARUPENEUS BIFASCIATUS (Munu)**

The young of this fish resembles *Parupeneus multifasciatus* as noted above, but as the fish grows older the whole body becomes darkly colored and the vertical bars indistinct.

The species seems to be considerably rarer than *P. multifasciatus* and to reach a somewhat larger size.

## Family SPARIDAE

The technical character distinguishing this family from other Hawaiian spine-finned fishes is the presence of low, rounded, molariform teeth in the back of the jaws. However, this feature is difficult to verify as the jaws are hard to open. Fortunately, the coloration of the single Hawaiian species in the family is quite distinctive with 2 to 4 white bands running vertically downward across the dark body. Additionally, the head is high (about as deep as long), and the maxillary is almost completely hidden by the cheekbones when the mouth is closed.

**MONOTAXIS GRANDOCULIS (Mu, Mamamu)**

Occasional specimens of this species may be seen on the reef and may be identified by the light vertical bands on a dark ground (see Fig. 122). It was said to have been a fairly abundant commercial fish, but we have seen few specimens in the market in the last few years. Reaches 2 feet in length.

## Family SCORPIDIDAE

The convict fish, *Microcanthus strigatus*, is the only Hawaiian member of this family. *Microcanthus* is at once distinguishable from all other Hawaiian fishes by the high body with several alternating dark and light stripes running more or less horizontally across it. In morphological characters it is close to the Chaetodontidae.

One species known from our waters.

**MICROCANTHUS STRIGATUS**

The form and coloration of this species make it very difficult to confuse with any other Hawaiian species (see Fig. 118).

Not uncommon in certain shallow-water areas. Reaches a length of about 6 inches.

## Family KYPHOSIDAE (Nenues or Rudder Fishes)

The common nenue (*Kyphosus cinerascens*) is a rather unattractive and non-descript fish but the apparently rare *Sector azureus* is a beautiful species with blue and gold stripes. The following characters are held in common by our two members of the family: a row of incisor teeth around the front of each jaw; nostrils in a slight longitudinal depression; gill covers broadly attached to one another by a free scaly fold across the isthmus; pelvics entirely behind the pectoral bases; scales running forward on top of head to above the nostrils and forming a heavy sheath on the dorsal and anal bases.

The kyphosids are herbivorous fishes, and the common nenue is said to give off a characteristic odor. For this reason many people object to it as a table fish, though others find it excellent.

Key to the Hawaiian species of the family Kyphosidae:

> Caudal only slightly forked, the longest rays shorter than the head length; soft dorsal rays 12; soft anal rays 11 . . . .*Kyphosus cinerascens*
>
> Caudal deeply forked, the longest rays considerably longer than the head length; soft dorsal rays 15 or 16; soft anal rays 13 or 14
> . . . . . . . . . . . . . . . . . . . . . . . . . . . . . . . . . . . . . . . . . . . . . . . . .*Sector azureus*

### KYPHOSUS CINERASCENS (Nenue, Nenue parii, Manaloa)

This is the common nenue. Apparently it also occurs in a yellow color variety, but it is possible that really two species are represented.

Attains a length of about 2 feet.

### SECTATOR OCYURUS

This species superficially resembles the little mahimahi (*Coryphaena equisetus*) and is apparently an offshore form. Apparently only two specimens are known, the type of the species and an individual taken in a trap off Waianae, which we have examined. Both are about 15 inches long.

## Family CHAETODONTIDAE (Butterfly Fishes)

Most of the butterfly fishes are extremely colorful, with bold markings that stand out conspicuously against any background in Hawaiian waters. Though the various species show combinations of blue, yellow, orange, red, white, and black, they seem to be lacking in greens. All are deep-bodied and have flexible, comblike teeth. Except in *Pomacanthus imperator* and *Hemitaurichthys*, the lateral line ends below the soft dorsal.

All butterfly fishes seem to be solitary in habit. None are ever found in Hawaii in great abundance, and some are exceedingly rare. In *Pomacanthus imperator* and *Chaetodon lunula* the color pattern changes considerably with growth, but the others obtain their adult markings and shape shortly after transforming from the larval form. The food of chaetodontids seems to consist of small invertebrates. The principal habitat of this family is the coral reef, though some forms are not lacking from rocky areas. Though none of the chaetodontids are truly deep-water fishes, there are a number that apparently never venture into depths of less than 100 feet.

Twenty-four species appear to have been validly recorded from Hawaii. Günther's Hawaiian record of *Holacanthus bicolor* is tentatively considered erroneous, and the species is not included here.

Key to the Hawaiian species of the family Chaetodontidae:

| | | |
|---|---|---|
| 1 | No strong spines projecting backward from the angle of the preopercle............................................................ | 7 |
| | One or more strong spines extending backward from the preopercle............................................................ | 2 |
| 2(1) | Scales in a longitudinal series 50 or fewer; lateral line ending below the soft dorsal............................................. | 3 |
| | Scales in a longitudinal series about 95; lateral line continued to base of tail. Body with 12 to 20 longitudinal or concentric light bars......................................*Pomacanthus imperator* | |
| 3(2) | No longitudinal barring on the body........................... | 4 |
| | A single broad dark bar extending from the eye backward to the edge of the soft dorsal fin.................*Holacanthus arcuatus* | |
| 4(3) | Scales about 45 in a longitudinal series; middle portion of caudal fin not yellow in life............................................ | 5 |
| | Scales about 28 in a longitudinal series; middle portion of caudal fin lemon-yellow in life.......................*Centropyge fisheri* | |
| 5(4) | No distinct round spots at the base of the pectoral and of the soft dorsal.......................................................... | 6 |
| | A distinct, roundish black spot about the size of the eye at the base of the pectoral, and another at the base of the soft dorsal. Known only from Johnston...................*Centropyge nigriocellus* | |
| 6(5) | Head (and body) with numerous alternating dark and light vertical bars.......................................*Centropyge potteri* | |
| | Head plain. Body reddish in life, with about 6 vertically elongate black blotches. Known only from Johnston....*Centropyge flammeus* | |
| 7(1) | Snout not greatly produced, less than half the head length......... | 8 |
| | Snout greatly produced, more than half the head length....... .............................................*Forcipiger longirostris* | |
| 8(7) | Fourth dorsal spine not very long, less than the head length; color pattern not of broad, alternating black and yellow vertical stripes............................................................ | 10 |
| | Fourth dorsal spine longer than the head length; color pattern of broad, alternating, more or less vertical black and yellow stripes.... | 9 |
| 9(8) | A dark band extending from dorsal origin through eye to the base of the cheek...............................*Heniochus excelsa* | |
| | Dark band above eye short, extending neither onto cheek nor to dorsal origin...............................*Heniochus acuminatus* | |
| 10(8) | Lateral line ending under the soft dorsal; scales in a longitudinal series 50 or fewer.................................................. | 12 |
| | Lateral line continued to caudal base; scales in a longitudinal series 60 or more.................................................. | 11 |
| 11(10) | Pectoral much longer than pelvic, reaching well beyond anal base; scales about 80 in a longitudinal series...*Hemitaurichthys thompsoni* | |

Pectoral and pelvic of about equal length, the former not reaching the anal origin; scales about 60 in a longitudinal series........
................................................*Hemitaurichthys zoster*

12(10) Color pattern includes a bar passing vertically through the eye..... 13

No bar passing vertically through the eye. About 8 nearly horizontal, narrow blue bars on body.................*Chaetodon fremblii*

13(12) Pelvic fins light in coloration................................. 15

Pelvic fins black or blackish.................................. 14

14(13) Anal fin and caudal peduncle mostly black........*Chaetodon reticulatus*

Anal fin and caudal peduncle the same light color as the rest of the body.......................................*Chaetodon corallicola*

15(13) Longest anal spine when depressed not reaching as far back as the tips of the soft dorsal rays; second dorsal spine more than half as long as third......................................... 16

Longest anal spine when depressed reaching farther back than tips of soft dorsal rays; second dorsal spine about half as long as third. Body abruptly black above and behind a line extending obliquely down and back from the third dorsal spine...*Chaetodon tinkeri*

16(15) None of the soft dorsal rays prolonged into a projecting filament.... 18

A few of the anterior soft dorsal rays elongated into a filament that projects well beyond the other rays........................ 17

17(16) Bar through eye much narrower than eye; black blotch on soft dorsal fin extending well down onto the body......*Chaetodon ephippium*

Bar through eye in part broader than eye; black spot on soft dorsal restricted to the fin rays.....................*Chaetodon auriga*

18(16) No single, large, black spot on the body just below the posterior dorsal spines........................................... 19

A single, large, roundish or vertically elongated, black spot just below the posterior dorsal spines..............*Chaetodon unimaculatus*

19(18) Vertical bar through eye at its broadest point narrower than the eye diameter................................................ 21

Vertical bar through eye at its broadest point much broader than the eye diameter......................................... 20

20(19) A white area just behind the dark bar through eye; no narrow vertical dark lines on the body...................*Chaetodon lunula*

No white area just behind the dark bar through eye; posterior portion of the body with a series of narrow, vertical, dark lines ................................................*Chaetodon lineolatus*

21(19) Bars through the 2 eyes not continuous with one another across the throat; color pattern not consisting of narrow, more or less horizontal bars........................................ 23

Black bars through the 2 eyes continuous with one another across the throat; color pattern consisting of narrow, more or less horizontal bars........................................ 22

22(21) Snout black to tip; body with about a dozen black bars.......
................................................*Chaetodon trifasciatus*

Tip of snout light; body with about 6 orange bars..........
................................................*Chaetodon ornatissimus*

23(21) No black area on the body below the dorsal fin.................. 24

A white spot enclosed in the dark area below the spinous dorsal
and another in the dark area below the soft dorsal............
......................................*Chaetodon quadrimaculatus*

24(23) No black band across the middle of the caudal fin............... 25

A black band across the middle of the caudal fin.. *Chaetodon multicinctus*

25(24) Spinous dorsal black-edged; spots on body forming rows that
ascend from front to rear......................*Chaetodon citrinellus*

Spinous dorsal without a black edge; spots on body forming
vertical rows..................................*Chaetodon miliaris*

### POMACANTHUS IMPERATOR

Only one specimen of this large and striking butterfly fish seems to have
been taken in Hawaii. Whether this was a straggler from southern waters is
unknown, but it is at least certain that no large population of so conspicuous
a fish as this would have gone unnoted about the high Hawaiian Islands.

To at least a foot in length.

### HOLACANTHUS ARCUATUS

The single dark band passing horizontally through the eye and obliquely
up to the edge of the soft dorsal fin will at once distinguish this species.

Taken from time to time in traps. To about 7 inches.

### CENTROPYGE FISHERI

One of the small, colorful, prickly chaetodontids with a very blunt snout.

This species is known only from 14 specimens dredged in about 180 feet
of water. To about 3 inches.

### CENTROPYGE NIGRIOCELLUS

A very strikingly spotted species known from a single specimen only 2
inches long.

### CENTROPYGE POTTERI

The only species of the genus and, in fact, the only chaetodontid of the
group with a preopercular spine known from less than 60 feet of water in
Hawaii. It is a very beautiful fish with russet and deep blue vertical barring.

Not rare. To about 4 inches.

### CENTROPYGE FLAMMEUS

A bright red fish with irregular dark vertical bars known only from Johnston Island.

To about 5 inches.

### FORCIPIGER LONGIROSTRIS (Lau-wiliwili-nukunuku-'oi'oi)

The long snout and high spines of this fish give it a shape that would be
difficult to confuse with any other Hawaiian species (see Frontispiece). The
color, too, is distinctive, though old individuals tend to become plain blackish.

Quite common. To about 5 inches.

**197**

### HENIOCHUS EXCELSA

A species known from one small specimen brought to the surface by the lava flow of 1919. The round black spot with a white border is unknown for any other species in the genus.

Presumably a deep-water form. The one specimen is 2 inches long.

### HENIOCHUS ACUMINATUS

Resembles the kihikihi or moorish idol (*Zanclus canescens*) in general shape and coloration, but has a less elongate snout and lacks the black on the caudal fin.

Not uncommon at a depth of about 100 feet. Reaches perhaps 7 inches in length.

### HEMITAURICHTHYS THOMPSONI

A dull blackish fish without noticeable markings. Quite rare. To about 7 inches.

### HEMITAURICHTHYS ZOSTER

This is by far the commoner of the two species of *Hemitaurichthys*. It has a peculiar flat-topped pyramid of light color on the sides bordered by darker areas.

Attains perhaps 7 inches in length.

### CHAETODON FREMBLII

As with the numerous other species of *Chaetodon*, this form is chiefly but readily distinguishable by color pattern. The absence of a vertical bar through the eye and the narrow blue bars on the body will identify *C. fremblii* at a glance (see Fig. 217a).

A relatively common, shallow-water form reaching about 5 inches in length.

### CHAETODON RETICULATUS

A very dark fish, the whole posteroventral portion of the body black with some light spotting on the scale centers (see Fig. 217b).

Recorded only twice from Hawaii, although it has been seen in the water off the Kona Coast several times. Reaches about 5 inches.

### CHAETODON CORALLICOLA

This is perhaps our most nondescript species of *Chaetodon*. Except for the dark bar through the eye, which extends downward and backward onto the pelvic fins, the only markings on the fish are some vague dark spots on the sides (see Fig. 217c).

Apparently restricted to depths of over 100 feet. Reaches about 4 inches in length.

### CHAETODON TINKERI

A handsome, recently described species with the whole posterodorsal portion of the body abruptly black (see Fig. 217d).

From relatively deep water. To about 6 inches.

### CHAETODON EPHIPPIUM

This is one of those fishes that is relatively common in more tropical waters to the south but rare in Hawaii (see Fig. 217e). The few Hawaiian specimens known have come from deep-water traps, although it has been sighted in water as shallow as 3 feet.

To about 6 inches.

### CHAETODON AURIGA

A rather common species with narrow dark lines in two series, one running at right angles to the other (see Fig. 217f).

To about 6 inches.

### CHAETODON UNIMACULATUS

The spot on the middle of the upper sides is distinctive (see Fig. 217g). Not rare; to about 6 inches.

### CHAETODON LUNULA

There is a considerable change in color pattern with growth in this species (see Fig. 217h). In specimens 2 inches long (see Fig. 217i) there is a prominent round, light-bordered, dark spot on the soft dorsal. By the time a length of 5 inches is attained, this spot is replaced by a rather indistinct vertical bar.

Common in shallow water. To about 6 inches.

### CHAETODON LINEOLATUS

The largest Hawaiian species of *Chaetodon* (see Fig. 217j). The narrow black lines running straight down from a black area at the dorsal base are sufficient to identify this fish.

Found in relatively deep water. To about a foot.

### CHAETODON TRIFASCIATUS

This species and *C. ornatissimus* are our only two *Chaetodons* with the snout blunt and the upper profile of the head evenly convex (see Fig. 217k).

*C. trifasciatus* seems to be most abundant in areas of enclosed reef, such as Kaneohe Bay. To about 5 inches.

### CHAETODON ORNATISSIMUS

The blunt snout and orange bands on the middle of the body will identify this species (see Fig. 217l).

Apparently not uncommon in relatively deep water. To about 7 inches.

Fig. 217

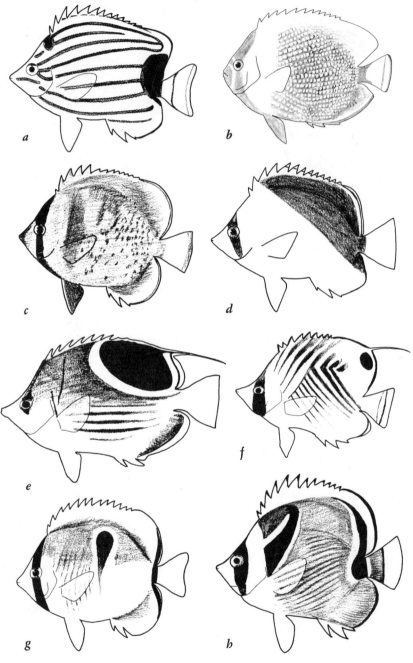

*a*

*b*

*c*

*d*

*e*

*f*

*g*

*h*

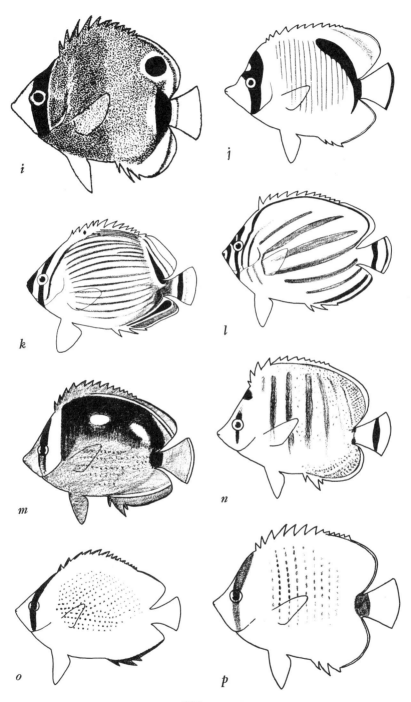

*i*

*j*

*k*

*l*

*m*

*n*

*o*

*p*

**201**

### CHAETODON QUADRIMACULATUS

A very striking fish, with 2 white areas on the upper sides more or less completely within a large black area (see Fig. 217m).

Fairly common in shallow water. To about 6 inches.

### CHAETODON MULTICINCTUS

A small, light-colored, rather fragile-looking chaetodontid somewhat similar to the next two species (see Fig. 217n). Aside from the spots, which do not form rows, there are several rather indistinct dark vertical bands on the sides.

Not rare. To about 4 inches.

### CHAETODON CITRINELLUS

Another species much commoner to the south than in Hawaii (see Fig. 217o). The black bar along the edge of the anal is a good spot character if it is not confused with the narrow dark border of several other species.

Definitely rare. To about 4 inches.

### CHAETODON MILIARIS

One of the commonest inshore species (see Fig. 217p). The black spots forming vertical rows will serve for identification.

To about 5 inches.

## Family HISTIOPTERIDAE

The family is represented in Hawaiian waters by one species.

### HISTIOPTERUS TYPUS

A deep-bodied, black-and-white fish said to have a patch of chin whiskers (see Fig. 102). Only one specimen recorded from Hawaii, though we have a second speared in about 100 feet of water.

Reaches perhaps 18 inches in length.

## Family HOPLEGNATHIDAE

This family is somewhat dubiously recorded on the basis of one specimen said to have been taken in Hawaii over 60 years ago.

### HOPLEGNATHUS FASCIATUS

A Japanese species easily recognizable by the fused teeth, which form a beak somewhat as in the parrot fishes (see Fig. 118). However, the scales are far smaller than in any scarid.

The length of the Hawaiian specimen was said to have been 20 inches.

## Family CHEILODACTYLIDAE

Very close to the Cirrhitidae, the one Hawaiian species differing in the longer dorsal fin, the coloration, and in the development of a bony projection over the eye in the adult.

There is no Hawaiian fish with which this species can be easily confused (see Fig. 105). The only other spiny-rayed fishes having a pattern of dark and light stripes have a very different shape, e.g., *Monotaxis*, *Microcanthus*, *Heniochus* and *Zanclus*.

Not uncommon in water about 100 feet deep. Reaches a length of perhaps a foot.

## Family CIRRHITIDAE (Hawkfishes)

The hawkfishes bear many features in common with the scorpaenids but lack the spines on the head and the bony strut running across the cheek of the Scorpaenidae (see Fig. 99). In the hawkfishes (as in the Scorpaenidae) the lower pectoral rays are simple, usually somewhat thicker than those in the upper part of the fin, and their tips project well beyond the interradial membranes. The presence of a fringe at the back of the anterior nostril is a characteristic feature of the Cirrhitidae.

Hawkfishes are perhaps most frequently seen sitting on large coral heads, from which they apparently make short dashes for food. Approached by a swimmer, they will dive into a crevice in the coral.

Five species in Hawaii, all of them found in rather shallow water and none attaining a length of more than about 10 inches.

For the generic classification of Hawaiian cirrhitids we intentionally follow the more conservative classification of Jordan and Evermann, rather than others more recently proposed. *Cirrhitichthys aprinus*, once taken from among the fouling on the bottom of a barge towed into Pearl Harbor from Guam, is not included here, though it may possibly have become established.

Key to the Hawaiian species of the family Cirrhitidae:

1      No oval, white-bordered, dark mark extending back from the posterior border of the eye.................................... 2

An ovoid, white-bordered, dark mark extending back from the posterior border of eye. Body relatively deep, its depth contained about 2.5 times in the standard length; no dark spots on the head.........................................*Paracirrhites arcatus*

2(1)   Body posteriorly without a wide longitudinal black band......... 3

Body posteriorly with a wide longitudinal black band. Head, including lips, with prominent roundish dark spots...*Paracirrhites forsteri*

3(2)   Scales on the cheek moderate, of about the same size as those on the body, in about 6 rows between the eye and the border of the preopercle; dorsal soft rays 12 to 14; maximum size about 5 inches.... 4

Scales on the cheek minute, much smaller than those on body, in about 30 rows between the eye and the edge of the preopercle; dorsal soft rays 11; maximum size at least 10 inches..*Cirrhitus alternatus*

4(3)   Snout pointed, the lips protruding; dorsal soft rays 12; lowermost 5 rays in the pectoral fin thickened and unbranched..*Cirrhitoidea bimacula*

Snout blunt, the lips little protruding; dorsal soft rays 14; lowermost 6 rays in the pectoral fin thickened and unbranched.......................................*Paracirrhites cinctus*

Fig. 218. PARACIRRHITES ARCATUS

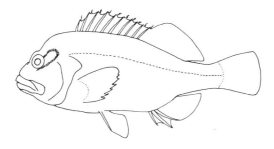

**PARACIRRHITES ARCATUS (Piliko'a)**

A small, deep-bodied, compressed species. The ovoid mark extending back and up from the eye is always present, though sometimes only in outline, sometimes solidly blocked in. In other respects the coloration of this species is highly variable.

To about 4 inches in length.

Fig. 219. PARACIRRHITES FORSTERI

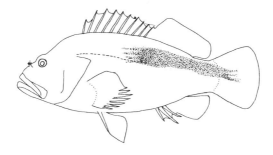

**PARACIRRHITES FORSTERI (Hilu piliko'a, Piliko'a)**

Perhaps the most oddly colored of our fishes in that the front half of the fish is distinctly spotted and the rear half equally distinctly banded. The two patterns do not seem appropriate for a single fish.

Attains a length of perhaps 9 inches; apparently restricted to somewhat deeper water than our other species.

**CIRRHITUS ALTERNATUS (Po'o-paa, 'O'opu-kai)**

The largest and in coloration the most nondescript of our hawkfishes, with red-and-brown spotting and mottling (see Fig. 106). It differs, however, from all our other species in having the cheek scales minute and thus strongly contrasting with those on the rest of the head and body.

Fairly common. To at least 10 inches.

**204**

Fig. 220. CIRRHITOIDEA BIMACULA

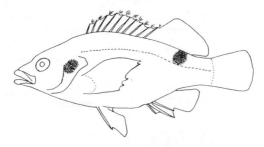

**CIRRHITOIDEA BIMACULA**

A small cirrhitid with a pointed snout in which the fringing on the inter-radial membranes between the dorsal spines is especially pronounced. The two large, roundish black spots, one on the gill cover and the other at the base of the last dorsal rays, are diagnostic; if black spots are present on other species, they are small and scattered or part of a series of vertical bars.

To about 3 inches; not uncommon.

### Fig. 221. PARACIRRHITES ·CINCTUS

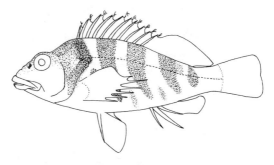

**PARACIRRHITES CINCTUS (Piliko'a, 'O'opu-kaha'ha'i, Po'opa'a)**

A small pinkish or reddish fish with black vertical bars.

Rather common in rocky surge channels. Attains a length of perhaps 5 inches.

## Family POMACENTRIDAE (Damselfishes)

The pomacentrids are blunt-headed, relatively deep-bodied fishes with the lateral line ending below the soft dorsal fin, or interrupted. Technically, the pomacentrids can be distinguished from all our other marine spiny-rayed fishes by the presence of only a single nostril on each side of the head.

Eleven species are recorded from the Hawaiian Islands, of which the mao-mao and kupipi are the most generally known. None of the species reach more than a foot in length, and are inshore forms occurring in less than 50 feet of water, though some are also taken to at least 150 feet.

**205**

Some of the pomacentrids, such as *Pomacentrus jenkinsi*, appear to be more or less solitary, but the majority may be frequently seen forming a small cloud over coral of proper type. Generally these clouds disappear into the coral on approach, but in one instance we have seen a school of some 400 maomao suspended like a curtain all the way between the surface and the bottom 40 feet below.

In habitat, *Dascyllus albisella* seems to be the most noticeably restricted, living in large heads of a certain type of finger coral. Wherever such heads exist, a small school of *Dascyllus* of various ages may be expected. Certain other species seem to be associated with coral of other types. *Abudefduf sindonis*, however, appears to favor areas of lava rock, while the maomao and *Pomacentrus jenkinsi* seem to be almost ubiquitous over hard bottom.

Even though all pomacentrids are inshore species there is a considerable difference in depth zonation among the various forms. The kupipi is basically a surge-pool form. At least, the young kupipi are among the most abundant of surge-pool inhabitants. The adults, however, move out to open water. The young of the maomao, and occasionally of other species, are found in surge pools but not nearly so frequently as the kupipi. *Abudefduf imparipennis* is one of the most characteristic of surge-zone fishes, living in small holes and crevices in the rock even in the more violent of surge areas. *Dascyllus albisella*, as noted, is restricted to coral heads of certain types, and these are found only in quiet water. However, they and *Dascyllus* may be found under proper conditions at 4 feet or at 50 feet. The other pomacentrids, except *Abudefduf sindonis*, seem to be restricted to areas off the reef and outside the surge zone.

In food habits, the species vary from herbivorous through omnivorous and carnivorous to detritus feeders. The relationship between feeding habits, tooth structure, and the digestive system in the various genera of pomacentrids seems never to have been adequately investigated.

Pomacentrids probably all spawn on the bottom, and the maomao, at least, guards its eggs. This species spawns all year round, but the spawning season on Oahu for *Pomacentrus jenkinsi* seems to be restricted to the period between December and March. The development of the young is direct; specimens 10 mm. long look very much like the adult. If there is a specialized planktonic larval stage, we have never taken it.

Key to the Hawaiian species of the family Pomacentridae:

(The species accounts are not in the same order as in the key)

1    Pelvic fins inserted somewhat behind the base of the uppermost pectoral ray; body ovate, the profile of the snout oblique, and the distance from the tip of snout to the origin of the pelvic fins contained less than 1.5 times in the body depth.............. 2

Pelvic fins inserted somewhat ahead of the base of the uppermost pectoral ray; body orbicular (see Fig. 223), the profile of the snout almost vertical, and the distance from the tip of snout to the origin of the pelvic fins contained more than 1.5 times in the body depth.................................*Dascyllus albisella*

2(1)    Body without dark vertical bars extending down the sides; no black mark on the body below the last dorsal ray............... 4

Body greenish yellow with 4 to 6 black vertical bands extending down the sides; a black spot or band usually present on the body just below the last dorsal ray.................................. 3

3(2)  No dark blotch on the bases of the last soft dorsal rays, but an intense dark spot on the caudal peduncle just below the last dorsal ray; dorsal soft rays 15 or 16...............*Abudefduf sordidus*

Bases of last soft dorsal rays dark; the dark bar on caudal peduncle, if present, no better defined than those ahead of it; dorsal soft rays 13 or 14.........................*Abudefduf abdominalis*

4(2)  Lips vertically furrowed; outline of raised dorsal fin almost horizontal, not notched, the third and succeeding dorsal spines subequal with the first soft dorsal ray; snout somewhat concave, relatively long, its length slightly greater than eye and equal to interorbital; gill rakers flaplike, as broad at base as long. Plain light-colored, with no black mark at pectoral base...........
..................................*Plectroglyphidodon johnstonianus*

Lips smooth; outline of raised dorsal fin more or less notched; snout usually somewhat convex, relatively short, its length less than eye diameter; gill rakers finger-shaped..................... 5

5(4)  Mouth originating slightly below eye level, in front directed more horizontally than obliquely downward (Fig. 222a); scales absent on snout from nostril level to upper lip, on preorbital, and on chin below sides of lower lip (Fig. 222a); dorsal soft rays 15–19; gill rakers on lower limb of first arch about 9–14; teeth long, brushlike, closely packed, directed as much forward as vertically...................................................... 6

Mouth originating about at level of lower edge of pupil, directed immediately downward at an angle of about 45° (Fig. 222b); scales present on most of snout, most of preorbital, and area on chin below sides of lower lip (Fig. 222b); dorsal soft rays 11–13(14); gill rakers 16–21 on lower limb of first arch; teeth triangular, small, well separated................................ 9

**Fig. 222**

a                              b

6(5)  Body light-colored, pelvic fins light; no dark spot at the base of the pectoral.............................*Abudefduf imparipennis*

Body basically dark-colored, pelvic fins very dark; a more or less prominent dark spot at the base of the pectoral................. •7

7(6)  Edge of preopercle smooth; dorsal XII, 18 or 19; anal soft rays 15........................................................ 8

Edge of preopercle serrate; dorsal XIII(XII–XIV), 15 or 16; anal soft rays 12 or 13. Body plain dark brown in specimens over 3 inches long.................................*Pomacentrus jenkinsi*

**207**

8(7)   Caudal peduncle and caudal fin uniformly blackish; body deep, depth contained about 1¾ times in standard length...*Abudefduf sindonis*

Caudal peduncle blackish, caudal fin abruptly white; body more elongate, depth contained about 2 times in standard length. Not known north of Johnston Island..............*Abudefduf phoenixensis*

9(5)   No black mark at base of pectoral; anal and caudal with dark bars; anal soft rays 11. Reaches only about 2½ inches..*Chromis vanderbilti*

A black mark at base of pectoral; anal and caudal uniform in color; anal soft rays 12–14................................. 10

10(9)  Pelvics light-colored; caudal peduncle narrow, its depth less than length of head to rear border of eye. Dorsal spines 14....*Chromis ovalis*

Pelvics dark-colored; caudal peduncle deeper, its depth equal to length of head to rear border of eye......................... 11

11(10) Dorsal spines 12; body light-colored or a mixture of black and light..........................................*Chromis leucurus*

Dorsal spines 14; body plain blackish................*Chromis verater*

**Fig. 223. DASCYLLUS ALBISELLA**

### DASCYLLUS ALBISELLA

Counts on five specimens: dorsal XII, 15 or 16; anal II, 15; total pectoral rays 20 or 21; total gill rakers on first arch 24 to 27.

A plain black fish with a striking white spot on the middle of the upper sides in the young. The head of this fish appears to have been pushed back into the body with the result that the anterior profile is very steep and the pelvic bases are under the gill cover. Preopercle serrate and scales rough.

Stomachs of this species examined contained mysids, calanoid copepods, and shrimp and crab larvae.

*Dascyllus* occurs in small schools around certain large coral heads. Not rare; attains a length of perhaps 5 inches.

### ABUDEFDUF SORDIDUS (Kupipi)

Counts on five specimens: dorsal XIII, 15 or 16; anal II, 15; total pectoral rays 18 or 19; total gill rakers on first arch 18 to 23.

The kupipi can readily be distinguished from the maomao by the black spot at the front of the caudal peduncle. Any doubt on the matter can be resolved by counting the soft dorsal rays.

Fig. 224. ABUDEFDUF SORDIDUS

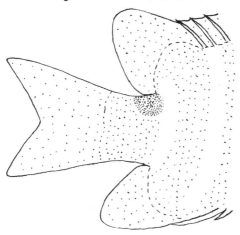

The young of the kupipi are very prominent tide-pool inhabitants. The adults tend to become a uniform dark gray-green, with the vertical striping obscure. These adults are much less frequently seen than the young. They apparently live just outside the reef edge and, like the maomao, are omnivorous.

To about 8 inches.

Fig. 225. ABUDEFDUF ABDOMINALIS

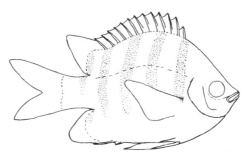

### ABUDEFDUF ABDOMINALIS (Maomao)

Counts on five specimens: dorsal XIII, 13 or 14; anal II, 13 to 15; total pectoral rays 17 to 19; total gill rakers on first arch 28 to 31.

The maomao is one of our two Hawaiian pomacentrids with dark vertical stripes. The chief color difference between them is shown in the figures.

The maomao is certainly not the most abundant of our pomacentrids. However, it is much the best known. This arises from the fact that it occurs in the same areas as the shore fisherman, will take his bait, and attains a sufficiently large size to be valued by him.

Spawning occurs all the year around, but with a peak of activity during April, May, and June.

The species appears to be omnivorous as an adult. Reaches a length of about 9 inches.

### ABUDEFDUF IMPARIPENNIS

Counts on five specimens: dorsal XII, 15 or 16; anal II, 11 or 12; total pectoral rays 18 to 20; total gill rakers on first arch 10 to 12.

The plain yellow coloration of this species is in itself almost distinctive. The only other pomacentrid with which it might be confused in color, *Plectroglyphidodon johnstonianus*, has 16 or 17 anal rays whereas *Abudefduf imparipennis* has only 11 or 12.

This bright-eyed little pomacentrid seems to occur over all rocky areas in the surge zone. It appears to be entirely carnivorous, with the predominant food organism a polychaet annelid.

Attains a maximum length of less than 3 inches.

### ABUDEFDUF SINDONIS

Counts on five specimens: dorsal XII, 19; anal II, 15; total pectoral rays 20 to 22; total gill rakers on first arch 11 to 13.

The young of this fish are very strikingly marked. Up to about 1 inch in length there is a large round, black, white-bordered spot on the soft dorsal fin. At a length of 2 to 3 inches this spot drops out and 2 narrow vertical white bands on the body develop. Fishes 4 inches long are a plain black and thus similar in coloration to *Pomacentrus jenkinsi* and *Chromis verater*. They differ from both these species in the lower number of dorsal spines and gill rakers and the higher soft anal ray count. The dorsal soft ray count of 19 is the highest for any of the Hawaiian pomacentrids.

The species seems to be restricted to surge areas among lava rocks and appears to be omnivorous. Reaches about 5 inches in length.

### ABUDEFDUF PHOENIXENSIS

Counts on two specimens: dorsal XII, 17 and 18; anal II, 15; total pectoral rays 21 and 22; total gill rakers on first arch 12 and 13.

This species was described from the Phoenix Islands and does not appear to occur north of Johnston. It is sufficiently distinguished from other members of the family by the dark caudal peduncle and abruptly light tail. There are 2 narrow vertical white bands on the body.

Reaches about 4 inches in length.

**Fig. 226. PLECTROGLYPHIDODON JOHNSTONIANUS**

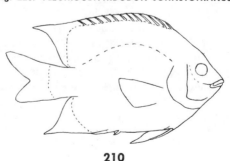

## PLECTROGLYPHIDODON JOHNSTONIANUS

Counts on five specimens: dorsal XII, 18; anal II, 16 or 17; total pectoral rays 18 to 20; total gill rakers on first arch 13 or 14.

A high-bodied pomacentrid; quite scaly, the scales on the operculum extending back beyond the membrane. The anal soft ray count is the highest of any Hawaiian pomacentrid.

Not uncommon at depths of 10 to 50 feet. Attains a length of about 4 inches.

## POMACENTRUS JENKINSI

Counts on five specimens (except for dorsal spine count): dorsal XIII (XII to XIV), 15 or 16; anal II, 12 or 13; total pectoral rays 21 or 22; total gill rakers on first arch 15 or 16. The dorsal spine count is almost always 13, but out of 53 specimens three had a count of 12 and one a count of 14.

A plain dark-brown fish with a yellowish eye in life. It is the only one of our pomacentrids except *Dascyllus albisella* with a distinctly serrate preopercle.

Certainly one of the most abundant of our pomacentrids, occurring in relatively quiet water both inside and outside the reef. It does not, however, live in the heavy surge zone with *Abudefduf imparipennis* or in the high tide pools with the young of the maomao and kupipi. It is a solitary fish, living in holes in the reef and feeding on algae and perhaps detritus.

Unlike the maomao, *Pomacentrus jenkinsi* is restricted to a winter spawning season on Oahu. On Midway with much colder water, ripe females have been taken in June. The young about an inch long have been caught around Oahu in June. Maturity in the species is reached at about 3½ inches and the maximum size is about 5 inches.

### Fig. 227. CHROMIS VANDERBILTI

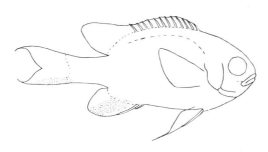

## CHROMIS VANDERBILTI

Counts on five specimens: dorsal XI or XII, 11; anal II, 10 or 11; total pectoral rays 17; total gill rakers on first arch 24 or 25.

A lovely little fish with the anterior soft anal rays black, the posterior few rays abruptly light; usually the lower caudal rays are blackish. The outer caudal rays are prolonged beyond the rest of the fin.

The food seems to consist of calanoid copepods.

It is quite abundant over coral beyond the surge zone but has never been taken in less than about 15 feet of water. Attains a length of about 2½ inches.

**Fig. 228. CHROMIS OVALIS**

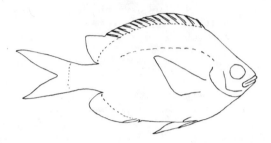

### CHROMIS OVALIS

Counts on five specimens: dorsal XIV, 11 or 12; anal II, 12 or 13; total pectoral rays 21 or 22; total gill rakers on first arch 34 to 38.

This steel-blue to silvery fish is quite unlike the rest of the pomacentrids in coloration. The caudal is deeply forked, and the body scales are relatively large and smooth. The young, which have been taken from a tide pool on one occasion, have longitudinal blue lines on the top of the head. The total gill raker count of 34 to 38 on the first arch is the highest for any of the Hawaiian pomacentrids.

Quite common in water of 30 to 50 feet, where they hover some 6 feet above the bottom. The stomach of one specimen contained a mass of copepods.

To about 6 inches in length.

### CHROMIS LEUCURUS

Counts on ten specimens: dorsal XII, 12 or 13; anal II, 12 to 14; total pectoral rays 16 to 18; total gill rakers on first arch 27 to 31.

*Chromis leucurus* has apparently two color phases: in one the body is all black anteriorly but abruptly white posteriorly; in the other the whole body except for the black pectoral base is a plain pinkish brown.

It is found in fairly deep water, usually over 15 feet; quite common on the outer side of the reef.

Reaches perhaps 5 inches in length.

### CHROMIS VERATER

Counts on five specimens: dorsal XIV, 13; anal II, 13 or 14; total pectoral rays 19 or 20; total gill rakers on first arch 28 to 31.

A relatively large, plain black pomacentrid, somewhat resembling *Pomacentrus jenkinsi* and the adult *Abudefduf sindonis*. It differs from both of these, however, in the 14 dorsal spines.

Apparently restricted to deeper water than any of our other members of the family, seldom taken in less than 40 feet. Also one of the largest, attaining a length of some 9 inches, and frequently seen in the market.

## Family LABRIDAE (Wrasses or Hinaleas)

The Labridae is the largest family of fishes in the Hawaiian Islands, with 22 genera and 48 species so far recorded. The species are among the gaudiest of fishes, with blues, greens, yellows, and reds abundantly represented. Often the color and color pattern of the juvenile is completely different from that of the adult. For this reason the salient color characters of both the adult and juvenile stages are given in the species accounts wherever young specimens have been available. The possibility that males and females of the same species differ in color and/or morphological characters has never adequately been, but should be, investigated. It is also possible that certain so-called species are really only color varieties of the same fish.

Despite the large number of species and their brilliant coloration, the labrids do not form an especially conspicuous element in the reef-fish fauna. For one thing, the individuals are more or less solitary, and many of the species are uncommon or rare. For another, labrids keep close to bottom cover, disappearing into the coral or sand upon approach. So far as is known, all of our labrids (except *Labroides*) bury themselves in the sand at night.

**Fig. 229**

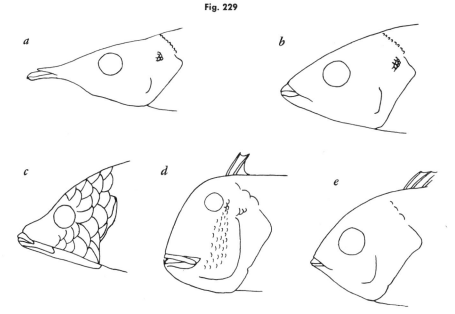

a. *Gomphosus varius.* b. *Thalassoma umbrostigma.* c. *Epibulus insidiator.*
d. *Hemipteronotus umbrilatus.* e. *Macropharyngodon geoffroyi.*

In size the members of the family vary greatly. Several of the species become adult at less than 3 inches in length, but at least one reaches a size of several feet. All labrids are carnivorous, and the members of this family form an important element in the catch of small boys fishing off the rocks. In the deeper water on the outer sides of reefs, different and larger species take a hook readily. Unfortunately, the flesh of labrids is soft, and the members of the family are not much esteemed as food. They rarely enter the Honolulu market today, although they did so formerly.

In morphological features the various labrids are extremely diverse, so that it becomes difficult to characterize the family as a whole. However, it may be distinguished from other Hawaiian fishes by the following combination of characters: pelvics separate from one another, with 4 or 5 soft rays; teeth separate, at least in the front of the jaws; caudal fin rounded, truncate, trilobate, or lunate, but never forked, with only 11 or 12 branched rays.

In view of the large number of Hawaiian species, the labrids are keyed out first to genera and then to species.

Key to the Hawaiian genera of the family Labridae:

| | | |
|---|---|---|
| 1 | Body compressed, its greatest width contained more than 2 times in the greatest depth, which in turn is contained fewer than 6 times in the standard length.................................. | 2 |
| | Body cigar-shaped, its greatest width contained about 1.5 times in the greatest depth, which in turn is contained about 7 times in the standard length...................................... *Cheilio* | |
| 2(1) | Lateral line either interrupted or with a sharp downward jog below the soft dorsal; dorsal spines 8 to 11.......................... | 4 |
| | Lateral line continuous, without a sharp downward jog below the soft dorsal; dorsal spines 12.................................. | 3 |
| 3(2) | Caudal truncate or lunate; base of dorsal and anal covered by a heavy sheath of scales made up of several scale rows.........*Bodianus* | |
| | Caudal rounded; basal sheath of scales on dorsal and anal either low or wanting....................................... *Verriculus* | |

**Fig. 230**

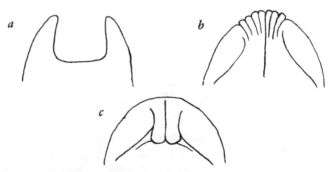

*a. Labroides phthirophagus.  b.  Thalassoma duperreyi.  c. Stethojulis axillaris.*

| | | |
|---|---|---|
| 4(2) | Lips normal, the lower without forwardly projecting lateral lobes (Fig. 230b and c), the upper without a median slit.............. | 5 |
| | Lower lip with 2 lateral lobes that project forward around a median interspace (Fig. 230a); upper lip with a median slit....*Labroides* | |

**214**

5(4) Opercle either naked (Fig. 229e) or with a patch of a few small scales above (Fig. 229 b and d); scales on body moderate to small, 26 or more in a longitudinal series; no enlarged scales on the caudal base; gill covers attached to the isthmus by a membrane..... 10

Opercle completely covered by a few large scales (Fig. 229c); scales on body large, 25 or fewer in a longitudinal series; 3 scales on the caudal base (these are easily rubbed off) that are even larger than those on body; gill covers free from the isthmus but attached to one another by a membrane that passes across the isthmus................................................... 6

6(5) Lower jaw normal, not projecting backward well behind the eye.... 7

Lower jaw bones projecting backward to within 3 scales of the pelvic origin (Fig. 229c). Not recorded north of Johnston Island................................................... *Epibulus*

7(6) Body not uniformly reddish; dorsal spines 9; preopercle not serrate................................................... 8

Body uniformly reddish in life; dorsal spines 11; preopercle serrate................................................... *Cirrhilabrus*

8(7) Preopercular edge exposed; 2 or more canines in each jaw; no large, round, black spot on the center of each pelvic fin.......... 9

Preopercular edge completely hidden by scales; no canines; a large, round, black spot on the center of each pelvic fin. Adult size: 2 inches................................................... *Wetmorella*

**Fig. 231**

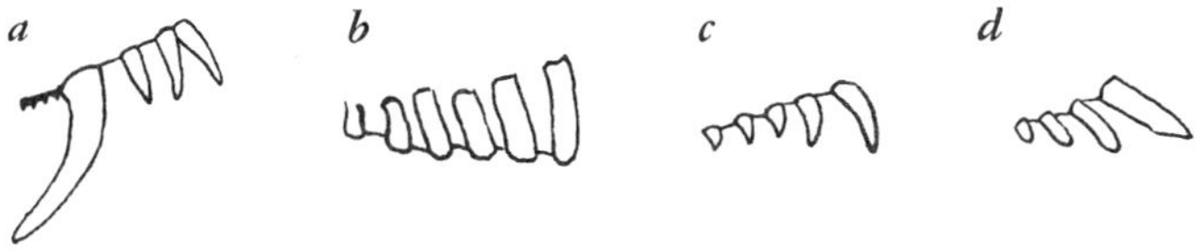

*a. Pseudocheilinus sp.   b. Stethojulis albovittata.   c. Novaculichthys bifer. d. Halichoeres ornatissimus.*

9(8) At least 3 pairs of canines in the upper jaw, the posteriormost the largest, curving backward like a pig's tusk (Fig. 231a); interorbital nearly flat, with a slight median depression; pupil of the eye double, one section lying directly in front of the other; adult size: 2 to 6 inches................................................... *Pseudocheilinus*

A single pair of downwardly projecting canines in the upper jaw; interorbital gently and evenly convex; pupil of eye normal; adult size: 5 to more than 30 inches................................................... *Cheilinus*

10(5) Eye nearer to the corner of mouth than to dorsal origin.......... 14

Eye nearer to dorsal origin than to corner of mouth.............. 11

11(10) Scales moderate, fewer than 30 in a longitudinal series; interorbital and snout with a sharp median ridge.................... 12

Scales small, more than 70 in a longitudinal series; interorbital gently convex in cross section.................................... *Cymolutes*

12(11) Cheek scaleless, except sometimes for a row of scales around the orbit.................................................... 13

Cheek more or less scaled (Fig. 229d)................. *Hemipteronotus*

13(12)  First 2 dorsal rays completely separated from the rest of the fin..*Iniistius*

First 2 dorsal rays incompletely separated from the rest of the fin, the first ray not especially elongate and equal to less than half the length of the head . . . . . . . . . . . . . . . . . . . . . . . . . . . . . . . . . *Xyrichthys*

14(10)  Upper portion of gill opening (above tip of opercular flap) not bordered by a single enlarged scale; free border of preopercle at least moderately long, its horizontal limb developed and its vertical limb usually longer than an eye diameter (Fig. 229d); dorsal spines 9 . . . . . . . . . . . . . . . . . . . . . . . . . . . . . . . . . . . . . . . .  16

Upper portion of gill opening entirely bordered by a single enlarged scale; free border of preopercle short, its horizontal limb rudimentary and its vertical limb about equal to an eye diameter in length (Fig. 229 a and b); dorsal spines 8 . . . . . . . . . . . . . . . . . . . .  15

15(14)  Jaws normal, not projecting as a birdlike beak; snout length less than postorbital head length . . . . . . . . . . . . . . . . . . . . . . . . . . *Thalassoma*

Jaws projecting as a birdlike beak (Fig. 229a); snout length equal to postorbital head length . . . . . . . . . . . . . . . . . . . . . . . . . *Gomphosus*

16(14)  Scales moderate, 35 or fewer in a longitudinal series . . . . . . . . . . . . . .  17

Scales small, 50 or more in a longitudinal series . . . . . . . . . . . . . . . . *Coris*

17(16)  Body moderately deep, the greatest depth contained less than 3.5 times in the standard length . . . . . . . . . . . . . . . . . . . . . . . . . . . .  18

Body relatively elongate, the greatest depth contained about 4.3 times in the standard length . . . . . . . . . . . . . . . . . . . . . . . . *Pseudojuloides*

18(17)  One or more pairs of enlarged teeth in the front of the jaws (Fig. 231 c and d); tip of chin without a single longitudinal ridge on either side of the midline (Fig. 230b) . . . . . . . . . . . . . . . . . . . . . . . . .  19

All of the front teeth incisiform, none of them particularly enlarged (Fig. 231b); lower lip with a longitudinal ridge on either side of the midline (Fig. 230c) . . . . . . . . . . . . . . . . . . . . . . . . . . . . *Stethojulis*

19(18)  Front pair of teeth in each jaw projecting forward at least as much as vertically (Fig. 231d); scales below pectoral reduced in size so that there are 4 or more major rows between the pectoral base and the pelvic origin . . . . . . . . . . . . . . . . . . . . . . . . . . . . . . . . . . . . .  20

Front pair of teeth in each jaw extending more vertically than forward (Fig. 231c); scales below pectoral little reduced in size so that there are only 2.5 or 3 major scale rows between the pectoral base and the pelvic origin . . . . . . . . . . . . . . . . . . . . . . *Novaculichthys*

20(19)  Numerous teeth in each jaw, all conical . . . . . . . . . . . . . . . . . . . . . . . .  21

Only 2 teeth in each jaw, these dorso-ventrally flattened and protruding almost horizontally from the front of the mouth . . . . . . *Anampses*

21(20)  Horizontal limb of free preopercular border well developed, extending forward to before middle of eye; depth moderate, contained about 3 times in standard length . . . . . . . . . . . . . . . . . . *Halichoeres*

Horizontal limb of free preopercular border short, not reaching forward to middle of eye; body deep and compressed, the greatest depth contained about 2.5 times in the standard length . . . .
. . . . . . . . . . . . . . . . . . . . . . . . . . . . . . . . . . . . . . . . . . . . . . *Macropharyngodon*

### Genus CHEILIO

The elongate form of the single species belonging to this genus is sufficient to distinguish it from all other Hawaiian labrids. Its closest affinities appear to be with the *Halichoeres*-like genera from which it differs in lacking a jog in the lateral line and in the small scales, there being about 48 in a longitudinal series in *Cheilio*.

### Fig. 232. CHEILIO INERMIS

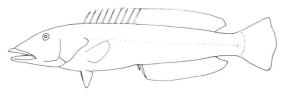

After J. and E.

**CHEILIO INERMIS (Kupoupou)**

This species is sufficiently characterized above. It is of a rather drab greenish or brownish color and is not uncommon in certain areas. Attains a length of perhaps 18 inches.

### Genus BODIANUS

*Bodianus* contains some of the largest labrids in our waters. The combination of compressed body, lateral line without a jog, and truncate or lunate caudal will distinguish it from other Hawaiian labrids.

Key to the Hawaiian species of the genus *Bodianus:*

> Profile of the snout straight in the young, rounded in the adult; no black spot on the membranes at the base of the seventh and eighth dorsal spines, though one may be present between the second and third. . . . . . . . . . . . . . . . . . . . . . . . . . . . . . .*Bodianus bilunulatus*
>
> Profile of the snout concave; a black spot on the base of the membrane between the seventh and eighth dorsal spines . . . . . . . . . .
> . . . . . . . . . . . . . . . . . . . . . . . . . . . . . . . . . . . . . . . . . .*Bodianus oxycephalus*

### Fig. 233. BODIANUS BILUNULATUS

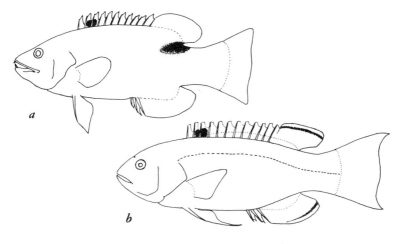

*a*

*b*

### BODIANUS BILUNULATUS ('A'awa)

The females of this species go through three color phases with growth. Curiously enough, none of the specimens we have examined have been males. Specimens up to about 4 inches long have a large black blotch extending between the soft dorsal and anal, followed abruptly by a light caudal peduncle. From 4 to 12 inches in length the body color is nearly plain red except for a horizontally elongate black spot extending forward on the body from the base of the last dorsal ray (Fig. 233a). Above 12 inches the fish is a plain bluish black (Fig. 233b).

The species attains a length of at least 2 feet and is frequently taken by hook and line at depths of 100 feet or so. It probably appears more frequently in the Honolulu market than any other labrid.

### BODIANUS OXYCEPHALUS

Known to us only from specimens recorded in the literature. It apparently differs from other species of *Bodianus* in the more elongate, piglike snout.

### Genus VERRICULUS

Appears to be very closely related to *Bodianus*, from which it differs chiefly in the characters given in the generic key. One species.

#### Fig. 234. VERRICULUS SANGUINEUS

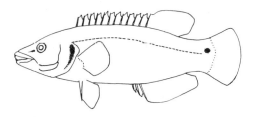

After J. and E.

### VERRICULUS SANGUINEUS

This genus and species is known from one specimen, 7.5 inches long "taken at Hilo with hook and line, in deep water." The specimen was red and yellow in life, with a small dark spot on the caudal peduncle just ahead of the tail.

### Genus LABROIDES

*Labroides* appears to be a highly specialized genus, the characters given in the generic key setting it apart quite distinctly from all other Hawaiian labrids.

### LABROIDES PHTHIROPHAGUS

This fish is perhaps the most brilliantly colored labrid in Hawaii, being a striking contrast of reddish violet and black (see Fig. 230a). It is not rare and can frequently be seen swimming in water of a few feet in depth. Attains a

**218**

length of about 5 inches and appears to have the habit of picking external parasites off larger fishes. It does not bury itself in the sand at night like other labrids but forms a gelatinous cocoon like the scarids.

### Genus EPIBULUS

*Epibulus* is unique among labrids in having a jaw structure which permits the mouth to be projected forward like a bellows. One species known.

#### EPIBULUS INSIDIATOR

This distinctive Indo-Pacific species is common at Johnston but apparently does not occur in the Hawaiian Islands (see Fig. 229e). Reaches a length of perhaps 2 feet.

### Genus CIRRHILABRUS

Differs from all other Hawaiian labrids in having 11 dorsal spines. Like *Pseudocheilinus* it has backwardly projecting tusks near the front of the upper jaw on either side.

#### Fig. 235. CIRRHILABRUS JORDANI

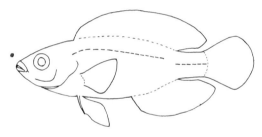

After J. and E.

#### CIRRHILABRUS JORDANI

Not known to reach a length of more than 4 inches. A rare fish, known from only two specimens. We have examined one of these, taken in a surge pool.

### Genus CHEILINUS

*Cheilinus* is probably the most familiar of the group of labrid genera with large scales covering the opercle, body, and caudal base. A further distinguishing character of this group is that they all have 8 or 9 soft anal rays instead of 11 or more. *Cheilinus* is the only genus in the group in Hawaii any of whose species reach more than about 6 inches in length. It is quite possible that more than the two species listed below occur in Hawaiian waters.

Key to the Hawaiian species of the genus *Cheilinus:*

Caudal fin rounded; no black spot behind the eye although there may be a pair of horizontal lines; size attained large......*C. rhodochrous*

Caudal trilobate, the central rays projecting in the adult; a black
spot just behind the eye; size small to about 6 inches....*C. bimaculatus*

### Fig. 236. CHEILINUS RHODOCHROUS

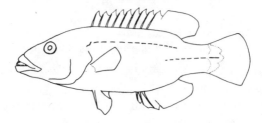

After J. and E.; see also Fig. 002c

**CHEILINUS RHODOCHROUS (Po'ou)**

Growth in this species appears to be accompanied by considerable color
change. Specimens 20 inches long are almost plain with black pelvics and dark
basal and central areas on the soft dorsal and anal. Ten-inch specimens have
no black areas on the soft dorsal and anal but have a white saddle across the
caudal peduncle; the pelvics are black basally. At 4.5 inches the fish is plain
except for the white saddle, a black spot at the base of the first dorsal spines,
and another at the base of the last soft dorsal rays; the pelvic rays are dusky.
In a specimen 2 inches in standard length the body and fins have dark markings and there are indications of 4 vertical light bars; 2 parallel lines extend
horizontally behind the eye; there is a small, intense ocellus in the middle of
the caudal peduncle.

The length attained by this species is at least 2 feet.

**CHEILINUS BIMACULATUS**

The dark spot behind the eye appears to be diagnostic. The elongation of
the central caudal rays does not occur until the fish is about 5 inches long.
The name *bimaculatus* is based on the fact that in specimens over 3 inches long
there is a second, small, intense black spot on the mid-sides.

A small but not uncommon fish, reaching about 6 inches in length.

### Genus *PSEUDOCHEILINUS*

The double eye of this genus is unique among labrids, and the lateral tusk
in the upper jaw is found elsewhere among Hawaiian forms only in *Cirrhilabrus*.
Key to the Hawaiian species of the genus *Pseudocheilinus:*

1      Four to 8 dark longitudinal bands running along the centers of
the upper scale rows.................................................. 2

No dark bands running along the centers of the scale rows..*P. evanidus*

2(1)   Body color primarily brownish; about 8 longitudinal black
bands.............................................................*P. octotaenia*

Body color primarily bluish; about 4 longitudinal black bands
...............................................................*P. tetrataenia*

### PSEUDOCHEILINUS EVANIDUS

Judging from our collections this species is rarer than the other two members of the genus. Reaches 4 inches.

**Fig. 237  PSEUDOCHEILINUS OCTOTAENIA**

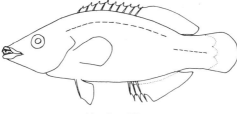

After J. and E.

### PSEUDOCHEILINUS OCTOTAENIA

In addition to the characters given in the key, this species can be separated from the other two Hawaiian members of the genus by the fact that it has 3 scale rows, instead of 2, on the cheek between the eye and the angle of the preopercle.

Attains a length of about 6 inches.

### PSEUDOCHEILINUS TETRATAENIA

The bright bluish body color is apparently sufficient to distinguish this from the other Hawaiian members of *Pseudocheilinus* (see Fig. 231a).

#### Genus WETMORELLA

A strange little genus unique in having the preopercular border completely invisible from the exterior.

**Fig. 238.  WETMORELLA ALBOFASCIATA**

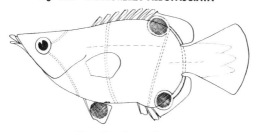

From Hawaiian specimen

### WETMORELLA ALBOFASCIATA

The coloration as well as the preopercular structure is diagnostic. There is a round, black ocellus on the dorsal and anal, a round black spot on the body under the pelvic fins, and a black blotch on each pelvic fin.

Known from one specimen about 2 inches long taken in shallow water in Kaneohe Bay.

This is the only high-headed genus of labrids in the Hawaiian Islands that has small scales. Only one species.

### CYMOLUTES LECLUSEI

The drab whitish or greenish color marked only by a small, sharply defined black spot on the upper part of the caudal peduncle just ahead of the tail is characteristic of this fish.

Not rare. Reaches at least 6 inches in length.

### Genus HEMIPTERONOTUS

*Hemipteronotus* is the only high-headed genus of labrids in Hawaii with scales on the cheek. It has the first 2 dorsal rays nearly or completely separated from the rest of the fin.

Key to the Hawaiian species of the genus *Hemipteronotus:*

> A large, diffuse black blotch on the sides, mostly or entirely below the lateral line; cheek scales in about 6 vertical rows..*H. umbrilatus*
>
> A small dark mark below the soft dorsal but above the lateral line; scales on cheek in 3 or 4 vertical rows...............*H. baldwini*

### Fig. 239. HEMIPTERONOTUS UMBRILATUS

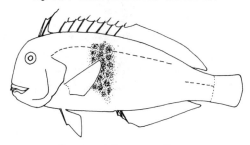

After J. and E.; see also Fig. 229

### HEMIPTERONOTUS UMBRILATUS

Reaches perhaps a foot in length.

### Fig. 240. HEMIPTERONOTUS BALDWINI

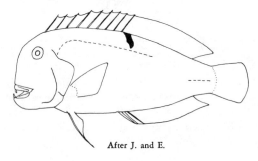

After J. and E.

### HEMIPTERONOTUS BALDWINI

This species, which we have not seen, apparently has a black spot on the anal in the young as well as the mark on the upper sides.

To at least 9 inches.

### Genus INIISTIUS

The elongate first ray in the separate first dorsal is diagnostic for this genus. Key to the Hawaiian species of the genus *Iniistius:*

> Body color in life green or gray; 3 more or less distinct crossbars
> . . . . . . . . . . . . . . . . . . . . . . . . . . . . . . . . . . . . . . . . . . . . . . . . . . . . . . . . . . . . .*I. pavoninus*
> Body color in life black or brown without crossbars . . . . . . . . . . .*I. niger*

### INIISTIUS PAVONINUS

In this species there is a single scale between the pectoral and the dorsal base that is notably darker than the others, giving a strikingly demarcated spot on the upper sides.

To at least 15 inches.

**Fig. 241. INIISTIUS NIGER**

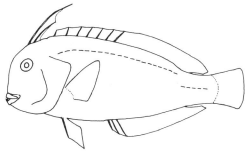

After J. and E.

### INIISTIUS NIGER

Seems to be considerably rarer than *I. pavoninus,* and is known only from a few specimens obtained in the Honolulu market.

Greatest known length 8 inches.

### Genus XYRICHTHYS

First 2 dorsal rays partly but incompletely separated from the rest of the fin. No scales on the cheek. One species known from Hawaii.

### XYRICHTHYS NIVEILATUS

A swimmer passing over sandy patches occasionally sees a fish ahead of him dive into the sand and disappear. Presumably such fishes belong to the high-headed labrid genera related to *Xyrichthys.*

Reaches a length of about 10 inches.

**Fig. 242. XYRICHTHYS NIVEILATUS**

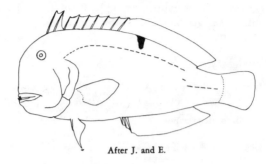

After J. and E.

### Genus THALASSOMA

*Thalassoma* is not only the largest labrid genus in Hawaii, but two of its species are as abundant as any members of the family. Morphologically, the genus has no conspicuous peculiarities, although it does differ from most related genera in the two characters given in the generic key.

One or more species of *Thalassoma* may be found in almost all clear-water inshore areas. Though one species, *T. umbrostigma*, is a cŏmmon inhabitant of deeper surge pools, most of the species are to be found in from 6 to 30 feet of water. Their proclivity for nibbling at a baited hook makes them a boon to small boys and may be responsible for the present scarcity of *T. purpureum* around the high islands.

At least one of the species, *T. duperreyi*, goes through rather drastic color changes with growth. For this and other reasons some suspicion should be directed toward the validity of those species separable only by color. Nevertheless, color is by far the easiest, and in some instances apparently the only, way of separating the Hawaiian species of *Thalassoma*. Under the circumstances, a key would largely duplicate features that are better shown by Fig. 243; the key has therefore been omitted.

### THALASSOMA FUSCUM

There are three species of *Thalassoma* that have the rows of upright rectangles along the sides shown in Fig. 243a: *T. fuscum*, *T. purpureum* (Fig. 243f), and *T. umbrostigma* (Fig. 243b). The first two of these have a coloration made up chiefly of reds and blues, whereas *T. umbrostigma* is green with black markings. The three may be further separated by the head markings: *T. fuscum* has none; *T. purpureum* has a black splotch running downward and backward from the eye that forks below; and *T. umbrostigma* has a whole series of dark spots and wormlike marks.

*T. umbrostigma* is obviously a separate species. However, the distinctness of *T. fuscum* and *T. purpureum* is open to some question. The two seem separable only on the basis of the head markings noted above. We have never seen specimens of *T. fuscum* as large as our smallest *T. purpureum*, and it seems possible that the latter is the mature adult of the former. However, our material is not adequate to prove or disprove this, as neither species is at all common about Oahu today.

T. *fuscum* is said to attain a length of 11.5 inches.

### THALASSOMA UMBROSTIGMA

This is the only greenish species of *Thalassoma* in Hawaiian waters; indeed, that feature together with the numerous, distinct dark marks on the upper

Fig. 243

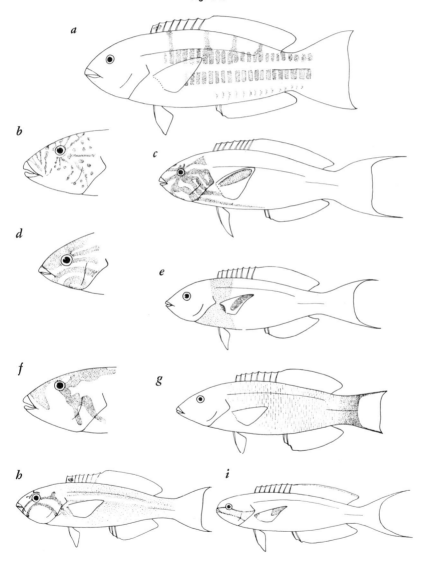

portion of the head will distinguish it from all our other labrids (see Figs. 243b and 239b).

The head markings (Fig. 243b) are diagnostic for specimens down to 50 mm. in standard length; below that size they are not present. Smaller specimens, down at least as far as 25 mm. have characteristic W-shaped marks on the sides; these are in 2 or 3 longitudinal rows, of which the one just above the middle of the sides is the most prominent.

*T. umbrostigma* is undoubtedly the commonest member of the genus in open, rocky, surge areas, frequently entering the deeper pools. It takes a hook readily. Attains a length of perhaps 11 inches.

### THALASSOMA LUNARE

We have never seen this species in Hawaiian waters, and it is included here on the basis of a single record 50 years old (see Fig. 243c).

In Line Island specimens, the adults are a bluish green with the very distinctive club-shaped mark on the pectoral shown in Fig. 243c. At all sizes the caudal peduncle is exceptionally deep and compressed, its depth being greater than the distance from the tip of the snout to the rear of the eye (in most other species of *Thalassoma* it is less). Young specimens (45 to 95 mm. in standard length) have a more or less distinct dark blotch at the base of the upper caudal rays.

Reaches about 6 inches in length.

### THALASSOMA LUTESCENS

This species is so like *Thalassoma duperreyi* in everything except color as to raise a suspicion concerning the validity of the two species (see Fig. 243d). However, the color differences are striking. *T. lutescens* has a plain yellowish body with a more or less faint series of dark vertical marks on each scale posteriorly. The head has several fairly well-defined curved dark bars (Fig. 243d).

*T. lutescens* has been recorded only a few times from Hawaiian waters. We have not seen it there, though we have taken it at Johnston. The largest recorded specimens from our area are about 7 inches long.

### THALASSOMA DUPERREYI (Hinalea lauwili, 'A'ala'ihi)

The striking light brown shoulder bar of the adults of this species is unique (see Figs. 243e and 230b). Unfortunately it disappears quickly in alcohol and is not present in the young. Indeed, the species goes through a very radical color change with growth. The adult coloration appears in specimens of 60 mm. in standard length, although the lunate caudal is not present in examples smaller than 95 mm. At 50 mm. the brown shoulder bar is not present and the fish is plain dark above the middle of sides, light below. At 35 mm. the sides are light both above and below a prominent longitudinal stripe with a width about equal to an eye diameter running just above the middle from the gill opening to the base of the caudal rays. This same stripe is prominent in a specimen 14 mm. in standard length.

*Thalassoma duperreyi* is probably the commonest Hawaiian species in the genus. It is found in some abundance both in rocky areas such as Waikiki and in pure reef areas such as Kaneohe Bay. The maximum length attained is about a foot.

### THALASSOMA PURPUREUM ('Olani, 'Olali, Palae'a, 'Awela, Hou)

For a comparison with *Thalassoma fuscum*, see the account of that species.

A large species for this genus (see Fig. 243f). The only specimen we have seen is about 15 inches long. Though it appears to have many old Hawaiian names, it seems to be rare around the high Hawaiian islands today.

### THALASSOMA BALLIEUI (Hinalea luahine)

Old specimens often become almost black, whereas the younger fishes are brownish-yellow forward, becoming darker in the region of the caudal peduncle. The vertical marks on each scale, though more noticeable in this species than any other, occur in several other members of *Thalassoma*. Except for the general darkening, there seems to be no color change with growth in *T. ballieui*, at least in specimens longer than 43 mm. in standard length.

This is one of the larger species of *Thalassoma*, attaining a length of perhaps 2 feet (see Fig. 243g).

### THALASSOMA QUINQUEVITTATA

Apparently the very small caudal fin of *T. quinquevittata* never becomes lunate (see Fig. 243h). In color the adults may be sufficiently characterized by the light lateral band and the dark bar across the posterior part of the lower jaw. The only dark mark on the dorsal lies between the first 2 spines. Below 80 mm. in standard length the adult color pattern gradually disappears and is replaced by a whole series of small dark dots, about 17 in number, at the base of the dorsal fin; of these the one at the front and another near the middle of the fin are the most prominent. In addition, specimens 32 to 50 mm. in standard length have a black spot at the base of the upper caudal rays, this being much more prominent in the smaller sizes.

An extremely small species for the genus, apparently never reaching more than about 5 inches in length. Not known north of Johnston.

### THALASSOMA MELANOCHIR

This is another species known from Hawaii on the basis of some old and perhaps questionable records (see Fig. 243i). It is a small and very distinct fish. Morphologically, it differs from all our other species of *Thalassoma* in the blunt head with the tip of the upper jaw above the level of the lower border of the eye and in lacking a median furrow under the chin. In color the adults have the very characteristic narrow lines running across the head; juveniles, however, have a single dark longitudinal band similar to that in the young of *T. duperreyi*.

The species appears to attain adult coloration at about 5 inches.

### Genus GOMPHOSUS

The tendency for the development of an elongate beak in labrids, exemplified by such genera as *Pseudocheilinus* and *Wetmorella*, reaches its maximum development in *Gomphosus*.

**Fig. 244. GOMPHOSUS VARIUS**

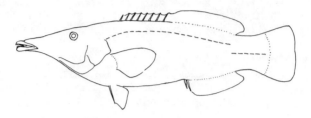

After J. and E.; see also Fig. 229a

**GOMPHOSUS VARIUS ('Aki-lolo, Hinalea 'i'iwi)**

The green and brown forms of this fish have long been considered separate species, but recent information indicates that the green fish is merely the adult male.

Attains a length of about 8 inches.

### Genus CORIS

*Coris* has no striking morphological peculiarities. On the one hand, it rather resembles the *Halichoeres* group of genera but is the only one of these with small scales. On the other, it has the general appearance of *Bodianus*, though it differs immediately in having only 9 spines in the dorsal and a downward jog in the lateral line below the soft dorsal. In coloration, *Coris* is one of the most brilliant of labrid genera. However the fact that the color may vary considerably from individual to individual and that certain species undergo a drastic color change with growth has made the classification of the species of *Coris* rather uncertain.

Key to the Hawaiian species of the genus *Coris:*

1     No longitudinal black band running from the tip of the snout to the caudal base. . . . . . . . . . . . . . . . . . . . . . . . . . . . . . . . . . . . . . . . . . . . . . . . . . . 2

A longitudinal black band running from the tip of the snout to the caudal base; other black bands running parallel to this at least above. . . . . . . . . . . . . . . . . . . . . . . . . . . . . . . . . . . . . . . . . . .*C. flavovittata*

2(1)   No black spot on the posterior tip of the gill cover. . . . . . . . . . . . . . 4

A black spot on the posterior tip of the gill cover that is strikingly darker than any other portion of the head or body. . . . . . . . . . 3

3(2)   Scales in a longitudinal series about 90; no longitudinal color bands on the anterior portion of the body. . . . . . . . . . . . . . . . . .*C. lepomis*

Scales in a longitudinal series about 60; longitudinal color bands on the anterior portion of the body in the adult. Maximum length less than 8 inches. . . . . . . . . . . . . . . . . . . . . . . . . . . . . . . .*C. venusta*

**228**

| 4(2) | Caudal yellow, contrasting strikingly with the dark body in the adult; scales in a longitudinal series about 75 . . . . . . . . . . . . .*C. gaimardi* |
|---|---|
| | Caudal with crossbars; scales in a longitudinal series about 54 . . . . . . 5 |
| 5(4) | Color bluish; first dorsal spine about as long as head . . . . . . . .*C. ballieui* |
| | Color reddish; first dorsal spine less than half the length of the head. . . . . . . . . . . . . . . . . . . . . . . . . . . . . . . . . . . . . . . . . . . . . . . . . . . .*C. rosea* |

### CORIS FLAVOVITTATA (Hilu)

The longitudinal black bands are diagnostic for this species throughout life. In the adult they are restricted to the upper sides but below 130 mm. in standard length the whole body is banded.

Reaches perhaps 18 inches in length.

### CORIS LEPOMIS (Hilu lauwili)

The only specimen of this species available to us is 21 inches long. In addition to a roundish black spot about the size of the eye on the gill cover, it has a series of alternating oblique black and green bars on the lower sides.

To at least 2 feet in length; specimens less than a foot long do not seem to have been recorded.

### CORIS VENUSTA

Extremely variable in coloration. In the adult a bright red band running from the edge of the gill cover to slightly beyond the tip of the pectoral fin is characteristic. There is also another, narrower band that curves up on either side of the nape to below the spinous dorsal. Specimens below 50 mm. in standard length lack these bands as well as those on the head and have instead about 5 more or less prominent dark crossbars extending down from the back.

The species apparently does not reach more than about 6 inches in length.

### CORIS GAIMARDI (Lolo)

A most strikingly colored species at all stages, though both color and color pattern change radically with growth. The adult can easily be distinguished by the abruptly yellow tail. At 90 mm. in standard length this is still present, but there are also traces of the juvenile banding on the snout. Up to 60 mm. in standard length this is a brick-red fish except for 5 black-bordered white areas extending down from the back plus a black line across the caudal base.

Attains at least a foot in length.

**Fig. 245. CORIS BALLIEUI**

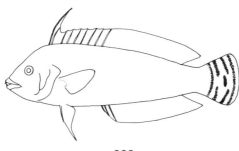

### CORIS BALLIEUI

A series of light blue spots running along the upper scale rows is characteristic.

Our only specimen is about 14 inches long.

### CORIS ROSEA (Malamalama)

Provisionally, we follow previous authors in recognizing *Coris ballieui* and *C. rosea* as distinct species. The latter is always red rather than blue, but it seems highly possible that the characters separating the two are due merely to differences in sex and maturity.

The largest specimens of *C. rosea* known are about 10 inches long.

### Genus PSEUDOJULOIDES

*Pseudojuloides* contains elongate labrids with rather pointed snouts. As in *Stethojulis* (Fig. 230c) a forward ridged section of the chin is separated from a posterior smooth section by a cross-furrow. *Pseudojuloides* differs immediately from *Stethojulis*, however, in having a pair of canines at the front of each jaw.

### Fig. 246. PSEUDOJULOIDES CERASINUS

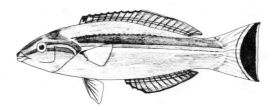

### PSEUDOJULOIDES CERASINUS

Among the four specimens available to us, two very different color patterns are present. The two smaller individuals, 3.5 and 3.8 inches in total length, in life were a plain bright red except for the yellowish tail and a dark mark between the first 2 dorsal spines. The two larger, 4.1 and 4.3 inches long, have the color pattern shown in Fig. 246. The ground color of these specimens was slaty blue. It is quite possible that these represent a different species, although we can find no morphological differences between them. All of our specimens were speared in about 100 feet of water.

### Genus STETHOJULIS

The species of this genus rather resemble small parrot fishes. The presence of incisiform teeth, which in the upper jaw leave a toothless gap in the middle, with the total absence of enlarged canines at the front of the jaws, is diagnostic. The two Hawaiian species can also be distinguished from all other labrids by the color characters given in the species key below.

Key to the Hawaiian species of the genus *Stethojulis:*

One or more small black dots along the middle of the caudal peduncle; no broad red band on sides....................S. *axillaris*

No small black dots along the middle of the caudal peduncle; a broad reddish or orange, blue-bordered band along the sides.
.......................................................S. *albovittata*

## STETHOJULIS AXILLARIS ('Omaka)

The 2, frequently 1 or 3, small black dots along the middle of the caudal peduncle are present from a very small size up (see Fig. 230c). In other color characters, however, there is considerable change with growth. Down to a standard length of 60 mm. the sides are plain greenish-brown, sometimes with white dotting, and besides the black dots on the caudal peduncle there is a cream-colored patch just above the pectoral base. Specimens smaller than 60 mm. are light green, and the light patch above the pectoral base is absent; instead, small black marks at the base of the last dorsal and anal rays and on the upper surface of the snout become prominent.

The species apparently never gets to be more than about 5 inches long. It is by far the most abundant labrid in certain areas.

### Fig. 247. STETHOJULIS ALBOVITTATA

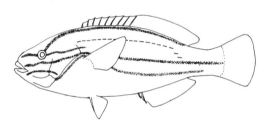

After J.and E.; see also Fig. 231b

## STETHOJULIS ALBOVITTATA

The red band along the sides makes this a very conspicuous and easily identified fish. It is not rare, but is less frequent than S. *axillaris*. Grows to a somewhat larger size, perhaps 7 inches, and we have never seen small specimens.

### Genus NOVACULICHTHYS

A moderately high-headed labrid intermediate in this respect between *Hemipteronotus* and its allies and the normal labrid type as represented by *Stethojulis*, etc. Two of the Hawaiian species are rather similar and quite different from the third.

Key to the Hawaiian species of the genus *Novaculichthys:*

1      Dark lines radiating from the eye; pelvics black................. 2

       No dark lines radiating from the eye; pelvics light..........N. *woodi*

2(1)   Four black lines radiating from the eye.................N. *taeniourus*

       About 8 black lines radiating from the eye..................N. *bifer*

**231**

### NOVACULICHTHYS WOODI

Aside from coloration this species differs from *N. bifer* and *N. taeniourus* in having a higher head, falcate pectorals with the upper rays much the longest, and the outer soft pelvic rays elongate. The small, intense, black spot on the membrane between each pair of dorsal spines will immediately distinguish this species from all other adult Hawaiian labrids.

Reaches about 7 inches in length.

**Fig. 248. NOVACULICHTHYS TAENIOURUS**

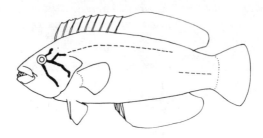

After J. and E.

### NOVACULICHTHYS TAENIOURUS

This species and *N. bifer* appear to differ only in color. In both, the first 2 dorsal rays may or may not be produced into elongate filaments, the pectorals are rounded with the upper rays little longer than the lower, and none of the pelvic rays are elongate.

Aside from the number of stripes leading from the eye, it differs from *N. bifer* in having the light bar at the base of the caudal of equal width throughout and in lacking alternating light and dark areas along the dorsal and anal, though both of these fins have numerous light spots.

To at least 10 inches.

### NOVACULICHTHYS BIFER

The major color differences between this species and *N. taeniourus* have been noted above. Actually *N. bifer* is exceedingly variable in coloration, ranging from a light grass green to a brownish black.

A smaller species than the other two members of the genus, reaching only about 6 inches in length.

### Genus MACROPHARYNGODON

A genus of deep-bodied fishes of rather small size. The chief peculiarity of the genus is its few large pharyngeal teeth. One species known from Hawaii.

### MACROPHARYNGODON GEOFFROYI (Hinalea 'aki-lolo)

This fish may be usually seen in about 30 feet of water. It apparently never gets to be more than about 5 inches long.

**Fig. 249. MACROPHARYNGODON GEOFFROYI**

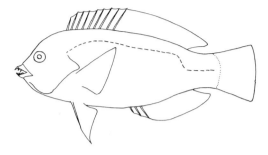

After J. and E.; see also Fig. 229e

### Genus ANAMPSES

The teeth of *Anampses* will immediately distinguish it from all other Hawaiian fishes. There are only 4 teeth in the mouth, 2 above and 2 below, and these are dorso-ventrally flattened and protrude almost horizontally from the front of the jaws.

The species of the genus are among the most colorful of Hawaiian fishes, and two of them reach more than a foot in length.

Key to the Hawaiian species of the genus *Anampses*:

1 White or blue spots or lines on the center of each scale; head and body essentially similar in coloration . . . . . . . . . . . . . . . . . . . . . . . . . 2

 No light spots or vertical lines on the center of each scale; head abruptly light, with bluish spots and bands . . . . . . . . . . *A. chrysocephalus*

2(1) Outer two-thirds of caudal not plain red in life; anal fin with 5 or 6 narrow, green, horizontal bands; depth of body contained about 2.7 times in the standard length . . . . . . . . . . . . . . . . . . . . . . . 3

 Outer two-thirds of caudal plain red in life; anal fin black except for a single row of small white spots anteriorly; depth of body about 3.5 times in standard length . . . . . . . . . . . . . . . *A. rubrocaudatus*

3(2) Each scale with a round blue spot . . . . . . . . . . . . . . . . . . . . . . . *A. cuvieri*
 Each scale with a narrow, vertical, light line . . . . . . . . . . . . . *A. godeffroyi*

## ANAMPSES CHRYSOCEPHALUS

The strongly contrasting color of the head and body will immediately distinguish this species. It differs further in having a plain dark brown or black tail, somewhat lighter basally.

Only three specimens of the species are known. Two of these were taken in traps; the third was speared in about 100 feet of water. The largest is about 7 inches long.

## ANAMPSES RUBROCAUDATUS

The bright red tail of this species will immediately distinguish it. In the white spotting of the body it resembles *Anampses cuvieri*.

**233**

Only a few specimens about 4 inches long are known, all of them taken in about 100 feet of water. Verbal information indicates that it is brought in by trap fishermen from time to time but has hitherto been confused with *A. cuvieri*.

### ANAMPSES CUVIERI ('Opule, Hilu)

Any shallow-water labrid with prominent, round, light spots on the center of each scale is undoubtedly this species. Specimens smaller than 3 inches long lack the spotting. A 2-inch specimen is a plain, light green and has a prominent black, oval ocellus on the base of the last dorsal and anal rays; it retains the tooth characters of the adult *Anampses*.

One of our commoner labrids. Single specimens can be frequently seen in rather shallow water. Attains a length of about 15 inches.

### ANAMPSES GODEFFROYI

Quite similar to *Anampses cuvieri*, except that a narrow vertical line replaces the round light spots on the scale centers.

Rather infrequent, but apparently inhabiting the same areas as *A. cuvieri*. Only large specimens, 10 to 15 inches in length, are known. It is possible that this "species" is made up of the adult males of *A. cuvieri*, but our material is insufficient to check this.

#### Genus HALICHOERES

A well-known and abundant genus of labrids throughout the Indo-Pacific. For some reason only one species occurs in Hawaii.

Fig. 250. HALICHOERES ORNATISSIMUS

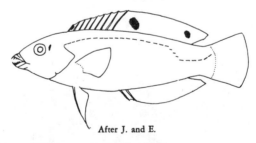

After J. and E.

### HALICHOERES ORNATISSIMUS (La'o, 'Ohua, Pa'awela)

A rather gaudy species, but quite variable in coloration. The small black mark behind the eye is, however, always present and will serve to distinguish this species from all other labrids except *Cheilinus bimaculatus*. Not uncommon in about 20 feet of water, attaining a length of perhaps 7 inches.

## Family SCARIDAE (Parrot Fishes or Uhus)

The combination of beaklike jaw teeth and large scales on the body (about 24 in a longitudinal series) will immediately identify most of our uhus to family. The species of *Calotomus* and *Scaridea*, which have the beak made up of many series of teeth fused at the base in the adult, are, when young, difficult to distinguish from certain of the large-scaled labrids. However, unlike the labrids, they have overlapping series of incisiform teeth at the front of both jaws even in specimens as small as 2 inches long.

Though the uhus are known to every spearfisherman in Hawaii, the classification of species within the family remains chaotic. The various species all have approximately the same lateral-line scale counts and fin counts. On the other hand, the scarids differ strikingly in color. Consequently color has been used almost exclusively in the description of species. Thus one whole series of green and another whole host of brown species have been described. However, recent investigations have strongly indicated that the green *Scarus perspicillatus* consists only of males. Following this lead, we sexed all of the green individuals available to us, and they all turned out to be males. The brown forms include immatures, females, and males. Apparently, some, or perhaps all, of our species of scarids have a gray, red, or brown phase in which maturity is reached in both sexes; however, old males become green whereas old females undergo no change in color. The same phenomenon has been demonstrated in at least one tropical labrid.

With the confusion that reigns in the classification of Hawaiian scarids, it has seemed best to us to recognize in this handbook only those species which we have been able to differentiate morphologically on the basis of specimens examined. Under this approach, some good species of Hawaiian scarids will probably have been omitted altogether; some of the species we recognize may turn out to contain complexes of two or more species. Nevertheless we prefer these risks to a continuation of the old system whereby the different stages of male maturity were classified as different species and each color variation was given a different specific name.

(For a revision of the members of this family on a world-wide basis, which has appeared since the present account was written, see Schultz, L.P., 1958, Review of the Parrotfishes Family Scaridae, U.S. National Museum Bulletin 214.)

Tentative key to the Hawaiian species of the family Scaridae:

1    Jaws in front made up of a hard beak from which no individual teeth protrude. . . . . . . . . . . . . . . . . . . . . . . . . . . . . . . . . . . . . . . . . . .  3

      Outer surface of jaws in front made up of numerous separate teeth which may be fused at base. . . . . . . . . . . . . . . . . . . . . . . . . . . . .  2

2(1)    Caudal fin with a narrow light border; dorsal spines flexible, without sharp tips. . . . . . . . . . . . . . . . . . . . . . . . . . . .*Calotomus sandvicensis*

      Caudal fin without a light border; dorsal spines sharp-tipped, though the tips may be covered by flesh. . . . . . . . . . . . .*Scaridea zonarcha*

3(1)    Three or 4 scales on the middorsal line in front of the dorsal fin. . . .  4

      Five or 6 scales on the middorsal line in front of the dorsal fin. Three rows of scales on the cheek. . . . . . . . . . . . . . . . . . . . . .*Scarus paluca*

4(3)    Lower limb of preopercular border relatively little developed (Fig. 253), the length of its free edge (measured to the point at which the border runs vertically) less than the distance from its most anterior point to the mid-ventral line; canine teeth at the corners of the mouth, if present, low and knoblike . . . . . . . . . . . . . .     5

Lower limb of preopercular border relatively elongate (Fig. 251), the length of its free edge greater than the distance from its anterior end to the mid-ventral line; adults usually with 1 to 3 conspicuous conical, pointed canines at the corners of the mouth. Two complete scale rows on the cheek with sometimes a third, incomplete row below; maximum size about 14 inches . . . . *Scarus dubius*

5(4)     Lower of the 2 scale rows on the cheek, if present, incomplete, consisting of 1 to 3 scales; head relatively small, its length considerably less than the greatest depth of body . . . . . . . *Scarus perspicillatus*

Lower of the 2 scale rows on the cheek almost as long as the upper, consisting of 5 to 7 scales; head relatively long and bullet-shaped, its length about equal to the greatest depth of body . . .
. . . . . . . . . . . . . . . . . . . . . . . . . . . . . . . . . . . . . . . . . . . . . . . . . . . . *Scarus sordidus*

### CALOTOMUS SANDVICENSIS

Four species of the genus *Calotomus* have been described from the Hawaiian Islands on the basis of color differences. Until some better distinguishing characters are found, there seems no certainty that more than one is represented.

All of our specimens, which range from 2 to 17 inches in total length, have a light border to the caudal, but this is about the only color marking that remains constant. The 2-inch specimen is a light grass green (a common, if not universal, coloration in scarids this size); it has a black bar across the base of the pectoral rays, 2 white bars across the chin, rather indefinite light cross-barring on the caudal, a dark blotch on the base of the pelvic rays, and several dark marks along the anal base; the teeth in the front of both jaws are in two irregular series of incisors so oriented that their tips form a single cutting edge; the snout is pointed; and the tail is rounded. A specimen 5.3 inches long differs chiefly in the gray-brown body coloration, in the more numerous teeth in the jaws, the slightly lunate caudal, the black blotch at the base of the last dorsal rays, and in the vague dark mark between the first 2 dorsal spines. In individuals 7.3 to 10.3 inches long the barring on the chin disappears, the snout becomes blunter, and the outer caudal rays more elongate. Our 17-inch specimen is in the green phase; it has no dark bar on the pectoral base but a series of white lines radiating from the eye.

Not uncommon. The largest recorded length is 20 inches.

### SCARIDEA ZONARCHA

If there is a large green phase for this species, it remains unknown in Hawaiian waters. Two species of the gray phase have been differentiated largely on the basis of color, but we are unable to recognize more than a single species in our material, which consists of four specimens, 2.3 to 9 inches in total length. All of these are more or less spotted and speckled. In the two specimens smaller than 3 inches long the body and fins are light (they were probably greenish in life) whereas in the two nearly 9 inches long the fins especially are much darker. Even in the two larger individuals the caudal fin is rounded. Of the two larger, one has a dark body with an arc of white spots along the edge of each scale, whereas the other has a dark spot at the base of each scale.

These two specimens may represent different species, but more and better preserved material will be necessary to determine this.

Judging from our material and from the literature, *Scaridea* is not common about Hawaii.

### SCARUS PALUCA

We provisionally identify as this species two large individuals which have in common the 2 distinctive characters given in the key. Aside from this the two specimens bear little resemblance to one another. The smaller, a male 13 inches in total length, is a rather cylindrical fish, the width going into the depth about 1⅔ times; in alcohol it is gray with dark spots on many of the scale centers. The larger, a spent female 28 inches long, was plain reddish brown in life, and is a more compressed fish, the greatest width going more than 2 times into the depth.

**Fig. 251. SCARUS DUBIUS**

### SCARUS DUBIUS

The young and half-grown of this species seem to be unique among our species of *Scarus* in that the lips completely cover the jaws when the mouth is closed and the jaws are retracted. However, the tooth plate is partially exposed if the jaws are even partially protruded (as in Fig. 251). The adults may be separated from our other species in the genus (except *S. paluca*) by the sharp canines at the corner of the mouth. Still another distinguishing character is the pectoral count. Excluding the very short splint above, the counts for our specimens of *Scarus* are as follows: usually 13 in *S. dubius*, nearly always 14 in *S. perspicillatus* and *S. sordidus*, and 15 in one specimen of *S. paluca*. In specimens 8.5 inches and over the outer caudal rays become considerably prolonged, more so than in any of our other species.

Immatures, females, and young males are dull brown to black in color. By contrast, old males are very striking. Two rather different color patterns are represented among the green individuals that we here assign to *Scarus dubius*. Both have the following features in common: 2 green bars across chin, a narrow one across the lip and a broader one just behind the lip; a green bar across upper lip continued backward to behind eye; the outer pelvic and caudal rays bright green, bordered abruptly inside by lighter; and a light band on the

**237**

base of the dorsal and the anal. A specimen 12 inches long differs from another 14 inches long, however, in the following features: a mid-ventral green bar extending from the throat to the anal origin; 2 indefinite green bars radiating from the back of the eye instead of a well-defined narrow bar passing through and interrupted by the upper portion of the eye; and an evenly bordered bar on the dorsal and anal as contrasted with 1 with extremely wavy borders. (The color pattern of the smaller specimen is essentially that shown in Günther's 1914 plate 155 of *Pseudoscarus forsteri*, whereas the larger is well represented by Jordan and Evermann's 1905 color plate 42 of *Scarus lavia*.)

One of our commonest scarids, attaining about 14 inches in length.

### Fig. 252. SCARUS PERSPICILLATUS

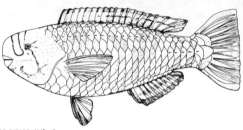

### SCARUS PERSPICILLATUS (Uhu)

Apparently our only *Scarus* with an incomplete second row of scales on the cheek. It is a deep-headed, compressed fish attaining a large size. Old males, 16 inches and over, have a very distinctive dark band running across the snout and down to below the eyes (as indicated in Fig. 253). Females are almost a plain red brown.

Perhaps our commonest species, reaching at least 2 feet in length.

### Fig. 253. SCARUS SORDIDUS

### SCARUS SORDIDUS

A small species with a relatively long, bullet-shaped head for which the dorsal and ventral profiles are about equally convex. The tooth plates of *Scarus sordidus* take on a greenish tinge in specimens more than about 5 inches long. The brown form often has a white band across the caudal peduncle with a black spot in the middle of it. Old males are green with an ill-defined darker area behind the eye.

Not uncommon. Apparently never exceeds more than about a foot in length.

## Family AMMODYTIDAE

The Hawaiian species of this family most closely resembles certain species of the Gempylidae in the elongate form, single long dorsal, and the absence of pelvic fins. However, the ammodytid has about 100 small scales in a longitudinal series; the incomplete lateral line runs close to the back; and there are no teeth.

### BLEEKERIA GILLII

*Bleekeria gillii* is obviously an offshore species (see Fig. 146). Only two Hawaiian specimens are known. The individual we have examined was taken from aku spewings. Both specimens are about 3 inches long.

## Family CHAMPSODONTIDAE

This family is represented in Hawaii by one species (see Fig. 88) known only from water over 700 feet deep. It has a number of peculiar features: for example, only 4 spines in the first dorsal fin and none in the anal; the scales each with a projecting flap; 2 longitudinal lateral lines with numerous cross-connections between them; preopercle with enlarged spines at the angle; and gill cover with a wide, membranous, coarsely fringed margin.

## Family PARAPERCIDAE

The family Parapercidae is represented in Hawaii by three poorly known species from rather deep water. They may be distinguished from other families by the following combination of characters: lateral line present, single, and complete, running along or above the middle of the sides for its full length; no bony stay across cheek; anal fin without spines and with 18 to 25 soft rays; caudal fin not forked; pelvic fins inserted ahead of pectorals and with the middle or inner rays longest; head and body scaled.

Key to the Hawaiian species of the family Parapercidae:

1      Spinous and soft dorsal fins connected; soft dorsal longer than anal; cheek at least partially scaled . . . . . . . . . . . . . . . . . . . . . . . . . . . . . 2

        Spinous and soft dorsal fins completely separate; soft dorsal shorter than anal; cheek scaleless . . . . . . . . . . . . . . . *Pteropsaron incisum*

2(1)    Caudal lunate; a deep notch in the outline of the dorsal fin between the spinous and soft portions . . . . . . . . . . . *Parapercis schauinslandi*

        Caudal rounded; outline of dorsal fin not notched between the spinous and soft portions . . . . . . . . . . . . . . . . . . . . . . *Neopercis roseoviridis*

### PTEROPSARON INCISUM

A small, large-eyed fish with about 30 cycloid scales in a longitudinal series. The anterior separate dorsal fin is composed of only 4 spines.

Dredged in several localities, all over 500 feet deep. To somewhat over 2 inches in length.

Unlike the last species, the spinous dorsal is partially attached to the soft portion by a low membrane and the scales in a longitudinal series number about 60. The series of dark spots along the dorsal fin is very distinctive.

Attains a length of about 7 inches. We have one specimen speared in about 100 feet of water, though the species is apparently common in deeper water.

### NEOPERCIS ROSEOVIRIDIS

The continuous, unnotched dorsal fin distinguishes this species from our other known members of the family (see Fig. 110).

Recorded from two specimens about 3 inches long taken in about 600 feet of water.

## Family BEMBROPSIDAE

A family of rather deep-water fishes. It resembles the Parapercidae in appearance but differs in having the lower jaw projecting and the lateral line running posteriorly well below the middle of the body. In the latter character it resembles the Trichonotidae, but the bembropsids always have 2 separate dorsal fins.

Key to the Hawaiian species of the family Bembropsidae:

1    Eye diameter about equal to snout length; second dorsal fin with 16 rays.................................................... 2

     Eye diameter contained nearly twice in snout length; second dorsal fin with 14 rays.............................*Bembrops filifera*

2(1)  Anal fin with 24 rays...........................*Chrionema chryseres*

      Anal fin with 18 rays........................*Chrionema squamiceps*

### BEMBROPS FILIFERA

Known from two specimens, the largest 9 inches long, dredged in over 1000 feet of water.

### CHRIONEMA CHRYSERES

Known from a single specimen, 8 inches long, dredged in about 1000 feet of water.

### CHRIONEMA SQUAMICEPS

One specimen from about 600 feet of water, a little over 2 inches long (see Fig. 87).

## Family TRICHONOTIDAE

The members of this family are small fishes that dive headlong into the sand and disappear at the slightest provocation. The pointed snout and fringed lip appear to be adaptations to life in the sand. The Hawaiian members of the family are unique in that the lateral line runs along the anal base and terminates behind the base of the last anal ray.

Two Hawaiian forms known.

Key to the Hawaiian species of the family Trichonotidae:

> Body scaleless except for the lateral-line series; dorsal and anal rays each about 37 . . . . . . . . . . . . . . . . . . . . . . . . . . . . . . . . *Crystallodytes cookei*
>
> Body completely scaled; dorsal and anal rays each about 24 . . . . . . . . . . . . . . . . . . . . . . . . . . . . . . . . . . . . . . . . . . . . . . . . *Limnichthys donaldsoni*

### CRYSTALLODYTES COOKEI

This elongate little fish seems to be abundant along shore in sandy areas (see Fig. 102). Whether it normally lives in the sand or just above the sand is unknown. About the only fish from the same habitat that it could be confused with is *Kraemeria bryani*, but the latter has a projecting lower jaw.

Attains a length of perhaps 4 inches.

### LIMNICHTHYS DONALDSONI

This seems to be a deeper-water counterpart to *Crystallodytes cookei*. It is known in Hawaii from only two specimens about 1 inch long taken in about 30 feet of water.

## THE MOORISH IDOLS AND SURGEONFISHES

The members of this suborder (Acanthuroidei) are distinguished from the typical sea basses primarily by a specialization in the head skeleton. The two families included also have in common the deep body, the small terminal mouth, and the shagreen-like scales. The kihikihi (moorish idol) resembles the butterfly fishes in the flexible teeth and omnivorous food habits, whereas the surgeonfishes are mostly herbivorous, cropping off algae with their peculiar incisiform teeth.

### Family ZANCLIDAE

The kihikihi or moorish idol is the only species in this family. The body of this fish is orbicular, somewhat deeper than long, with the snout projecting. The teeth are flexible; the first dorsal rays are greatly prolonged; and the markings consist chiefly of broad, bold, vertical black and yellow bands. The only fishes with which the kihikihi might be confused are the chaetodontids of the genus *Heniochus*. In these, however, the body is longer than deep and, unlike *Zanclus*, have no black on the tail.

### ZANCLUS CANESCENS (Kihikihi, Moorish idol)

When young this species has a knifelike spine behind each corner of the mouth (see Fig. 98). These, however, drop off when the fish is about 3 inches long. In old adults a pair of hornlike protuberances develop in front of the eyes.

A conspicuous and fairly common fish, often to be seen in water as shallow as 5 feet. Reaches a length of about 7 inches.

## Family ACANTHURIDAE (Surgeonfishes)

### (By JOHN E. RANDALL)

The surgeon fishes or tangs (manini, pualu, maiko, kole, la'i-pala, kala, etc.) are characterized by a single sharp folding spine or pair of fixed spines at the base of the tail. These spines may inflict deep gashes; therefore, these fishes should be handled cautiously. Surgeonfishes feed on algae (limu) and represent one of the most abundant families of Hawaiian fishes. Their late larval stages are transparent with silvery abdomen; they are scaleless with narrow vertical ridges on the body; and the caudal spine(s) are rudimentary. A painful sting may result from being stuck with the dorsal, anal, or pelvic spines of these larvae. According to fishermen, the poisonous nature of these spines is retained in the adult of at least some species of *Naso* (kala).

The identification of the larval fishes may be difficult. In these, counts of the spines of the dorsal and anal fins and of the pelvic fin rays readily separate the genera. Counts of the soft rays of the fins and the size at transformation to the juvenile stage are useful in distinguishing the larval forms of some of the species. When known and when diagnostic, these characters will be included in the discussion of individual species.

The one record by Fowler of *Acanthurus gahhm* (as *Hepatus nigricans*) from the Hawaiian Islands appears to be an error, and this species has been omitted from the following account. *A. gahhm* is similar to *A. olivaceus* (na'ena'e), but has a black horizontal bar on the shoulder instead of a dark-edged orange bar.

Key to the Hawaiian fishes of the family Acanthuridae:

| | | |
|---|---|---|
| 1 | A spine folding forward into a groove on each side of caudal peduncle; pelvic fin with an initial spine and 5 rays; 3 anal spines; 4, 5, 8, or 9 dorsal spines............................... | 2 |
| | Two fixed spines or bony tubercles on each side of caudal peduncle; pelvic fin with an initial spine and 3 rays; 2 anal spines; 6 (rarely 5) dorsal spines................................... | 17 |
| 2(1) | Dorsal fin with 8 or 9 spines; dorsal and anal fins not high, the first soft ray of the dorsal fin contained 4.5 to 7.5 times in standard length...................................... | 3 |
| | Dorsal fin with 4 or 5 spines; dorsal and anal fins high, the first soft ray of the dorsal fin contained 2 to 3.7 times in the standard length...................................... | 16 |
| 3(2) | Teeth lobate, not freely movable, and not numerous (not more than 24 in lower jaw); 9 dorsal spines......................... | 4 |
| | Teeth elongate with tips slightly expanded, freely movable, and numerous (more than 30 in lower jaw of specimens over 70 mm. long); 8 dorsal spines................................... | 15 |
| 4(3) | Body not light gray and not crossed with 6 vertical black bars; 22 to 29 soft rays in the anal fin........................... | ·5 |
| | Body light gray, crossed with 6 vertical black bars (the first on head passing through eye); 20 to 22 soft rays in the anal fin... .............................................*Acanthurus sandvicensis* | |
| 5(4) | Posterior half of body without white spots; body without 3 broad vertical pale bands; body depth not great, the greatest depth contained 1.7 to 2.2 times in the standard length........... | 6 |

Posterior half of body and dorsal and anal fins with numerous white spots on a brown background; body with 3 broad vertical pale bands; body depth great, the greatest depth contained 1.4 to 1.5 times in the standard length..................*Acanthurus guttatus*

6(5)    Body not black and without a pale band basally in dorsal and anal fins; 23 to 28 soft rays in the dorsal fin; 22 to 26 soft rays in the anal fin............................................... 8

Body black with a single pale (orange or yellow in life) band basally in dorsal and anal fins, this band becoming broader posteriorly; 28 to 33 soft rays in the dorsal fin; 26 to 29 soft rays in the anal fin.................................................. 7

**Fig. 254**

7(6)   Body with a large elliptical pale yellow (orange in life) spot pos-
       teriorly, enclosing caudal peduncle spine (this pale area absent in
       specimens less than about 65 mm. in length); no pale area under
       eye; pale line on chin not extending above corner of mouth; 29
       to 33 soft rays in the dorsal fin....................*Acanthurus achilles*

       Body without a large pale spot posteriorly; a pale area under eye;
       pale line on chin extends above corner of mouth; 28 to 31 soft
       rays in the dorsal fin......................*Acanthurus glaucopareius*

8(6)   A black spot at base of the last dorsal and anal rays (anal spot
       small in *A. leucopareius*); 14 or fewer upper teeth (except large
       *A. leucopareius* which may have 16)...........................   9

       No black spot at base of the last dorsal and anal rays; 16 to 22
       upper teeth in adults........................................   11

9(8)   No pale vertical band, broadly bordered in dark brown, on pos-
       terior part of head; body not deep, greatest depth about 1.8 to
       2 in standard length.........................................   10

       A pale vertical band, broadly bordered in dark brown, on pos-
       terior part of head (see Fig. 254d); body moderately deep,
       greatest depth about 1.7 in standard length......*Acanthurus leucopareius*

10(9)  Caudal fin strongly lunate, caudal concavity (the horizontal dis-
       tance from the posterior tip of the upper lobe of the caudal fin to
       the most anterior portion of the hind margin of the fin) con-
       tained 4.5 to 6 times in the standard length (see Fig. 254g); a
       definite black edge around caudal peduncle spine groove; white
       posterior margin of caudal fin relatively broad, its width con-
       tained about 2 times in pupil of eye; black spot at rear base of
       dorsal fin large, its greatest diameter contained less than 2 times
       in the diameter of the eye.....................*Acanthurus nigrofuscus*

       Caudal fin not strongly lunate, caudal concavity contained 6.7
       to 11 times in the standard length (see Fig. 254h); no black edge
       around caudal peduncle spine groove; white posterior margin of
       caudal fin narrow, its width contained 3 to 4 times in pupil of
       eye; black spot at rear base of dorsal fin not large, its greatest di-
       ameter contained more than 2 times in diameter of eye.........
       ..........................................*Acanthurus nigroris*

11(8)  Snout not short, the distance from edge of eye to front of upper
       lip contained 4 to 5.2 times in standard length; no dark brown
       spot extending below axil of pectoral fin......................   12

       Snout short, the distance from edge of eye to front of upper lip
       contained about 8 times in standard length; a dark brown spot
       extending slightly below axil of pectoral fin.......*Acanthurus thompsoni*

12(11) No horizontal, black-edged, yellow bar on shoulder; 25 to 27 soft
       rays in the dorsal fin; 24 to 26 soft rays in the anal fin............   13

       A horizontal, black-edged, yellow (orange in life) bar on shoul-
       der region above and just posterior to gill opening in adults
       (the young lack the bar but are distinctive in being solid
       orange-yellow in life); 23 to 25 soft rays in the dorsal fin; 22 to
       24 soft rays in the anal fin....................*Acanthurus olivaceus*

13(12) Caudal fin marked with numerous blackish spots; sheath of
       caudal spine white and in sharp contrast to black surrounding
       caudal spine groove; a pale (yellow in life) band crossing or
       nearly crossing interorbital space from eye to eye; body with
       numerous, fine, slightly wavy, light blue, lengthwise lines.....
       ..........................................*Acanthurus dussumieri*

       Caudal fin not marked with numerous blackish spots; sheath of
       caudal spine brown; no pale band crossing interorbital space (a

pale yellow area may extend anterior to eye but not as a definite band); body without numerous, slightly wavy, light blue lines (although rows of spots or very irregular gray lines may be visible)...................................................... 14

14(13)  Dorsal fin with about 4 lengthwise dark (blue in life) bands; outer ⅓ of pectoral fin pale (yellow in life) and contrasting with darker basal ⅔ of fin (in specimens over about 120 mm. in standard length); caudal spine usually small, its length about 4.5 to 5.5 in the head length.....................*Acanthurus xanthopterus*

Dorsal fin with about 8 lengthwise dark (blue in life) bands; pectoral fin uniform brown; caudal spine usually not small, its length about 3 to 4.2 in the head length............*Acanthurus mata*

15(3)  A pale (yellow in life) ring around eye; posterior margin of caudal fin moderately concave; membranes of pectoral fin hyaline.... ...............................................*Ctenochaetus strigosus*

No pale ring around eye; posterior margin of caudal fin truncate or slightly emarginate; membranes of pectoral fin dark brown ...............................................*Ctenochaetus hawaiiensis*

16(2)  Body uniformly pale (bright yellow in life), without bands or other contrasting markings; dorsal fin with 5 spines and from 23 to 25 rays...............................*Zebrasoma flavescens*

Body dark brown with 5 vertical pale yellow bands; dorsal fin with 4 spines and from 30 to 32 rays..............*Zebrasoma veliferum*

17(1)  Caudal peduncle spines and a broad area surrounding each spine not paler than rest of body; preopercular grooves continuous under chin; no pale band from corner of mouth to eye; a horn or bony prominence may or may not be present on forehead......... 18

Caudal peduncle spines and a broad area surrounding each spine pale (orange in life); preopercular grooves not continuous under chin; a pale (yellow in life) band from corner of mouth to eye; no horn or bony prominence present on forehead........*Naso lituratus*

18(17)  A definite horn or bony prominence present on forehead in all but young; teeth not small, central teeth as long or longer than greatest diameter of posterior nasal opening.................... 19

No horn or bony prominence present on forehead; teeth small, their length about half the greatest diameter of posterior nasal opening.......................................*Naso hexacanthus*

19(18)  Pectoral rays 17 or 18; distance from upper edge of upper lip along profile to lower edge of horn of adults about equal to the diameter of the eye...................................... 20

Pectoral rays 15 or 16; distance from upper edge of upper lip along profile to lower edge of horn about half the diameter of the eye.......................................*Naso brevirostris*

20(19)  Caudal spines blackish (blue in life); 6 dorsal spines; axis of horn above center of eye; posterior margin of pectoral fin not paler than rest of fin......................................*Naso unicornis*

Caudal spines not blackish; 5 dorsal spines; axis of horn below center of eye; posterior margin of pectoral fin broadly white and contrasting with basal dusky portion of fin............*Naso annulatus*

## ACANTHURUS SANDVICENSIS (Manini, Convict tang)

The manini is readily distinguished from other surgeonfishes by its pale color and vertical black bars (see Fig. 254a). It has fewer fin rays (dorsal IX,

23 or 24; anal III, 20 to 22) than any other species of *Acanthurus* and the smallest caudal spine.

*A. sandvicensis*, known only from Hawaii, differs from the widely distributed *A. triostegus* (Africa to the Gulf of California, but not Hawaii) in the greater length of the mark at the base of the pectoral fin and slightly higher dorsal and anal fin ray counts. Here regarded as a species, *sandvicensis* could also be treated as a subspecies of *triostegus*.

The manini is the most abundant of Hawaiian surgeonfishes and occurs in nearly all habitats occupied by reef fishes. It may be seen singly, in small aggregations, or in large schools. Like other surgeonfishes it grazes on algae most of the time during the day and is quiescent at night.

In the Hawaiian Islands, manini spawn from early December to late July. The eggs are pelagic, about .7 mm. in diameter, and contain a single oil globule. Hatching occurs in about 24 hours and feeding commences on the fifth day. The late larval form enters shallow water where it transforms to the juvenile stage. Transforming fish are found in tide pools on Oahu from the middle of February to early October, thus the duration of larval life is estimated at 2½ months.

The late larval stage enters shallow water from the pelagic realm only at night and predominantly during the time of new moon. The fluctuation in abundance of incoming young is probably due to cyclic spawning by adults rather than any direct lunar effect on the young. The period of transformation requires about 4 to 5 days, the first obvious alteration being the appearance of the vertical dark bars on the body and the last the complete formation of the scales. The toxic quality of the second dorsal, second anal, and pelvic spines is lost on the third day. During transformation, the digestive tract lengthens nearly three-fold, reflecting the change-over in food habits from feeding on zooplankton to feeding on algae.

The young are highly resident to the shallow-water area which they first enter as larvae. With increasing size the juveniles show a progressive tendency to move into deeper water. Recovery of tagged adults has indicated that this species remains in the same general area and does not normally make extensive migrations along the reef.

Growth of juveniles is rapid, about 12 mm. (½ inch) per month. As the fish become larger, the rate of growth diminishes; a 100 mm. manini increases less than 2 mm. per month, and a 120 mm. fish about 1 mm. per month. During winter months in the Hawaiian Islands growth of juveniles and adults ceases completely.

The largest of over 2000 adult manini from Oahu measured nearly 9 inches in total length.

### ACANTHURUS GUTTATUS

The white spots, 3 vertical white bars, deep body, and nearly truncate tail preclude the confusion of this species with any other (see Fig. 254b). The dorsal soft rays are 27 to 30. In life, the pelvic fins are bright yellow. It occurs in inshore turbulent water and is often seen in small schools. Attains nearly

12 inches. The transforming young have occasionally been taken in tide pools, their size averaging about 35 mm. in standard length.

### ACANTHURUS ACHILLES (Paku'iku'i, Achilles tang)

The adult paku'iku'i is unmistakable with its black body and large, vivid orange, elliptical spot which encloses the caudal spine; however, fish less than about 2½ inches in length lack the orange spot and might be confused with *Acanthurus glaucopareius* (see Fig. 254c). The latter has an elongate white spot just under the eye whereas *achilles* has a white marking at the edge of the gill cover; *achilles* has a more lunate caudal fin and the highest number of dorsal soft rays (29 to 33) of any species of *Acanthurus*.

Paku'iku'i are found inshore in moderately turbulent water of exposed reef areas. Large individuals may be as long as 10 inches. The transforming young are unusually large, about 60 mm. in standard length. They have round, dark brown spots on the body, mostly dorsally.

### ACANTHURUS GLAUCOPAREIUS

This species, black with bright yellow at the base of the dorsal and anal fins (this band of color broader posteriorly), is abundant in the South Pacific but rare in Hawaii (see Fig. 254f). It is closely related to *Acanthurus achilles* (see above), and appears to occupy approximately the same habitat. Like *achilles* it has few teeth, adults with at most 10 in the upper jaw and 12 in the lower. Dorsal soft rays 28 to 31. Attains 8 inches.

### ACANTHURUS LEUCOPAREIUS (Maikoiko)

The white, near vertical band behind the eye, broadly bordered in dark brown, is the most characteristic feature of this common species (see Fig. 254d). A white band may be seen at the base of the tail and a small black spot occurs at the rear base of the dorsal fin. In life, faint bluish longitudinal lines are visible, which are fewer in number and more evident in smaller fish. On the upper part of the body these lines consist of rows of spots. Dorsal soft rays 25 to 27 (usually 26). Large adults reach a length of 10 inches and have as many as 16 upper and 20 lower teeth. Transformation of the larvae occurs at a standard length of about 33 mm. Formerly believed to be restricted to the Hawaiian Islands, it is now known to occur at Marcus Island and Easter Island. Usually seen in relatively shallow water on reefs and may occur in schools.

### ACANTHURUS NIGROFUSCUS

This species is frequently confused with *Acanthurus nigroris*. The best means of separation lie in the shape and color of the caudal fin and the size of the black spots at the rear base of the dorsal and anal fins (see Fig. 254 g). In life *nigrofuscus* is lavender brown with small orange spots on the head. Both species have from 24 to 27 soft dorsal rays (usually 25 for *nigrofuscus* and 26 for *nigroris*), transform to the juvenile stage at a standard length of about 34 to 40 mm., and as adults have at most 14 upper and 16 lower teeth.

*A. nigrofuscus* is probably second in abundance among reef surgeonfishes in Hawaii only to the manini. It is a small species, rarely exceeding 7 inches in total length.

### ACANTHURUS NIGRORIS (Maiko)

When alive, *Acanthurus nigroris* is dark brown with narrow, irregular, longitudinal, blue lines on the body (see Fig. 254h). The median fins are brownish yellow with lengthwise dull blue bands. A white band is usually evident at the base of the tail. See section above on *nigrofuscus* for further discussion of this species.

*A. nigroris* is a common reef fish and reaches a length of 10 inches.

### ACANTHURUS THOMPSONI

*Acanthurus thompsoni* is dark olive drab in life with a dark brown spot at and extending slightly below the axil of the pectoral fin (see Fig. 254e). The dorsal and anal fins have a narrow dark blue margin and submarginally 2 or 3 narrow yellowish brown bands. The snout is short, the body moderately elongate (depth about 2.3 in standard length), and the caudal fin lunate. The mouth is small and the teeth small and numerous, about 20 in the upper and 24 in the lower jaw.

A rare species, it has been observed in Hawaii at depths from 40 to 90 feet. It has been seen singly and in small aggregations, and may swim well off the bottom when not disturbed, unlike other species of *Acanthurus*. Although most of the fish appear nearly black underwater, some may be light bluish gray. Probably does not exceed 8 inches in length.

### ACANTHURUS OLIVACEUS (Na'ena'e)

The adult na'ena'e is easily identified by the large, elongate, dark-edged, bright orange band on the body extending posteriorly from the upper end of the gill opening (see Fig. 254i). The young are also distinctive in being entirely orange-yellow. The change-over in color from solid yellow to brown takes place at a length of about 2 inches. The number of dorsal and anal soft rays are fewer than any species except the manini, 23 to 25 in the dorsal and 22 to 24 in the anal fin. The size at transformation is about 29 mm. in standard length.

Large adults develop a convexity to the dorsal profile of the snout, this being more prominent in the male. The same is true to a lesser degree of the three species which follow below. Also characteristic of the na'ena'e and these three species is a large, subspherical, gizzard-like stomach. Considerable inorganic sediment is usually found in the diet.

The na'ena'e is common around reefs where much of the bottom is sandy. It reaches a length of at least 12 inches.

### ACANTHURUS DUSSUMIERI (Palani)

*Acanthurus dussumieri*, *A. xanthopterus*, and *A. mata* are the largest species of the genus *Acanthurus*, large individuals exceeding 18 inches in length (see Fig. 254j). All have relatively numerous teeth; adults have as many as 20 upper and 22 lower teeth. Individuals as small as 45 mm. in standard length have 14 or more teeth in the jaws. Juveniles or preserved specimens of these three species may be difficult to distinguish, since adult color pattern affords the easiest separation. *A. dussumieri* has a slightly larger eye than either of the other species when individuals the same length are compared. Usually *A. dussumieri* has 25 anal soft rays, whereas the other two species generally have 24. Degree of concavity of the caudal fin, size of caudal spine, and number of gill rakers are useful in separating *A. dussumieri* from *xanthopterus* (see below).

The palani is a colorful fish with its black-spotted, bright-blue caudal fin, fine blue lines on the body, yellow interocular band, white caudal spine broadly edged in black, and yellow dorsal and anal fins (banded with blue like *A. mata* when young, these bands persisting distally in the fins into small adult size).

Although it ranges from southern Japan through the Philippines and East Indies to South Africa and occurs in Australia, *A. dussumieri* is known from Oceania only in the Hawaiian Islands where it is a very common species and forms a major component of the surgeonfish catch of trap fishermen. Fishermen handle this fish with special care, for it is prone to inflict wounds with its long caudal spine. The palani occurs in bays and outer reef areas.

### ACANTHURUS XANTHOPTERUS (Pualu)

This wide-ranging species (Western Mexico to South Africa) is probably the largest of the genus, attaining a length of about 20 inches (see Fig. 254k). Its most distinguishing color markings are the yellow of the outer third of the pectoral fin and the 3 or 4 lengthwise blue bands of the brownish yellow dorsal and anal fins. The body is usually uniform purplish gray; however, the fish may rapidly assume a color phase in which highly irregular, dark purplish gray lines (of about 2 scales in width) alternate with lighter lines of about the same width.

*A. xanthopterus* has a more lunate caudal fin than *A. dussumieri* or *A. mata*, and a smaller caudal spine. The length of the caudal spine is contained about 4.5 to 5.5 times in the head length (the spine is relatively longer in longer fish). Over the same size range the spine length of *A. dussumieri* and *A. mata* is contained about 3 to 4.5 times in the head length). Although difficult to obtain, a count of the number of gill rakers provide a helpful separation of *A. xanthopterus* from *A. mata* or *A. dussumieri*. *A. xanthopterus* has from 17 to 22 rakers on the first gill arch (including all rudiments); *A. dussumieri* has from 23 to 26; *A. mata* has 20 to 26 (usually 21 to 23).

Unlike most species of *Acanthurus*, *xanthopterus* is often taken with hook and line. It is found in bays and harbors and in deeper outer reef areas.

### ACANTHURUS MATA (Pualu)

*Acanthurus mata* bears the same Hawaiian name as *A. xanthopterus;* nevertheless, most commercial fishermen distinguish the two species (see Fig. 254l). The differences between them and between *mata* and *A. dussumieri* are discussed in the two previous species accounts.

*A. mata* is dark greenish gray with close-set lengthwise rows of small lighter gray spots on the body. The caudal fin is dark blue with indistinct dark vertical wavy lines in the middle and a white band at the base; a prominent yellow spot occurs between the eye and the upper end of the gill opening; there are 8 or 9 lengthwise blue lines in the dorsal and 5 or 6 in the anal fins; the pectoral fin lacks yellow color and is uniform brown in preservative. Under water this species appears almost black except for the white band at the base of the tail.

*A. mata* is a relatively common species in Hawaii and is most prevalent in clear water well offshore and away from harbors.

### CTENOCHAETUS STRIGOSUS (Kole)

The kole belongs to a genus of surgeonfishes characterized chiefly by numerous tiny elongate teeth and 8 dorsal spines. The teeth are movable and appear to function in the picking up of fine detrital algal material from the bottom. The kole's most distinctive color marking is a yellow ring around the eye. The body is brown with numerous light blue longitudinal lines which extend diagonally out on the basal part of the dorsal and anal fins. There are small blue spots on the head. One of the most abundant of inshore reef fishes in Hawaii, this species appears to be rare elsewhere in Oceania where another species, *Ctenochaetus striatus*, is a dominant form. The kole is a small species, not exceeding 7 inches in length. The standard length at transformation is about 27 mm.

### CTENOCHAETUS HAWAIIENSIS

This species is known only from the island of Hawaii where it is moderately abundant in deeper water and is often seen in schools. It is dark olive brown with numerous yellowish gray lengthwise lines on the head and body. Underwater it appears black. Attains a length of at least 10 inches.

### ZEBRASOMA FLAVESCENS (Lau'i-pala, Yellow tang)

The lau'i-pala is entirely bright yellow in life except for a white sheath which encloses the caudal spine. Juveniles are also solid yellow without dark markings. Transformation occurs at a standard length of about 22 mm. Adults do not exceed 8 inches in length. This species appears to be more common on leeward sides of islands.

### ZEBRASOMA VELIFERUM (Sailfin tang)

Although *Z. flavescens* has very elevated dorsal and anal fins, those of *Z. veliferum* are exceedingly high, resulting in the common name, sailfin tang. The head and body of the sailfin tang have alternating narrow yellowish and broad brown vertical bands. The snout is covered with small yellow spots. It is not as common as the lau'i-pala, and is seen more often in bays than more exposed areas. Attains a length of about 15 inches.

## NASO LITURATUS

The most colorful of the Hawaiian species of *Naso*, *N. lituratus* has a curved yellow stripe running from the eye to the corner of the mouth, a bright blue band at the base of the dorsal fin, and a bright orange area around the prominent, forward-curved, caudal spines. The bright color around these spines, like that of the paku'iku'i (*A. achilles*) and the blue of the spines of *N. unicornis*, probably functions as warning coloration. A long filament develops from the upper and another from the lower lobe of the caudal fin of adult males of *N. lituratus*. This species is more common on reefs in relatively shallow than in deeper water. It probably reaches about 15 inches in length.

## NASO HEXACANTHUS

Like *N. lituratus*, *N. hexacanthus* never develops a horn or prominence on the forehead. There are 17 (rarely 18) pectoral rays. The color in life is either dark olive gray or light purplish blue. The caudal fin is dark blue shading to greenish posteriorly. The dorsal and anal fins are brownish yellow with light blue lengthwise bands. This species usually occurs in large schools, individuals of which may be seen well above the bottom. It is more common in relatively deep water (i.e., more than 30 feet), and judging from the catch of trap fishermen, it is the most abundant species of the genus in Hawaiian waters. Reaches a length of at least 20 inches.

## NASO BREVIROSTRIS

*N. brevirostris* is one of the horned species of *Naso*, and, its scientific name notwithstanding, the horn is long in large adults. The horn is lacking in the young, although a prominent bump on the forehead of specimens as small as 6 inches clearly indicates the future site of the horn. There are 16 (rarely 15) pectoral rays. The color in life is dark greenish gray with numerous vertical rows of small dark spots or short lines on the side of the body (these dark markings may not persist in preservative). Dorsal and anal fins are grayish brown with dark mottlings basally. The outer third of the caudal fin is greenish. Attains a length of at least 18 inches.

## NASO UNICORNIS (Kala, Unicorn fish)

Although the Hawaiian name "Kala" appears to be applied most specifically to this species, it is often used for the other species of *Naso*. *N. unicornis* is light olive drab in color. The dorsal and anal fins have alternate bands of light blue and brownish yellow. The caudal spines are light blue. The horn, which first becomes evident (as a bony prominence) at a length of about 5 inches, originates at the level of the eye. There are usually 18 pectoral rays. Transformation occurs at a standard length of about 65 mm., and the young are occasionally taken in tide pools. In spite of their large size (up to 2 feet), adults are prone to enter shallow water, apparently to feed on algae, such as *Sargassum* and other leafy types.

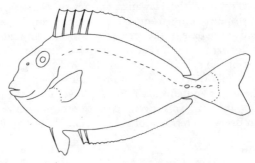

**Fig. 255. NASO ANNULATUS**

**NASO ANNULATUS**

This species is included here with some doubt, for no specimens have been examined, and its record from Hawaii is based entirely on a single small specimen originally described as *Naso incipiens* ( Jenkins). Most authors assign a dorsal spine count of 5 to the species, a characteristic which would serve to separate it from other species of *Naso* in the Hawaiian Islands which have 6 dorsal spines. The dorsal fin has a submarginal black line and a narrow white margin. The pectoral and caudal fins have broad white margins. The axis of the horn is below the center of the eye. There are 17 or 18 pectoral rays.

## THE GEMPYLID FISHES

The gempylid fishes (suborder Trichiuroidei) differ from the Percoidei in the fixed premaxillaries. In this they resemble the tunas, but the tunas have in addition a very specialized tail structure.

### Family GEMPYLIDAE

An exceedingly variable family of high-seas fishes, many of which grow to a considerable size. The following characters are held in common by Hawaiian gempylids: coloration black or silvery; scales small or absent; lower jaw more or less projecting beyond the upper; vomer with backwardly slanting, fanglike teeth; and one or more finlets behind the dorsal and anal.

Key to the Hawaiian species of the family Gempylidae:

1      Scales smooth or absent; lateral line prominent..................2

        Skin covered with bony tubercles; lateral line obscure...*Ruvettus pretiosus*

2(1)    Five to 7 finlets behind the soft dorsal and anal; pelvic fins with a spine and 3 to 5 soft rays....................................3

        A single finlet behind the soft dorsal and anal; pelvic fins consisting of a single spine only................*Promethichthys prometheus*

3(2)    Spinous dorsal short, of about 9 spines; lateral line undulating. ......................................*Lepidocybium flavobrunneum*

        Spinous dorsal long, of about 28 spines; lateral line straight... ..............................................*Gempylus serpens*

### RUVETTUS PRETIOSUS (Walu)

*Ruvettus pretiosus* is a large fish of circumtropical distribution first described from the Mediterranean (see Fig. 72). In some areas it once supported a considerable deep-water hook-and-line fishery, but appears to be rarely taken around Hawaii.

Attains a length of perhaps 5 feet. We have never seen it.

**Fig. 256. PROMETHICHTHYS PROMETHEUS**

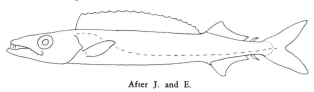

After J. and E.

### PROMETHICHTHYS PROMETHEUS

This oceanic species was first described from the Atlantic. Several specimens about 15 inches long have been recorded from Hawaiian waters. We have an additional smaller specimen.

### LEPIDOCYBIUM FLAVOBRUNNEUM

This fish resembles the tunas at first glance, but can readily be distinguished by the wavy lateral line and the enlarged vomerine teeth (see Fig. 74). It is occasionally taken around Hawaii by the long-line tuna fishermen.

Attains a length of about 4 feet. Two specimens examined.

### GEMPYLUS SERPENS (Hauliuli-puhi)

An elongate, snakelike fish with large fangs, occasionally taken in the open sea about Hawaii. Reaches at least 3 feet in length.

## THE MACKERELS, TUNAS, SPEARFISHES, AND THEIR ALLIES

The members of this group comprise the suborder Scombroidei of the order Perciformes. They can be distinguished from all other fishes by the tail structure, for the bases of the caudal rays completely overlap and conceal the caudal skeleton (in other fishes the caudal rays merely articulate with the edge of the caudal skeleton). Thus, in the scombroids the end of the vertebral column and the tail form a single, nearly inflexible unit instead of the normal hinged junction. This specialization is merely one of the numerous adaptations for a fast swimming life in the high seas. All of the members of the suborder are predators and many are large.

### Family SCOMBRIDAE (Tunas and Mackerels)

Members of this family possess finlets, 5 or more in number; 9 or more spines in the first dorsal fin; and do not have any lateral bony scutes. Many species have a median lateral keel on the caudal peduncle.

**253**

The mackerels and tunas, together with the billfishes and broadbill sword-fish, are characteristically fishes of the high seas, the pelagic zone. The true mackerels are, by and large, temperate-water species that sustain important commercial fisheries where they occur abundantly. A single species occurs in Hawaii, which is more abundant in the leeward than in the main islands of the group. The tunas represent the culmination of the family of mackerels in size and in their adaption for life in the open ocean. Although some, like the giant bluefin and the albacore, occur as far north as the coast of Norway or in the Gulf of Alaska during the summer months, tunas are essentially fish of tropical and subtropical waters. They are schooling fish, and the schools may be for some species, such as the skipjack, of great size at some seasons and places. They are all carnivorous fishes, feeding upon others or on squid, crustacea, or other creatures of the high seas. As far as is known, spawning occurs in the waters of the open ocean, where minute eggs are laid. These soon hatch into tiny transparent larvae, very different in appearance from the adult.

These fishes are of great commercial value, being by far the most important group of species landed from tropical waters. In Hawaii, the tunas account for more than 80 percent of the total catch taken by commercial fishermen.

Key to the Hawaiian species of the family Scombridae:

1     Gill filaments separate; gill rakers present...................... 2

Gill filaments fused into a net; no gill rakers. Ono...........
.................................Fig. 257a, *Acanthocybium solandri*

**Fig. 257a. ACANTHOCYBIUM SOLANDRI**

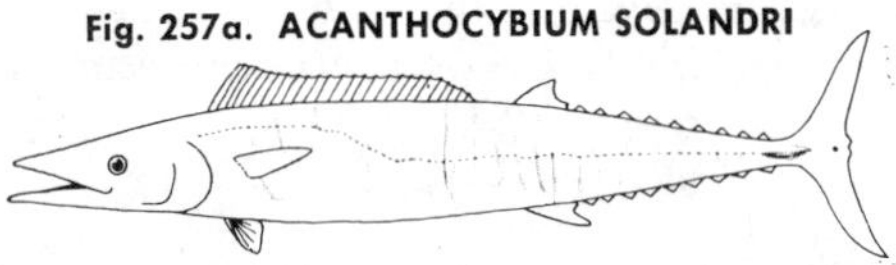

2(1)    Eye without transparent gelatinous membrane over outer portions; 7 or more finlets present............................. 3

Eye with transparent gelatinous membrane over outer portions;
5 finlets present. Mackerel...............Fig. 257b, *Scomber japonicus*

3(2)    Body completely scaled, scales may be enlarged in corselet and
lateral line....................................................... 7

Body naked, without scales, except for scaly corselet and lateral
line........................................................... 4

4(3)    The last spine in the first (spinous) and the first ray in the second
(soft-rayed) dorsal fins close together, separated by a distance
equal to about $\frac{1}{5}$ of head length........................... 6

The first and second dorsal fins far apart, separated by a distance
equal to about $\frac{1}{2}$ the head length or more.................... 5

5(4)    Corselet scales along lateral line 2 to 4 scale rows wide under
origin of second dorsal. Corselet abruptly tapering to narrow
band of 3 to 4 scales along lateral line at midway between first
and second dorsals. Total gill-raker count of first gill arch 37 to
43. Frigate mackerel......................Fig. 257c, *Auxis thazard*

Corselet scales along lateral line in a wide band 7 to 12 irregular
scale rows wide under origin of second dorsal. Corselet tapers
gradually and evenly throughout length, ends under about second dorsal finlet. Total gill-raker count of first gill arch 44 to 48.
.................................................*Auxis thynnoides*

**254**

6(4)  Four dark longitudinal stripes present below lateral line on lower surface of side and on belly. Aku........Fig. 257d, *Katsuwonus pelamis*

No dark longitudinal stripes below lateral line, about 12 dark wavy streaks on back. Kawakawa............Fig. 257e, *Euthynnus yaito*

7(3)  Gill rakers more than 20 in number on upper and lower branch of first gill arch........................................  8

Gill rakers less than 15 on upper and lower branch of first gill arch; back with a pattern of longitudinal wavy dark bands. Bonito................................ .......Fig. 257f, *Sarda orientalis*

8(7)  Gill rakers on upper and lower branch of first gill arch fewer than 32 in number, usually fewer than 30..........................  10

Gill rakers on upper and lower branch of first gill arch 36 to 39 in number; pectoral fin does not reach to a vertical through second dorsal fin insertion. Bluefin tuna.............................. ............................Fig. 257h, *Thunnus thynnus orientalis*

9(8)  Anal finlets with yellow or orange color; a vertical line through tip of pectoral fin usually falls anterior to front of anal fin base, at least in larger specimens of over 70 or 80 pounds.............  11

Anal finlets dusky without yellow or orange color; a vertical line through tip of pectoral fin usually falls posterior to end of anal fin base; size medium to small, rarely more than 70 or 80 pounds, usually much less. Albacore..............Fig. 257i, *Thunnus alalunga*

10(9) Dorsal and anal finlets a clear yellow, very narrowly black-edged; some large individuals of this species may have elongate second dorsal and anal fins, reaching nearly to the caudal fin or beyond; number of gill rakers on upper and lower limb of first gill arch usually 30 (27 to 31); liver without marginal striations. Yellowfin tuna..............................Fig. 257j, *Thunnus albacares*

Dorsal and anal finlets with a broad black border, anal finlets often with an orange rather than yellow color; second dorsal and anal fins never greatly elongated, a little longer than the longest spines of the first dorsal fin and much shorter than pectoral fin; number of gill rakers on upper and lower limb of first gill arch usually 27 (24–29); liver with marginal striations. Bigeye tuna ............................................................*Thunnus obesus*

### ACANTHOCYBIUM SOLANDRI (Ono, Wahoo)

A long, slender mackerel or tuna-like fish, dark blue in color on the back with about 30 irregular dark purplish gray bars on the sides (see Fig. 257a). The gills are without rakers or filaments, like a fine net. The head is slender and sharp-pointed; the mouth has rather close-set, triangular-shaped teeth. It reaches a weight of 120 pounds; the average fish caught in Hawaii weighs around 30 pounds.

It is seemingly circumtropical in distribution, the same species apparently occurring on both sides of the Pacific and in the Atlantic Ocean.

The ono is a pelagic species, solitary in habit, living in the isothermal (pelagic zone) upper water layer of the tropical ocean. It is a carnivorous species, frequently with fragments of aku in the stomach when taken in Ha-

Fig. 257

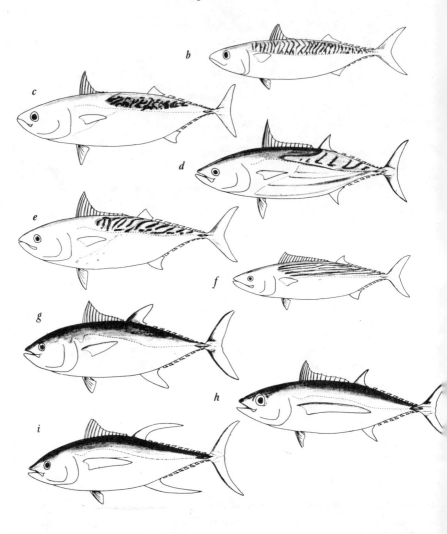

b. *Scomber Japonicus; c. Auxis thazard; d. Katsuwonus pelamis; e. Euthynnus yaito; f. Sarda orientalis; g. T. thynnus orientalis; h. Thunnus alalunga; i. Thunnus albacares.*

waiian waters, and feeding largely on fish (90%) and to a minor extent on cephalopods (10%).

The ono is taken usually by trolling and is regarded as a fine food fish; one meaning of the Hawaiian word ono is "to have sweet taste." The amount taken in Hawaiian waters by commercial fishermen has varied from 30,000 to 40,000 pounds for the last few years.

### SCOMBER JAPONICUS (Japanese mackerel, Saba)

This species resembles a tuna in its possession of finlets, but, unlike any of the tunas, it has a transparent membrane covering much of the outer portions of the eye (see Fig. 257b). The back is bluish green, with about 30 darker irregular, vertical bands, more or less branched. The body is covered with small scales of about equal size.

Japanese mackerel are occasionally taken about the main islands of the Hawaiian groups, being not rare in some years, such as 1957. This species appears to be more numerous in the leeward islands; however, it is of slight economic value in Hawaii. It feeds on smaller fish and various planktonic invertebrates. Spawning occurs in May in Japan, according to Kishinouye.

### AUXIS THAZARD (Frigate mackerel, Keokeo)

A small tuna-like fish with wavy oblique bars on the posterior ⅗ of the back, a silvery belly without markings and the interspace between the first and second dorsal fins greater than the longest dorsal fin spine (see Fig. 257c). The frigate mackerel is generally less than 10 pounds in weight. The frigate mackerel is often hooked when fishing kawakawa. No food studies of this species have yet been made in Hawaii; however, it is carnivorous and pelagic in habitat.

The commercial importance is slight. Occasional catches are made of this species sometimes mixed with schools of kawakawa.

### AUXIS THYNNOIDES

The species closely resembles the frigate mackerel in size, appearance, and probably in habits. Fish identified as this species, mixed with a school of frigate mackerel, were recently taken in Hawaiian waters by the U. S. Fish and Wildlife Service.

### KATSUWONUS PELAMIS (Aku, Skipjack, Striped tuna, Oceanic skipjack, Katsuwo)

A small tuna with a plump streamlined body, short pectoral fin and longitudinal dark stripes on a silvery belly (see Fig. 257d). Dorsal XII + XVII, 11–14, 8 finlets. Anal 11–15, 7 finlets. Gill rakers 15–20 + 36–39, very thin, their inner margin undulating. Vertebrae 41 in number.

The aku approaches 40 inches in length and 50 pounds in weight. This is a pelagic fish of the open tropical sea, entering subtropical and temperate areas during the warmer months of the year. Circumtropical in distribution.

The spawning period in Hawaii begins in March or April and closes sometime in September. It is possible that individual fish spawn a number of times during this period. The rate of growth is rapid, an average length of 45 centimeters being attained by the end of the first year, 70 centimeters by the end of the second, and 80 centimeters by the end of the third. Seemingly very few aku live longer than this.

The aku is a carnivorous fish feeding upon the crustacea, squid, and small fishes of the open ocean. The relative importance of these foods as found in a number of aku stomachs examined by the Fish and Game Division was: fish, 72 percent of the food mass; cephalopods, 22 percent; and crustacea, 5 percent.

This is a schooling species, occasionally occurring in schools of enormous size; ordinarily, however, they are composed of 10 tons or less of fish. The schooling fish usually move rapidly and erratically in pursuit of food, driving the smaller creatures upon which they feed from the depths to the surface, where flocks of sea birds, largely noddy terns, join the pursuit and incidentally serve to mark the location of aku schools for the fishermen.

This species is one of the most pelagic of the tunas, and may be expected to occur wherever water temperatures are suitable, without direct regard to the presence of land. The abundance of this species through its range is probably related to the abundance of suitable food organisms, which by way of food chains depend upon the relative concentration of nutrient salts and finally upon the hydrographic situation.

This species sustains the most important Hawaiian fishery—landings averaged 9,000,000 to 14,000,000 pounds per annum for the past few years. The catch is largely utilized for canning; however, an important part is consumed fresh.

Aku is taken about the Hawaiian Islands throughout the year; however, the fishery is ordinarily supported, except during the summer months, by small fish of 5 to 12 pounds in weight, which are a year or a little more in age. During the summer months schools of larger fish occur, fish averaging between 18 to 22 pounds and of two years or more in age. It is these fish which supply the bulk of the catch during the summer season; without them the Hawaiian fishery would not be productive nor particularly profitable.

**EUTHYNNUS YAITO (Kawakawa, Little tuna, Black skipjack, Bonito)**

A small tuna with a pattern of a dozen wavy oblique dark bands on the back (see Fig. 257e). Aside from a corselet of scales, on the anterior portion of the side, the body is naked. There are usually a few round dark spots on the head and below the pectoral fins on the side.

A small species rarely exceeding 30 inches in length. The average weight of fish landed in Hawaii is around 4 to 5 pounds. This is an Indo-Pacific species, found from Japan and the Philippines through Oceania to the Hawaiian Islands.

The kawakawa is an inshore pelagic species not taken remote from land. The food of this species is, by bulk, more than half crustacea—largely crab and 'alo'alo larvae—the remainder being largely fish, with a small volume of cephalopods. A large portion of the food animals are reef- or bottom-dwelling species, indicating that kawakawa does forage for food away from the surface.

The species is of minor importance in the record of commercial landings; the catch was 23,000 pounds in 1954, 40,000 in 1955, and 61,000 in 1956.

## SARDA ORIENTALIS (Bonito)

A small tuna-like fish with dark longitudinal bands on the back and a silvery belly, and the body entirely covered with small scales (see Fig. 257f). Reaches a weight of about 7 pounds.

This bonito is an Indo-Pacific species, not common in Hawaii. It apparently does not occur in the eastern Pacific where the related *Sarda chilensis* occurs.

Where abundant this species is usually found in coastal waters. Its comparative rarity around Hawaii may be a reflection of the lack of continental coastal conditions. No studies have been made of the feeding or reproductive habits of this species in Hawaii.

Commercial importance is slight. It is not segregated from other small tuna-like fishes in the catch statistics.

## THUNNUS THYNNUS ORIENTALIS (Bluefin tuna, Black tuna, Maguro)

This species is rare in Hawaiian waters being occasionally landed by longline fishermen (see Fig. 257g). It is characterized by short pectoral fins, small eye, a sharp bend in the lateral line, and alternate rows of transverse colorless lines and dots on the greyish belly. This is one of the largest of the tunas, exceeding 800 pounds (Japanese examples) in weight.

The bluefin tuna is found in largely subtropical and temperate waters. While fish of all sizes are taken in the Japanese fisheries in the Western Pacific, the most abundant sizes taken in the Eastern Pacific off Lower California and Southern California are from 10 to 45 pounds in weight. These fish are immature and seasonal in their abundant occurrence. Bluefin tuna, tagged in the Eastern Pacific, were subsequently recaptured in the Western Pacific off Japan. This suggests the possibility of a migratory movement of a portion of the immature bluefin tuna across the North Pacific and that perhaps there is a single stock of this species in the North Pacific. A similar distributional and migratory pattern appears to also characterize part of the immature albacore stock in the North Pacific.

Both mature and immature sizes of bluefin tuna occur in the eastern and western sides of the North Atlantic. Fish tagged in the western North Atlantic have been recaptured on the eastern side. The bluefin tuna is highly regarded in Japan for eating as sashimi and brings a good price there when fresh. The world catch of bluefin is of minor importance in the total tuna landings and the occasional capture of this species in Hawaiian waters suggests that such fish as are taken are strays. It is, of course, of negligible commercial value in Hawaii.

## THUNNUS ALALUNGA (Albacore, Ahipahala)

This is another small species, less than 90 pounds in weight, with long pectoral fins reaching beyond the anal fin insertion, a large eye, and anal finlets without yellow color (see Fig. 257h).

The albacore has a wide range, being found in both Northern and Southern hemispheres and in all oceans. This is a temperate-water species, preferring temperatures in the high 50's to the low 60's. In temperate waters it occurs at the surface and can often be taken in quantity by trolling; in the tropics it inhabits the deeper-water layers and is taken by long-line gear where the hook depth is sufficient to reach these layers. Fish tagged off southern California have been taken off Japan and northwest of Midway Island, which, when considered together with its seasonal occurrence in the continental coastal fisheries (summer) and in the offshore Midway fishery (winter), may suggest a migratory pattern of major extent in the Pacific.

It feeds upon smaller pelagic fishes and invertebrates. The coastal fisheries appear to take small immature fish, at least along the Pacific coast of North America, while large mature fish are not uncommon in the winter Hawaiian landings, where the average size of fish landed has varied from 45 to 80 pounds during the last three years. This fact, when considered together with the seasonal pattern of the fisheries, suggests that the immature portion of the stock may feed in coastal waters while the mature portion remains well offshore or perhaps in the subsurface waters in tropical or subtropical areas.

Albacore is the most valuable of the tunas from the standpoint of quality for the conventional canned tuna pack, and brings therefore the highest price from the American canner. In volume of landings it ranks low. It is of minor importance in the Hawaiian catch; some 29,000 pounds were taken in 1954, 21,000 in 1955, and 13,000 in 1956.

**THUNNUS ALBACARES (Yellowfin tuna, 'Ahi, Shibi)**

This is the most abundant large tuna of the tropics, a fish of great value commercially and highly regarded as a game fish (see Fig. 257i). The common name "yellowfin" refers to the bright yellow tips of the second dorsal fin, the anal fin, and the dorsal and anal finlets. The Hawaiian name "'ahi" is used for all species of large tunas and has the meaning of "fire," in reference, perhaps, to the speed with which the fishing line is pulled out with a fish on the hook.

Small yellowfin are sometimes taken in Hawaiian waters by commercial fishermen with live-bait chumming; large adults are commonly taken by long-line fishermen. All sizes are taken by trolling; however, in the Eastern Pacific the smaller sizes would seem to be more of a surface-dwelling species than the larger sizes, a trend present, but perhaps less strongly marked in Hawaiian waters. This species approaches 300 pounds in weight; however the average fish taken by long line has been about 80 pounds during the periods 1954, 1955, and 1956. The large fish have elongate second dorsal and anal fins.

Yellowfin commonly feed on crustacea, squid, and pelagic fishes, with a tendency, as might be expected, to feed on larger creatures as the tuna become larger. This causes an increase in the proportion of fish eaten with increasing size and proportionately less of pelagic invertebrates.

The growth is rapid, according to Moore (1951), with average weights of about 50 pounds at the end of the second year, 110 pounds at the end of the third, 170 at the end of the fourth, and 210 at the end of the fifth. Spawning occurs to some extent throughout the year, according to Yuen and June

(1957), with the least spawning during fall and early winter months. Some spawning may be done by fish a little over 2 feet long. Fish are generally mature at a little over 3 feet.

This is an important tuna in Hawaiian commercial fish landings; however in recent years it has been replaced in volume by the bigeye. The landings were 525,600 pounds in 1954, 445,800 pounds in 1955, and 304,000 pounds in 1956.

### THUNNUS OBESUS (Bigeye tuna, Po'o-nui, Mebachi shibi)

This species has a relatively large head (the Hawaiian name "po'o-nui," meaning "big head") and a large eye. Small fish, a yard or less in length, have long pectoral fins reaching to the anal insertion, while large ones, a hundred pounds or more, have a relatively short pectoral hardly reaching to the second dorsal fin insertion—somewhat shorter than that of a yellowfin of comparable size but longer than that of a black tuna (*Thunnus orientalis*).

The bigeye tuna approaches 2 meters (80 inches) in length and 300 pounds in weight; the average weight of fish taken in the commercial catch is around 160 pounds.

It occurs throughout the tropical and subtropical Pacific Ocean. *Parathunnus* is perhaps somewhat more subtropical in habitat than either *Neothunnus* or *Katsuwonus*.

This species is not abundant in surface waters, at least during the day. Occasionally small fish are taken by trolling or live-bait fishing—both are methods which take fish near the surface; the commercial catch is taken by long line which fishes at depths of 20 fathoms or greater.

This species ranks second in volume of landings and in value of all fish taken in Hawaiian waters. Ten years ago the 'ahi (yellowfin tuna) ranked second among the commercial landings, but has been replaced by the bigeye today. With the increase in the volume of the bigeye catch, some shift of fishing effort from leeward to windward areas has occurred. The commercial catch has fluctuated between 2,000,000 and 2,700,000 pounds per year for the past several years.

## Family ISTIOPHORIDAE (Sailfishes and Marlins or A'us)

This is a family of large pelagic fishes of the tropical and subtropical oceans. Until recently the identity of the various species has been confused, a situation not yet entirely clarified, and as a result the range of some may be greater than is commonly recognized. Members of this family are big-game fishes par excellence and are eagerly pursued by sport-fishermen. Istiophorids characteristically possess a bill or sword—an elongated bony projection of the upper jaw—which is commonly assumed to be useful in subduing prey, but which may serve in reality to streamline the fish, since marlin apparently can successfully exist without the sword. Some species attain weights well in excess of 1000 pounds, and these large fish are capable of high speeds in the water. They are predators, even on large tuna, marlin having been taken that have ingested a 150-pound tuna.

**261**

The scientific nomenclature used is from Royce (1958).

Key to the Hawaiian species of the family Istiophoridae:

1      Head length, measured from nostril to posterior margin of gill cover, less than length of pectoral fin or of sword, measured from its tip to nostril . . . . . . . . . . . . . . . . . . . . . . . . . . . . . . . . . . . . . . . . . . . . . .  2

Head length, measured from nostril to posterior margin of gill cover, about the same as or usually greater than length of pectoral fin or of sword, measured from its tip to nostril. Short-nosed spearfish . . . . . . . . . . . . . . . . . . . . . . . . .Fig. 258a, *Tetrapterus angustirostris*

2(1)    Length of middle rays of dorsal fin much less than greatest depth of body and less than length of anterior dorsal rays . . . . . . . . . . . . . .  3

Length of middle rays of dorsal fin greater than greatest depth of body and greater than length of anterior rays. Sailfish . . . . . . . . . . . . . . . . . . . . . . . . . . . . . . . . . . . . . . . . . . . . . . . . .Fig. 258b, *Istiophorus orientalis*

3(2)    Pectoral fin capable of being folded back along the sides, a flexible joint existing at its juncture with the body . . . . . . . . . . . . . . . . . .  4

Pectoral fin extending rigidly out, almost at right angles to longitudinal axis of body, not capable of being folded back along side and without a flexible joint at its juncture with body. Black marlin . . . . . . . . . . . . . . . . . . . . . . . . . . . . . . . . . . . .Fig. 258c, *Istiompax marlina*

4(3)    Length of first dorsal ray less than greatest depth of body; body not laterally compressed at origin of anal fin. Pacific blue marlin . . . . . . . . . . . . . . . . . . . . . . . . . . . . . . . . . . . . .Fig. 258d, *Makaira ampla*

Length of first dorsal ray equal to or greater than greatest depth of body, which is compressed laterally at origin of anal fin. Striped marlin . . . . . . . . . . . . . . . . . . . . . . . . . . . .Fig. 258e, *Makaira audax*

### TETRAPTERUS ANGUSTIROSTRIS (Short-nosed spearfish)

This species is easily recognized (see Fig. 258a). The lower jaw is more than ⅔ as long as the upper, measured from the corner of the mouth; the dorsal fin is low and long; and the fish is slender and lightly built.

The species is one of the smallest of the spearfishes, reaching a weight of 50 to 60 pounds and 6 feet in length.

It occurs in the Central and Western Tropical Pacific.

Little is known of the life history of the short-nosed spearfish. In Asiatic waters it apparently lives well offshore, never in coastal areas.

Commercial landings are few in Hawaiian waters.

### ISTIOPHORUS ORIENTALIS (Sailfish, A'u-lepe)

The characteristic which permits a ready identification of this species is its enormous dorsal fin, which is much higher than the depth of the body and is highest about the middle of its length (see Fig. 258b).

This is a small species, attaining a weight of approximately 150 pounds. The average fish landed weighs about 50 pounds.

It occurs in the Central and Western Tropical Pacific and is pelagic in habitat. Rarely taken by surface fishing methods, it is, however, occasionally caught by long-line fishing.

The commercial catch around Hawaii is slight, the annual landings ranging from 6,000 to 11,000 pounds during the last few years.

**Fig. 258.**

*a. Tetrapterus angustirostris; b. Istiophorus orientalis; c. Istiompax marlina* (black);
*d. Makaira ampla* (blue); *e. Makaira audax* (striped); *f. Xiphius gladius.*

**263**

### ISTIOMPAX MARLINA (Black marlin, Shirokajiki, Silver marlin, White marlin)

This species is usually called white marlin (from the Japanese name) or silver marlin in Hawaii (see Fig. 258c). In New Zealand and Central and South America it is known as the black marlin, a name applied in Hawaii to the Pacific blue marlin. It is easily distinguished from all other spearfishes by a rigid pectoral fin that cannot be folded against the body.

This is a large, heavy-bodied species attaining a weight substantially over 1250 pounds and a length greater than 11.5 feet, though the average weight of fish taken by long line falls between 200 and 350 pounds. A tropical Pacific species, possibly also occurring in the Indian Ocean.

It is not abundant in our commercial catch, between 11,000 and 20,000 pounds being landed annually during the last few years.

### MAKAIRA AMPLA (Pacific blue marlin, Kurokajiki, Black marlin)

This species has a relatively low dorsal fin; the anterior rays are shorter than the greatest depth of the body (see Fig. 258d). The lateral line is obscure and divided. The body is robust and deep. When the fish is first taken from the water, vertical stripes are usually in evidence, sometimes causing this species to be confused with the striped marlin, from which it can readily be distinguished by a low dorsal fin and a more robust form.

The weight of this large species may exceed 1400 pounds and the length 11 feet, though the average weight is between 300 and 400 pounds. It is a pelagic fish found in the tropical Pacific and possibly the Indian Ocean. According to Nakamura, it spawns in June in Formosan waters.

This is an abundant species in Hawaiian waters, being taken by surface trolling and by long-line fishing. It is the most important member of the family in the commercial fishery, the annual landings varying between 400,000 and 800,000 pounds per year.

### MAKAIRA AUDAX (Striped marlin, Kajiki)

The first dorsal rays are longer than the greatest depth of the body (see Fig. 258e). The middorsal rays are relatively long in small fish and short in large ones, causing one authority to distinguish the small ones as a separate species. There are more than 10 cobalt vertical stripes on the sides of the body. The lateral line is simple, but obscure. The body is laterally compressed.

This species reaches a weight of 250 pounds and more; the average weight of those taken by commercial fishermen is around 80 pounds. The identification of specimens of 400 or 500 pounds and greater should be made with great care since it is possible to confuse it with the Pacific blue marlin (*Makaira ampla*).

It is pelagic in habitat and is found throughout the tropical and subtropical Pacific. According to Nakamura, the peak of the spawning season occurs in May in Formosan waters.

This species is the second most important in volume of landings in the Hawaiian commercial spearfish catch; for the last few years something over 200,000 pounds per year have been taken. It is commonly taken by long line and by trolling with a lure or bait.

## Family XIPHIIDAE

This family has but a single species which is cosmopolitan in range and is the most highly specialized of the billfishes.

### XIPHIAS GLADIUS (Broadbill swordfish)

This species is readily distinguished from the marlins by a sword that is flattened rather than round in cross section and by a short, high dorsal fin not extending behind the middle of the body (see Fig. 258f). It is a good food fish and one of the prime game fishes of the world. The broadbill approaches 1000 pounds in weight and 15 feet in total length. The average weight of fish taken commercially in Hawaii is about 250 pounds.

The broadbill is remarkably tolerant to various water temperatures, occurring in the tropics and in temperate seas in water as cool as 50°F. Major commercial fisheries for this species are in temperate waters, where it is harpooned at the surface of the ocean. Such fisheries exist off California, off the east coast of the United States, and off the Pacific Coast of South America. The fish are pursued during the summer. This species is taken in small numbers in Hawaii by commercial fishermen using long-line gear set principally for tuna.

Broadbills feed upon other fishes—both surface-schooling species and species living near the bottom. Evidence from the stomach contents would indicate that they may occasionally feed deeper than one hundred fathoms.

Little is known of its spawning habits; however, small broadbills, 3 or 4 feet in length, are not uncommonly taken by long-line fishermen in Hawaii.

The weight of broadbills landed by Hawaiian commercial fishermen is minor, being 11,000 pounds in 1954, 38,000 pounds in 1955, and 29,000 pounds in 1956.

## THE GOBIES AND THEIR ALLIES

To have the gobies (suborder Gobioidei) immediately follow the marlins is a bit ludicrous, as the gobies include some of the smallest of fishes. Nevertheless, in their minor way this group has been quite successful. If one cracks open a large piece of coral, several types of fishes may fall out, but the most abundant is a member of this group. If one swims over holes in the silt between dead coral, a flock of fishes may disappear down the holes; these fishes will be members of this group. Still another goby is probably the commonest inhabitant of sandy pools. Others have gone up the various fresh-water streams; two of these are rather unusual for this group in attaining a size of a foot or more. The true gobies can be readily distinguished from all our other fishes by the median sucking disc on the abdomen; but some of the goby relatives without this feature are nondescript forms difficult to characterize externally. Yet, skeletally, all gobioid fishes are readily identifiable.

## Family ELEOTRIDAE

The eleotrids are small nondescript fishes without distinctive features. About the best that can be done for the Hawaiian forms is to state that they have the following features in common: body completely scaled, but the lateral line absent; 2 separate dorsal fins, the first of 6 spines; pelvic fins separate; pectoral and caudal rounded; gill covers united to the isthmus.

Key to the Hawaiian species of the family Eleotridae:

| | | |
|---|---|---|
| 1 | Scales large, fewer than 30 in a longitudinal series; jaws about equal; maximum size 3 inches; marine species.................. | 2 |
| | Scales small, about 75 in a longitudinal series; lower jaw projecting; reaches at least 9 inches in length; an estuarine and fresh-water species.................................... *Eleotris sandwicensis* | |
| 2(1) | Each scale with a dark crescent-shaped mark; no spines on preopercle; maximum size about 1 inch.............. *Eviota epiphanes* | |
| | No markings on scales; a few blunt spines on preopercle; maximum size about 3 inches.................. *Asterropteryx semipunctatus* | |

### ELEOTRIS SANDWICENSIS ('O'opu 'akupa)

*Eleotris sandwicensis* is one of the prominent stream fishes of the Hawaiian Islands. In general appearance it resembles the gobies of the genus *Sicydium* that are often found in the same streams, but can immediately be separated from these by the separate pelvic fins. Though *Eleotris sandwicensis* is also abundant in brackish water, it seems to be rare or lacking in fully marine areas.

To 9 inches.

### EVIOTA EPIPHANES

In maximum length attained this is probably the smallest of Hawaiian fishes (see Fig. 85). It seems to be abundant everywhere in coralline areas at depths from 5 to at least 30 feet and can easily be obtained by breaking up coral heads.

If a microscope is available, *Eviota epiphanes* may be readily distinguished from all our other fishes by the peculiar pelvic rays. There are 4 main rays, but each of these gives off numerous side branches creating a rather feather-like appearance.

Maximum length 1 inch.

### ASTERROPTERYX SEMIPUNCTATUS

This species may be distinguished from the other Hawaiian members of the family both by the blunt spines on the preopercle and by the fact that the first 3 dorsal spines are usually prolonged into filaments.

The species may be found in great numbers in front of holes in the silt that collects between the dead coral in such areas as Kaneohe Bay. It may be taken in water as shallow as 2 feet in depth. Reaches about 3 inches in length.

## Family GOBIIDAE (Gobies)

The members of the Gobiidae are unique among Hawaiian fishes in having the two pelvic fins fused to form a sucking disc (see Fig. 5f). Like the Eleotridae, the gobies all have a separate first dorsal fin composed of 6 (rarely 7) spines.

The gobies are quite variable in habitat. They are among the most prominent of our native fresh-water fishes and were formerly found in the lower reaches of all Hawaiian streams. In fresh water, members of the genera *Sicydium*, *Lentipes*, and *Chonophorus* are to be expected, along with the eleotrid *Eleotris sandwicensis*. Some of these grow to a relatively large size and support a fishery. Two other gobies, *Oxyurichthys lonchotus* and *Bathygobius fuscus*, penetrate at least as far as brackish water. Of our purely marine forms, none attain a length of more than 3 inches, and two, *Kelloggella* and *Vitraria*, have a maximum size of about an inch. *Kelloggella* and *Bathygobius fuscus* are surge-pool forms. The transparent *Vitraria* is said to burrow in the sand. *Bathygobius cotticeps* is found among the rocks in surge areas, and *Quisquilius eugenius* is very abundant in dead coral. The Hawaiian gobies that are not mentioned above seem to stay out below the surge zone.

Key to the known Hawaiian species of the family Gobiidae:

| | | |
|---|---|---|
| 1 | Caudal rounded or pointed................................... | 2 |
| | Caudal distinctly forked. Body elongate, the depth contained about 6.7 times in the standard length..............*Vitraria clarescens* | |
| 2(1) | Caudal rounded; no distinct median crest on nape running forward from the first dorsal nearly to the level of the eyes; anal and second dorsal each with 13 or fewer rays...................... | 3 |
| | Caudal distinctly pointed; a well-developed, fleshy crest on nape extending forward from the first dorsal nearly to the level of the eyes; anal and second dorsal each with 14 or more rays.......  ..........................................*Oxyurichthys lonchotus* | |
| 3(2) | United pelvic fins entirely free from the body posteriorly.......... | 6 |
| | United pelvic fins forming a nearly circular sucking disc which is everywhere closely attached to the body. Fresh-water forms...... | 4 |
| 4(3) | Body naked or nearly so..................................... | 5 |
| | Body completely scaled.........................*Sicydium stimpsoni* | |
| 5(4) | Tail without scales; dorsal rays 10...................*Lentipes concolor* | |
| | Tail covered with small scales; dorsal rays 11........*Lentipes seminudus* | |
| 6(3) | Body scaled, at least posteriorly............................. | 7 |
| | Body naked. A series of vertical stripes running across body...  .....................................*Kelloggella oligolepis* | |
| 7(6) | Interorbital width less than or equal to the eye diameter; no knoblike, fleshy projections extending forward from the lower portion of the shoulder girdle inside the gill openings................. | 9 |
| | Interorbital width considerably greater than the eye diameter; a few prominent, knoblike, fleshy projections extending forward from the lower portion of the shoulder girdle inside the gill openings. Brackish and fresh-water forms...................... | 8 |
| 8(7) | A broad, slaty blotch extending from below eye downward and backward across cheek; anal rays 13............*Chonophorus genivittatus* | |
| | No broad, slaty blotch on cheek; anal rays 10.....*Chonophorus stamineus* | |
| 9(7) | Head more or less compressed, higher than broad.............. | 12 |

Head depressed, broader than high........................ 10

10(9)    Upper pectoral rays terminating in free, silky filaments; nape scaled; color dark or with light and dark markings, but without prominent dark spots at the base of the caudal and at the base of the upper pectoral rays.................................... 11

Upper pectoral rays not terminating in free, silky filaments; nape scaleless; color mostly light but with a black blotch on caudal peduncle and a small dark mark on the base of the upper pectoral rays.........................................*Ctenogobius tongarevae*

11(10)   Head strongly flattened, as broad or broader than long; cheeks and opercles scaled in adults......................*Bathygobius cotticeps*

Head longer than broad; cheeks and opercles naked...*Bathygobius fuscus*

12(9)    A membrane (sometimes quite narrow and transparent) running across the front of the pelvic fins (see Fig. 6f) and attached to the outermost rays.......................................... 16

No membrane running across the front of the pelvic fins, the 2 pelvics attached to one another along the mid-ventral line but otherwise unmodified...................................... 13

13(12)   Mid-line of back scaled forward of the dorsal fin nearly to the eyes; no dark-bordered light lines running across the top of head and down the cheek...................................... 14

Mid-line of the back naked forward of the dorsal fin; about 3 prominent, dark-bordered light lines running across the top and down the sides of head.........................*Zonogobius farcimen*

14(13)   Upper half of cheek and operculum naked; body not very dark and not with alternating darker and lighter vertical stripes......... 15

Upper half of cheek and operculum scaled (except in very small specimens); body very dark, usually with alternating darker and lighter vertical stripes..........................*Quisquilius eugenius*

15(14)   A series of pigment spots outlining the border of each scale; head relatively flat, its depth contained about 2 times in its length, and the eyes directed more upward than outward; scales in a longitudinal series about 27; 10 or 11 rays in second dorsal......
................................................*Quisquilius limbatosquamis*

Scales without pigment spots outlining their borders; head relatively compressed, its depth contained about 1.7 times in its length, and the eyes directed more out than up; scales in a longitudinal series about 31; 11 or 12 rays in second dorsal........
................................................*Quisquilius aureoviridis*

16(12)   Gill covers broadly attached to throat, the distance between the lower ends of the gill openings greater than an eye diameter....... 18

Gill openings extending forward to in front of the preopercular border, the distance between their lower ends equal to or less than a pupil diameter...................................... 17

17(16)   First spine in both dorsal fins not heavy and sharp-tipped; each dorsal fin with a narrow black border..............*Hazeus unisquamis*

First spine in both dorsal fins relatively heavy and sharp-tipped; dorsal fins without a narrow black border..............*Opua nephodes*

18(16)   Snout blunt, the lower jaw not projecting beyond its tip; midline of nape completely scaled; a dark bar extending down across cheek from below eye.........................*Gnatholepis anjerensis*

Snout sharp, the lower jaw projecting beyond its tip; mid-line of nape scaleless; no dark vertical bar below eye.....*Fusigobius neophytus*

## VITRARIA CLARESCENS

A small but quite distinctive goby. It is the only Hawaiian member of the family with a forked caudal. In addition, the pelvics are entirely in front of the first dorsal, and the caudal peduncle is about as long as the second dorsal base. The fish is practically transparent in life.

We have seen only one specimen, but the species is probably not at all rare. Maximum length about 1 inch.

## OXYURICHTHYS LONCHOTUS

Aside from the peculiarities mentioned in the key, this species is unique among Hawaiian gobies in having a small but distinct black mark on each anterior nostril. The body is scaleless in front of the ventrals and along the mid-line in front of the first dorsal.

Apparently primarily a brackish-water species living over muddy bottoms. Reaches 5 inches in length.

## SICYDIUM STIMPSONI

A small-scaled fresh-water species with a high first dorsal fin. Known from at least Hawaii, Maui, and Oahu. Attains a length of 7 inches.

## LENTIPES CONCOLOR

A naked, fresh-water species recorded long ago from the streams about Hilo.

## LENTIPES SEMINUDUS

Said to differ from *Lentipes concolor* in having scales on the tail. Described from fresh water around Honolulu in 1880 and does not seem to have been taken since.

The type specimen was about 2 inches long.

## KELLOGGELLA OLIGOLEPIS

This is one of the smallest of Hawaiian fishes and without much doubt the smallest of our gobies. It is a scaleless, elongate species with alternating dark and light vertical bars. In habitat it appears to be restricted to the rocky pools in the upper tidal zone.

Attains almost an inch in length.

## CHONOPHORUS GENIVITTATUS ('O'opu)

This is said to be a common form in streams and estuaries. Apparently it can be easily distinguished from *Chonophorus stamineus* by the characters given in the key.

To 6 inches.

## CHONOPHORUS STAMINEUS ('O'opu nakea)

Undoubtedly the largest goby in the Islands, reaching a foot in length. Widely distributed in the streams of the high Hawaiian islands.

### CTENOGOBIUS TONGAREVAE

Three small specimens less than an inch long, presumed to be this species, have been taken in about 30 feet of water off Waikiki reef.

### BATHYGOBIUS COTTICEPS

*Bathygobius* is the only genus of Hawaiian gobies in which the upper rays of the pectoral fin extend as free, hairlike filaments. *B. cotticeps* differs from *B. fuscus* in having a broad depressed head the bottom surface of which forms a nearly flat plate.

Apparently restricted to rocky areas in shallow water. To about 5 inches in length.

### BATHYGOBIUS FUSCUS

Probably the commonest "tide-pool" fish in the Hawaiian Islands. Its presence can almost be counted on in any area in which pools occur; in the smaller of these *Bathygobius fuscus*, *Istiblennius zebra*, and perhaps *Kelloggella oligolepis* may be the only fishes. The rounded head and silky upper pectoral rays are diagnostic for *Bathygobius fuscus*. In color the species ranges from a light tan over sandy bottoms to black over basalt. Attains perhaps 4 inches in length.

### ZONOGOBIUS FARCIMEN

A small, yellowish-brown fish in which the fins always seem to be retained in an erect position. The banding on the head (not shown in the figure) is diagnostic (see Fig. 65).

Though the fish is not infrequently taken in rotenone poison stations, it has never been found alive, and consequently its exact habitat is unknown. To about 1.5 inches.

### QUISQUILIUS EUGENIUS

*Quisquilius* and *Zonogobius* are our two goby genera in which there is no fleshy membrane across the front of the pelvic fins. In addition, the membrane connecting the pelvics of the two sides is easily torn in *Quisquilius;* indeed the type specimen of *Q. eugenius* apparently had the pelvics separated and the species was consequently misplaced in the family Eleotridae. A dark brown fish, usually with more or less distinct darker vertical stripes.

A common species in shallow water, occurring in great numbers in certain areas. To about 3 inches.

### QUISQUILIUS LIMBATOSQUAMIS

A very small species of *Quisquilius*, known only from over 20 feet of water. It differs from the other species in that each body scale has a light center and a dark rim.

Our only specimens are about an inch long.

### QUISQUILIUS AUREOVIRIDIS

This species differs from *Q. eugenius* immediately in general coloration, for in life it is yellowish. Not known from less than 15 feet of water. To about 3 inches.

**HAZEUS UNISQUAMIS**

Superficially this species resembles *Eviota epiphanes*. Known from two specimens about an inch long taken in approximately 20 feet of water.

**OPUA NEPHODES**

Our only collection of this species is from a few feet of water in Kaneohe Bay. The largest specimen is about 2 inches long.

**GNATHOLEPIS ANJERENSIS**

Our only strictly marine goby with a black bar extending down from the eye. It is perhaps the most ubiquitous of our marine gobies, found from a few feet down to depths of at least 50 feet. In shallow water it may be seen, along with *Asterropteryx semipunctatus*, sitting on the sand at the base of coral heads. To about 3 inches.

**FUSIGOBIUS NEOPHYTUS**

This species may be identified by the heavy projecting lower jaw that juts forward nearly horizontally, giving the front of the head a very pointed appearance.
To about 4 inches.

## Family KRAEMERIIDAE

The Kraemeriidae is a family of small, naked, burrowing fishes. It can be immediately distinguished from the Trichonotidae, which it superficially resembles, by the strongly projecting lower jaw.

**KRAEMERIA BRYANI**

In the burrowing habit, projecting chin, and small eye this species resembles the moringuid eels; however, it has the pectorals, pelvics, and caudal of a normal fish.
The maximum known length is about 1 inch.

# THE DRAGONETS

The suborder Callionymoidei is characterized chiefly by skeletal peculiarities. Externally, the members all have spines on the cheek or gill cover and the pelvics well in advance of the pectorals and with the innermost rays longest.

## Family CALLIONYMIDAE

The Hawaiian fishes of the family Callionymidae have a flattened head with a well-developed preopercular spine and a small, terminal mouth. There is considerable difference between the sexes in the adult, the males having a much more striking coloration and longer fins; in the adult male the caudal fin may be as long as the body.
Four species are here recognized from Hawaiian waters. So far as known

our species vary in maximum length from about 2 to 11 inches. All are decidedly uncommon.

Key to the Hawaiian species of the family Callionymidae:

1     Innermost pelvic ray connected with the base of the pectoral by a membrane; gill openings restricted to small holes above the opercle. . . . . . . . . . . . . . . . . . . . . . . . . . . . . . . . . . . . . . . . . . . . . . . . . .  2

Innermost pelvic ray not connected with the base of the pectoral by a membrane; gill openings relatively broad, not restricted to above the opercle. . . . . . . . . . . . . . . . . . . . . . . . . *Pogonemus pogognathus*

2(1)    A spine (concealed in the flesh) projecting forward from the base of the preopercular spine on its outer surface, inner surface of preopercular spine with 4 to 8 anteriorly directed pointed spinelets; snout length equal to or greater than the eye diameter. . . .  3

No spine projecting forward from the outer surface of the pre-opercular spine, 3 to 5 hooked spinelets upturned from its dorsal surface; snout length about ⅔ an eye diameter. . .*Synchiropus rubrovinctus*

3(2)    Width of head contained about 1½ times in length of head (measured to the tip of the opercle); no enlarged teeth in the lower jaw. . . . . . . . . . . . . . . . . . . . . . . . . . . . . . . .*Callionymus decoratus*

Width of head contained 2 times in head length; 2 or 3 enlarged teeth in the inner series on each side of the lower jaw. Not known from less than 250 feet of water. . . . . . . . . . . . .*Callionymus caeruleonotatus*

### POGONEMUS POGOGNATHUS

This little fish is promptly distinguishable from other Hawaiian calliony-mids by the fringe of conspicuous tentacles projecting directly forward from the edge of the lower jaw. The preopercular spine is short, its length about equal to the pupil diameter, and upturned.

The species has been taken only once, over sand in a few feet of water near Hanalei, Kauai, but it was the most abundant fish taken there. Maximum known length about 1.5 inches.

### SYNCHIROPUS RUBROVINCTUS

We have two specimens presumably of this species, the larger about 1 inch in length, taken in about 30 feet of water on the western shore of Maui (see Fig. 77). They differ from the original description in lacking the first dorsal spine filament; also, the maxillary does not reach past the eye, the snout is not so convex as in the figure, and the larger has 5 instead of 3 hooked spinelets on the preopercular spine.

### CALLIONYMUS DECORATUS

Though several species of *Callionymus* have been described from the Hawaiian Islands, we have not been able to ascertain that more than two are valid. This is a tentative arrangement forced upon us by the fact that the number of specimens known is insufficient to work out the limits of the obviously great ontogenetic and sexual differentiation that occurs within species.

Our specimens all appear to belong to this species. The adult males have striking black lines on the throat and a very long tail. To about 11 inches in length. Occurs not infrequently in shallow water.

##### CALLIONYMUS CAERULEONOTATUS

This species appears to differ from the last in the narrower head, upturned tip of the preopercular spine, and the presence of a few enlarged teeth in the lower jaw.

Known from a few specimens about 4 inches long dredged at depths of 300 to over 600 feet.

### Family DRACONETTIDAE

Another of those deep-water families recorded from Hawaii on the basis of one specimen. This individual, 2 inches long and described as *Draconetta hawaiiensis* (see Fig. 78), was dredged in over 600 feet of water between Molokai and Maui.

## THE SCHINDLERIAS

### Family SCHINDLERIIDAE

The family Schindleriidae is made up of two described species of most aberrant fishes. In many respects, for example, the cartilaginous skull and the form of the pectoral fin, they appear to be larval fishes. However, their maturity may be frequently demonstrated by the presence of large eggs. The vertebral column is unique in having the last few vertebrae fused into a pipe-like structure.

The species are transparent and among the smallest of fishes, attaining a length of about an inch. It is almost impossible to see them in the water, and they are usually inadvertently taken in fine-meshed nets. Nevertheless, they occur in great numbers near the surface around Hawaii and a quart jarful has been collected off one of the Honolulu piers; indeed, it is not impossible that they are the commonest Hawaiian fishes.

Key to the Hawaiian species of the family Schindleriidae:

> Anal rays 11 to 13; vertebrae 38 to 40 including the urostyle...
> ..............................................*Schindleria praematurus*
> Anal rays 14 to 17; vertebrae 34 to 38 including the urostyle...
> ..............................................*Schindleria pietschmanni*

##### SCHINDLERIA PRAEMATURUS

Both species of *Schindleria* were originally described from Hawaiian waters, but no attempt has been made to determine the relative abundance of the two (see Fig. 137).

Total length about 1 inch.

##### SCHINDLERIA PIETSCHMANNI

Total length about 1 inch.

**273**

# THE BLENNIES

## (By Donald W. Strasburg)

The blennies are small, agile fishes, characterized chiefly by the location and number of rays of the pelvic fins. These fins are jugular in position (just back of the throat), and the rays number from 2 to 4, exclusive of a very small spine which is not externally visible. The Hawaiian blennies are grouped in two families, the Tripterygiidae and the Blenniidae. Members of the Tripterygiidae have scales and 3 dorsal fins, whereas the Blenniidae are naked and have a single dorsal fin which is frequently divided into 2 portions by a deep notch.

Although of no commercial importance, other than occasionally as bait in surf-casting, the blennies are a diverse and interesting group of fishes. Their habitats range from depths of at least 120 feet to tide pools less than an inch deep. Between these extremes there are species which dwell among dead coral, in areas of pounding surf, and on shallow reef flats. The habits of only two species, *Istiblennius zebra* and *Entomacrodus marmoratus*, are well known, although food studies and other observations have been made on most of the other Hawaiian forms.

In general terms, the blennies are shy and secretive, dwelling in or retreating to holes or crevices when disturbed. They lack an air bladder and are demersal, except possibly for *Runula*. The eggs of *Istiblennius zebra* are spherical and attached to the undersides of rocks or the walls of holes by an adhesive disc. The eggs hatch in about one week; the young *I. zebra* then become a part of the plankton or drifting life of the open ocean. Here they grow to about an inch in length, and ultimately return to shore as distinctive postlarvae. These are glassily transparent fish, with teeth, digestive tracts, and fins adapted to a much different way of life from the adult. Apparently most Hawaiian blennies have these peculiar postlarval forms, many of which have been described as new genera and species. Upon reaching a suitable adult habitat the postlarval *I. zebra* metamorphose into small juveniles which resemble the adults except for size. Growth to breeding size probably requires about a year.

The blennies of Hawaii are relatively well-known taxonomically, being recently reviewed by Strasburg (1956). The Tripterygiidae are represented by a single species and the Blenniidae by twelve. Of the latter group, two have been recorded from Hawaii under most peculiar circumstances, and it is likely that only ten species are actually well established. The Blenniidae are usually divided into two subfamilies, the Salariinae and the Blenniinae. In the Salariinae the teeth (exclusive of canines) are movably set in the gums, whereas in the Blenniinae all teeth are rigidly attached to the jaws. The genera *Ecsenius* and *Exallias*, although regarded as salariin, have the upper teeth movable and the lower teeth fixed. The following key will separate the adults of all thirteen Hawaiian blennioid fishes, but usually cannot be used for the postlarval stages. The use of fin-ray counts has been avoided in the key insofar as possible. Where ray counts are necessary (*Cirripectus*) it should be noted that the last dorsal spine is minute and easily overlooked.

Key to the Hawaiian blennioid fishes:

1       Body scaled; 3 dorsal fins (family Tripterygiidae)....*Tripterygion atriceps*

        Body naked; 1 or 2 dorsal fins (family Blenniidae)............... 2

2(1)    A fringe of 25 to 45 tentacles across neck...................... 3

        No fringe of tentacles on neck; if tentacles occur on neck they
        total only 4................................................. 6

3(2)    Body yellowish-brown to orange, covered with clusters of dark
        dots; a pair of short tentacles on each side of chin.......*Exallias brevis*

        Body dark brown or black, unmarked or with dark or light spots;
        no tentacles on chin......................................... 4

4(3)    First dorsal fin plain blackish; a dark spot behind eye; dorsal rays
        XII, 16.............................................*Cirripectus obscurus*

        First dorsal fin abruptly pale or transparent anteriorly and distally;
        no dark spot behind eye; dorsal rays XII, 14 or 15.............. 5

5(4)    Body with rows of small white or yellow dots; dorsal rays XII,
        15...............................................*Cirripectus lineopunctatus*

        Body unmarked; dorsal rays XII, 14.............*Cirripectus variolosus*

6(2)    A small tentacle over eye.................................... 7

        No tentacle over eye........................................ 9

7(6)    Tentacle over eye with numerous branches; a pair of tentacles on
        each side of neck........................*Entomacrodus marmoratus*

        Tentacle over eye unbranched; no tentacles on neck............. 8

8(7)    Adults and large juveniles with a fleshy crest on mid-line of head
        and with last soft dorsal ray attached to caudal fin by a mem-
        brane; no canine teeth in jaws.....................*Istiblennius zebra*

        No crest on head; last dorsal ray not attached to caudal fin; a
        short canine tooth posteriorly in lower jaw.......*Istiblennius gibbifrons*

9(6)    Gill opening large, extending to ventral side of throat; teeth in
        upper jaw loosely set in gums and freely movable...*Ecsenius hawaiiensis*

        Gill opening extending ventrally only to level of middle pectoral
        rays; teeth in both jaws firmly attached and practically immovable.... 10

10(9)   Dorsal and anal fins attached to caudal by membranes; trunk and
        tail deep brownish black or black..............*Enchelyurus brunneolus*

        Dorsal and anal fins free from caudal; trunk and tail marked with
        dark stripes or bars on a lighter background.................... 11

11(10)  Throat with 5 or 6 dark V-shaped marks; a dark spot behind eye;
        body with oblique and vertical dark bars.......*Omobranchus elongatus*

        Throat plain pale; no spot behind eye; body with dark length-
        wise stripes on a lighter background.......................... 12

12(11)  A pair of black-edged blue stripes running length of body;
        ground color pale (brick red in life).................*Runula ewaensis*

        No black-edged blue stripes; upper half of body brown, lower
        half abruptly white, brown area divided into 2 lengthwise stripes
        by a narrow white line...............................*Runula goslinei*

## Family TRIPTERYGIIDAE

**TRIPTERYGION ATRICEPS**

The single Hawaiian member of this family rarely attains more than an inch in length (see Fig. 75). In life the body is bright red, and in males the head is black, making the fish distinctively colorful. It is common but secretive, usually living in crevices in dead coral or among rocks. So far as is known, it is found only in the Hawaiian Islands.

## Family BLENNIIDAE

**EXALLIAS BREVIS (Pao'o kauila, 'O'opu pao'o)**

This blenny is a handsomely marked but uncommon fish found at depths of 4 to at least 35 feet. Its leopard-like spotting and, in the case of males, bright orange coloration, make it easily recognizable. It attains a length of 6 inches, and is distributed throughout the tropical Indo-Pacific. As with *Cirripectus* (see below) males are distinguished from females in having the anal spines enclosed in bulbous fleshy pads.

**CIRRIPECTUS OBSCURUS**

*Cirripectus obscurus* is a giant among the Hawaiian blennies, with specimens 7 inches in length rather common. In addition to the characters noted in the key, the life colors of dusky rose (male) or golden brown (female) covered with tiny white dots serve to distinguish it. It abounds at depths of 4 to 20 feet, particularly where the bottom is rocky and water movement is moderately strong. The species is found only in the Hawaiian Islands.

**Fig. 259. CIRRIPECTUS LINEOPUNCTATUS**

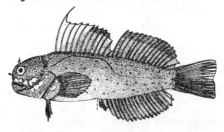

**CIRRIPECTUS LINEOPUNCTATUS**

This blenny can be distinguished from other species of *Cirripectus* by the fact that the tentacle over the eye is typically unbranched. The fish reaches a length of about 3 inches, and is fairly common at depths of 4 to 10 feet along rocky coasts having a strong surf. It is apparently limited to the Hawaiian and Johnston islands, with a close relative, *C. quagga*, occurring in the Marshalls, Gilberts, and elsewhere.

**CIRRIPECTUS VARIOLOSUS**

Anyone using a face mask can watch this dark-colored blenny flit from crevice to crevice among dead coral reefs such as characterize Waikiki. An abundant species, *Cirripectus variolosus* occurs in water 2 to 30 feet deep throughout the Hawaiian Islands, and is also widely distributed throughout the Indo-Pacific. Many specimens have bright red marks on the head when fresh. A 4-inch specimen is large.

### Fig. 260.  ENTOMACRODUS MARMORATUS

### ENTOMACRODUS MARMORATUS

This fish dwells principally in the surf zone of rocky coasts, inhabiting small holes or crevices away from the full force of the sea. When frightened it leaps into the surf, skittering across the frothing water just clear of the foam. Its diet includes detritus, algae, and small invertebrates. Native only to the Hawaiian chain, *Entomacrodus marmoratus* reaches 4 or 5 inches about Oahu, and about 6 inches at Midway Island.

### ISTIBLENNIUS ZEBRA (Rockskipper, Zebra, Panoa, Pao'o, Gori)

Rockskippers, or zebra blennies, derive the first of these names from their ability to cross considerable stretches of rocky shoreline by leaping, and the second from their coloration of vertical bars (see Fig. 93). They dwell in tide pools and abound in many parts of the Hawaiian Islands. The pools inhabited are subject to considerable evaporation and heating by the sun, and also to dilution by heavy rains, so these blennies must be able to withstand a wide range of temperature and salinity. They are of particular interest because of the timing and accuracy of their leaps when pursued. They hop from pool to pool, seemingly knowing the location of each escape route, and showing considerable "intelligence" in eluding the pursuer. Their diet consists almost solely of precipitated detritus. *I. zebra* can be distinguished from *I. edentulus*, a close relative from many other Pacific islands, by its lack of a tiny tentacle on each side of the neck. Large specimens are 6 inches or more in length. The species is found only in the Hawaiian Islands.

### ISTIBLENNIUS GIBBIFRONS

In the field, this blenny is most commonly confused with *Istiblennius zebra*, from which it differs in having a prominent bulging of the forehead so that the snout slopes backward from the eye to the mouth. In *zebra* the forehead is nearly vertical, or if rounded, there is no conspicuous bulging. There are well-marked color pattern differences between the sexes of *gibbifrons*, with males having numerous blue-white ocelli on the sides and females not. This blenny inhabits permanently submerged reef flats of depths less than about 4 feet. It is abundant but secretive, and most reefs contain far more of this fish than one would suspect. The species attains a length of about 5 inches, and is found on all the Hawaiian Islands, Johnston Island, Wake Island, and possibly elsewhere.

### ECSENIUS HAWAIIENSIS

The fourteen known specimens of this blenny were taken from the fouling on the bottom of a barge brought from Guam to Pearl Harbor and there placed in drydock. At present the blenny is unknown from any other part of the world, and has not been retaken in Hawaii. It is possible that the species occurs in Hawaii, either naturally or as a result of introduction via the barge, but intensive collecting has failed to reveal it. The species apparently reaches 4 or 5 inches in length.

### ENCHELYURUS BRUNNEOLUS

*E. brunneolus* is an inch-long, nearly jet-black inhabitant of dead coral heads. It is common but seldom seen alive because of its small size and shy nature. Specimens can be collected by splitting masses of coralline material. Its shape and coloring cause it to resemble-juvenile *Cirripectus*, from which it can be distinguished by its lack of tentacles on the neck and above the eye.

### OMOBRANCHUS ELONGATUS

Like *Ecsenius hawaiiensis*, this species is known from the Hawaiian Islands under odd circumstances. The four known Hawaiian specimens were obtained from a concrete-walled tank on Coconut Island, Oahu, which had at one time contained masses of coral rock brought from American Samoa. Even though the fish were collected after the rocks had been discarded and the tank drained and painted, it would seem that they entered Hawaii by this means. Populations may now be established on Oahu as a result of escapes from the tank. Living specimens are readily distinguishable from other Hawaiian blennies by the fact that the body is translucent and the vertebral column clearly visible. The largest specimen taken in Hawaii was about 3 inches but even at this small size it bit the hand (and drew blood) when handled.

### RUNULA EWAENSIS

This is a brilliantly-colored deep-water blenny; the depths of capture range down to at least 120 feet. The species may live in tubes or burrows, for two of the five known specimens were taken from pipes hauled to the surface. The brick-red ground color with blue lengthwise stripes make it an unmistakable fish. So far it is known only from the Hawaiian Islands. Attains a length of about 5 inches.

Fig. 261. RUNULA GOSLINEI

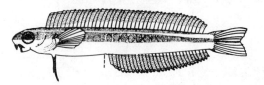

This blenny is apparently a wide-ranging form as far as depth is concerned. Several specimens have been recovered from the stomachs of dolphin (*Coryphaena hippurus*) and yellowfin tuna, and others have been collected at depths as shallow as 3 to 5 feet. Like its close relative, *Runula tapeinosoma* of the Central Pacific and elsewhere, *R. goslinei* "attacks" swimmers by biting legs or other exposed parts of the body. Because of its small size, 2- to 3-inch maximum length, these bites are ineffectual, but they are probably not so to smaller organisms similarly attacked, for the blenny has enormous fangs in the lower jaw which are undoubtedly used in feeding. *R. goslinei* has only been reported from Hawaii.

## THE BROTULIDS AND CARAPIDS

These two groups belong to the perciform suborder Ophidioidei, characterized in part by having the pelvic fins, if present at all, made up of 1 or 2 filaments far forward. The brotulids are primarily deep-water fishes, whereas the carapids seem to be mostly inshore forms; nevertheless it is the latter family that is the more specialized.

### Family BROTULIDAE

In superficial appearance the brotulids resemble the codlike fishes. The Hawaiian species all have the pelvic fins reduced to 1 or a pair of filaments, and the dorsal and anal are continuous with the caudal fin. Unlike the Hawaiian codlike fishes, the brotulids have only a single, continuous dorsal fin.

The brotulids are basically deep-water fishes, but a few members of this large family have become adapted to shallow-water life. In Hawaii, four shallow-water and five deep-water species are known. In adult size these species vary from 2 inches to about 18 inches.

Key to the Hawaiian shallow-water species of the family Brotulidae:

| | | |
|---|---|---|
| 1 | No barbels on snout and chin.................................. | 3 |
| | Barbels present on snout and chin............................ | 2 |
| 2(1) | Eye large, its horizontal diameter greater than or equal to the width of the fleshy interorbital; lips dark, contrasting strikingly with chin, which is white except at tip...........*Brotula multibarbata* | |
| | Eye relatively small, its horizontal diameter considerably less than the width of the fleshy interorbital; lips and chin uniformly greenish brown in life...........................*Brotula townsendi* | |
| 3(1) | Caudal rays not longer than the adjacent dorsal and anal rays; a distinct, downwardly projecting point at the posteroventral angle of the maxillary; size small to about 3 inches.............. | 4 |
| | Caudal rays longer than the adjacent dorsal and anal rays, projecting posteriorly as a more or less well-defined caudal fin; no downwardly projecting point at the posteroventral angle of the maxillary; length 5 inches or more...............Deep-water species | |
| 4(3) | Body black.....................................*Microbrotula nigra* | |
| | Body red in life, pale in alcohol.................*Microbrotula rubra* | |

**279**

### BROTULA MULTIBARBATA

A dark brown species with a submarginal black band and a narrow white border on the dorsal and anal fins. The maxillary reaches about the rear border of the eye (see Fig. 95).

Young specimens about 3 inches long are light (more or less transparent) with dark speckling.

The commonest Hawaiian brotulid. Reaches at least 18 inches in length.

### BROTULA TOWNSENDI

Similar to *Brotula multibarbata*, but greenish to orange brown, and the dorsal and anal with a broad orange border in life. The maxillary reaches about an eye diameter behind eye.

Only a few specimens of this species are known, some of them taken along with *B. multibarbata*. The largest of these is about 8 inches long.

### MICROBROTULA NIGRA

A small, chunky, black fish.

Only one specimen known, taken off Waikiki in about 30 feet of water. It is 3 inches long.

### MICROBROTULA RUBRA

A bright red fish known only from the reefs in Kaneohe Bay. A specimen less than 2 inches long had large eggs.

## Family CARAPIDAE

The members of this family have a long tapering body and the dorsal and anal continuous or almost continuous around the tip of the tail. Consequently, they may be easily mistaken for eels. However, unlike the eels, they have the anal fin commencing far forward, below the pectoral fins.

Many of the species of the family live in the cavities of invertebrates, living in oysters, starfishes, and sea cucumbers.

Key to the Hawaiian species of the family Carapidae:

| | | |
|---|---|---|
| 1 | Anal fin commencing in advance of the dorsal; pectoral fin shorter than head............................................ | 2 |
| | Anal fin commencing behind the dorsal; pectoral fin equal to the head length....................................*Snyderidia canina* | |
| 2(1) | Maxillary free from the skin of snout; eye not covered by adipose tissue; pectoral fin at least half the head length................. | 3 |
| | Maxillary bound to the head for most of its length; eye covered by a heavy layer of adipose tissue; pectoral fin about ⅓ the head length........................................*Encheliophis gracilis* | |
| 3(2) | Maxillary extending well behind eye; chest in front of anal sharply keeled.............................*Carapus margaritiferae* | |
| | Maxillary about reaching posterior border of eye; chest rounded in front of anal. No fanglike teeth in jaws.............*Carapus homei* | |

### SNYDERIDIA CANINA

This is a deep-water species with large fangs in the jaws. It is known from one specimen a foot long dredged in over 2000 feet of water.

### ENCHELIOPHIS GRACILIS

The upper jaw is bound to the snout for most of its length and the eye is so heavily covered with flesh as to be almost invisible in preserved specimens.

All the Hawaiian specimens of the species have been taken from sea cucumbers. The fish reaches about 10 inches in length.

### CARAPUS MARGARITIFERAE

In alcohol this species is completely white except for the dusky tail and a dark mark showing through the back of the head. In some specimens there are 2 tremendous fangs at the front of the lower jaw, but these are not always present; indeed they are never present in specimens less than 3 inches long.

Our material all came from rock oysters, and our largest specimen is about 4 inches long.

### CARAPUS HOMEI

Known in Hawaii from a single specimen 4 inches long taken in about 200 feet of water (see Fig. 129).


## THE NOMEID FISHES AND THEIR ALLIES

This group (suborder Stromateoidei) is made up of a number of externally nondescript fishes, but all of them have a large muscular gullet, rather like a bird's crop, with small teeth in the lining. This structure is unique among fishes.

### Family NOMEIDAE

The nomeids are, aside from *Nomeus gronovii*, rather nondescript; all are high-seas forms. The diagnostic feature of the family, held in common with the Tetragonuridae among Hawaiian fishes, is a heavy-walled pouch at the back of the throat; unfortunately, dissection is necessary to find this.

Though the members of the family are rarely seen, they must be common offshore, judging from aku spewings.

Key to the Hawaiian species of the family Nomeidae:

| | | |
|---|---|---|
| 1 | Pelvics not greatly expanded, shorter than the pectorals . . . . . . . . . . | 2 |
| | Pelvics greatly expanded, longer than the pectorals . . . . . *Nomeus gronovii* | |
| 2(1) | Body approximately cylindrical, the depth contained more than 3 times in the standard length . . . . . . . . . . . . . . . . . . . . . . . . . . . . . | 4 |
| | Body deep and compressed, the depth contained somewhat less than 2 times in the standard length . . . . . . . . . . . . . . . . . . . . . . . . | 3 |
| 3(2) | Scales in lateral line about 45 . . . . . . . . . . . . . . . . . . . . *Psenes arafurensis* | |
| | Scales in lateral line 56–63 . . . . . . . . . . . . . . . . . . . . . . *Psenes cyanophrys* | |

4(2)     Cheek with at most a single row of large scales, the upper portion
         of the cheek covered by a horny layer of adipose tissue; least
         depth of caudal peduncle less than an eye diameter............... 5

         Cheek completely scaled to the orbital border, with several lon-
         gitudinal rows of scales; least depth of caudal peduncle equal to
         or greater than an eye diameter................*Cubiceps pauciradiatus*

5(4)     Scales on top of head not extending forward over eye; adipose
         eyelids little developed, not reaching pupil; pelvics nearly as
         long as pectorals, which in turn are about ⅔ as long as the caudal
         lobes.................................................*Ariomma evermanni*

         Scales on top of head extending forward to over middle of eye;
         adipose eyelids well developed, the posterior extending forward
         to pupil; pelvics about half the length of the pectorals, which in
         turn are longer than the caudal lobes................*Ariomma lurida*

### NOMEUS GRONOVII

This fish appears to live chiefly among the tentacles of such planktonic
animals as the Portuguese man-of-war, and either avoids the stinging cells or
is not harmed by them (see Fig. 86). Only two groups of fishes are normally
found in this habitat. One is *Nomeus*, which can be readily recognized by the
blackish, expanded pelvic fins; the other is the young of certain uluas. Around
Hawaii, the latter group appears to be more frequently represented.

Maximum size about 3 inches.

### PSENES ARAFURENSIS

A species known from two Hawaiian specimens, the larger 4 inches long
taken beside a tern's nest. This individual, collected over 30 years ago, can
no longer be found. A smaller specimen, 23 mm. in standard length, is preserved in the Pacific Oceanic Fishery Investigations collections.

### PSENES CYANOPHRYS

Here recorded from Hawaiian waters for the first time. One individual,
118 mm. in standard length, was scooped up beside a glass ball between Oahu
and Kauai, and a second smaller one was taken in a plankton haul. In addition
to the smaller scales, the soft dorsal and soft anal counts for these specimens
are somewhat greater (24–25) than for *Psenes arafurensis* (19–22).

### CUBICEPS PAUCIRADIATUS

This species is also recorded here from Hawaiian waters for the first time.
Two specimens were taken from among aku spewings brought in to Hilo.
Other larger and better-preserved individuals are in the Pacific Oceanic Fishery
Investigations nite-lite collections. These show a median glandular protu-
berance on the snout and another in front of each eye.

To 6 inches.

### ARIOMMA EVERMANNI

Judging from available specimens, this is larger than other Hawaiian
nomeids. We have one specimen about a foot long, and there is a cast of

another in the Bishop Museum (the type of *Cubiceps thompsoni* Fowler) a little over 2 feet in length.

### ARIOMMA LURIDA

This fish has an elongate, cigar-shaped head that is contained about 2.7 times in the standard length and a tremendous eye with a well-developed adipose lid over its posterior portion.

The largest known specimen is a little over a foot long.

## Family TETRAGONURIDAE

A family of small, high-seas fishes known in Hawaiian waters from a single specimen. The long, low spinous dorsal and the keeled scales are distinguishing features.

### TETRAGONURUS CUVIERI

The one specimen recorded from our area was about 4 inches long (see Fig. 80).

# THE SCORPAENOID FISHES

The scorpaenoid fishes look and act very much like the sea basses. Nevertheless, they are allotted a separate order because of the development of a bony stay that runs across the cheek between the suborbital bones and the preopercle. However, this stay is only one element in a fairly general trend among scorpaenoids toward armature. Frequently this is expressed in spines or bony plates on the head, and at times in plates on the sides of the body.

## Family SCORPAENIDAE

If it were not for their excessive spininess the scorpaenids would be a rather typical group of bottom-living percoid fishes. They may be easily separated from the perchlike fishes by the presence of backwardly projecting spines on the rear of the head and by a rough or spiny ridge that runs across the cheek below the eye.

Scorpaenids spend their lives on the bottom, making short lunges to capture the animals on which they feed. This mode of life is reflected in their appearance: large mouth, large, rounded pectoral fins, often flaps of flesh on the head, and a coloration that makes them very difficult to see against the background on which they rest.

Certain scorpaenids have in their spines an apparatus for injecting poison. Of our Hawaiian forms, *Pterois* and *Dendrochirus* are the most notorious in this respect, but all scorpaenids should be handled with care. Fortunately for Hawaii, the stonefish, which has an extremely evil reputation throughout the tropical Pacific, is not found here.

Members of the Scorpaenidae occur at all depths from a few feet of water to at least half a mile. Indeed, this appears to be one of the predominant groups of bottom fishes in depths of about 500 feet.

Eighteen species of scorpaenids are recognized here as valid. Of these, seven have never been seen by us; six of the seven are from dredge hauls in over 200 feet of water. Among the remaining species an abundance of taxonomic problems remain. Though the scorpaenids have, literally, taxonomic characters sticking out all over them, there is often great variation from individual to individual. This has led to considerable confusion in the classification of the family, not only in Hawaii, but in the Pacific as a whole.

Key to the Hawaiian species of the family Scorpaenidae:

1  Body covered by normal scales, though fleshy flaps may also be present. . . . . . . . . . . . . . . . . . . . . . . . . . . . . . . . . . . . . . . . . . . . . . . . . .  2

Body without normal scales, its surface covered by papillae. Last dorsal ray connected to the basal portion of the uppermost caudal ray by a membrane. . . . . . . . . . . . . . . . . . . . .*Taenianotus triacanthus*

2(1)  Longest pectoral rays shorter than the head length. . . . . . . . . . . . . . .  4

Longest pectoral rays considerably longer than the head length. . . . .  3

3(2)  All of the pectoral rays unbranched, the upper forming long free filaments that usually reach beyond the caudal base. . . . . . . .*Pterois sphex*

Most of the upper pectoral rays branched, not extending beyond the interradial membranes. . . . . . . . . . . . . . . . . . .*Dendrochirus brachypterus*

4(2)  None of the dorsal spines notably produced beyond the others, several of the longest spines being of nearly equal length. . . . . . . . . . .  6

Either the third or the fourth dorsal spine produced well beyond the others. Lower jaw projecting. . . . . . . . . . . . . . . . . . . . . . . . . . . . . .  5

5(4)  Third dorsal spine produced, considerably longer than the second or fourth; cheeks scaleless; a moderately deep-water species. . . . . . . . . . . . . . . . . . . . . . . . . . . . . . . . . . . . . . . . . . . . . . . . . . . . . .*Peloropsis xenops*

Fourth dorsal spine produced, at least half again as long as the third or fifth; cheeks mostly scaled; an inshore species. .*Iracundus signifer*

6(4)  Upper edge of caudal base without low, sharp, backwardly pointed spines; dorsal spines 12, rarely 11. . . . . . . . . . . . . . . . . . . . . .  8

Upper edge of caudal base with 2 or more low, sharp, backwardly pointed spines (that are easily felt by running a finger forward along the dorsal surface of the caudal peduncle); dorsal spines 13, rarely 12. No palatine teeth. . . . . . . . . . . . . . . . . . . . . . . . .  7

7(6)  Pectoral fin extending to above anal origin; longest dorsal spine about twice the interorbital width. . . . . . . . . . . . . . .*Scorpaenodes guamensis*

Pectoral fin not reaching anal origin; longest dorsal spine slightly longer than the interorbital width. . . . . . .*Scorpaenodes parvipinnis*

8(6)  Jaws equal or the lower included; palatine teeth usually present. . . .  10

Lower jaw projecting; no palatine teeth. . . . . . . . . . . . . . . . . . . . . . . .  9

9(8)  Gray in life (except for the inside of the pectoral fins); width of bony interorbital about equal to the snout length. . .*Scorpaenopsis gibbosa*

Red in life; width of bony interorbital contained more than 1.5 times in the snout length. . . . . . . . . . . . . . . . . . . . . . . .*Scorpaenopsis cacopsis*

10(8)   Lateral line not contained in a wide, scaleless trough; not more
        than 1 preopercular spine longer than half-an-eye diameter......... 11

        Lateral line contained in a wide, scaleless trough; at least 3 pre-
        opercular spines that are longer than half-an-eye diameter. Scales
        small, cycloid; a deep-water species.................*Setarches remiger*

11(10)  Second dorsal fin consisting of 1 spine and 9 to 11 soft rays....... 12

        Second dorsal fin consisting of 2 spines and 7 soft rays. Body
        relatively elongate, the depth going about 4 times into the stand-
        ard length; a deep-water species.................*Plectrogenium nanum*

12(11)  At least some of the upper pectoral rays branched............... 13

        None of the pectoral rays branched. Supraocular tentacle cylin-
        drical in cross section; a moderately deep-water species.......
        ....................................*Merinthe macrocephala*

13(12)  No scattered, small but conspicuous dark spots on the body,
        head, and dorsal fin.......................................... 14

        Many scattered, small but conspicuous dark spots on the body,
        head, and basal portion of the dorsal fin............*Scorpaena coniorta*

14(13)  Head below the horizontal cheek strut with small but normal
        scales. Deep-water species................................... 17

        Head below the horizontal cheek strut without normal scales...... 15

15(14)  Maxillary reaching posterior border of eye..................... 16

        Maxillary not reaching posterior border of pupil. Eye diameter
        much greater than the snout length; a rather deep-water species
        ..............................................*Scorpaena coloratus*

16(15)  Last dorsal ray attached to the back by a membrane; palatine
        teeth present...................................*Scorpaena ballieui*

        Last dorsal ray free from the back; palatine teeth absent. A mod-
        erately deep-water species.....................*Scorpaenopsis altirostris*

17(14)  Eye diameter greater than the snout length; no black blotch on
        the posterior portion of the spinous dorsal.........*Helicolenus rufescens*

        Eye diameter less than the snout length; a black blotch on the
        posterior portion of the spinous dorsal..............*Pontinus spilistius*

## TAENIANOTUS TRIACANTHUS

This is the most compressed of all our scorpaenids; it is also one of the
most striking. The first dorsal spine is inserted less than an eye diameter behind the eye and the dorsal fin runs like a sail from there to its attachment
with the caudal.

Though the species is rather rare it has been taken from depths of a few
feet to over 300 feet. Perhaps the deep-water form is a different species, but
we do not have the material to check this.

To about 4 inches.

## PTEROIS SPHEX

This is the lion-fish of aquarists. The extremely elongate spines are said to
form an extremely efficient poison-injection apparatus. Probably for this
reason *Pterois* makes no attempt to escape and can easily be caught in a net.

Fig. 262. PTEROIS SPHEX

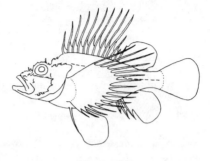

After J. and E.

Two species of *Pterois* undoubtedly occur in Hawaii, but what the second species is and how it may be characterized remain unknown to us.

Reaches about 10 inches in length.

Fig. 263. DENDROCHIRUS BRACHYPTERUS

After J. and E.

### DENDROCHIRUS BRACHYPTERUS

A more normal relative of *Pterois*. Like that genus, the fins are long and the interradial membranes between the dorsal spines are usually deeply incised.

Far commoner than *Pterois* in shallow water. To about 7 inches in length.

### PELOROPSIS XENOPS

One of our numerous scorpaenids described from dredge hauls in moderately deep water long ago and never taken in Hawaii since. This one has the look of *Scorpaenopsis* except for the elongate third dorsal spine.

One known specimen 6 inches long.

### IRACUNDUS SIGNIFER

This species is supposed to be an inshore form, but we have never seen it. Among other peculiarities, it has a black spot on the membrane between the second and third dorsal spines.

Two specimens known, the larger 4.2 inches long.

## SCORPAENODES GUAMENSIS

Much the rarer of our two species of *Scorpaenodes*. *S. guamensis* seems to be distinctive among our scorpaenids in having a small median knob at the tip of the lower jaw that fits into a median depression in the upper. The body and fins are covered with brown crossbars and specklings.

Our specimens are less than 3 inches long.

**Fig. 264. SCORPAENODES PARVIPINNIS**

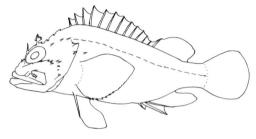

After J. and E.

## SCORPAENODES PARVIPINNIS

*Scorpaenodes parvipinnis* has probably the lowest spinous dorsal fin of any of our scorpaenids, the length of the longest spine going 3½ times (stepped) into the spinous dorsal base. It is unique among Hawaiian members of the family in having the basal portion of the whole dorsal fin covered with a rather heavy sheath of scales. The fish is basically red in life.

A rather abundant shallow-water form attaining a length of about 6 inches.

## SCORPAENOPSIS GIBBOSA (Nohu, Omakaha)

An ugly gray fish with numerous flaplike appendages. There is no striking coloration in the resting fish, but when it moves the violent reds and yellows on the insides of the pectoral fin flash into view. The young have prominent broad crossbars on the body and fins.

In appearance, this species strongly resembles the notorious stonefish of the tropical Pacific, but we know of no records of ill effects from being spined by the nohu.

A common inshore species attaining perhaps 12 inches in length.

**Fig. 265. SCORPAENOPSIS CACOPSIS**

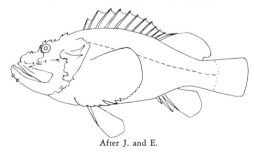

After J. and E.

**287**

### SCORPAENOPSIS CACOPSIS (Nohu)

This fish has the general appearance of *Scorpaenopsis gibbosa* but is reddish in life. It seems to replace *S. gibbosa* on the outside of the reef; indeed it is never found in less than 20 feet of water.

Unlike *S. gibbosa* it attains a size of at least 20 inches and is much sought after as food.

### SETARCHES REMIGER

A peculiar deep-water form that resembles only *Pterois* and *Dendrochirus* among Hawaiian scorpaenids in having the third anal spine notably longer than the second.

Apparently common at depths from 500 to 1000 feet. To at least 7 inches in length.

### PLECTROGENIUM NANUM

Another peculiar deep-water form, this one with very large scales for a scorpaenid, there being about 27 in a longitudinal series below the lateral line.

Taken in about the same depth with *Setarches*. To about 4 inches in length.

**Fig. 266.  MERINTHE MACROCEPHALA**

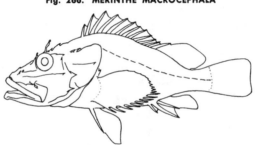

After J. and E.

### MERINTHE MACROCEPHALA ('O'opu kai nohu)

*Merinthe* is peculiar in usually having a long, cylindrical, muscular, supra-ocular tentacle. Unfortunately, as in other scorpaenids, the supraocular tentacle is quite variably represented in different specimens of the same species.

We have never seen adult specimens of *Merinthe*, but the species is said to attain a weight of 4 or 5 pounds.

### SCORPAENA CONIORTA

This is one of our two inshore members of the genus *Scorpaena* (see Fig. 100). The small spots (not shown in the figure) are distinctive, but, in addition, it is the only member of the genus in which the cheeks below the strut have normal scales. There is never any large dark blotch on the posterior portion of the spinous dorsal.

### SCORPAENA COLORATUS

A deep-water form apparently related to *S. ballieui*, from which it differs in having a larger eye and one more pectoral ray.

The only known specimens were dredged off Molokai in 240 to 400 feet of water. The type is 3 inches long.

### SCORPAENA BALLIEUI

Probably the commonest Hawaiian shallow-water scorpaenid. It is quite variable and has apparently been described as several different species. For one thing, the black blotch on the spinous dorsal does not appear until specimens reach a length of 2 inches. For another, the development of dermal flaps on the head and body varies greatly from specimen to specimen.

Occurs everywhere in shallow water and reaches about 4 inches in length.

### SCORPAENOPSIS ALTIROSTRIS

That this species belongs to the genus *Scorpaenopsis* seems extremely doubtful. It looks much less like the other members of that genus than like *Scorpaena*, from which it is said to differ in lacking palatine teeth.

Six specimens known, dredged in 240 to 400 feet. The type is less than 3 inches long.

### HELICOLENUS RUFESCENS

Another small, generalized, and dubious form described from two specimens dredged in more than 240 feet of water. The type is 4 inches long.

### PONTINUS SPILISTIUS

Quite similar to the last in appearance. Known from a few specimens about 4 inches long taken from water some 500 feet deep.

## Family PERISTEDIIDAE

A very unusual-looking family of deep-water fishes with the head completely armored, the armor usually with 2 forwardly projecting prongs.

Two species known from Hawaii, both recorded from depths of more than 1000 feet (Fig 67).

## Family CARACANTHIDAE

A very peculiar family of small compressed, deep-bodied fishes with the head and body covered by papillae; in fact the adult caracanthid would bear a distinct resemblance to a furry fifty-cent piece. They have a strong preorbital spine just above the rear of the jaw that can be extended outward, and their pelvic fins are so small as to be easily overlooked.

These fishes seem to wedge themselves between the branches of coral.

Two species recorded from the Hawaiian Islands though the record of one of these seems questionable.

Key to the recorded Hawaiian species of the family Caracanthidae:

> Head and body with light spots; a deep notch in the outline of
> of the dorsal fin between the spinous and the soft dorsal......
> ..............................................*Caracanthus maculatus*

Head and body without light spots; outline of the dorsal fins nearly continuous, the last dorsal spine nearly as long as the longest dorsal ray...........................*Caracanthus unipinna*

### CARACANTHUS MACULATUS

A not uncommon species in areas of live coral (see Fig. 90). Reaches about 1.5 inches in length.

### CARACANTHUS UNIPINNA

There is only one ancient record (1874) of this fish from Hawaii. That it occurs here seems dubious. Apparently a somewhat smaller species than *Caracanthus maculatus*.

## Family PLATYCEPHALIDAE

Another scorpaenoid family represented in Hawaii only in deep water. Only one species recorded from here, described from two specimens dredged in some 800 feet of water (Fig 66).

## Family HOPLICHTHYIDAE

Two Hawaiian species recorded, both from depths of over 500 feet (Fig. 68).

## Family DACTYLOPTERIDAE

This family comprises some of the most bizarre of fishes. One Hawaiian species.

### DACTYLOPTENA ORIENTALIS (Lolo-'oau)

The long, spotted, winglike pectorals resemble those of the flying fishes but the head is completely armored, a combination found elsewhere only in *Pegasus* (see Fig. 63). As if these peculiarities were not enough, *Dactyloptena* has a single, flagpole-like dorsal ray standing straight up from the back of the head.

Not rare in shallow water. Attains a length of at least 14 inches.

## THE PEGASIDS

## Family PEGASIDAE

The fishes in this family are so odd that it has been impossible to reach any agreement on what they are related to. One species in Hawaiian waters.

### PEGASUS PAPILIO

As the specific name implies, this species acts in an aquarium like a not very large butterfly (see Fig. 92). Aside from the winglike pectorals and armored head, this fish possesses a peculiar club-shaped snout and a single filament instead of the usual pectoral fin.

**290**

So far as is known, the species does not get to be more than 2 inches long. It is brought in from time to time from moderately deep water.

## THE REMORAS

### Family ECHENEIDAE

The remoras or shark-suckers have the first dorsal fin transformed into a sucking disc. By the use of this they ride along on sharks and other large marine animals, detaching themselves to pick up the scraps from the meals of their hosts. The species of remoras seem to be as widespread in distribution as the various animals to which they attach themselves.

Several species probably occur here, but only one seems to have been definitely recorded. Remoras are probably much commoner than records indicate, for they have a habit of slipping off their hosts when the latter are brought into a boat.

#### REMORA REMORA

A common and widespread species (see Fig. 101). There are 17 or 18 cross ridges in the dorsal sucking disc; other species that may occur here will probably have either more than 20 (the genus *Echeneis*) or fewer than 12 (*Ptheirichthys*).

Attains a length of about 18 inches.

## THE HUMUHUMUS, PUFFERS, AND THEIR ALLIES

The various members of the order Tetraodontiformes have few superficial traits in common except, perhaps, that they all look absurd. Nevertheless, an examination of their skeletons quickly demonstrates their relationship to one another and how specialized they are. It also demonstrates their derivation from an acanthuroid-like fish. Superficially, none of the group has normal pelvic fins or normal scales.

The members of this group are all slow swimmers. Probably in relation to this they have almost all developed protective devices of one sort or another, though the methods of protection employed are quite varied, including spines, armor, poisonous flesh, and ability to inflate.

### Family BALISTIDAE (Triggerfishes or Humuhumus)

The humuhumus are rather conspicuous, if uncommon, fishes on Hawaiian reefs. Solitary individuals may be seen swimming slowly over the reef bottom. If approached they will swim into a small hole in the coral, wedging themselves tightly against the sides.

The balistids have a reduced number of flattened teeth in the small mouth and no pelvic fins. They may be most easily differentiated from their closest relatives by their platelike scales; in the related monacanthids, by contrast, the individual scales cannot be distinguished, and the surface of the body is fuzzy to the touch.

Ten species recognized from our area. All of these reach at least 6 inches in length.

Key to the Hawaiian species of the family Balistidae:

1      Anterior soft dorsal and anal rays relatively short, not reaching beyond the tips of the last rays when depressed, shorter than the snout length . . . . . . . . . . . . . . . . . . . . . . . . . . . . . . . . . . . . . . . . . . . . . . 2

Anterior soft dorsal and anal rays high, reaching beyond the tips of the last rays when the fins are depressed, longer than the snout plus eye . . . . . . . . . . . . . . . . . . . . . . . . . . *Canthidermis maculatus*

2(1)    Cheek below eye without 5 longitudinal, dark-bottomed grooves . . . . 3

Cheek below eye with 5 nearly longitudinal, dark-bottomed grooves. Lower jaw projecting . . . . . . . . . . . . . . . . . . . . *Xanthichthys ringens*

3(2)    No conspicuous dark band extending downward and backward from the pectoral to the anus; forwardly projecting spines on caudal peduncle, if present, not in 2 to 4 longitudinal rows . . . . . . . . 5

A conspicuous dark band extending downward and backward from the pectoral region to the anus; forwardly projecting spines on caudal peduncle in 2 to 4 longitudinal rows . . . . . . . . . . . . . . . . . 4

4(3)    Caudal peduncle with a forwardly projecting, black wedge which includes the spinelets; pectoral base black . . . . . . *Rhinecanthus rectangulus*

Caudal peduncle pale except for the black spinelets; pectoral base pale . . . . . . . . . . . . . . . . . . . . . . . . . . . . . . . . . . . . *Rhinecanthus aculeatus*

5(3)    Lips thick and well delimited, their widths at least ⅔ the diameter of the pupil of the eye; snout protruding, the jaws equal or the upper longer . . . . . . . . . . . . . . . . . . . . . . . . . . . . . . . . . . . . . . . . . . . . . . . . . 8

Lips thin and poorly delimited except at sides, their widths less than ½ a pupil diameter; snout rounded, the lower jaw protruding . . . . 6

6(5)    Dorsal and anal light with a black border; pectoral yellow or pink in life; outer caudal rays not projecting . . . . . . . . . . . . . . . . . . . . . 7

Dorsal and anal black except for a light blue line along the base; pectoral dark; outer caudal rays projecting beyond the others . . 
. . . . . . . . . . . . . . . . . . . . . . . . . . . . . . . . . . . . . . . . . . . . . . . . *Melichthys buniva*

7(6)    First rays of dorsal and anal somewhat longer than the others, forming a slight lobe; basal portion of dorsal and anal plain pink in life . . . . . . . . . . . . . . . . . . . . . . . . . . . . . . . . . . . . . . . . . *Melichthys vidua*

Dorsal and anal outlines rounded; basal portion of dorsal and anal crossed by 4 narrow, parallel, black lines . . . . . . . . . . . *Balistes nycteris*

8(5)    Outer caudal rays not produced beyond the others; distance from upper angle of gill opening to eye contained more than 3 times in snout length . . . . . . . . . . . . . . . . . . . . . . . . . . . . . . . . . . . . . . . . . . . . . 9

Outer caudal rays produced well beyond the others; distance from upper angle of gill opening to eye contained about 2½ times in snout length . . . . . . . . . . . . . . . . . . . . . . . . . . . . . . . *Balistes fuscus*

9(8)    Base of pectoral dark; a dark semicircular band running down to in front of pectoral; no light lines running across chin . . . . *Balistes bursa*

Base of pectoral light; no dark semicircular band running down to in front of pectoral; 2 light lines running across chin . . . . . . . 
. . . . . . . . . . . . . . . . . . . . . . . . . . . . . . . . . . . . . . . . . . . . . . . *Balistes capistratus*

### CANTHIDERMIS MACULATUS

This high-finned fish is quite unlike all of the other Hawaiian balistids in appearance. The caudal fin is lunate and a technical character that it shares only with *Xanthichthys ringens* is that there are no especially enlarged plates just behind the gill opening.

Apparently rather rare, though it comes into the aquarium from time to time. To over a foot.

### XANTHICHTHYS RINGENS

The longitudinal grooves between the scale rows on the cheek will distinguish this species. In addition it has a lunate caudal with a light border.

Not common. To about 9 inches.

**Fig. 267. RHINECANTHUS RECTANGULUS**

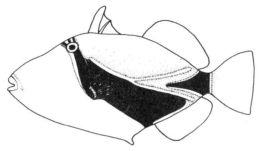

After J. and E.

### RHINECANTHUS RECTANGULUS (Humuhumu-nukunuku-a-pua'a)

The humuhumus of the genus *Rhinecanthus*, although famous in Hawaiian song, are actually rather brainless-looking fishes. The black, forwardly projecting wedge on the tail will distinguish *R. rectangulus* from other Hawaiian fishes.

Not uncommon. To about 9 inches.

**Fig. 268. RHINECANTHUS ACULEATUS**

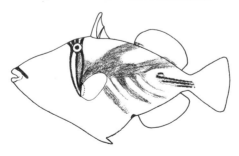

After J. and E.

**293**

### RHINECANTHUS ACULEATUS (Humuhumu-nukunuku-a-pua'a)

Easily distinguished by the 3 or 4 rows of black spinelets on the caudal peduncle which stand out against the light background.

Fairly common. To about 9 inches.

**Fig. 269. MELICHTHYS BUNIVA**

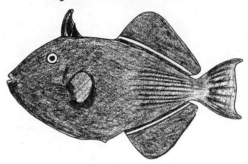

After J. and E.

### MELICHTHYS BUNIVA (Humuhumu-'ele'ele)

This is one of the two or three glossy black humuhumus. The narrow blue line along the dorsal and anal base is an immediate means of species identification.

Not uncommon. To at least a foot.

**Fig. 270. MELICHTHYS VIDUA**

After J. and E.

### MELICHTHYS VIDUA (Humuhumu-hi'u-kole, Humuhumu-uli)

Another of the glossy black species, this one with plain white dorsal and anal fins below the black borders but with a pink tail.

Not uncommon. To about 10 inches.

### BALISTES NYCTERIS

Apparently close to *Melichthys vidua* in appearance, differing in the lines on the fin (see Fig. 140).

Not seen by us. The three known specimens are 5 to 7 inches long.

#### BALISTES FUSCUS

A large and plain-colored triggerfish. Uncommon. To at least 20 inches.

#### BALISTES BURSA

The scimitar-shaped dark bar running down from the eye and hooking into the base of the pectoral fin is diagnostic for this species.
Fairly common. To about 8 inches.

#### BALISTES CAPISTRATUS

A plain fish except for the light markings around mouth.
Rather uncommon. To at least 12 inches.

## Family MONACANTHIDAE

This family is most easily distinguished from the Balistidae, its closest relative, by the velvety surface to the body. Additionally, the first dorsal spine (the trigger) lies about over the middle of the eye in Hawaiian monacanthids, over the rear of or behind the eye in our balistids.

*Pervagor spilosoma*, at least, appears at certain times in great numbers. The species vary considerably in size from the 5-inch *Pervagor* to *Alutera* at least 2 feet in length. All of the species may be rather pernicious nibblers of bait and none are worth anything commercially.

Key to the Hawaiian species of the family Monacanthidae:

| | | |
|---|---|---|
| 1 | A bony tubercle projecting on the mid-ventral line; gill openings entirely below or behind the eye; dorsal spine stiff and sharp.... | 3 |
| | No bony tubercle projecting from the mid-ventral line; gill openings extending forward of the eye; dorsal spine over eye long and fragile................................................. | 2 |
| 2(1) | Upper profile of snout evenly convex; outer caudal rays as long as those in middle..............................*Alutera monoceros* | |
| | Upper profile of snout concave; middle caudal rays longer than outer.......................................*Alutera scripta* | |
| 3(1) | No movable knob on the tip of the pelvic tubercle; caudal fin plain...................................................... | 5 |
| | A movable, spiny knob at the tip of the pelvic tubercle; caudal fin with a pale base and a blackish border...................... | 4 |
| 4(3) | Body spotted; head with dark longitudinal lines; dorsal rays 37 or 38.......................................*Pervagor spilosoma* | |
| | Head and body plain blackish; dorsal rays 32 or 33........... ............................................*Pervagor melanocephalus* | |
| 5(3) | Body plain brown or variously mottled and barred but never with round white spots; soft dorsal rays 34 or 35................ | 6 |
| | Body covered with round white spots; soft dorsal rays 38..... ..........................................*Amanses albopunctatus* | |
| 6(5) | No enlarged spinelets on caudal peduncle; pectoral rays 12 or 13.... | 7 |
| | Four forwardly-hooked spinelets on either side of the caudal peduncle; pectoral rays 15 or 16......................*Amanses carolae* | |

**295**

7(6)    Body plain brown; caudal fin dark brown at base, with a pink border in life; first dorsal spine long, longer than the middle rays of the truncate caudal fin....................*Amanses sandwichiensis*

Body usually barred and spotted; caudal with light bars across base, but the posterior third plain dark gray in life; first dorsal spine relatively short, shorter than the middle rays of the rounded caudal fin........................................*Amanses pardalis*

**Fig. 271. ALUTERA MONOCEROS**

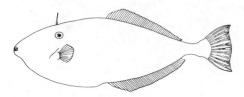

**ALUTERA MONOCEROS (Loulu)**

One of the two species of *Alutera* that are taken by fishermen from time to time. It seems to be the smaller of the two. Our specimen is 17 inches long.

**Fig. 272. ALUTERA SCRIPTA**

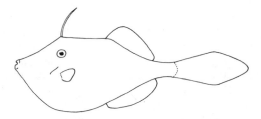

**ALUTERA SCRIPTA ('O'ili lepa, 'Ohua)**

The long whiskbroom-like tail and greatly compressed body are diagnostic for this fish.

To at least 2 feet in length.

**PERVAGOR SPILOSOMA ('O'ili uwiwi)**

The bright orange tail with a dark border will immediately identify this species. In the adult the body is yellow with black spots; at 2 inches long the body is plain silvery (see Fig. 139).

In some years this fish seems to be abundant everywhere; in others it is rather rare. Attains a length of only 5 inches.

**PERVAGOR MELANOCEPHALUS**

This plain blackish-bodied fish seems to be the only representative of the genus at Johnston. However, we have only identified one specimen of it in our Hawaiian material.

To about 5 inches.

### AMANSES ALBOPUNCTATUS

This species does not seem to have been recorded from Hawaiian waters since it was originally described over 40 years ago. Judging from the published account and figure it should be a readily recognizable form.

The only known specimen is 8 inches long.

**Fig. 273. AMANSES CAROLAE**

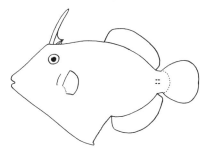

### AMANSES CAROLAE

Apparently the largest of our species of *Amanses*. We have specimens over a foot long. Since our smallest is 7.5 inches we are unable to say whether small specimens have the spinelets on the tail; however the difference in pectoral count should make this species differentiable from *A. sandwichiensis* at all stages. Another feature that should distinguish these two species is that *A. carolae* has a submarginal light band around the mouth.

### AMANSES SANDWICHIENSIS

This plain brown species is perhaps our commonest *Amanses*. In life the dorsal, anal, pectoral, and caudal borders are all pink. None of our specimens are longer than 7 inches.

### AMANSES PARDALIS

The species that we provisionally and probably erroneously identify as *Amanses pardalis* seems to be both the smallest and most deep-bodied of our *Amanses*. The body and caudal are variously barred, blotched, and dark spotted, and the dorsal, anal, and pectoral are plain gray in life.

The largest of our specimens is about 5 inches long.

## Family OSTRACIONTIDAE (Boxfishes or Cowfishes)

The boxfishes or cowfishes are among the most peculiar of our fishes. The bony box in which the body is enclosed is sufficient identification. The members of the family are not strong swimmers and can often be approached quite closely.

None of the Hawaiian species attain a length of more than 9 inches. Only one, *Ostracion lentiginosus*, is at all common.

Key to the Hawaiian species of the family Ostraciontidae:

| 1 | Carapace without a mid-ventral keel, closed behind the dorsal and anal fins.................................................... | 2 |
| | Carapace with a mid-ventral keel, not enclosing the dorsal and anal fins posteriorly...........................*Aracana aculeata* | |
| 2(1) | Carapace with 2 spines in front of eye........................ | 4 |
| | Carapace without spines in front of eye....................... | 3 |
| 3(2) | Body with numerous small white spots, especially on the dorsal surface; no striping...........................*Ostracion lentiginosus* | |
| | Upper sides with alternating dark and light stripes, the dark stripes continuous, but the light ones broken up into segments. Not known north of Johnston....................*Ostracion solorensis* | |
| 4(2) | No small spines on the dorso-lateral ridges behind the eye.... ............................................*Lactoria fornasini* | |
| | At least 1 small spine on each dorso-lateral ridge behind the eye ............................................*Lactoria diaphanus* | |

### ARACANA ACULEATA

Known from Hawaiian waters from two specimens, the larger 4 inches long, dredged at a depth of some 500 feet.

### OSTRACION LENTIGINOSUS (Moa, Mamoa waa, Oopakaku)

This spotted fish is often brilliantly colored with yellow and blue tints in life (see Fig. 141). It can frequently be seen swimming around in leisurely fashion in quite shallow water. The males are blue and yellow, the females relatively drab. The species appears to give off a substance poisonous to other fishes in the vicinity when excited.

Rather common. To about 6 inches.

### OSTRACION SOLORENSIS

The species is included here on the basis of a single, small Johnston Island specimen.

### LACTORIA FORNASINI (Makukana)

The name cowfish, used for this and related species, refers to the horns projecting in front of the eyes. All of our specimens of *Lactoria* belong to this species. The largest is about 6 inches long.

### LACTORIA DIAPHANUS

Closely allied to the preceding species. Attains at least a foot in length.

## Family TETRAODONTIDAE (Puffers or Balloonfishes)

The puffers are among the ugliest of fishes. They not only have the power of inflating themselves like a balloon but have the reputation of being poisonous if eaten. However, by proper preparation certain puffers at least can be made into a rather esoterically flavored soup. This is done extensively in Japan and to some extent in Hawaii.

Five species known from our waters, only one of which is at all common. The largest reach perhaps 20 inches in length.

Key to the Hawaiian species of the family Tetraodontidae:

1      Head and body with backwardly projecting prickles that are easily felt by running a finger forward over the body; body with some spotting or banding.................................... 2

        Head and body without prickles and without markings of any sort........................................*Sphoeroides cutaneus*

2(1)    Dorsal and anal fins rounded, the first ray not reaching beyond the others when the fin is laid back; no ridge of flesh along the the lower sides posteriorly; nostrils in a 2-lobed flap without visible openings............................................ 4

        Dorsal and anal fins falcate, the first rays reaching well beyond the others when the fin is laid back; a fleshy ridge along the lower sides posteriorly; nostrils in a tube with 2 holes............ 3

3(2)    Dorsal and anal each with 12 rays; no longitudinal dark band running backward from above the pectoral base..............
       .......................................*Lagocephalus lagocephalus*

        Dorsal and anal each with 7 to 9 rays; a longitudinal dark band running backward from above the pectoral base..............
       .....................................*Lagocephalus hypselogeneion*

4(2)    Bony eye sockets nowhere raised above the level of the inter-orbital, which is flat; dorsal rays 10. No longitudinal dark lines on the ventral portion of body....................*Arothron meleagris*

        Bony eye sockets slightly raised above the level of the interorbital; dorsal rays 9. White spotting, if present, not extending across abdomen.................................*Arothron hispidus*

### SPHOEROIDES CUTANEUS

Known only from one Hawaiian record of a specimen 9 inches long.

### LAGOCEPHALUS LAGOCEPHALUS

This species has only been recorded from Hawaii a few times. The only specimen we have seen is an extremely elongate (perhaps emaciated) individual nearly 2 feet long that died in the Honolulu aquarium.

### LAGOCEPHALUS HYPSELOGENEION

Judging by the specimens taken, this is much the commoner of our two Hawaiian species of *Lagocephalus*. The largest available to us is about a foot in length.

### AROTHRON MELEAGRIS

The white spotting all over the body is distinctive. Not common. Reaches about a foot in length.

### AROTHRON HISPIDUS ('O'opu-hue, Makimaki, Keke)

Quite variable in color pattern but never approaching the other Hawaiian species in appearance (see Fig. 143). Usually the body is gray with black circles around the pectoral base and longitudinal dark lines on the abdomen. There is frequently white spotting on the back but never across the ventral part of the body.

**299**

By far the commonest of our puffers. The young are often abundant inhabitants of mullet ponds and other brackish-water areas. Reaches about 10 inches in length.

## Family CANTHIGASTERIDAE (Sharpbacked Puffers)

The canthigasterids are small puffers, distinguishable from the tetraodontid puffers by a number of minor external features. In an uninflated condition, canthigasterids are deeper than broad, whereas the tetraodontids are approximately round in cross section. The gill openings of the canthigasterids are relatively shorter (see family key), and the outer border of the pectoral is either straight or slightly indented, whereas it is rounded in the tetraodontids.

The canthigasterids are beautifully colored little fishes, but both the color and color pattern of the species may be subject to considerable variation. This last feature has led to considerable confusion in the classification of the group.

None of the four Hawaiian species recognized here occur in great numbers in any locality though solitary individuals may frequently be seen. None of the species reach more than 5 inches in length.

Key to the Hawaiian species of the family Canthigasteridae:

| | | |
|---|---|---|
| 1 | Ventral profile of the body rounded; not more than 1 black saddle extending downward from the back........................ | 2 |
| | Ventral profile of the body nearly straight from the chin to the base of the tail; 3 black saddles extending downward and forward into the light coloration of the body..........*Canthigaster cinctus* | |
| 2(1) | No large white blotches on upper sides, though a series of small white as well as dark dots may occur; usually a series of lines radiating from the eye; dorsal rays 10 or more................... | 3 |
| | Color pattern on the upper part of body consisting entirely of white blotches on a dark ground; no lines radiating from the eye; dorsal rays 9................................*Canthigaster jactator* | |
| 3(2) | Dorsal rays 11 or more. No dark lines running out onto the caudal; no dark median line running from chin to anus....... ........................................*Canthigaster amboinensis* | |
| | Dorsal rays 10..............................*Canthigaster rivulatus* | |

**Fig. 274. CANTHIGASTER CINCTUS**

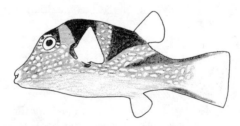

**CANTHIGASTER CINCTUS**

Compared to the other species of *Canthigaster*, *C. cinctus* appears emaciated. The 3 black saddles are also distinctive. The coloration of this fish in life is

**300**

black and white, with orange spots and yellow fins.

Apparently rare. Reaches about 5 inches in length.

**Fig. 275. CANTHIGASTER JACTATOR**

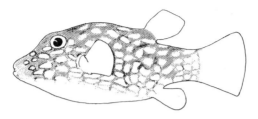

**CANTHIGASTER JACTATOR**

The plain white spotting on a dark ground is diagnostic for this species. The spotting does not extend on to the tail. A closely related tropical Pacific species, *Canthigaster solandri*, has been recorded once from Hawaiian waters, but the record needs substantiation. *C. solandri* differs from *C. jactator* in having lines radiating from the eye and white spotting on the caudal.

*C. jactator* is probably the commonest as well as the smallest of Hawaiian canthigasterids. Reaches perhaps 3 inches in length.

**Fig. 276. CANTHIGASTER AMBOINENSIS**

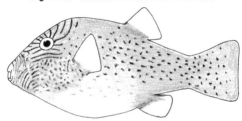

**CANTHIGASTER AMBOINENSIS (Pu'u-ola'i)**

About the only certain distinguishing character for this species is the dorsal-ray count; no other Hawaiian canthigasterid has more than 10. In color *Canthigaster amboinensis* is usually dark and may have small light as well as dark spots. The lines running back from the eye extend up and across the top of the head.

Not uncommon. To about 5 inches.

**Fig. 277. CANTHIGASTER RIVULATUS**

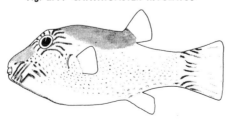

Unless we have confused two species here, the color pattern of *Canthigaster rivulatus* is quite variable. The young, described by Jenkins as *C. bitaeniatus*, have 2 longitudinal bars on each side running from the pectoral to the base of the tail; these meet one another in front by running around the front of the pectoral base; there is also a dark spot on the pectoral base but apparently no other markings are present. In large specimens the whole sides are covered with reticulations; a series of dark lines runs out onto the base of the tail; and there is a dark mid-ventral line from the chin to the anus. Two of our three specimens are intermediate between the 2 patterns just described.

Apparently rare. To about 5 inches.

## Family DIODONTIDAE (Spiny Puffers)

The porcupine fishes, or spiny puffers, are exceedingly difficult to handle. On provocation they blow themselves up with air or water, and when inflated all the spines of the body stand erect. Judging by the number of times the jaws are picked up on the beach, at least one species must be common about Hawaii. These jaws are beaklike and are often misidentified as those of parrot fishes, but in *Diodon* there are a number of transverse grooves on the inside of the jaw behind the beak itself.

Three species are known from the Hawaiian Islands.

Key to the Hawaiian species of the family Diodontidae:

1        Spines elongate, movable, and needle-like; no brown bars extending down the sides...................................... 2

         Spines short, immovable, triangular and broad-based, 4 brown bars extending down the sides from the back.......*Chilomycterus affinis*

2(1)    No dark bars across back; a dusky bar across rear of chin; fins spotted.........................................*Diodon hystrix*

         About 3 dark bars across back, the first extending across between the eyes; no dusky bar across rear of chin; fins plain..*Diodon holocanthus*

### CHILOMYCTERUS AFFINIS ('O'opu-hue)

The broad-based, rigid, protuberances will distinguish this fish from the species of *Diodon*.

Apparently a relatively rare form; we have not seen it. Reaches 20 inches.

### DIODON HYSTRIX ('O'opu-kawa)

This seems to be the common large Hawaiian spiny puffer (see Fig. 142). It apparently occurs both inshore and offshore. It is frequently seen dead on the beach.

To approximately 2 feet in length.

### DIODON HOLOCANTHUS

This may prove to be the young of *Diodon hystrix*, although its coloration is quite different and its spines appear to be relatively longer. However, we have never seen specimens of *D. holocanthus* longer than 10 inches in length or of *D. hystrix* shorter than 15 inches.

## Family MOLIDAE (Ocean Sunfishes)

The ocean sunfishes are peculiar oceanic fishes that look as if they had had their tails bitten off.

The three known genera of the family are all represented from Hawaii, each apparently by a single species.

Key to the Hawaiian species of the family Molidae:

| | | |
|---|---|---|
| 1 | Depth of body about equal to the distance from the snout to the base of the dorsal fin...................................... | 2 |
| | Depth of body contained about 2 times in the distance from the snout to the dorsal fin............................ *Ranzania laevis* | |
| 2(1) | "Tail" ending in a distinct point................ *Masturus lanceolatus* | |
| | "Tail" bluntly rounded.............................. *Mola mola* | |

### RANZANIA LAEVIS ('Apahu, Makua)

This is the only member of the family for which adults are frequently seen in Hawaii (see Fig. 126). Unlike the other two species, the lips project around the mouth, which gives the impression of the intake valve of a jet engine.

Adult specimens about 2 feet in length are sometimes washed ashore.

### MASTURUS LANCEOLATUS

The pointed-tail sunfish is said to reach a length of 11 feet, but, aside from the cast of a large individual in the Bishop Museum, only small specimens up to some 6 inches long are known from Hawaiian waters. These small individuals are not of infrequent occurrence in tuna stomachs.

### MOLA MOLA

This species also gets to be 11 feet long. One adult from Kauai was said to have appeared in the Honolulu market in 1921. Its length was apparently not recorded.

## THE ANGLER FISHES AND THEIR ALLIES

The members of this group are unique in two respects. One is that they have the gill opening reduced to a small hole in or behind the "armpit." The other is that they have run the dorsal fin out onto the head and have converted the first ray into a "fishing pole" with a "bait" at the tip. These features alone would seem to justify their position at the very end of any book on fishes.

## Family LOPHIIDAE

This family, which includes the goosefishes of northern seas, is known from Hawaiian waters on the basis of a single specimen (Fig. 26) taken in over 1000 feet of water.

## Family ANTENNARIIDAE

The frogfishes do not look much like frogs, but neither do they resemble any other Hawaiian inshore fishes (see Fig. 23). The body is globular; the pectoral fin base appears to have a joint in it; and the gill opening is a small hole below or behind the pectoral base. The dorsal spines have moved far forward on the head, and the first of them has become transformed into a flexible "fishing pole" with a fleshy "bait" at its tip. This apparatus is waved until a passing fish is attracted sufficiently near, at which point a single gulp frequently results in its disappearance. Judging from the rotund form, frogfishes must be rather successful fishermen, and this raises several questions for the human angler. For example, different frogfishes use rather differently shaped baits: is each bait type selected with a particular species of prey in mind? An abnormal specimen in our collections has two "poles" and two "baits": how did the bearer operate these and with what success? Another quite fat specimen was obviously blind in one eye; apparently this did not greatly impair his fishing operations. Finally, what does a frogfish do when it loses its bait?

The well-known ability of certain frogfishes to change color may also be associated with fishing activities. In aquaria at least, they frequently take on a coloration in violent contrast to the background; nevertheless, however conspicuous they may be as lumps, they do not look like fishes, and very rarely is there any fin movement to give their real nature away.

Seven species are known from Hawaiian waters. None of them is abundant. Key to the Hawaiian species of the family Antennariidae:

| | | |
|---|---|---|
| 1 | Gill openings in front of anal base........................... | 2 |
| | Gill openings above the anterior anal rays.........*Abantennarius analis* | |
| 2(1) | Gill openings much nearer to the pectoral base than to the anal origin...................................................... | 3 |
| | Gill openings about midway between the pectoral base and the anal origin.................................*Abantennarius duescus* | |
| 3(2) | First stiff dorsal spine (not the fishing pole) not attached to the back behind it by a membrane................................ | 6 |
| | First stiff dorsal spine attached to the back behind it by a membrane................................................ | 4 |
| 4(3) | "Bait" made up of 3 equal lobes radiating from a central base; dark lines radiating from the eye..............*Phrynelox cunninghami* | |
| | "Bait" various but not of 3 equal lobes; color various but without lines radiating from the eye.............................. | 5 |
| 5(4) | Pectoral rays 11; last anal ray connected for over half its length by a membrane to the caudal peduncle above it.....*Antennarius moluccensis* | |
| | Pectoral rays 10; last anal ray connected only at its base by a membrane to the caudal peduncle above it.......*Antennarius chironectes* | |
| 6(3) | First stiff dorsal spine sharply recurved...........*Antennarius drombus* | |
| | First stiff dorsal spine nearly straight..............*Antennatus bigibbus* | |

### ABANTENNARIUS ANALIS

It is peculiar enough to have the gill openings in the "armpits," but this species has them far back above the anal base, thus resembling a globular jet propulsion engine. The "bait" in the only known specimen is bifurcate, with one prong longer than the other. The first stiff dorsal spine is recurved, without a membrane attaching it to the back, and is very slightly prickly at the tip. The second dorsal spine forms a low middorsal ridge with slightly enlarged prickles above. There are no conspicuous flaps of skin on the head or body. Pelvic projecting points 5; pectorals 10. Dorsal rays 12; anal rays 7. Head and body mottled brown; caudal fin crossbanded.

The type, 4 inches long, was taken off Waikiki in about 30 feet of water.

### ABANTENNARIUS DUESCUS

This species seems to be intermediate between the preceding and the following members of the Antennariidae in the position of the gill openings. The first stiff dorsal spine is erect and has a prickly, knobbed tip. Second dorsal spine prickly above, attached to the back by a membrane. A few hairlike, elongate projections on the body. Dorsal rays 12; anal rays 7.

Known only from a few specimens, the largest less than 2 inches long, taken many years ago between Maui and Lanai in a dredging station.

### PHRYNELOX CUNNINGHAMI

Known from a single specimen about 4 inches long.

### ANTENNARIUS MOLUCCENSIS

This seems to be the largest antennariid around Hawaii, reaching a length of perhaps 10 inches. In appearance it is very similar to *Antennarius chironectes* but has one more ray in the dorsal and anal (13 and 8 respectively) as well as in the pectoral.

### ANTENNARIUS CHIRONECTES

Similar to the above species and exceedingly variable in color (see Fig. 23). To perhaps 6 inches.

### ANTENNARIUS DROMBUS

An especially lumplike species with heavy layers of flesh often almost engulfing the first soft dorsal ray. The "fishing pole" is short, barely reaching the tip of the first stiff dorsal spine, and the "bait" is a globular mass of short filaments. The first dorsal spine is short and recurved and usually has a pair of pronglike filaments projecting from the tip. The second dorsal spine barely extends above the level of the back but its upper surface does have some rather elongate prickles. Head and body with numerous, scattered, arborescent flaps, those on the chin the most conspicuous. Pelvic projections 6; pectoral 12. Dorsal soft rays 12; anal soft rays 7 or 8. Color very variable: plain, spotted or blotched; the only constant feature seems to be a series of about 4 dark crossbars on the caudal.

Attains about 4 inches in length.

So far as available specimens are concerned, this species seems to have a unique and constant color pattern. The head and body are light, but the fins, except the dorsal, have a narrow black edge with another black bar running along the middle of the fin. Unlike our other antennariids, *Antennatus bigibbus* has no groove running between the upper jaw and the base of the fish pole, and the second dorsal spine is visible externally merely as a lump on the back covered by undifferentiated skin. Pelvic projections 5; pectoral 11. Dorsal rays 11 to 13; anal rays 7.

Apparently a small species, reaching a maximum length of about 2 inches.

### Family CHAUNACIDAE

A family of deep-water angler fishes known only from a single Hawaiian specimen (Fig. 24).

### Family OGCOCEPHALIDAE

In some areas of the world the very peculiar bat fishes (Fig. 27) come into shallow water, but in Hawaii they have not been taken at depths less than 300 feet. The five species recorded from our waters were all taken in dredge hauls.

### Family CERATIIDAE

Still another family of deep-water angler fishes with but one recorded Hawaiian specimen (Fig. 25).

# *Appendix A*

## LIST OF SPECIES OF MARINE FISHES INTRODUCED INTO THE WATERS OF THE HAWAIIAN ISLANDS

| Name | Place of Origin | Date of Introduction |
| --- | --- | --- |
| *Harengula vittata* | Marquesas Islands | various: from Dec. 1955 to Jan. 1958 |
| *Epinephelus merra* | Moorea | Oct. 1956 |
| *Epinephelus* | Moorea | Oct. 1956 |
| *Cephalopholis argus* | Moorea | Oct. 1956 |
| *Lutianus vaigiensis* | Moorea | Oct. 1956 |

Certain other species have been introduced incidentally with the Marquesan sardine, *Harengula vittata*, for example, but only in small numbers. It is unlikely that any of these more or less fortuitous releases will ever become established.

# *Appendix B*

## CHECK LIST OF NATIVE HAWAIIAN FISHES

This Appendix provides references for those who wish further information on the species dealt with in the body of the handbook. It is arranged in the form of species synonymies, but synonymies of a rather special type. For each species the original description and the best available account of the Hawaiian form are listed. Since Jordan and Evermann (1905, see below) and Gilbert (1905) are undoubtedly the most useful reference works on Hawaiian fishes, the accounts of all species dealt with in these two books are cited. All species described as new from Hawaiian waters have been included. However, no attempt has been made to cite all Hawaiian records for each species. Such records, up to 1949, may be found in Fowler (1928–1949, see below). Nor has any serious attempt been made to cite and rectify all the misidentifications of Hawaiian fishes recorded by various authors. Deep-water Hawaiian species are included; introduced fishes are not.

In the synonymies that follow, certain frequently cited works are referred to in more or less abbreviated form. Thus:

**Bigelow and Schroeder** refers to their 1948 work on sharks in vol. 1 of "Fishes of the Western North Atlantic."

**Fowler, 1928** refers to his "Fishes of Oceania" and **Fowler, 1931, Fowler, 1934,** and **Fowler, 1949** refer to the supplements to this volume.

**Gilbert** refers to "The Deep-Sea Fishes of the Hawaiian Islands" in vol. 23, part 2 of the Bulletin of the U. S. Fish Commission for 1903, actually published in 1905.

**J. and E.** represents Jordan and Evermann's 1905 volume on "The Shore Fishes of the Hawaiian Islands," published as part 1 of the same vol. 23 with **Gilbert.**                                    •

**Schultz** refers to vol. 1 of "Fishes of the Marshall and Marianas Islands," 1953, Bulletin 202 of the U. S. National Museum.

When the citation in the synonymy deals with Hawaiian specimens no locality is listed, but where fishes from other areas are dealt with the locality from which the fishes came is given in parentheses at the end of the citation. The absence of a comma between species name and author indicates that the species is described as new in the paper cited; the presence of a comma indicates a redescription. Figure numbers on plates are omitted. Citations to original descriptions are usually cited from recent literature and, in general, have not been verified.

## ISURIDAE

### Isurus glaucus

*Oxyrhina glauca* Müller and Henle, 1841, Plagiostomen, p. 69, pl. 29 (Japan).
*Isuropsis glauca,* J. and E., p. 43, fig. 5.
*Isurus glaucus,* Bigelow and Schroeder, pp. 124, 128, and 129 (no material cited); Strasburg, 1958, Fish Bull. U. S. Fish Wildlife Serv., vol. 58, p. 339.

## ALOPIIDAE

### Alopias vulpinus

*S q u a l u s vulpinus* Bonnaterre, 1788, Tableau Encycl. Ichthy., p. 9 (Mediterranean).
*Alopias vulpes,* J. and E., p. 42, fig. 4.
*Alopias vulpinus,* Bigelow and Schroeder, p. 167, figs. 27 and 28 (Atlantic and Eastern Pacific).

## RHINCODONTIDAE

### Rhincodon typus

*Rhincodon typus* Smith, 1829, Zool. Jour., vol. 4, p. 443 (South Africa); Bigelow and Schroeder, p. 189, fig. 130 (Atlantic).

## SCYLIORHINIDAE

### Apristurus spongiceps

*Catulus spongiceps* Gilbert, p. 579.

## TRIAKIDAE

### Triaenodon obesus

*Carcharias obesus* Rüppell, 1835, Neue Wirbelthiere: Fische, p. 64, pl. 18, fig. 2 (Red Sea).
*Triaenodon obesus,* Fowler, 1928, p. 22, fig. 7.

## CARCHARHINIDAE

### Carcharodon carcharias

*Squalus carcharias* Linnaeus, 1758, Systema Naturae, Ed. X, p. 235 (Europe).
*Carcharodon carcharias,* J. and E., p. 44; Bigelow and Schroeder, p. 134, figs. 20–22 (Atlantic).

### Prionace glauca

*Squalus glaucus* Linnaeus, 1758, Systema Naturae, Ed. X, pp. 235 (Europe).
*Prionace glauca,* J. and E., p. 37, fig. 3; Bigelow and Schroeder, p. 282, figs. 47 and 48 (Atlantic and Japan); Stras-

burg, 1958, Fish Bull. U. S. Fish Wildlife Serv., vol. 58, p. 339.

### Galeocerdo cuvieri

*Squalus cuvier* Lesueur, 1822, Jour. Acad. Nat. Sci. Philadelphia, vol. 2, p. 351 (Australia).
*Galeocerdo tigrinus,* J. and E., p. 36.
*Galeocerdo cuvier,* Bigelow and Schroeder, p. 266, fig. 44 (Atlantic).

### Galeorhinus galeus

*Squalus galeus* Linnaeus, 1758, Systema Naturae, Ed. X, p. 234 (Europe).
*Galeus vulgaris,* Steindachner, 1900, Denkschr. Math.-Naturwiss. Classe K. Akad. Wiss., vol. 70, p. 37. (One specimen recorded, with a wholly inadequate description, from Laysan; as the species has never been recorded from the central Pacific since, the record must be regarded as questionable.)

### Pterolamiops longimanus

*Squalus longimanus* Poey, 1861, Memorias, vol. 2, p. 338 (Cuba).
*Carcharias insularum* Snyder, 1904, Bull. U. S. Fish Comm., vol. 22, p. 513, pl. 1; J. and E., p. 40, pl. 3.
*Pterolamiops longimanus,* Backus, Springer, and Arnold, 1956, Deep-Sea Research, vol. 3, p. 178 (Atlantic material); Strasburg, 1958, Fish Bull. U. S. Fish Wildlife Serv., vol. 58, p. 339.

### Carcharhinus melanopterus

*Carcharias melanopterus* Quoy and Gaimard, 1824, Voyage de l'Uranie: Zoologie, p. 194, pl. 43, figs. 1 and 2 (Vaigiou Island); J. and E., p. 38, pl. 1.
*Carcharhinus melanopterus,* Schultz, p. 13, pl. 3A (Marshall Islands and Guam).

### Carcharhinus nesiotes

*Carcharias nesiotes* Snyder, 1904, Bull. U. S. Fish Comm., vol. 22, p. 514, pl. 1; J. and E., p. 40, pl. 3.

### Eulamia phorcys

*Carcharias phorcys* Jordan and Evermann, 1903, Bull. U. S. Fish Comm., vol. 22, p. 163; J. and E., p. 39, pl. 2.

### Eulamia floridanus

*Carcharinus floridanus* Bigelow, Schroeder and Springer, 1943, Proc. New England

Zool. Club, vol. 22, p. 71, pl. 13 (Florida).

Carcharhinus floridanus, Bigelow and Schroeder, p. 333, figs. 58, 59 (Atlantic material).

Eulamia floridanus, Strasburg, 1958, Fish Bull. U. S. Fish Wildlife Serv., vol. 58, p. 339.

### SPHYRNIDAE

#### Sphyrna lewini

Zygaena lewini Griffith, 1834, Animal Kingdom, vol. 10, p. 640, pl. 50 (Australia).

?Sphyrna zygaena, J. and E., p. 41.

Sphyrna diplana, Bigelow and Schroeder, p. 415, figs. 12A and 81 (Atlantic).

Sphyrna lewini, Fraser-Brunner, 1950, Rec. Australian Mus., vol. 22, pp. 218 and 219, figs. 2 and 3 (locality?).

### SQUALIDAE

#### Squalus fernandinus

Squalus mitsukurii Jordan and Snyder, 1903, Proc. U. S. Nat. Mus., vol. 26, p. 629 (Japan); J. and E., p. 45; Gilbert, p. 580.

Squalus fernandinus, Bigelow and Schroeder, p. 454, footnote 20 (Japan); Bigelow and Schroeder, 1957, Bull. Mus. Comp. Zool., vol. 117, p. 33.

#### Centroscyllium nigrum

Centroscyllium nigrum Garman, 1899, Mem. Mus. Comp. Zool., vol. 24, p. 28, pls. 1, 4, 5, and 69 (Eastern Pacific); Bigelow and Schroeder, p. 481; Bigelow and Schroeder, 1957, Bull. Mus. Comp. Zool., vol. 117, p. 43.

Centroscyllium ruscosum Gilbert, p. 580, fig. 230.

#### Etmopterus villosus

Etmopterus villosus Gilbert, p. 580, pl. 66; Bigelow and Schroeder, p. 488, footnote 3; Bigelow and Schroeder, 1957, Bull. Mus. Comp. Zool., vol. 117, p. 57.

#### Isistius brasiliensis

Scymnus brasiliensis Quoy and Gaimard, 1824, Voy. "Uranie," Zool., p. 198 (Brazil).

Isistius brasiliensis, Fowler, 1928, p. 23; Bigelow and Schroeder, p. 509, figs. 98 and 99 (Bahamas, Japan, and Galapagos).

#### Euprotomicrus bispinatus

Scymnus bispinatus Quoy and Gaimard, 1824, Voy. "Uranie," Zool., p. 197, pl. 44 (Mauritius).

Euprotomicrus hyalinus R. S. Eigenmann,

1890, Proc. California Acad. Sci., ser. 2, vol. 3, p. 35 (from between Honolulu and San Francisco).

Euprotomicrus bispinatus, King and Ikehara, 1956, Pacific Sci., vol. 10, p. 17, fig. 1 (340 miles WNW of Johnston).

#### Echinorhinus brucus

Squalus brucus Bonnaterre, 1788, Tableau Encycl. Ichthy., p. 11 (Atlantic); Bigelow and Schroeder, p. 527, fig. 102 (Atlantic).

Echinorhinus cookei Pietschmann, 1930, Bull. B. P. Bishop Mus. no. 73, pp. 3 and 4, pl. 1 and fig. 1.

### DASYATIDAE

#### Dasyatis hawaiiensis

Dasyatis hawaiiensis Jenkins, 1903, Bull. U. S. Fish Comm., vol. 22, p. 420, pl. 1; J. and E., p. 48, pl. 4, fig. 1.

#### Dasyatis lata

Trygon lata Garman, 1880, Bull. Mus. Comp. Zool., vol. 6, p. 170.

Dasyatis sciera, J. and E., p. 47, pl. 4, fig. 2.

Dasyatis lata, J. and E., p. 47.

### MYLIOBATIDAE

#### Aetobatus narinari

Raja narinari Euphrasen, 1790, Vet. Akad. Nya. Handl., vol. 11, p. 217 (Brazil).

Stoasodon narinari, J. and E., p. 49, fig. 7.

Aetobatus narinari, Bigelow and Schroeder, 1953, Fishes of the Western North Atlantic, p. 453, figs. 105, 106 (various localities including Hawaii).

### MOBULIDAE

#### Mobula japonica

Cephaloptera japonica Müller and Henle, 1841, Plagiostomen, p. 185 (Japan).

Mobula japonica, J. and E., p. 50; Fowler, 1927, Bull. B. P. Bishop Mus., vol. 38, p. 3, pl. 1.

#### Manta alfredi

Deratoptera alfredi Krefft, 1868, Illus. Sydney News, vol. 5, pp. 3 and 9, fig. (Australia).

Manta birostris, Fowler, 1928, p. 26.

Manta alfredi, Schultz, p. 20, fig. 6 (Marshalls).

### CHIMAERIDAE

#### Hydrolagus purpurescens

Chimaera purpurescens Gilbert, p. 582, fig. 231.

Hydrolagus purpurescens, Bigelow and Schroeder, 1953, Fishes of the Western North Atlantic, no. 1, pt. 2, p. 536.

**ELOPIDAE**

### Elops hawaiensis

*Elops saurus,* J. and E., p. 53, fig. 8; Hildebrand, 1943, Jour. Washington Acad. Sci., vol. 33, pp. 90–94 (Atlantic; affinity, anatomy, and development).
*Elops hawaiensis* Regan, 1909, Ann. Mag. Nat. Hist., ser. 8, vol. 3, p. 39.
*Elops machnata,* Hiatt, 1947, Trans. American Fisheries Soc., vol. 74, p. 255 (food habits).

**ALBULIDAE**

### Albula vulpes

*Esox vulpes* Linnaeus, 1758, Systema Naturae, Ed. X, p. 313 (Bahamas).
*Albula vulpes,* J. and E., p. 55, fig. 9.
*Albula virgata* Jordan and Jordan, 1922, Mem. Carnegie Mus., vol. 10, no. 1, p. 6, pl. 1.

**DUSSUMIERIDAE**

### Etrumeus micropus

*Clupea micropus* Schlegel, 1846, Fauna Japonica, Poiss., p. 236, pl. 107 (Japan).
*Etrumeus micropus,* J. and E., p. 58, fig. 11.

### Spratelloides delicatulus

*Clupea delicatula* Bennett, 1831, Proc. Zool. Soc. London, pt. 1, p. 168 (Mauritius).
*Spratelloides delicatulus,* Fowler, 1928, p. 29.

**ENGRAULIDAE**

### Stolephorus purpureus

*Stolephorus purpureus* Fowler, 1900, Proc. Acad. Nat. Sci. Philadelphia for 1900, p. 497, pl. 19; Gosline, 1951, Pacific Sci., vol. 5, p. 272 (use of the generic name); Tester, 1951, *ibid.,* vol. 5, pp. 321–346 (eggs and larvae); Hiatt, 1951, *ibid.,* vol. 5, pp. 347–358 (food habits); Tester and Hiatt, 1952, *ibid.,* vol. 6, pp. 59–70 (vertebral variation).

**GONOSTOMATIDAE**

### Gonostoma elongatum

*Gonostoma elongatum* Günther, 1878, Ann. Mag. Nat. Hist., ser. 5, vol. 2, p. 187 (off New Guinea); Norman, 1930, "Discovery" Repts., vol. 2, p. 283 (South Atlantic).
*Cyclothone rhodadenia* Gilbert, p. 602, pl. 71.

### Cyclothone atraria

*Cyclothone atraria* Gilbert, p. 605, pl. 72.

### Cyclothone canina

*Cyclothone canina* Gilbert, p. 604, pl. 71.

### Vinciguerria poweriae

*Gonostomus poweriae* Cocco, 1838, Nuovi Ann. Sci. Nat., vol. 2, p. 167 (Mediterranean).
*Vinciguerria poweriae,* Ahlstrom and Counts, 1958, Fish Bull. U. S. Fish Wildlife Serv., vol. 58, p. 400.

### Vinciguerria nimbaria

*Zalarges nimbarius* Jordan and Williams, in Jordan and Starks, 1896, Proc. California Acad. Sci., ser. 2, vol. 5, p. 793, pl. 76 (Pacific).
*Vinciguerria nimbaria,* Ahlstrom and Counts, 1958, Fish Bull. U. S. Fish Wildlife Serv., vol. 58, p. 405.

### Argyripnus ephippiatus

*Argyripnus ephippiatus* Gilbert and Cramer, 1897, Proc. U. S. Nat. Mus., vol. 19, p. 414, pl. 39; Gilbert, p. 601.

**STERNOPTYCHIDAE**

### Sternoptyx diaphana

*Sternoptyx diaphana* Hermann, 1781, Naturforscher, vol. 16, pp. 8 and 33, pl. 1 (Jamaica); Gilbert, p. 609; Haig, 1955, Pacific Sci., vol. 9, p. 319.

### Polyipnus nuttingi

*Polyipnus spinosus* (not of Günther), Gilbert and Cramer, 1897, Proc. U. S. Nat. Mus., vol. 19, p. 416.
*Polyipnus nuttingi,* Gilbert, p. 609, pl. 73; Haig, 1955, Pacific Sci., vol. 9, p. 319.

### Argyropelecus affinis

*Argyropelecus affinis* Garman, 1899, Mem. Mus. Comp. Zool., vol. 24, p. 237 (West Indies); Haig, 1955, Pacific Sci., vol. 9, p. 321.

### Argyropelecus heathi

*Argyropelecus heathi* Gilbert, p. 601, pl. 72; Haig, 1955, Pacific Sci., vol. 9, p. 321.

### Argyropelecus sladeni

*Argyropelecus sladeni* Regan, 1908, Trans. Linnaean Soc. London, Zoology, vol. 12, p. 218 (Indian Ocean); Haig, 1955, Pacific Sci., vol. 9, p. 322.

**ASTRONESTHIDAE**

### Astronesthes lucifer

*Astronesthes lucifer* Gilbert, p. 605, pl. 71; Regan and Trewavas, 1929, Danish "Dana" Expeditions 1920–22, Rept. No. 5, p. 18, fig. 8 (Japan).

**311**

**STOMIATIDAE**

*Leptostomias macronema*

*Leptostomias macronema* Gilbert, p. 606, pl. 72; Regan and Trewavas, 1930, Danish "Dana" Expeditions 1920–22, Rept. No. 6, p. 60 (redescription from Gilbert).

**CHANIDAE**

*Chanos chanos*

*Mugil chanos* Forskål, 1775, Descript. Animal., p. 74 (Red Sea).
*Chanos cyprinella* Cuvier and Valenciennes, 1846, Hist. Nat. Poiss., vol. 19, p. 198.
*Chanos chanos*, J. and E., p. 57, fig. 10; Hiatt, 1947, Trans. American Fisheries Soc., vol. 74, pp. 254–255 (food habits); Mane, Villaluz, and Rabanal, 1953, Philippine Fisheries, pp. 133–137 (Philippine pondfish culture).

**GONORHYNCHIDAE**

*Gonorhynchus gonorhynchus*

*Cyprinus gonorhynchus* Linnaeus, 1766, Systema Naturae, Ed. XII, p. 528 (South Africa).
*Gonorhynchus moseleyi* J o r d a n and Snyder, 1923, Jour. Washington Acad. Sci., vol. 13, p. 347.

**CHLOROPHTHALMIDAE**

*Chlorophthalmus agassizi*

*Chlorophthalmus Agassizii* Bonaparte, 1840, Fauna Italica, Pesci, p. 100, pl. 121 (Mediterranean).
*Chlorophthalmus proridens* Gilbert and Cramer, 1897, Proc. U. S. Nat. Mus., vol. 19, p. 406, pl. 36; Gilbert, p. 589.
*Chlorophthalmus agassizi,* K a m o h a r a, 1956, Res. Repts., Kochi Univ., vol. 5, no. 15, p. 4 (apparently based on the literature).

**SYNODONTIDAE**

*Trachinocephalus myops*

*Salmo myops* Forster, 1801, in Schneider, Syst. Ichth., p. 421 (St. Helena).
*Saurus limbatus* Eydoux and Souleyet, 1841, Voyage "Bonite," Poiss., p. 199.
*Trachinocephalus myops,* J. and E., p. 62, fig. 13.

*Saurida gracilis*

*Saurus gracilis* Quoy and Gaimard, 1824, Voy. "Uranie," Zool., p. 224.
*Synodus sharpi* Fowler, 1900, Proc. Acad. Nat. Sci. Philadelphia, p. 497, pl. 19; Fowler, 1911, *ibid.,* p. 599.
*Saurida gracilis,* J. and E., p. 65; Schultz, p. 32, pl. 6 (Marshall Islands).

*Synodus kaianus*

*Saurus kaianus* Günther, 1880, "Challenger" Repts., Shore Fishes, p. 50, pl. 23 (Kei Islands).
*Synodus kaianus,* Gilbert, p. 558; Schultz, p. 31 (presumably based on Gilbert's specimens).

*Synodus binotatus*

*Synodus binotatus* Schultz, p. 35, fig. 8 (Marshall Islands and Johnston).

*Synodus dermatogenys*

*Synodus varius* (not of Lacépède), J. and E., p. 63 (in part), col. pl. 2, fig. 14.
*Synodus dermatogenys* Fowler, 1911, Proc. Acad. Nat. Sci. Philadelphia, p. 566, fig. 3.
*Synodus ulae* Schultz, p. 38.

*Synodus variegatus*

*Salmo variegatus* Lacépède, 1803, Hist. Nat. Poiss., vol. 5, p. 157, pl. 3 (Ile de France).
*Synodus varius,* J. and E., p. 63 (in part).
*Synodus variegatus,* Schultz, p. 39, pl. 3 (Marshall Islands).

**BATHYPTEROIDAE**

*Bathypterois antennatus*

*Bathypterois antennatus* Gilbert, p. 590, fig. 235.
*Bathypterois atricolor antennatus,* Parr, 1928, Bull. Bingham Ocean. Coll., vol. 3, art. 3, p. 31; Matsubara, 1954, Japanese Jour. Ichthy., vol. 3, p. 62, fig. 1 (Japan).

**MYCTOPHIDAE**

*Neoscopelus macrolepidotus*

*Neoscopelus macrolepidotus* Johnson, 1863, Proc. Zool. Soc., p. 44, pl. 7 (Madeira); Gilbert, p. 601; Fraser-Brunner, 1949, Proc. Zool. Soc. London, vol. 118, p. 1039, fig. (temperate and warm seas).

*Hygophum reinhardti*

*Scopelus Reinhardtii* Lütken, 1892, Spolia Atlantica, vol. 2, p. 257, fig. 16 (Atlantic).
*Myctophum braueri* (not of Lönnberg) Gilbert, p. 598, pl. 70.
*Hygophum reinhardti,* Fraser-Brunner, 1949, Proc. Zool. Soc. London, vol. 118, p. 1050 fig. (Atlantic, Indian, and Pacific Oceans).

*Benthosema fibulata*

*Myctophum fibulatum* Gilbert and Cramer, 1897, Proc. U. S. Nat. Mus., vol. 19, p. 411, pl. 38; Gilbert, p. 596.

*Benthosema fibulata*, Fraser-Brunner, 1949, Proc. Zool. Soc. London, vol. 118, p. 1052, fig. (Indian and Pacific Oceans).

### Myctophum evermanni

*Myctophum evermanni* Gilbert, p. 597, pl. 70; Fraser-Brunner, 1949, Proc. Zool. Soc. London, vol. 118, p. 1055, fig. (Pacific Ocean).

### Myctophum affine

*Scopelus affinis* Lütken, 1892, Spolia Atlantica, vol. 2, p. 32 (Atlantic).
*Rhinoscopelus oceanicus* Jordan and Evermann, 1903, Bull. U. S. Fish Comm., vol. 22, p. 168; J. and E., p. 68, fig. 15.
*Myctophum margaritatum* G i l b e r t, p. 596, pl. 68.
*Myctophum affine*, Gilbert, 1908, Mem. Mus. Comp. Zool., vol. 26, p. 217 (South Pacific and Hawaii); Fraser-Brunner, 1949, Proc. Zool. Soc. London, vol. 118, p. 1056 (Atlantic, Indian, and Pacific Oceans).

### Myctophum spinosum

*Scopelus spinosus* Steindachner, 1867, Sitz. akad. wiss. Wien, vol. 55, p. 711, pl. 3 (China).
*Dasyscopelus spinosus*, Gilbert, p. 599; Gilbert, 1908, Mem. Mus. Comp. Zool., vol. 26, p. 220 (South Pacific and Hawaii).
*Myctophum spinosum*, Fraser-Brunner, 1949, Proc. Zool. Soc. London, vol. 118, p. 1057, fig. (South Atlantic, Indian, and Pacific Oceans).

### Myctophum brachygnathos

*Scopelus brachygnathos* Bleeker, 1856, Act. Soc. Sc. Indo-Neerl., vol. 1, p. 65 (East Indies).
*Dasyscopelus pristilepis* G i l b e r t and Cramer, Proc. U. S. Nat. Mus., vol. 19, p. 412, pl. 39; Gilbert, p. 601.
*Myctophum brachygnathos*, Fraser-Brunner, 1949, Proc. Zool. Soc. London, vol. 118, p. 1058, fig. (Pacific Ocean).

### Myctophum hollandi

*Myctophum hollandi* Jordan and Jordan, 1922, Mem. Carnegie Mus., vol. 10, p. 11, pl. 1.

### Centrobranchus chaerocephalus

*Centrobranchus chaerocephalus* Fowler, 1904, Proc. Acad. Nat. Sci. Philadelphia for 1903, p. 754; Gilbert, p. 594, pl. 69 (this species is tentatively s y n o n y m i z e d with *C. nigri-ocellatus* (Günther) by Fraser-Brunner, 1949, p. 1062).

### Diaphus urolampus

*Diaphus urolampus* Gilbert and Cramer, 1897, Proc. U. S. Nat. Mus., vol. 19, p. 408, pl. 38; Gilbert, p. 591; Fraser-Brunner, Proc. Zool. Soc. London, vol. 118, p. 1067, fig.

### Diaphus chrysorhynchus

*Diaphus chrysorhynchus* Gilbert and Cramer, 1897, Proc. U. S. Nat. Mus., vol. 19, p. 409, pl. 38; Gilbert, p. 592; Fraser-Brunner, 1949, Proc. Zool. Soc. London, vol. 118, p. 1073, fig. (Pacific Ocean).

### Diaphus adenomus

*Diaphus adenomus* Gilbert, p. 592, pl. 68.

### Lampanyctus reinhardti

*Nyctimaster reinhardti* Jordan, 1921, Proc. U. S. Nat. Mus., vol. 59, p. 645, fig. 2. (The validity and relationships of this species seem to be in considerable doubt. Fraser-Brunner, 1949, p. 1082, states that he is quite unable to place the species, which was based on sun-dried specimens.)

### Lampanyctus niger

*Nannobranchium nigrum* Günther, 1887, "Challenger" Reports, Deep-sea Fishes, p. 199, pl. 52 (south of Philippines); Gilbert, p. 591.
*Lampanyctus niger*, Fraser-Brunner, 1949, Proc. Zool. Soc. London, vol. 118, p. 1085, fig. (southern Atlantic, Indian, and Pacific Oceans).

## PARALEPIDIDAE

### Lestidium nudum

*Lestidium nudum* Gilbert, p. 607, fig. 236; Harry, 1953, Proc. Acad. Nat. Sci. Philadelphia, vol. 105, p. 202, figs. 23, 27 (redescription of type).

### Lestidium mirabile

*Paralepis mirabilis* Ege, 1933, Vidensk. Medd. fra Dansk naturh. Forening, vol. 94, p. 228 (East Indies).
*Lestidium mirabile*, Harry, 1953, Proc. Acad. Nat. Sci. Philadelphia, vol. 105, p. 197, figs. 19, 21.

## ALEPISAURIDAE

### Alepisaurus borealis

*Caulolepis borealis* Gill, 1862, Proc. Acad. Nat. Sci. Philadelphia, p. 128 (Pacific coast of North America).

## ATELEOPIDAE

### Ateleopus plicatellus

*Ateleopus plicatellus* Gilbert, p. 653, fig. 253.

## MURAENIDAE

### Rabula fuscomaculata
Rabula fuscomaculata Schultz, p. 147, fig. 30 (Marshall Islands, Johnston, and Hawaii).

### Uropterygius sealei
Scuticaria unicolor Seale, 1917, Mus. Comp. Zool., vol. 61, p. 94 (Society Islands).
Uropterygius sealei, Schultz, p. 140 (based on cotype); Gosline, 1958, Pacific Sci., vol. 12, p. 222.

### Uropterygius tigrinus
Ichthyophis tigrinus Lesson, 1829, Mem. Soc. Hist. Nat. Paris, vol. 4, p. 399 (Society Islands).
Scuticaria tigrina, J. and E., p. 112, pl. 22.
Uropterygius tigrinus, Schultz, p. 140 (no locality given); Gosline, 1958, Pacific Sci., vol. 12, p. 223.

### Uropterygius polyspilus
Gymnomuraena polyspila Regan, 1909, Ann. Mag. Nat. Hist., ser. 8, vol. 4, p. 438 (Tahiti, Zanzibar).
Uropterygius polyspilus, Schultz, p. 140 (no locality given); Gosline, 1958, Pacific Sci., vol. 12, p. 223.

### Uropterygius knighti
Anarchias knighti Jordan and Starks, in Jordan and Seale, 1906, Bull. Bur. Fish., vol. 25, p. 205, fig. 10 (Samoa).
Uropterygius marmoratus, J. and E., p. 111 (but not fig. 33 which is labeled as this species).
Uropterygius knighti, Gosline, 1958, vol. 12, p. 227.

### Uropterygius inornatus
Uropterygius inornatus Gosline, 1958, Pacific Sci., vol. 12, p. 225, figs. 1e, 2a.

### Uropterygius fuscoguttatus
Uropterygius fuscoguttatus Schultz, pp. 142, 156, fig. 33 (Marshall Islands and Johnston); Gosline, 1958, Pacific Sci., vol. 12, p. 224.

### Uropterygius supraforatus
Gymnomuraena supraforata Regan, 1909, Ann. Mag. Nat. Hist., ser. 8, vol. 4, p. 439 (Samoa).
Uropterygius dentatus Schultz, p. 152, fig. 32 (Johnston); Gosline, 1955, Pacific Sci., vol. 9, p. 446 (Johnston).
Uropterygius supraforatus, Gosline, 1958, Pacific Sci., vol. 12, p. 224.

### Anarchias leucurus
Uropterygius leucurus Snyder, 1904, Bull.

U. S. Fish Comm., vol. 22, p. 521, pl. 6; J. and E., p. 112, pl. 13.
Anarchias leucurus, Schultz, pp. 139, 144, fig. 29 (Marshall Islands).

### Anarchias cantonensis
Uropterygius cantonensis Schultz, 1943, U. S. Nat. Mus. Bull. 180, p. 27, pl. 14 (Phoenix Islands).
Anarchias cantonensis, Schultz, pp. 139, 146, fig. 29 and pl. 15 (Marshall Islands).

### Anarchias allardicei
Anarchias allardicei Jordan and Starks, 1906, in Jordan and Seale, Bull. U. S. Bur. Fisheries, vol. 25, p. 204, fig. 9 (Samoa); Schultz, pp. 139, 143 (Marshalls, Guam, Saipan).

### Muraena pardalis
Muraena pardalis Schlegel, 1846, Fauna Japonica, Pisces, p. 268, pl. 119 (Japan).
Muraena kailuae Jordan and Evermann, 1903, Bull. U. S. Fish Comm., vol. 22, p. 165; J. and E., p. 88, pl. 9 and figs. 20, 21.
Muraena lampra Jenkins, 1903, Bull. U. S. Fish Comm., vol. 22, p. 413, fig. 3.
Muraena kauila Jenkins, 1903, Bull. U. S. Fish Comm., vol. 22, p. 424, fig. 4.

### Enchelynassa canina
Muraena canina Quoy and Gaimard, 1824, Voyage "Uranie" et "Physicienne," Poissons, p. 247 (Vaigiou and Rawak).
?Muraena acutirostris Abbott, 1860, Proc. Acad. Nat. Sci. Philadelphia, p. 476.
Gymnothorax vinolentus Jordan and Evermann, 1903, Bull. U. S. Fish Comm., vol. 22, p. 165.
Enchelynassa bleekeri, J. and E., p. 90, pl. 10.
Enchelynassa vinolentus, J. and E., p. 91, pl. 11.
?Eurymyctera acutirostris, J. and E., p. 105.

### Echidna zebra
Gymnothorax zebra Shaw, 1797, Natural. Miscell., vol. 9, pl. 322 (American seas).
Echidna zebra, J. and E., p. 106, pl. 20.

### Echidna nebulosa
Muraena nebulosa Ahl, 1789, De Muraena et Ophichtho, p. 5, pl. 1 (East Indies).
Echidna nebulosa, J. and E., p. 110, col. pl. 1.

### Echidna leucotaenia
Echidna leucotaenia Schultz, 1943, U. S. Nat. Mus. Bull. 180, p. 22, pl. 3 (Phoenix and Samoan Islands);

Schultz, p. 105, fig. 21 and pl. 12 (Marshalls, Guam, and Saipan).

### Echidna polyzona

Muraena polyzona Richardson, 1844, Zoology of the "Sulphur," Ichthyology, p. 112, pl. 55 (no locality).
Poecilophis tritor Vaillant and Sauvage, 1875, Rev. et Mag. Zool., ser. 3, vol. 3, p. 287.
Echidna zonata Fowler, 1900, Proc. Acad. Nat. Sci. Philadelphia, p. 495, pl. 18; J. and E., p. 108, fig. 31.
Echidna zonophaea Jordan and Evermann, 1903, Bull. U. S. Fish Comm., vol. 22, p. 167; J. and E., p. 109, pl. 21.
Echidna leihala Jenkins, 1903, Bull. U. S. Fish Comm., vol. 22, p. 428, fig. 9; J. and E., p. 109, fig. 32.
Echidna vincta Jenkins, 1903, Bull. U. S. Fish Comm., vol. 22, p. 429, fig. 10.
Echidna obscura Jenkins, 1903, Bull. U. S. Fish Comm., vol. 22, p. 430, fig. 11; J. and E., p. 107, fig. 30.
Echidna psalion Jenkins, 1903, Bull. U. S. Fish Comm., vol. 22, p. 430, fig. 12, J. and E., p. 106, fig. 29.
Echidna polyzona, Schultz, p. 102, fig. 21 (Marshalls).

### Gymnothorax hepaticus

Muraena hepatica Rüppell, 1828, Atlas Reis. Nord. Afrika, Fisch., p. 120 (Red Sea).
Lycodontis hepatica, Fowler, 1928, p. 58, pl. 2.

### Gymnothorax moluccensis

Priodonophis moluccensis Bleeker, 1864, Atlas Ichthyol. Indes Orientales Néerland., vol. 4, p. 108, pl. 187 (Amboina).
Gymnothorax moluccensis, Schultz, p. 113, fig. 10 (Bikini).

### Gymnothorax pictus

Muraena picta Ahl, 1789, De Muraena et Ophichtho, p. 8 (Red Sea).
Gymnothorax pictus, J. and E., p. 103, pl. 19; Schultz, p. 123, fig. 23 and pl. 13 (Marshalls and Guam).

### Gymnothorax melatremus

Gymnothorax melatremus Schultz, p. 120, figs. 23 and 25 (Marshalls).

### Gymnothorax flavimarginatus

Muraena flavimarginata Rüppell, 1828, Atlas Reis. Nord. Afrika, Fisch., p. 119, pl. 30 (Red Sea).
Gymnothorax thalassopterus J e n k i n s, 1903, Bull. U. S. Fish Comm., vol. 22, p. 427, pl. 2.

Gymnothorax flavimarginatus, J. and E., p. 99, pl. 17; Schultz, p. 130, fig. 27 (Marshalls and Guam).

### Gymnothorax meleagris

Muraena meleagris Shaw and Nodder, 1795, Natural. Miscell., vol. 7, p. A2, pl. 220 ("Southern Ocean").
Gymnothorax goldsboroughi Jordan and Evermann, 1903, Bull. U. S. Fish Comm., vol. 22, p. 167; J. and E., p. 100, fig. 26.
Gymnothorax leucostictus Jenkins, 1903, Bull. U. S. Fish Comm., vol. 22, p. 425, fig. 5; J. and E., p. 96, fig. 25.
Gymnothorax nuttingi Snyder, 1904, Bull. U. S. Fish Comm., vol. 22, p. 518, pl. 4; J. and E., p. 103, pl. 15.
Gymnothorax xanthostomus Snyder, 1904, Bull. U. S. Fish Comm., vol. 22, p. 519, pl. 5; J. and E., p. 104, pl. 14.
Gymnothorax meleagris, J. and E., p. 94; Schultz, p. 114, fig. 23, pl. 14 (Marshalls and Guam).

### Gymnothorax eurostus

Thyrsoidea eurostus Abbott, 1860, Proc. Acad. Nat. Sci. Philadelphia, p. 478.
Muraena laysana Steindachner, 1900, Anzeiger Denkschr. Akad. Wiss. Wien, vol. 16, p. 177.
Lycodontis parvibranchialis Fowler, 1900, Proc. Acad. Nat. Sci. Philadelphia, p. 494, pl. 18.
Gymnothorax ercodes Jenkins, 1903, Bull. U. S. Fish Comm., vol. 22, p. 428, fig. 8; J. and E., p. 95, fig. 23.
Gymnothorax laysanus, J. and E., p. 93, fig. 22.
Gymnothorax eurostus, J. and E., p. 92; Schultz, p. 120.

### Gymnothorax buroensis

Muraena buroensis Bleeker, 1857, Nat. Tijd. Ned. Ind., vol. 13, p. 79 (East Indies).
Gymnothorax buroensis Schultz, p. 118, fig. 23 (Marshalls and Guam).

### Gymnothorax steindachneri

Gymnothorax steindachneri Jordan and Evermann, 1903, Bull. U. S. Fish Comm. vol. 22, p. 166; J. and E., p. 101, fig. 28.

### Gymnothorax berndti

Gymnothorax berndti Snyder, 1904, Bull. U. S. Fish Comm., p. 518, pl. 4; J. and E., p. 98, pl. 15.

### Gymnothorax petelli

Muraena petelli Bleeker, 1856, Nat. Tijd. Ned. Ind., vol. 11, p. 84 (Java).

**315**

*Gymnothorax leucacme* Jenkins, 1903, Bull. U. S. Fish Comm., vol. 22, p. 427, fig. 7.
*Gymnothorax waialuae* Snyder, 1904, Bull. U. S. Fish Comm., vol. 22, p. 520, pl. 6; J. and E., p. 97, pl. 13.
*Gymnothorax petelli,* J. and E., p. 100, fig. 27; Schultz, p. 133, fig. 10.

### Gymnothorax hilonis

*Gymnothorax hilonis* Jordan and Evermann, 1903, Bull. U. S. Fish Comm., vol. 22, p. 167; J. and E., p. 102, pl. 18.

### Gymnothorax undulatus

*Muraenophis undulatus* Lacepede, 1803, Hist. Nat. Poiss., vol. 5, pp. 629, 642, 644, pl. 641 (no locality).
*Muraena valenciennei* Eydoux and Souleyet, 1842, Voy. "Bonite," Poiss., p. 207, pl. 8.
*Thyrsoidea kaupii* Abbott, 1860, Proc. Acad. Nat. Sci. Philadelphia, p. 477.
*Gymnothorax undulatus,* J. and E., p. 98, pl. 16; Schultz, p. 137, fig. 27 and pl. 14 (Marshalls).

### Gymnothorax gracilicaudus

*Gymnothorax gracilicauda* Jenkins, 1903, Bull. U. S. Fish Comm., vol. 22, p. 426, fig. 6; J. and E., p. 94, fig. 23.
*Heteromyrus atolli* Pietschmann, 1938, B. P. Bishop Mus. Bull. 156, p. 14, pl. 6.
*Gymnothorax gracilicaudus,* Schultz, p. 135, fig. 27 (Marshall Islands).

### Gymnothorax mucifer

*Gymnothorax mucifer* Snyder, 1904, Bull. U. S. Fish Comm., vol. 22, p. 519, pl. 5; J. and E., p. 97, pl. 14.

## XENOCONGRIDAE

### Kaupichthys diodontus

*Kaupichthys diodontus* Schultz, 1943, U. S. Nat. Mus. Bull. 180, p. 50, fig. 5 and pl. 6 (Samoan Islands); Gosline, 1950, Pacific Sci., vol. 4, p. 309.

### Chilorhinus platyrhynchus

*Brachyconger platyrhynchus* N o r m a n, 1922, Ann. Mag. Nat. Hist., ser. 9, vol. 10, p. 218, fig. (New Britain).
*Chilorhinus brocki* Gosline, 1951, Copeia, p. 195, fig. 1.
*Chilorhinus platyrhynchus,* Böhlke, 1956, Proc. Acad. Nat. Sci. Philadelphia, vol. 108, p. 82 (on the type).

## MORINGUIDAE

### Moringua macrochir

*Moringua macrochir* Bleeker, 1855, Nat. Tijd. Ned. Ind., vol. 9, p. 71 (East Indies); Gosline and Strasburg, 1956, Copeia, p. 9, fig. 1.
*Moringua hawaiiensis* Snyder, 1904, Bull. U. S. Fish Comm., vol. 22, p. 517, pl. 3; J. and E., p. 86, pl. 8.

## SERRIVOMERIDAE

### Serrivomer beani

*Serrivomer Beanii* Gill and Ryder, 1883, Proc. U. S. Nat. Mus., vol. 6, pp. 260, 261 (Atlantic); Goode and Bean, 1895, Oceanic Ichthyology, p. 155, fig. 175 (on the type); Gilbert, p. 586.

### Stemonidium hypomelas

*Stemonidium hypomelas* Gilbert, p. 586, pl. 67.

## NEMICHTHYIDAE

### Nematoprora polygonifera

*Nematoprora polygonifera* Gilbert, p. 587, fig. 234; Trewavas, 1932, Proc. Zool. Soc. London, p. 648 (Atlantic).

## MURAENESOCIDAE

### Rhechias armiger

*Rhechias armiger* Jordan, 1921, Proc. U. S. Nat. Mus., vol. 59, p. 644, fig. 1.

## NETTASTOMIDAE

### Metapomycter denticulatus

*Metapomycter denticulatus* Gilbert, p. 585, fig. 233.

## CONGRIDAE

### Veternio verrens

*Veternio verrens* Snyder, 1904, Bull. U. S. Fish Comm., vol. 22, p. 516, pl. 2; J. and E., p. 79, pl. 5.

### Promyllantor alcocki

*Promyllantor alcocki* Gilbert and Cramer, 1897, Proc. U. S. Nat. Mus., vol. 19, p. 405, pl. 37; Gilbert, p. 584.

### Congrellus aequoreus

*Congermuraena aequorea* Gilbert and Cramer, 1897, Proc. U. S. Nat. Mus., vol. 19, p. 405, pl. 37.
*Congrellus aequoreus,* J. and E., p. 77, fig. 17.
*Leptocephalus aequoreus,* Gilbert, p. 584.

### Ariosoma bowersi

*Congrellus bowersi* Jenkins, 1903, Bull. U. S. Fish Comm., vol. 22, p. 422, fig. 1; J. and E., p. 77, fig. 77.

### Conger marginatus

*Conger marginatus* Valenciennes, 1841, Voyage "Bonite," Poiss., p. 201, pl. 9.
*Leptocephalus marginatus,* J. and E., p. 76. (The Hawaiian fish here called *C. marginatus* is identified as *C. cinereus*

*marginatus,* Kanazawa, 1958, Proc. U. S. Nat. Mus., vol. 108, p. 232, figs. 4–6 in a revision of the genus *Conger* which appeared after this book went to press.)

### Conger wilsoni
*Gymnothorax wilsoni* Schneider, 1801, Syst. Ichth., p. 529 (New Holland).
*Conger wilsoni* Fowler, 1928, p. 38, pl. 1. (Since this book went to press the Hawaiian species identified above as *C. wilsoni* has been described as *C. oligoporus* Kanazawa, 1958, Proc. U. S. Nat. Mus., vol. 108, p. 251, pls. 1B, 3B.)

## OPHICHTHIDAE
### Schultzidia johnstonensis
*Muraenichthys johnstonensis* Schultz and Woods, 1949, Jour. Washington Acad. Sci., vol. 39, p. 172, fig. 1 (Johnston and Bikini).
*Schultzidia johnstonensis,* Schultz, pp. 71, 82, fig. 17 (Johnston and Bikini).

### Leptenchelys labialis
*Muraenichthys labialis* Seale, 1917, Bull. Mus. Comp. Zool., vol. 61, no. 4, p. 79 (Marshall Islands).
*Leptenchelys labialis,* Schultz, pp. 71, 80 (Marshall Islands).

### Muraenichthys schultzei
*Muraenichthys schultzei* Bleeker, 1857, Nat. Tijd. Ned. Ind., vol. 13, p. 366 (Java); Schultz, pp. 73, 75, fig. 13 (Marshall Islands).

### Muraenichthys cookei
*Muraenichthys cookei* Fowler, 1928, p. 41, fig. 9; Schultz, p. 72 (no locality).

### Muraenichthys gymnotus
*Muraenichthys gymnotus* Bleeker, 1864, Atlas Ichthyol. Indes Orientales Néerland., vol. 4, p. 33, pl. 150 (Amboina); Schultz, pp. 73, 76, fig. 13 and pl. 10 (Marshall Islands).

### Caecula platyrhyncha
*Caecula platyrhyncha* Gosline, 1951, Pacific Sci., vol. 5, p. 312, fig. 14.

### Caecula flavicauda
*Sphagebranchus flavicaudus* Snyder, 1904, Bull. U. S. Fish Comm., vol. 22, p. 517, pl. 2; J. and E., p. 80, pl. 5; Gosline, 1951, Pacific Sci., vol. 5, p. 311, fig. 14.

### Callechelys luteus
*Callechelys luteus* Snyder, 1904, Bull. U. S. Fish Comm., vol. 22, p. 517, pl. 3; J. and E., p. 86, pl. 8.

### Cirrhimuraena macgregori
*Microdonophis macgregori* Jenkins, 1903,

Bull. U. S. Fish Comm., vol. 22, p. 422, fig. 2; J. and E., p. 82, fig. 18.
*Cirrhimuraena macgregori,* Gosline, 1951, Pacific Sci., vol. 5, p. 315, figs. 6, 10b, 16.

### Myrichthys maculosus
*Muraena maculosa* Cuvier, 1817, Règne Animal, vol. 2, p. 232 (European Seas?).
*Pisoodonophis magnifica* Abbott, 1861, Proc. Acad. Nat. Sci. Philadelphia, p. 476.
*Ophichthus stypurus* Smith and Swain, 1882, Proc. U. S. Nat. Mus., vol. 5, p. 120 (Johnston).
*Myrichthys magnificus,* J. and E., p. 84.
*Myrichthys stypurus,* J. and E., p. 85, fig. 19 (Johnston).

### Phyllophichthus xenodontus
*Phyllophichthus xenodontus* G o s l i n e, 1951, Pacific Sci., vol. 5, p. 316, fig. 17.

### Leiuranus semicinctus
*Ophisurus semicinctus* Lay and Bennett, 1839, Zool. Beechey's Voy., Fishes, p. 66, pl. 20.
*Leiuranus semicinctus,* J. and E., p. 81.

### Ophichthus polyophthalmus
*Ophichthus polyophthalmus* B l e e k e r, 1864, Atlas Ichthyol. Indes Orientales Néerland., vol. 4, p. 43 (Amboina).
*Microdonophis fowleri* Jordan and Evermann, 1903, Bull. U. S. Fish Comm., vol. 22, p. 164; J. and E., p. 82, pl. 6.

### Brachysomophis sauropsis
*Brachysomophis sauropsis* Schultz, 1943, U. S. Nat. Mus. Bull. 180, p. 18, pl. 2 and fig. 2 (Samoan Islands); Gosline, 1955, Pacific Sci., vol. 9, p. 443 (Johnston).

### Brachysomophis henshawi
*Brachysomophis henshawi* Jordan and Snyder, 1904, Proc. U. S. Nat. Mus., vol. 27, p. 940; J. and E., p. 82, pl. 7.

## SYNAPHOBRANCHIDAE
### Synaphobranchus brachysomus
*Synaphobranchus brachysomus* Gilbert, p. 583, fig. 232.

## HALOSAURIDAE
### Halosauropsis kauaiensis
*Halosauropsis kauaiensis* Gilbert, p. 611, pl. 74.

### Halosauropsis verticalis
*Halosauropsis verticalis* Gilbert, p. 611, pl. 75.

*Halosauropsis proboscidea*
*Halosauropsis proboscidea* Gilbert, p. 612, pl. 76.

**SCOMBERESOCIDAE**
*Cololabis adocetus*
*Cololabis adocetus* Böhlke, 1951, Trans. Kansas Acad. Sci., vol. 54, p. 83 (coast of Peru).

**BELONIDAE**
*Belone platyura*
*Belone platyurus* Bennett, 1830, Proc. Comm. Zool. Soc. London, p. 138 (Mauritius).
*?Belone carinata* Cuvier and Valenciennes, 1846, Hist. Nat. Poiss., vol. 18, p. 437.
*Belone platyura,* J. and E., p. 122, fig. 128; Gosline, 1955, Pacific Sci., vol. 9, p. 47.
*Belone persimilis* Günther, 1909, Fische der Südsee, p. 349, fig.; Schultz, p. 160 (Johnston).

*Ablennes hians*
*Belone hians* Cuvier and Valenciennes, 1846, Hist. Nat. Poiss., vol. 18, p. 432, pl. 548 (Brazil).
*Athlennes hians,* J. and E., p. 125, fig. 40.

*Strongylura gigantea*
*Belone gigantea* Temminck and Schlegel, 1846, Fauna Japonica, pt. 5, p. 245 (Japan).
*Tylosurus giganteus,* J. and E., p. 124, fig. 39.
*Strongylura gigantea,* Schultz, p. 162.

**HEMIRAMPHIDAE**
*Euleptorhamphus viridis*
*Hemiramphus viridis* van Hasselt, 1824, Bull. Sci. Nat. Férussac, vol. 2, p. 374 (India).
*Euleptorhamphus longirostris,* J. and E., p. 128, fig. 43.

*Hyporhamphus pacificus*
*Hemirhamphus pacificus* Steindachner, 1900, Denkschr. Ak. Wiss. Wien, vol. 70, p. 511.
*Hyporhamphus pacificus,* J. and E., p. 126, fig. 41.

*Hemiramphus depauperatus*
*Hemiramphus depauperatus* Lay and Bennett, 1839, Zool. Beechey's Voy., p. 66; J. and E., p. 127, fig. 42.

**EXOCOETIDAE**
*Oxyporhamphus micropterus*
*Exocoetus micropterus* Cuvier and Valenciennes, 1846, Hist. Nat. Poiss., vol. 19, p. 127, pl. 563 (New Holland, etc.).

*Evolantia microptera,* J. and E., p. 130, fig. 44.

*Fodiator rostratus*
*Exocoetus rostratus* Günther, 1866, Cat. Fishes British Mus., vol. 6, p. 280.
*Parexocoetus rostratus,* J. and E., p. 131.
*Fodiator rostratus,* Bruun, 1935, Dana-Rept. No. 6, p. 20.

*Parexocoetus brachypterus*
*Exocoetus brachypterus* Solander, in Richardson, 1846, Ichth. China, p. 265 (Tahiti).
*Parexocoetus brachypterus,* J. and E., p. 131, col. pl. 3; Bruun, 1935, Dana-Rept. No. 6, p. 24 (on the type); Schultz, p. 188.
*Ptenonotus melanogeneion* Pietschmann, 1930, B. P. Bishop Mus. Bull. 73, p. 8, pl. 2.

*Exocoetus volitans*
*Exocoetus volitans* Linnaeus, 1758, Systema Naturae, Ed. X, p. 316 (no locality); J. and E., p. 132 (but not fig. 45); Schultz, p. 178 (near Johnston in part).

*Prognichthys gilberti*
*Exonautes gilberti* Snyder, 1904, Bull. U. S. Fish Comm., vol. 22, p. 522, pl. 7; J. and E., p. 134.
*Prognichthys gilberti,* Schultz, p. 189.
*?Prognichthys albimaculatus,* Schultz, p. 189 (off Johnston in part).

*Cypselurus speculiger*
*Exocoetus speculiger* Valenciennes, 1846, Hist. Nat. Poiss., vol. 19, p. 94 (Society Is., etc.).
*Cypsilurus speculiger,* Jordan and Seale, 1906, Bull. U. S. Fish Comm., vol. 25, p. 209, fig. 13 (Tasman Sea); Schultz, p. 188 (Hawaii in part).

*Cypselurus simus*
*Exocoetus simus* Cuvier and Valenciennes, 1846, Hist. Nat. Poiss., vol. 19, p. 105; J. and E., p. 134 (in part), fig. 46; Schultz, p. 186.

*Cypselurus spilonotopterus*
*Exocoetus spilonotopterus* Bleeker, 1866, Nederl. Tijdr. Dierk., vol. 3, p. 113 (Sumatra).
*Cypsilurus bahiensis,* J. and E., p. 136.
*Cypsilurus spilonotopterus,* Jordan and Dickerson, 1908, Proc. U. S. Nat. Mus., vol. 34, p. 606, fig. 2.

*Cypselurus atrisignis*
*Cypsilurus atrisignis* Jenkins, 1903, Bull. U. S. Fish Comm., vol. 22, p. 436, pl. 3; J. and E., p. 136, pl. 25.

?*Cypsilurus gregoryi* Pietschmann, 1930,
B. P. Bishop Mus. Bull. 73, p. 7, pl. 2.

### Cypselurus spilopterus
*Exocoetus spilopterus* Valenciennes, 1846,
Hist. Nat. Poiss., vol. 19, p. 82 (Carolines).
*Cypselurus spilopterus,* Schultz, p. 186.

## FISTULARIIDAE
### Fistularia petimba
*Fistularia petimba* Lacépède, 1803, Hist.
Nat. Poiss., vol. 5, p. 349 (New
Britain); J. and E., p. 116.
*Fistularia serrata,* J. and E., p. 116.

### Fistularia villosa
*Fistularia villosa* Klunzinger, 1871, Zool.
bot. Ges. Wien, Verh., vol. 21, p. 516
(Red Sea); Duncker and Mohr, 1925,
Zool. Mus. Hamburg, Mitt., vol. 41,
p. 4.

## AULOSTOMIDAE
### Aulostomus chinensis
*Fistularia chinensis* Linnaeus, 1766, Systema Naturae, Ed. XII, p. 515 (India).
*Aulostomus valentini,* J. and E., p. 114,
fig. 34.

## MACRORHAMPHOSIDAE
### Macrorhamphosus gracilis
*Centriscus gracilis* Lowe, 1839, Proc.
Zool. Soc. London, p. 86 (Madeira).
*Macrorhamphosus hawaiiensis* Gilbert, p.
613, fig. 237.
*Macrorhamphosus gracilis,* Mohr, 1937,
Dana-Rept. No. 13, p. 33, text fig. 19
(various localities).

## CENTRISCIDAE
### Centriscus strigatus
*Amphisile strigata* Günther, 1861, Cat.
Fishes British Mus., vol. 3, p. 528
(Java).
*Centriscus strigatus,* Fowler, 1928, p. 118;
Mohr, 1937, Dana-Rept. No. 13, p. 25,
text fig. 15 (various localities).

## SYNGNATHIDAE
### Hippocampus histrix
*Hippocampus histrix* Kaup, 1856, Cat.
Lophobranch. Fishes, p. 17, pl. 2, fig.
5 (Japan); Fowler, 1928, p. 115.

### Hippocampus kuda
*Hippocampus kuda* Bleeker, 1852, Nat.
Tijd. Ned. Ind., vol. 3, p. 82 (Singapore).
*Hippocampus hilonis* Jordan and Evermann, 1903, Bull. U. S. Fish Comm.,
vol. 22, p. 169; J. and E., p. 119, pl. 23.
*Hippocampus fisheri* Jordan and Ever-

mann, 1903, Bull. U. S. Fish Comm.,
vol. 22, p. 169; J. and E., p. 119, fig.
36.

### Syngnathus balli
*Micrognathus balli* Fowler, 1925, Bull. B.
P. Bishop Mus., vol. 22, p. 24; Fowler,
1928, p. 114, fig. 25.

### Ichthyocampus erythraeus
*Ichthyocampus erythraeus* Gilbert, p. 613,
fig. 238.

### Doryrhamphus melanopleura
*Syngnathus melanopleura* Bleeker, 1858,
Nat. Tijd. Ned. Ind., vol. 15, p. 464
(Cocos Island).
*Doryichthys pleurotaenia* Günther, 1880,
"Challenger" Repts., Shore Fishes,
Zool., vol. 1, pt. 6, p. 62, pl. 26.
*Doryrhamphus pleurotaenia,* J. and E., p.
121, fig. 37.
?*Doryrhamphus melanopleura melanopleura,* Herald, in Schultz, p. 246.
*Doryrhamphus melanopleura pleurotaenia,*
Herald, in Schultz, p. 245.

### Micrognathus brachyrhinus
*Micrognathus brachyrhinus* Herald, in
Schultz, p. 262, fig. 39.

### Micrognathus edmondsoni
*Ichthyocampus edmondsoni* Pietschmann,
1930, B. P. Bishop Mus., Bull. 73, p. 24.
*Micrognathus edmondsoni,* Herald, in
Schultz, p. 258, fig. 39.

## MACROURIDAE
### Bathygadus bowersi
*Gadomus bowersi* Gilbert, p. 659, fig. 257.
*Bathygadus bowersi,* Gilbert and Hubbs,
1920, U. S. Nat. Mus. Bull. 100, vol. 1,
pt. 7, p. 379.

### Bathygadus micronema
*Melanobranchus micronema* Gilbert, p.
661, fig. 258.
*Bathygadus micronema,* Gilbert and
Hubbs, 1920, U. S. Nat. Mus. Bull.
100, vol. 1, pt. 7, p. 380.

### Gadomus melanopterus
*Gadomus melanopterus* Gilbert, p. 658,
fig. 256; Gilbert and Hubbs, 1920,
U. S. Nat. Mus. Bull. 100, vol. 1, pt.
7, p. 393.

### Coryphaenoides longicirrhus
*Macrourus longicirrhus* Gilbert, p. 672,
fig. 263; Gilbert and Hubbs, 1916,
Proc. U. S. Nat. Mus., vol. 51, p. 143.

### Coelorhynchus gladius
*Coelorhynchus gladius* G i l b e r t and
Cramer, 1897, Proc. U. S. Nat. Mus.,
vol. 19, p. 421, pl. 41; Gilbert, p. 673;

Gilbert and Hubbs, 1920, U. S. Nat.
Mus. Bull. 100, vol. 1, pt. 7, p. 428.

## Coelorhynchus aratrum

Coelorhynchus aratrum Gilbert, p. 674,
fig. 264; Gilbert and Hubbs, 1920,
U. S. Nat. Mus. Bull. 100, vol. 1, pt.
7, p. 432.

## Coelorhynchus doryssus

Coelorhynchus doryssus Gilbert, p. 675,
pl. 94; Gilbert and Hubbs, 1920, U. S.
Nat. Mus. Bull. 100, vol. 1, pt. 7, p.
432.

## Hymenocephalus antraeus

Hymenocephalus antraeus Gilbert and
Cramer, 1897, Proc. U. S. Nat. Mus.,
vol. 19, p. 428, pl. 46; Gilbert, p. 663;
Gilbert and Hubbs, 1920, U. S. Nat.
Mus. Bull. 100, vol. 1, pt. 7, p. 521.

## Hymenocephalus striatulus

Hymenocephalus striatulus Gilbert, p. 665,
fig. 259; Gilbert and Hubbs, 1920,
U. S. Nat. Mus. Bull. 100, vol. 1, pt.
7, p. 521.

## Hymenocephalus aterrimus

Hymenocephalus aterrimus Gilbert, p.
666, pl. 93; Gilbert and Hubbs, 1920,
U. S. Nat. Mus. Bull. 100, vol. 1, pt. 7,
p. 521.

## Hymenocephalus tenuis

Hymenocephalus tenuis Gilbert and
Hubbs, 1917, Proc. U. S. Nat. Mus.,
vol. 54, p. 173; Gilbert and Hubbs,
1920, U. S. Nat. Mus. Bull. 100, vol.
1, pt. 7, p. 520.

## Ventrifossa ctenomelas

Chalinura ctenomelas Gilbert and Cramer,
1897, Proc. U. S. Nat. Mus., vol. 19,
p. 430, pl. 45; Gilbert, p. 662.
Ventrifossa ctenomelas, G i l b e r t and
Hubbs, 1920, U. S. Nat. Mus. Bull.
100, vol. 1, pt. 7, p. 544.

## Ventrifossa atherodon

Optonurus atherodon Gilbert and Cramer,
1897, Proc. U. S. Nat. Mus., vol. 19, p.
431, pl. 46; Gilbert, p. 663.
Ventrifossa atherodon, Gilbert and Hubbs,
1920, U. S. Nat. Mus. Bull. 100, vol.
1, pt. 7, p. 544.

## Lionurus ectenes

Macrourus ectenes Gilbert and Cramer,
1897, Proc. U. S. Nat. Mus., vol. 19,
p. 423, pl. 44; Gilbert, p. 667.
Lionurus ectenes, Gilbert and Hubbs,
1916, Proc. U. S. Nat. Mus., vol. 51,
p. 146.

## Lionurus propinquus

Macrourus propinquus G i l b e r t and
Cramer, 1897, Proc. U. S. Nat. Mus.,
vol. 19, p. 424, pl. 42; Gilbert, p. 667.
Lionurus propinquus, Gilbert and Hubbs,
1916, Proc. U. S. Nat. Mus., vol. 51,
p. 196.

## Lionurus holocentrus

Macrourus holocentrus G i l b e r t and
Cramer, 1897, Proc. U. S. Nat. Mus.,
vol. 19, p. 425, pl. 43; Gilbert, p. 668.
Lionurus holocentrus, Gilbert and Hubbs,
1916, Proc. U. S. Nat. Mus., vol. 51,
p. 196.

## Lionurus gibber

Macrourus gibber Gilbert and Cramer,
1897, Proc. U. S. Nat. Mus., vol. 19,
p. 426, pl. 44; Gilbert, p. 668.
Lionurus gibber, Gilbert and Hubbs, 1916,
Proc. U. S. Nat. Mus., vol. 51, p. 196.

## Lionurus burragei

Macrourus burragei Gilbert, p. 668, fig.
260.
Lionurus burragei, Gilbert and Hubbs,
1916, Proc. U. S. Nat. Mus., vol. 51,
p. 146.

## Lionurus obliquatus

Macrourus obliquatus Gilbert, p. 670, fig.
261.
Lionurus obliquatus, Gilbert and Hubbs,
1916, Proc. U. S. Nat. Mus., vol. 51,
p. 146.

## Lionurus hebetatus

Macrourus hebetatus Gilbert, p. 671, fig.
272.
Lionurus hebetatus, Gilbert and Hubbs,
1916, Proc. U. S. Nat. Mus., vol. 51,
p. 146.

## Mataeocephalus acipenserinus

Coelocephalus acipenserinus Gilbert and
Cramer, 1897, Proc. U. S. Nat. Mus.,
vol. 19, p. 422, pl. 42.
Mataeocephalus acipenserinus, Gilbert, p.
676; Gilbert and Hubbs, 1920, U. S.
Nat. Mus. Bull. 100, vol. 1, pt. 7, p.
564.

## Malacocephalus hawaiiensis

Malacocephalus hawaiiensis Gilbert, p.
677, fig. 265; Gilbert and Hubbs, 1916,
Proc. U. S. Nat. Mus., vol. 51, p. 190.

## Trachonurus sentipellis

Trachonurus sentipellis G i l b e r t and
Cramer, 1897, Proc. U. S. Nat. Mus.,
vol. 19, p. 429, pl. 45, fig. 1; Gilbert,
p. 679; Gilbert and Hubbs, 1916, Proc.
U. S. Nat. Mus., vol. 51, p. 146.

## MORIDAE

### Antimora microlepis

*Antimora microlepis* Bean, 1890, Proc. U. S. Nat. Mus., vol. 13, p. 38 (off Queen Charlotte Islands); Gilbert, p. 656.

### Laemonema rhodochir

*Laemonema rhodochir* Gilbert, p. 657, fig. 255.

### Physiculus grinnelli

*Physiculus grinnelli* Jordan and Jordan, 1922, Mem. Carnegie Mus., vol. 10, p. 22, pl. 1; Norman, 1937, "Discovery" Repts., vol. 16, p. 54.

## BERYCIDAE

### Beryx decadactylus

*Beryx decadactylus* Cuvier, in Cuvier and Valenciennes, 1829, Hist. Nat. Poiss., vol. 3, p. 151 (no locality); Fowler, 1928, p. 96, pl. 5.

## POLYMIXIIDAE

### Polymixia japonica

*Polymixia japonica* Günther, 1877, Ann. Mag. Nat. Hist., ser. 4, vol. 20, p. 436 (Japan); Lachner, 1955, Proc. U. S. Nat. Mus., vol. 105, p. 201 (various localities).

*Polymixia berndti* Gilbert, p. 616, pl. 78.

## CAULOLEPIDAE

### Caulolepis longidens

*Caulolepis longidens* Gill, 1884, Proc. U. S. Nat. Mus., vol. 6, p. 258 (Atlantic); Gilbert, p. 616.

## MELAMPHAIDAE

### Melamphaes unicornis

*Melamphaes unicornis* Gilbert, p. 615, pl. 77.

## HOLOCENTRIDAE

### Holocentrus sammara

*Sciaena sammara* Forskål, 1775, Descript. Animal., p. 48 (Red Sea).

*Flammeo sammara,* J. and E., p. 155, fig. 56.

### Holocentrus spinifer

*Sciaena spinifera* Forskål, 1775, Descript. Animal., p. 49 (Red Sea).

*Holocentrus spinifer,* J. and E., p. 161, col. pl. 8 (this plate is either very poor or does not represent this species at all).

### Holocentrus xantherythrus

*Holocentrus xantherythrus* Jordan and Evermann, 1903, Bull. U. S. Fish Comm., vol. 22, p. 175; J. and E., p. 164, col. pl. 9.

### Holocentrus ensifer

*Holocentrus ensifer* Jordan and Evermann, 1903, Bull. U. S. Fish Comm., vol. 22, p. 176; J. and E., p. 165, col. pl. 11 and pl. 28.

### Holocentrus scythrops

*Flammeo scythrops* Jordan and Evermann, 1903, Bull. U. S. Fish Comm., vol. 22, p. 174; J. and E., p. 157, col. pl. 7 and fig. 57.

### Holocentrus diadema

*Holocentrus diadema* Lacépède, 1802, Hist. Nat. Poiss., vol. 4, pp. 335, 372, 374, pl. 32 (South Seas); J. and E., p. 159, pl. 10.

### Holocentrus microstomus

*Holocentrum microstoma* Günther, 1859, Cat. Fishes British Mus., vol. 1, p. 34 (East Indies).

*Holocentrus microstomus,* J. and E., p. 160, fig. 58.

### Holocentrus tiere

*Holocentrum tiere* Cuvier and Valenciennes, 1829, Hist. Nat. Poiss., vol. 3, p. 202 (Tahiti).

*Holocentrus erythraeus,* J. and E., p. 161, fig. 59.

*Holocentrus tiere,* Woods, in Schultz, p. 221 (Marshall Islands and Johnston).

### Holocentrus lacteoguttatus

*Holocentrum lacteo-guttatum* Cuvier, in Cuvier and Valenciennes, 1829, Hist. Nat. Poiss., vol. 3, p. 214 (East Indies).

*Holocentrus gracilispinis* Fowler, 1904, Proc. Acad. Nat. Sci. Philadelphia, p. 228, fig. 4.

*Holocentrus punctatissimus,* J. and E., p. 162, fig. 60.

### Ostichthys japonicus

*Myripristis japonicus* Cuvier, in Cuvier and Valenciennes, 1829, Hist. Nat. Poiss., vol. 3, p. 129, pl. 58 (Japan).

*Myripristis pilwaxii* Steindachner, 1893, Sitz. akad. wiss. Wien, vol. 102, p. 215, pl. 1.

*Ostichthys pilwaxii,* J. and E., p. 148.

### Holotrachys lima

*Myripristis lima* Cuvier and Valenciennes, 1831, Hist. Nat. Poiss., vol. 7, p. 493 (Ile de France).

*Holotrachys lima,* J. and E., p. 147, pl. 4.

### ?Myripristis occidentalis

*Myripristis sealei* Jenkins, 1903, Bull. U. S. Fish Comm., vol. 22, p. 439, fig. 13; J. and E., p. 151, fig. 53. (The type of this species has been examined and appears to be a perfectly normal specimen of *M. occidentalis,* a west American species. Since no Hawaiian specimens have been forthcoming since Jenkins' original record, we tentatively believe that the original specimens were not from Hawaii.)

### Myripristis chryseres
*Myripristis chryseres* Jordan and Evermann, 1903, Bull. U. S. Fish Comm., vol. 22, p. 171; J. and E., p. 150, col. pl. 6.

### Myripristis multiradiatus
*Myripristis multiradiatus* Günther, 1874, Fische der Südsee, vol. 1, p. 93 (Vavau); J. and E., p. 149.

### Myripristis berndti
*Myripristis berndti* Jordan and Evermann, 1903, Bull. U. S. Fish Comm., vol. 22, p. 170; J. and E., p. 153, fig. 54.
*Myripristis murdjan,* J. and E., p. 152, col.

### Myripristis argyromus
pl. 5.
*Myripristis argyromus* Jordan and Evermann, 1903, Bull. U. S. Fish Comm., vol. 22, p. 172; J. and E., p. 154, pl. 27 and fig. 55.
*Myripristis symmetricus* Jordan and Evermann, 1903, Bull. U. S. Fish Comm., vol. 22, p. 173; J. and E., p. 151, pl. 26.

### LAMPRIDAE
#### Lampris regius
*Zeus regius* Bonnaterre, 1788, Encycl. Ichth., p. 72, pl. 39 (England).
*Lampris regius,* J. and E., p. 166; Fowler, 1928, p. 89, fig. 17.

### VELIFERIDAE
#### Velifer multispinosus
*Velifer multispinosus* Smith, 1951, Ann. Mag. Nat. Hist., ser. 12, vol. 4, pls. 11 and 12 and text fig. 2 (South Africa).

### LOPHOTIDAE
#### Lophotus capellei
*Lophotes capellei* Schlegel, 1845, Fauna Japonica, Poiss., p. 132, pl. 71 (Japan); Fowler, 1928, p. 88.

### ZEIDAE
#### Stethopristes eos
*Stethopristes eos* Gilbert, p. 622, fig. 241.

### CAPROIDAE
#### Cyttomimus stelgis
*Cyttomimus stelgis* Gilbert, p. 624, pl. 80.

### ANTIGONIIDAE
#### Antigonia steindachneri
*Antigonia steindachneri* Jordan and Evermann in Jordan and Fowler, 1903, Proc. U. S. Nat. Mus., vol. 25, p. 522; J. and E., p. 361, col. pl. 45; Gilbert, p. 621.

#### Antigonia eos
*Antigonia eos* Gilbert, p. 621, pl. 80.

### GRAMMICOLEPIDAE
#### Grammicolepis brachiusculus
*Grammicolepis brachiusculus* Poey, 1873, Anal. Soc. Española Hist. Nat., vol. 2, p. 403, pl. 12 (Cuba); Myers, 1937, Proc. U. S. Nat. Mus., vol. 84, p. 150 (Hawaii in part).
*Vesposus egregius* Jordan, 1922, Proc. U. S. Nat. Mus., vol. 59, p. 650, fig. 5.

### BOTHIDAE
#### Taeniopsetta radula
*Taeniopsetta radula* Gilbert, p. 680, fig. 266; Norman, 1934, Monograph of Flatfishes, p. 123, fig. 79.

#### Pelecanichthys crumenalis
*Pelecanichthys crumenalis* Gilbert and Cramer, 1897, Proc. U. S. Nat. Mus., vol. 19, p. 433, pl. 47; J. and E., p. 510, fig. 226; Gilbert, p. 690; Norman, 1934, Monograph of Flatfishes, p. 252, fig. 193.

#### Chascanopsetta prorigera
*Chascanopsetta prorigera* Gilbert, p. 689, fig. 271; Norman, 1934, Monograph of Flatfishes, p. 251, fig. 192.

#### Bothus pantherinus
*Rhombus pantherinus* Rüppell, 1830, Atlas Reis. Nord. Afrika, Fisch., p. 121, pl. 31 (Red Sea).
*Platophrys pantherinus,* J. and E., p. 512.
*Bothus pantherinus,* Norman, 1934, Monograph of Flatfishes, p. 233, fig. 177.

#### Bothus mancus
*Pleuronectes mancus* Broussonet, 1782, Ichthyol., pls. 3 and 4 (Pacific).
*Platophrys mancus,* J. and E., p. 513.
*Bothus mancus,* Norman, 1934, Monograph of Flatfishes, p. 131, fig. 174 (various localities).

#### Bothus bleekeri
*Bothus bleekeri* Steindachner, 1861, Verh. zool.-bot. Ges. Wien, vol. 11, p. 178 (East Indies); Norman, 1934, Monograph of Flatfishes, p. 235, pl. 178 (Ceylon and East Indies).
*Platophrys thompsoni* Fowler, 1923, Occ. Pap. B. P. Bishop Mus., vol. 8, p. 388; Fowler, 1928, p. 91, pl. 4.

#### Arnoglossus debilis
*Anticitharus debilis* Gilbert, p. 683, pl. 97.

*Arnoglossus debilis,* Norman, 1934, Monograph of Flatfishes, p. 194, fig. 142.

## Parabothus chlorospilus

*Platophrys chlorospilus* Gilbert, p. 684, fig. 267.
*Platophrys inermis* Gilbert, p. 685, fig. 268.
*Parabothus chlorospilus,* Norman, 1934, Monograph of Flatfishes, p. 241, fig. 242.

## Parabothus coarctatus

*Platophrys coarctatus* Gilbert, p. 686, fig. 269.
*Parabothus coarctatus* Norman, 1934, Monograph of Flatfishes, p. 243, fig. 185.

## Engyprosopon hawaiiensis

*Engyprosopon hawaiiensis* Jordan and Evermann, 1903, Bull. U. S. Fish Comm., vol. 22, p. 207; J. and E., 1905, p. 514, fig. 227; Gilbert, 1905, p. 514, fig. 227; Norman, 1934, Monograph of Flatfishes, p. 212, fig. 159.
*Engyprosopon arenicola* Jordan and Evermann, 1903, Bull. U. S. Fish Comm., vol. 22, p. 207; J. and E., 1905, p. 515, pl. 62; Norman, 1934, Monograph of Flatfishes, p. 211, fig. 158.

## Engyprosopon xenandrus

*Engyprosopon xenandrus* Gilbert, p. 687, fig. 270; Norman, 1934, Monograph of Flatfishes, p. 205, fig. 206.

## PLEURONECTIDAE

### Poecilopsetta hawaiiensis

*Poecilopsetta hawaiiensis* Gilbert, p. 391, pl. 95; Norman, 1934, Monograph of Flatfishes, p. 391, fig. 280.

### Samariscus triocellatus

*Samariscus triocellatus* Woods, U. S. Nat. Mus. Bull. 202, vol. 3, p. 00 (Marshalls).

### Samariscus corallinus

*Samariscus corallinus* Gilbert, p. 682, pl. 96; Norman, 1934, Monograph of Flatfishes, p. 409, fig. 297.

## SOLEIDAE

### Aseraggodes kobensis

*Solea (Achirus) kobensis* Steindachner, 1896, Reise "Aurora," p. 218 (Japan).
*Aseraggodes kobensis,* Jordan and Starks, 1906, Proc. U. S. Nat. Mus., vol. 31, p. 230, fig. 24 (Japan); Chabanaud, 1930, Zool. Mededeelingen, vol. 13, pp. 184 and 189 (Japan).

## CYNOGLOSSIDAE

### Symphurus undatus

*Symphurus undatus* Gilbert, p. 690, pl. 98; Chabanaud, 1956, Arch. du Muséum National d'Histoire naturelle, ser. 7, vol. 4, p. 94, figs. 1 and 2, pls. 1 and 4 (on the type).

### Symphurus strictus

*Symphurus strictus* Gilbert, p. 691, fig. 272.

## SPHYRAENIDAE

### Sphyraena barracuda

*Esox barracuda* Walbaum, 1792, Ichthyol., vol. 3, p. 94 (West Indies).
*Sphyraena snodgrassi* Jenkins, 1901, Bull. U. S. Fish Comm., vol. 19, p. 388, fig. 2; J. and E., p. 142, fig. 50.
*Sphyraena barracuda,* Schultz, p. 283, pl. 23 (Marshalls and Guam).

### Sphyraena helleri

*Sphyraena helleri* Jenkins, 1901, Bull. U. S. Fish Comm., vol. 19, p. 387, fig. 1; J. and E., p. 143, fig. 51; Schultz, p. 281.

## ATHERINIDAE

### Pranesus insularum

*Atherina insularum* Jordan and Evermann, 1903, Bull. U. S. Fish Comm., vol. 22, p. 170; J. and E., p. 138, fig. 47.
*Pranesus insularum insularum,* Schultz, p. 307.

### Iso hawaiiensis

*Iso hawaiiensis* Gosline, 1952, Pacific Sci., vol. 6, p. 47, fig. 1.

## MUGILIDAE

### Mugil cephalus

*Mugil cephalus* Linnaeus, 1758, Systema Naturae, Ed. X, p. 316 (Europe); J. and E., p. 139, fig. 48.
*Mugil cephalotus* Eydoux and Souleyet, 1841, Voy. "Bonite," vol. 1, p. 175, fig. 4.
?*Myxus pacificus* Steindachner, 1900, Denkschr. K. Akad. Wiss. Wien, vol. 70, p. 500.

### Neomyxus chaptalii

*Mugil chaptalii* Eydoux and Souleyet, 1841, Voy. "Bonite," vol. 1, p. 171, pl. 4.
*Myxus (Neomyxus) sclateri* Steindachner, 1878, Sitz. K. Akad. Wiss. Wien, vol. 77, p. 384 (Kingsmill and Hawaiian Islands).
*Chaenomugil chaptalii,* J. and E., p. 140, fig. 49.

*Neomyxus chaptalii,* Schultz, p. 315 (Marshalls, Saipan, and Guam).

### POLYNEMIDAE
#### *Polydactylus sexfilis*
*Polynemus sexfilis* Cuvier and Valenciennes, 1831, Hist. Nat. Poiss., vol. 7, p. 515 (Ile de France).
*Polydactylus sexfilis,* J. and E., p. 144.

### SERRANIDAE
#### *Pteranthias longimanus*
*Pteranthias longimanus* Weber, 1913, "Siboga" Exped., Fische, p. 209 (East Indies); Weber and de Beaufort, 1931, Fishes of the Indo-Australian Archipelago, vol. 6, p. 112, fig. 18 (East Indies).

#### *Grammatonotus laysanus*
*Grammatonotus laysanus* Gilbert, p. 619, fig. 240.

#### *Caprodon schlegelii*
*Caprodon schlegelii* Günther, 1859, Cat. Fishes British Mus., vol. 1, p. 93 (Japan); Jordan and Snyder, 1907, Bull. Bur. Fish., vol. 26, p. 211, pl. 12.
*Caprodon longimanus,* Fowler, 1928, p. 185, pl. 15.

#### *Epinephelus quernus*
*Epinephelus quernus* Seale, 1901, Occ. Pap. B. P. Bishop Mus., vol. 1, no. 4, p. 3, fig. 1; J. and E., p. 223, figs. 89 and 90.
*?Serranus (Epinephelus) dictyophorus,* Steindachner, 1893, Sitz. K. Akad. Wiss. Wien, vol. 102, p. 219.

#### *Epinephelus tauvina*
*Perca tauvina* Forskål, 1775, Descript. Animal, pp. 11 and 39 (Red Sea).
*Serranus phaeostigmus* Fowler, 1907, Proc. Acad. Nat. Sci. Philadelphia, p. 255, fig. 2.
*?Stereolepoides thompsoni* Fowler, 1923, Occ. Pap. B. P. Bishop Mus., vol. 8, p. 382; Fowler, 1928, p. 172, pl. 14.
*?Epinephelus lanceolatus,* Jordan, Evermann and Tanaka, 1927, Proc. California Acad. Sci., ser. 4, vol. 16, p. 654.

#### *Pikea aurora*
*Pikea aurora* Jordan and Evermann, 1903, Bull. U. S. Fish Comm., vol. 22, p. 176; J. and E., p. 220, pl. 14.

#### *Caesioperca thompsoni*
*Caesioperca thompsoni* Fowler, 1923, Occ. Pap. B. P. Bishop Mus., vol. 8, p. 379; Fowler, 1928, p. 185, fig. 43.

#### *Pseudanthias kelloggi*
*Anthias kelloggi* Jordan and Evermann, 1903, Bull. U. S. Fish Comm., vol. 22, p. 179.
*Pseudanthias kelloggi,* J. and E., p. 226, fig. 92.

#### *Odontanthias fuscipinnis*
*Anthias fuscipinnis* Jenkins, 1901, Bull. U. S. Fish Comm., vol. 19, p. 389, fig. 3.
*Odontanthias fuscipinnis,* J. and E., p. 225, pl. 15 and fig. 91.

#### *Odontanthias elizabethae*
*Odontanthias elizabethae* Fowler, 1923, Occ. Pap. B. P. Bishop Mus., vol. 8, p. 379; Fowler, 1928, p. 187, fig. 44.

### PSEUDOCHROMIDAE
#### *Pseudogramma polyacantha*
*Pseudochromis polyacanthus* B l e e k e r, 1856, Nat. Tijd. Ned.-Ind., vol. 10, p. 375 (East Indies).
*Pseudogramma polyacantha,* Schultz, p. 395 (Marshalls).

#### *Aporops bilinearis*
*Aporops bilinearis* Schultz, 1943, U. S. Nat. Mus. Bull. 180, p. 112, fig. 9 (Phoenix Islands); Schultz, p. 396, fig. 64 (Marshalls).

### KUHLIIDAE
#### *Kuhlia sandvicensis*
*Moronopsis argenteus* var. *sandvicensis* Steindachner, 1876, Sitz. K. Akad. Wiss. Wien, vol. 74, p. 205.
*Kuhlia malo,* J. and E., p. 207.
*Kuhlia sandvicensis,* Tester and Takata, 1953, Hawaii Industrial Research Advisory Council Grant No. 29, Final Report, 54 pp., 14 figs. (biology of the species); Schultz, p. 325.

### GREGORYINIDAE
#### *Gregoryina gygis*
*Gregoryina gygis* Fowler and Ball, 1924, Proc. Acad. Nat. Sci. Philadelphia, p. 270; Fowler, 1928, p. 223, fig. 46.

### PRIACANTHIDAE
#### *Priacanthus boops*
*Anthias boops* Schneider, 1801, Syst. Ichth., p. 308 (Atlantic).
*Priacanthus boops,* Fowler, 1928, p. 190, pl. 15.

#### *Priacanthus cruentatus*
*Labrus cruentatus* Lacépède, 1801, Hist. Nat. Poiss., vol. 3, p. 522 (West Indies).
*Priacanthus cruentatus,* J. and E., p. 229, fig. 94.

## Priacanthus alalaua

*Priacanthus alalaua* Jordan and Evermann, 1903, Bull. U. S. Fish Comm., vol. 22, p. 181; J. and E., p. 228, fig. 93.

### Priacanthus meeki

*Priacanthus meeki* Jenkins, 1903, Bull. U. S. Fish Comm., vol. 22, p. 450, fig. 20; J. and E., p. 231, fig. 95; Jordan, Evermann and Tanaka, 1927, Proc. California Acad. Sci., ser. 4, vol. 16, p. 663, pl. 23.
*Priacanthus helvolus* Jordan, Evermann and Tanaka, 1927, Proc. California Acad. Sci., ser. 4, vol. 16, p. 664, pl. 23.

## APOGONIDAE

### Pseudamiops gracilicauda

*Gymnapogon gracilicauda* Lachner, in Schultz, p. 497 (Marshalls).
*Pseudamiops gracilicauda,* Gosline, 1955, Pacific Sci., vol. 9, p. 450.

### Epigonus atherinoides

*Hynnodus atherinoides* Gilbert, p. 618, pl. 18.
*Sceptarias fragilis* Jordan and Jordan, 1922, Mem. Carnegie Mus., vol. 10, p. 45, pl. 2.
*Epigonus atherinoides,* Matsubara, 1936, Jour. Imp. Fisheries Institute, Tokyo, vol. 31, p. 120, fig. 1 (Japan).

### Synagrops argyrea

*Melanostoma argyrea* Gilbert and Cramer, 1896, Proc. U. S. Nat. Mus., vol. 19, pl. 39.
*Synagrops argyrea,* J. and E., p. 218, fig. 87; Gilbert, p. 618; Schultz, 1940, Proc. U. S. Nat. Mus., vol. 88, p. 416.

### Apogon evermanni

*Apogon evermanni* Jordan and Snyder, 1904, Proc. U. S. Nat. Mus., vol. 28, p. 123.
*Amia evermanni,* J. and E., p. 213, fig. 84.

### Apogon brachygrammus

*Fowleria brachygrammus* Jenkins, 1903, Bull. U. S. Fish Comm., vol. 22, p. 447, fig. 18.
*Foa brachygramma,* J. and E., p. 211, fig. 82.

### Apogon waikiki

*Apogonichthys waikiki* Jordan and Evermann, 1903, Bull. U. S. Fish Comm., vol. 22, p. 179.
*Mionurus waikiki,* J. and E., p. 210, pl. 35.

### Apogon erythrinus

*Apogon erythrinus* Snyder, 1904, Bull. U. S. Fish Comm., vol. 22, p. 526, pl. 9; Lachner, in Schultz, p. 446 (Marshalls and Guam).

*Amia erythrina,* J. and E., p. 217, pl. 34.

### Apogon maculiferus

*Apogon maculiferus* Garrett, 1863, Proc. California Acad. Sci., vol. 3, p. 105.
*Amia maculifera,* J. and E., p. 212, fig. 83.

### Apogon snyderi

*Apogon snyderi* Jordan and Evermann, 1903, Bull. U. S. Fish Comm., vol. 22, p. 180; Lachner, in Schultz, p. 453, pl. 33 (Marshalls and Guam).
*Amia snyderi,* J. and E., p. 214, pl. 36 and fig. 85.

### Apogon menesemus

*Apogon menesemus* Jenkins, 1903, Bull. U. S. Fish Comm., vol. 22, p. 448, fig. 19; Lachner, in Schultz, p. 437.
*Amia menesema,* J. and E., p. 215, col. pl. 13, and fig. 86.

## MALACANTHIDAE

### Malacanthus hoedtii

*Malacanthus hoedtii* Bleeker, 1859, Act. Soc. Sci. Indo-Neerl., vol. 6, p. 18 (New Guinea).
*Malacanthus parvipinnis* Vaillant and Sauvage, 1875, Rev. et Mag. Zool., ser. 3, vol. 3, p. 283; J. and E., p. 275, fig. 118.

## CARANGIDAE

### Scomberoides sanctipetri

*Chorinemus sancti-petri* Cuvier, in Cuvier and Valenciennes, 1831, Hist. Nat. Poiss., vol. 8, p. 379, pl. 236 (Malabar).
*Scomberoides tolooparah,* J. and E., p. 180.
*Scomberoides sancti-petri,* J. and E., p. 181.

### Elagatis bipinnulatus

*Seriola bipinnulatus* Quoy and Gaimard, 1824, Voy. "Uranie," vol. 1, p. 363, pl. 61 (East Indies).
*Elagatis bipinnulatus,* J. and E., p. 185.

### Naucrates ductor

*Gasterosteus ductor* Linnaeus, 1758, Systema Naturae, Ed. X, p. 295 (no locality).
*Naucrates ductor,* J. and E., p. 182, fig. 68.

### Seriola dumerilii

*Caranx dumerilii* Risso, 1810, Ichth. Nice, p. 175 (Mediterranean).
*Seriola purpurascens,* J. and E., p. 183, fig. 69.

### Seriola aureovittata

*Seriola aureovittata* Schlegel, 1842, Fauna Japonica, Poiss., p. 115, pl. 62 (Japan).

*Seriola sparna* Jenkins, 1903, Bull. U. S. Fish Comm., vol. 22, p. 442, fig. 14; J. and E., p. 184, fig. 70.

### Megalaspis cordyla

*Scomber cordyla* Linnaeus, 1758, Systema Naturae, Ed. X, p. 248 (America).
*Megalaspis cordyla,* Jordan, Evermann and Tanaka, 1927, Proc. California Acad. Sci., ser. 4, vol. 16, p. 655.

### Decapterus pinnulatus

*Caranx pinnulatus* Eydoux and Souleyet, 1841, Voy. "Bonite," Zool., vol. 1, p. 165, pl. 3.
*Decapterus canonoides* Jenkins, 1903, Bull. U. S. Fish Comm., vol. 22, p. 442, pl. 4.
*Decapterus pinnulatus,* J. and E., p. 186, pl. 30.

### Decapterus maruadsi

*Caranx maruadsi* Schlegel, 1844, Fauna Japonica, Poiss., p. 109, pl. 58 (Japan).
*Decapterus maruadsi,* Nichols, 1922, American Mus. Novitates, no. 50, p. 2.

### Carangoides gymnostethoides

*Carangoides gymnostethoides* Bleeker, 1852, Verh. Bat. Gen., vol. 24, p. 61 (Batavia); J. and E., p. 199.

### Gnathanodon speciosus

*Scomber speciosus* Forskål, 1775, Descript. Animal., pp. xii and 54 (Red Sea).
*Caranx speciosus,* J. and E., p. 197, pl. 12.

### Alectis ciliaris

*Zeus ciliaris* Bloch, 1788, Ichthyol., vol. 6, p. 27, pl. 191 (East Indies).
*Alectis ciliaris,* J. and E., p. 200, fig. 78.

### Alectis indica

*Scyris indicus* Rüppell, 1828, Atlas Reis. Nord. Afrika, Zool., p. 128, pl. 33 (Red Sea); Fowler, 1938, p. 151.

### Trachurops crumenophthalmus

*Scomber crumenophthalmus* Bloch, 1793, Ichthyologia, pl. 343 (Guinea).
*Trachurops crumenophthalmus,* J. and E., p. 187, fig. 71.

### Carangoides ferdau

*Scomber ferdau* Forskål, 1775, Descript. Animal., p. 55 (Red Sea).
*Carangoides ferdau,* J. and E., p. 199, fig. 77.

### Uraspis reversa

*Uraspis reversa* Jordan, Evermann and Wakiya, in Jordan, Evermann and Tanaka, 1927, Proc. California Acad. Sci., ser. 4, vol. 16, p. 658, pl. 22.

### Carangoides ajax

*Carangoides ajax* Snyder, 1904, Bull. U. S.

Fish Comm., vol. 22, p. 524, pl. 8; J. and E., p. 200, pl. 33.

### Carangoides equula

*Caranx equula* Schlegel, 1844, Fauna Japonica, Poiss., p. 111, pl. 60 (Japan).
*Caranx dasson* Jordan and Snyder, 1907, Bull. Bur. Fish., vol. 26, p. 210, fig. 2.

### Caranx helvolus

*Scomber helvolus* Forster, 1775, Descript. Animal., pp. 414 and 415 (probably Tahiti).
*Carangus helvolus,* J. and E., p. 196, pl. 33.
*Leucoglossa candens* Jordan, Evermann and Tanaka, 1927, Proc. California Acad. Sci., ser. 4, vol. 17, p. 660.
*Leucoglossa albilinguis* Jordan, Evermann and Tanaka, 1927, *op. cit.,* p. 661, pl. 22.

### Caranx ignobilis

*Scomber ignobilis* Forskål, 1775, Descript. Animal., p. 55 (Red Sea).
*Caranx hippoides* Jenkins, 1903, Bull. U. S. Fish Comm., vol. 22, p. 443, fig. 15.
*Caranx rhabdotus* Jenkins, 1903, *op. cit.,* p. 444, fig. 16; J. and E., p. 193, fig. 74.
*Caranx ignobilis,* J. and E., p. 188, fig. 72.

### Caranx cheilio

*Carangus cheilio* Snyder, 1904, Bull. U. S. Fish Comm., vol. 22, p. 524, pl. 8; J. and E., p. 196, pl. 33.

### Caranx melampygus

*Caranx melampygus* Cuvier and Valenciennes, 1833, Hist. Nat. Poiss., vol. 9, p. 116 (Waigiou, Rauwak, etc.).
*Caranx stellatus* Eydoux and Souleyet, 1841, Voy. "Bonite," Poiss., p. 167, pl. 3.
*Carangus melampygus,* J. and E., p. 192, fig. 73.

### Caranx sexfasciatus

*Caranx sexfasciatus* Quoy and Gaimard, 1825, Voy. "Uranie," Zool., p. 358, pl. 65 ("Iles des Papous").
*Carangus elacate* Jordan and Evermann, 1903, Bull. U. S. Fish Comm., vol. 22, p. 177; J. and E., p. 190, pl. 31.
*Carangus marginatus,* J. and E., p. 191.
*Carangus forsteri,* J. and E., p. 191.

### Caranx lugubris

*Caranx lugubris* Poey, 1861, Memorias, vol. 2, p. 222 (Cuba); Fowler, 1928, p. 149, pl. 13.

### Caranx mate

*Caranx mate* Cuvier and Valenciennes,

1833, Hist. Nat. Poiss., vol. 9, p. 40 (Pondicherry, etc.).
*Carangus politus* Jenkins, 1903, Bull. U. S. Fish Comm., vol. 22, p. 445, fig. 17; J. and E., p. 194, fig. 75.
*Carangus affinis,* J. and E., p. 195, fig. 76.
*Caranx affinis lundini* Nichols, 1922, American Mus. Novitates, no. 50, p. 1.

## Caranx kalla

*Caranx kalla* Cuvier, in Cuvier and Valenciennes, 1833, Hist. Nat. Poiss., vol. 9, p. 37 (Malabar, etc.).

**BRAMIDAE**

### Pteraclis velifer

*Coryphaena velifera* Pallas, 1769, Spicilegia zoologica, fasc. 8, p. 19, pl. 3 (Indian Ocean).

### Taractes longipinnis

*Brama longipinnis* Lowe, 1843, Proc. Zool. Soc. London, p. 82 (Madeira).
*Taractes steindachneri,* Fowler, 1928, p. 138, pl. 10.
*Taractes longipinnis,* Mead, 1957, Zoologica, vol. 42, p. 56 (synonymy).

### Collybus drachme

*Collybus drachme* Snyder, 1903, Bull. U. S. Fish Comm., vol. 22, p. 525, pl. 9; J. and E., p. 203, pl. 34; Mead, 1957, Zoologica, vol. 42, p. 58 (Gulf of Mexico).

### Eumegistus illustris

*Eumegistus illustris* Jordan and Jordan, 1922, Mem. Carnegie Mus., vol. 10, p. 36, pl. 2; Mead, 1958, Bull. Mus. Comp. Zool., vol. 119, p. 407.

**CORYPHAENIDAE**

### Coryphaena hippurus

*Coryphaena hippurus* Linnaeus, 1758, Systema Naturae, Ed. X, p. 261 (high seas); J. and E., p. 204, fig. 79.

### Coryphaena equisetus

*Coryphaena equisetus* Linnaeus, 1758, Systema Naturae, Ed. X, p. 261 (high seas); J. and E., p. 205, fig. 80.

**EMMELICHTHYIDAE**

### Erythrocles schlegelii

*Erythrichthys schlegelii* Günther, 1859, Cat. Fishes British Mus., vol. 1, p. 395 (Japan); J. and E., p. 245, col. pl. 19 and fig. 102.

**LUTJANIDAE**

### Symphysanodon typus

*Symphysanodon typus* Bleeker, 1878, Arch. Neerl. Sci. Nat., vol. 13, p. 61 (East Indies).

*Rhyacanthias carlsmithi* Jordan, 1921, Proc. U. S. Nat. Mus., vol. 59, p. 647, fig. 3.

### Rooseveltia brighami

*Serranus brighami* Seale, 1901, Occ. Pap. B. P. Bishop Mus., vol. 1, no. 4, p. 7.
*Apsilus brighami,* J. and E., p. 233, pl. 16.
*Rooseveltia aloha* Jordan and Snyder, 1907, Bull. U. S. Fish Comm., vol. 26, p. 212, fig. 3.

### Aphareus furcatus

*Labrus furcatus* Lacépède, 1802, Hist. Nat. Poiss., vol. 3, pp. 429, 477, pl. 21 (Pacific Ocean).
*Aphareus flavivultus* Jenkins, 1901, Bull. U. S. Fish Comm., vol. 19, p. 390, fig. 4; J. and E., p. 235, fig. 96; Jordan, Evermann and Tanaka, 1927, Proc. California Acad. Sci., ser. 4, vol. 16, p. 671.
*Aphareus furcatus,* Jordan, Evermann and Tanaka, 1927, Proc. California Acad. Sci., ser. 4, vol. 16, p. 672.

### Aphareus rutilans

*Aphareus rutilans* Cuvier and Valenciennes, 1830, Hist. Nat. Poiss., vol. 6, p. 490 (Red Sea); Jordan, Evermann and Tanaka, 1927, Proc. California Acad. Sci., ser. 4, vol. 16, p. 673, pl. 24.
*Aphareus thompsoni* Fowler, 1923, Occ. Pap. B. P. Bishop Mus., vol. 8, p. 382.

### Pristipomoides microlepis

*Chaetopterus microlepis* Bleeker, 1869, Versl. Kon. Akad. Wet. Amsterdam, ser. 2, vol. 3, p. 80 (East Indies).
*Apsilus microdon,* J. and E., p. 234.
*Bowersia violescens* Jordan and Evermann, 1903, Bull. U. S. Fish Comm., vol. 22, p. 183; J. and E., p. 236, fig. 97.
*Pristipomoides microlepis,* Smith, 1954, Ann. Mag. Nat. Hist., ser. 14, vol. 7, p. 488, pl. 10 (South Africa).

### Pristipomoides sieboldii

*Chaetopterus sieboldii* Bleeker, 1857, Verh. Bat. Gen., vol. 26, p. 20 (Japan).
*Aprion microdon* Steindachner, 1876, Sitz. K. Akad. Wiss. Wien, vol. 74, p. 158.
*Bowersia ulaula* Jordan and Evermann, 1903, Bull. U. S. Fish Comm., vol. 22, p. 183; J. and E., p. 238, fig. 98.
?*Arnillo auricilla* Jordan, Evermann and Tanaka, 1927, Proc. California Acad. Sci., ser. 4, vol. 16, p. 668, pl. 23.
*Pristipomoides sieboldii,* Smith, 1954, Ann. Mag. Nat. Hist., ser. 12, vol. 7, p. 490, pl. 10 (South Africa).

### Etelis marshi

Eteliscus marshi Jenkins, 1903,. Bull. U. S.
Fish Comm., vol. 22, p. 452, fig. 21.
Etelis marshi, J. and E., p. 240, col. pl.
17 and fig. 100.

### Etelis carbunculus

Etelis carbunculus Cuvier, 1828, Hist. Nat.
Poiss., vol. 2, p. 94, pl. 18 (Seychelles).
Etelis evurus Jordan and Evermann, 1903,
Bull. U. S. Fish Comm., vol. 22, p. 184;
J. and E., p. 242, col. pl. 18 and pl. 38.

## LOBOTIDAE

### Lobotes surinamensis

Holocentrus surinamensis Bloch, 1790,
Naturges. Ausl. Fische, vol. 4, p. 98
(Surinam).

## MULLIDAE

### Upeneus arge

Upeneus arge Jordan and Evermann, 1903,
Bull. U. S. Fish Comm., vol. 22, p.
187; J. and E., p. 264, pl. 39; Lachner,
1954, Proc. U. S. Nat. Mus., vol. 103,
p. 518, pl. 14.

### Mulloidichthys samoensis

Mulloides samoensis Günther, 1874,
Fische der Südsee, p. 57, pl. 43 (Samoa); J. and E., p. 253, fig. 105.
Upeneus preorbitalis Smith and Swain,
1882, Proc. U. S. Nat. Mus., vol. 5,
p. 132 (Johnston Island).
Pseudupeneus preorbitalis, J. and E., p.
263, fig. 111.
Mulloides vanicolensis, J. and E., p. 254.

### Mulloidichthys auriflamma

Mullus auriflamma Forskål, 1775, Descript. Animal., p. 30 (Red Sea).
Mulloides auriflamma, J. and E., p. 250,
fig. 103.
Mulloides erythrinus, J. and E., p. 251.

### Mulloidichthys pflugeri

Mulloides pflugeri Steindachner, 1900,
Denkschr. Akad. Wiss. Wien, vol. 70,
p. 485, pl. 3; J. and E., p. 251.
Mulloides flammeus Jordan and Evermann, 1903, Bull. U. S. Fish Comm.,
vol. 22, p. 186; J. and E., p. 251, fig.
104.

### Parupeneus pleurostigma

Upeneus pleurostigma Bennett, 1830,
Proc. Zool. Soc. London, p. 59 (Mauritius).
Pseudupeneus pleurostigma, J. and E., p.
260, fig. 108.

### Parupeneus chryserydros

Mullus chryserydros Lacépède, 1801, Hist.
Nat. Poiss., vol. 3, p. 406 (Ile de
France).
Pseudupeneus chryserydros, J. and E., p.
255, fig. 106.

### Parupeneus porphyreus

Pseudupeneus porphyreus Jenkins, 1903,
Bull. U. S. Fish Comm., vol. 22, p.
454, fig. 22; J. and E., p. 262, fig. 110.

### Parupeneus chrysonemus

Pseudupeneus chrysonemus Jordan and
Evermann, 1903, Bull. U. S. Fish
Comm., vol. 22, p. 186; J. and E., p.
258, col. pl. 21.

### Parupeneus multifasciatus

Mullus multifasciatus Quoy and Gaimard,
1824, Voy. "Uranie," Zool., p. 330, pl.
59.
Upeneus velifer Smith and Swain, 1882,
Proc. U. S. Nat. Mus., vol. 5, p. 130
(Johnston).
Pseudupeneus multifasciatus, J. and E., p.
256, col. pl. 22.

### Parupeneus bifasciatus

Mullus bifasciatus Lacépède, 1801, Hist.
Nat. Poiss., vol. 3, pl. 14 (no locality).
Pseudupeneus bifasciatus, J. and E., p. 258,
fig. 107.
Pseudupeneus crassilabrus, J. and E., p.
259.

## SPARIDAE

### Monotaxis grandoculis

Sciaena grandoculis Forskål, 1775, Descript. Animal., p. 53 (Red Sea).
Monotaxis grandoculis, J. and E., p. 243,
fig. 101.

## SCORPIDIDAE

### Microcanthus strigatus

Chaetodon strigatus Cuvier and Valenciennes, 1831, Hist. Nat. Poiss., vol. 7, p.
25, pl. 170.
Microcanthus strigatus, J. and E., p. 376.
Microcanthus hawaiiensis Fowler, 1941,
Proc. Acad. Nat. Sci. Philadelphia, vol.
93, p. 254, figs. 6 and 7.

## KYPHOSIDAE

### Kyphosus cinerascens

Kyphosus cinerascens Forskål, 1775, De-
script. Animal., pp. xii and 53 (Red
Sea).
Pimelepterus sandwicensis Sauvage, 1880,
Bull. Soc. Philom., ser. 7, vol. 4, p. 221.
Kyphosus sandwicensis, J. and E., p. 247.
Kyphosus fuscus, J. and E., p. 248.

## Sector azureus

Sector azureus Jordan and Evermann, 1903, Bull. U. S. Fish Comm., vol. 22, p. 185; J. and E., p. 248.

## CHAETODONTIDAE

### Pomacanthus imperator

Chaetodon imperator Bloch, 1787, Naturgeschichte der ausländischen Fische, vol. 3, p. 51, pl. 174 (Japan).
Pomacanthus (Pomacanthodes) imperator, Fraser-Brunner, 1933, Proc. Zool. Soc. London, p. 556, pl. 1 (various localities).
Pomacanthodes imperator, Brock, 1948, Pacific Sci., vol. 2, p. 298.

### Holacanthus arcuatus

Holacanthus arcuatus Gray, 1831, Zool. Miscell., p. 33; J. and E., p. 378, fig. 164; Fraser-Brunner, 1933, Proc. Zool. Soc. London, p. 578, fig. 19.

### Centropyge fisheri

Holacanthus fisheri Snyder, 1904, Bull. U. S. Fish Comm., vol. 22, p. 532, pl. 11; J. and E., p. 379, pl. 46.

### Centropyge nigriocellus

Centropyge nigriocellus Woods and Schultz, in Schultz, p. 608, fig. 89 (Johnston).

### Centropyge potteri

Holacanthus potteri Jordan and Metz, 1912, Proc. U. S. Nat. Mus., vol. 42, p. 525, pl. 71.

### Centropyge flammeus

Centropyge flammeus Woods and Schultz, in Schultz, p. 605, fig. 88 (Johnston).

### Heniochus excelsa

Loa excelsa Jordan, 1922, Proc. U. S. Nat. Mus., vol. 59, p. 652, fig. 6.

### Heniochus acuminatus

Chaetodon acuminatus Linnaeus, 1758, Systema Naturae, Ed. X, p. 272 (East Indies).
Heniochus acuminatus, J. and E., p. 376, col. pl. 55.

### Hemitaurichthys thompsoni

Hemitaurichthys thompsoni Fowler, 1923, Occ. Pap. B. P. Bishop Mus., vol. 8, p. 384; Fowler, 1928, p. 257, fig. 48.

### Hemitaurichthys zoster

Chaetodon zoster Bennett, 1831, Proc. Zool. Soc. London, p. 61 (Mauritius).
Hemitaurichthys zoster, Fowler, 1928, p. 257, pl. 27.

### Chaetodon fremblii

Chaetodon fremblii Bennett, 1829, Zool. Jour., vol. 4, p. 42; J. and E., p. 375, col. pl. 51.

### Chaetodon reticulatus

Chaetodon reticulatus Cuvier, 1831, Hist. Nat. Poiss., vol. 7, p. 24, pl. 171 (Tahiti); Fowler, 1928, p. 249, pl. 24 (Hawaii in part).

### Chaetodon corallicola

Chaetodon corallicola Snyder, 1904, Bull. U. S. Fish Comm., vol. 22, p. 531, pl. 11; J. and E., p. 374, pl. 46.

### Chaetodon tinkeri

Chaetodon tinkeri Schultz, 1951, Proc. U. S. Nat. Mus., vol. 101, p. 485, pl. 15.

### Chaetodon ephippium

Chaetodon ephippium Cuvier, 1831, Hist. Nat. Poiss., vol. 7, p. 61, pl. 174 (Molucca, Borabora, Tahiti); Fowler, 1928, p. 245 (Hawaii in part).

### Chaetodon auriga

Chaetodon auriga Forskål, 1775, Descript. Animal., pp. xiii and 60 (Red Sea).
Chaetodon setifer, J. and E., p. 364, col. pl. 47.

### Chaetodon unimaculatus

Chaetodon unimaculatus Bloch, 1788, Ichthyologie, vol. 6, pl. 201 (East Indies); J. and E., p. 368, fig. 161.
Chaetodon sphenospilus Jenkins, 1901, Bull. U. S. Fish Comm., vol. 19, p. 395, fig. 162.

### Chaetodon lunula

Pomacentrus lunula Lacépède, 1802, Hist. Nat. Poiss., vol. 4, pp. 507, 510, and 513 (no locality).
Chaetodon lunulatus Quoy and Gaimard, 1824, Voy. "Uranie," p. 381.
Chaetodon lunula, J. and E., p. 366, fig. 160 and col. pl. 54.

### Chaetodon trifasciatus

Chaetodon trifasciatus Mungo Park, 1797, Trans. Linn. Soc. London, vol. 3, p. 34 (East Indies); J. and E., p. 372, pl. 52.

### Chaetodon ornatissimus

Chaetodon ornatissimus Solander, in Cuvier and Valenciennes, 1831, Hist. Nat. Poiss., vol. 7, p. 22 (Tahiti); J. and E., p. 373, col. pl. 53.
Chaetodon ornatus Gray, 1831, Zool. Miscell., p. 31.

### Chaetodon quadrimaculatus

Chaetodon quadrimaculatus Gray, 1831, Zool. Miscell., p. 33; J. and E., p. 373, col. pl. 49.

## Chaetodon multicinctus

Chaetodon multicinctus Garrett, 1863, Proc. California Acad. Sci., vol. 3, p. 65; Woods, in Schultz, p. 595, pl. 58.
Chaetodon punctatofasciatus, J. and E., p. 369, fig. 162.

## Chaetodon citrinellus

Chaetodon citrinellus Cuvier, 1831, Hist. Nat. Poiss., vol. 7, p. 27 (Guam, Tahiti); Woods, in Schultz, p. 589, pl. 51 (Marshalls, Guam, Rota).

## Chaetodon miliaris

Chaetodon miliaris Quoy and Gaimard, 1824, Voy. "Uranie," Zool., p. 380, pl. 62; J. and E., p. 371, col. pl. 48 and fig. 163.
Chaetodon mantelliger Jenkins, 1901, Bull. U. S. Fish Comm., vol. 19, p. 394, fig. 7.

### HISTIOPTERIDAE

## Histiopterus typus

Histiopterus typus Schlegel, 1844, Fauna Japonica, Poiss., p. 86, pl. 45 (Japan); Fowler, 1928, p. 223, pl. 19.

### HOPLEGNATHIDAE

## Hoplegnathus fasciatus

Scarodon fasciatus Schlegel, 1844, Fauna Japonica, Poiss., p. 89, pl. 46 (Japan).
Hoplegnathus fasciatus, Steindachner, 1893, Sitz. akad. wiss. Wien, vol. 102, p. 222.

### CHEILODACTYLIDAE

## Cheilodactylus vittatus

Cheilodactylus vittatus Garrett, 1864, Proc. California Acad. Nat. Sci., vol. 3, p. 103; J. and E., p. 447, pl. 54.

### CIRRHITIDAE

## Paracirrhites arcatus

Cirrhites arcatus Cuvier and Valenciennes, 1829, Hist. Nat. Poiss., vol. 3, p. 274 (Ile de France).
Paracirrhites arcatus, J. and E., p. 450, col. pl. 69.

## Paracirrhites forsteri

Grammistes forsteri Bloch and Schneider, 1801, Syst. Ichth., p. 191 (Marquesas).
Paracirrhites forsteri, J. and E., p. 450, col. pl. 67.

## Cirrhitus alternatus

Cirrhitus alternatus Gill, 1862, Proc. Acad. Nat. Sci. Philadelphia, p. 122; Schultz, 1950, Proc. U. S. Nat. Mus., vol. 100, pp. 548, 552, pl. 13.
Cirrhitus marmoratus, J. and E., p. 452, col. pl. 70.

## Cirrhitoidea bimacula

Cirrhitoidea bimacula Jenkins, 1903, Bull. U. S. Fish Comm., vol. 22, p. 489, fig. 36; J. and E., p. 448, fig. 197.

## Paracirrhites cinctus

Cirrhites cinctus Günther, 1860, Cat. Fishes British Mus., vol. 2, p. 73.
Paracirrhites cinctus, J. and E., p. 449, col. pl. 48.

### POMACENTRIDAE

## Dascyllus albisella

Dascyllus albisella Gill, 1862, Proc. Acad. Nat. Sci. Philadelphia, p. 149; J. and E., p. 266.
Dascyllus edmondsoni Pietschmann, 1934, Anz. Akad. Wiss. Wien, vol. 71, p. 100.

## Abudefduf sordidus

Chaetodon sordidus Forskål, 1775, Descript. Animal., p. 62 (Red Sea).
Abudefduf sordidus, J. and E., p. 274, fig. 117.

## Abudefduf abdominalis

Glyphisodon abdominalis Quoy and Gaimard, 1824, Voy. "Uranie," Zool., p. 390.
Abudefduf abdominalis, J. and E., p. 274, fig. 116.

## Abudefduf imparipennis

Glyphisodon imparipennis Sauvage, 1875, Rev. Mag. Zool., vol. 3, p. 279.
Chromis elaphrus Jenkins, 1903, Bull. U. S. Fish Comm., vol. 22, p. 457, fig. 23; J. and E., p. 268, fig. 113.
Abudefduf imparipennis, J. and E., p. 274.

## Abudefduf sindonis

Glyphisodon sindonis Jordan and Evermann, 1903, Bull. U. S. Fish Comm., vol. 22, p. 188; J. and E., p. 272, pl. 40.

## Abudefduf phoenixensis

Abudefduf phoenixensis Schultz, 1943, U. S. Nat. Mus. Bull. 180, p. 190, fig. 15 (Phoenix Islands).

## Plectroglyphidodon johnstonianus

Plectroglyphidodon johnstonianus Fowler and Ball, 1924, Proc. Acad. Nat. Sci. Philadelphia, p. 271 (Johnston Island); Fowler, 1928, p. 326, fig. 58 (on the type).

## Pomacentrus jenkinsi

Pomacentrus jenkinsi Jordan and Evermann, 1903, Bull. U. S. Fish Comm., vol. 22, p. 189; J. and E., p. 270, fig. 115.
Pomacentrus vanderbilti Fowler, 1941, Proc. Acad. Nat. Sci. Philadelphia, vol. 93, p. 263, fig. 14.

### Chromis vanderbilti

*Pycnochromis vanderbilti* Fowler, 1941, Proc. Acad. Nat. Sci. Philadelphia, vol. 93, p. 260, fig. 12.

### Chromis ovalis

*Heliastes ovalis* Steindachner, 1900, Denkschr. K. Akad. Wiss. Wien, vol. 70, p. 502.
*Chromis velox* Jenkins, 1899, Bull. U. S. Fish Comm., vol. 19, p. 393, fig. 6.
*Chromis ovalis,* J. and E., p. 269, fig. 114 (the usage of this name is dubious, as it is a secondary homonym of the cichlid described as *Chromis ovalis* by Steindachner in 1866).

### Chromis leucurus

*Chromis leucurus* Gilbert, p. 620, pl. 77.

### Chromis verater

*Chromis verater* Jordan and Metz, 1912, Proc. U. S. Nat. Mus., vol. 42, p. 526, pl. 71.

### LABRIDAE

### Cheilio inermis

*Labrus inermis* Forskal, 1775, Descript. Animal., p. 34 (Red Sea).
*Cheilio inermis,* J. and E., p. 314, col. pl. 33.

### Bodianus bilunulatus

*Labrus bilunulatus* Lacépède, 1802, Hist. Nat. Poiss., vol. 3, pp. 454, 526, pl. 31, fig. 2 (Pacific Ocean).
*Cossyphus albotaeniatus* Cuvier and Valenciennes, 1839, Hist. Nat. Poiss., vol. 13, p. 141.
*Crenilabrus modestus* Garrett, 1864, Proc. California Acad. Sci., vol. 3, p. 106.
*Lepidaplois strophodes* Jordan and Evermann, 1903, Bull. U. S. Fish Comm., vol. 22, p. 190; J. and E., p. 280, col. pl. 23.
*Lepidaplois albotaeniatus,* J. and E., p. 278, col. pl. 24.
*Lepidaplois modestus,* J. and E., p. 279, fig. 119.
*Lepidaplois atrorubens* E. K. Jordan, 1926, Proc. U. S. Nat. Mus., vol. 66, art. 23, p. 23, pl. 1.

### Bodianus oxycephalus

*Cossyphus oxycephalus* Bleeker, 1862, Versl. Kon. Akad. Wet. Natur. Amsterdam, vol. 14, p. 129 (Japan?).
*Verreo oxycephalus,* J. and E., p. 281, fig. 120 (the fig. is of a Japanese specimen).

### Verriculus sanguineus

*Verriculus sanguineus* Jordan and Evermann, 1903, Bull. U. S. Fish Comm.,
vol. 22, p. 191; J. and E., p. 281, col. pl. 25.

### Labroides phthirophagus

*Labroides phthirophagus* Randall, 1958, Pacific Sci., vol. 12, p. 337, pl. 1A.

### Epibulus insidiator

*Sparus insidiator* Pallas, 1770, Spicilegia Zoologica . . . , pt. 8, p. 41, pl. 5 (Java).

### Cirrhilabrus jordani

*Cirrhilabrus jordani* Snyder, 1904, Bull. U. S. Fish Comm., vol. 22, pl. 10; J. and E., p. 315, pl. 42.

### Cheilinus rhodochrous

*Cheilinus rhodochrous* Günther, 1866, Fishes of Zanzibar, p. 90 (Zanzibar).
*Cheilinus zonurus* Jenkins, 1900, Bull. U. S. Fish Comm., vol. 19, p. 56, fig. 13.
*Cheilinus hexagonatus,* J. and E., p. 319, fig. 254.

### Cheilinus bimaculatus

*Cheilinus bimaculatus* Cuvier and Valenciennes, 1839, Hist. Nat. Poiss., vol. 14, p. 96; J. and E., p. 320, col. pl. 38.

### Cheilinus sinuosus

*Cheilinus sinuosus* Quoy and Gaimard, 1824, Voy. "Uranie" et "Physicienne," Zool., p. 278. (This species, based on a specimen 3.5 inches long, does not seem to agree with any fish taken since in Hawaii. J. and E., p. 322, have synonymized it with *Cheilinus trilobatus,* but we do not feel that even a generic allocation for this fish can be made with any great certainty. It has therefore been omitted from our text.)

### Pseudocheilinus evanidus

*Pseudocheilinus evanidus* Jordan and Evermann, 1903, Bull. U. S. Fish Comm., vol. 22, p. 192; J. and E., p. 317, pl. 43.

### Pseudocheilinus octotaenia

*Pseudocheilinus octotaenia* Jenkins, 1900, Bull. U. S. Fish Comm., vol. 19, p. 64, fig. 22; J. and E., p. 317, fig. 135.

### Pseudocheilinus tetrataenia

*Pseudocheilinus tetrataenia* Schultz, 1959, U. S. Nat. Mus. Bull. 202, vol. 2, p. (?) (Marshalls).

### Wetmorella albofasciata

*Wetmorella albofasciata* Schultz and Marshall, 1954, Proc. U. S. Nat. Mus., vol. 103, p. 446, pl. 12 (Philippines).

### Cymolutes leclusei

*Xyrichthys lecluse* Quoy and Gaimard, 1824, Voy. "Uranie," Zool., p. 284, pl. 65.

*Xyrichthys microlepidotus* Cuvier and Valenciennes, 1839, Hist. Nat. Poiss., vol. 14, p. 52.
*Cymolutes lecluse,* J. and E., p. 327.

### Hemipteronotus umbrilatus

*Hemipteronotus umbrilatus* Jenkins, 1900, Bull. U. S. Fish Comm., vol. 19, p. 53, fig. 10; J. and E., p. 333, fig. 141.

### Hemipteronotus baldwini

*Hemipteronotus baldwini* Jordan and Evermann, 1903, Bull. U. S. Fish Comm., vol. 22, p. 192; J. and E., p. 334, col. pl. 39.
*Hemipteronotus jenkinsi* Snyder, 1904, Bull. U. S. Fish Comm., vol. 22, p. 530, pl. 10; J. and E., p. 336, pl. 42.

### Iniistius pavoninus

*Xyrichthys pavoninus* Cuvier and Valenciennes, 1839, Hist. Nat. Poiss., vol. 14, p. 63.
*Iniistius leucozonus* Jenkins, 1900, Bull. U. S. Fish Comm., vol. 19, p. 54, fig. 11.
*Iniistius pavoninus,* J. and E., p. 329, fig. 139 and col. pl. 42.

### Iniistius niger

*Novacula (Iniistius) nigra* Steindachner, 1900, Anz. Denkschr. K. Akad. Wiss. Wien, no. 16, p. 176.
*Iniistius verater* Jenkins, 1900, Bull. U. S. Fish Comm., vol. 19, p. 55, fig. 12.
*Iniistius niger,* J. and E., p. 331, fig. 140.

### Xyrichthys niveilatus

*Xyrichthys niveilatus* Jordan and Evermann, 1903, Bull. U. S. Fish Comm., vol. 22, p. 194; J. and E., p. 337, fig. 142.

### Thalassoma fuscum

*Labrus fuscus* Lacépède, 1801, Hist. Nat. Poiss., vol. 3, p. 437 (no locality).
*Thalassoma fuscum,* J. and E., p. 299, col. pl. 34.

### Thalassoma umbrostigma

*Julis umbrostigma* Rüppell, 1838, Neue Wirbelthiere, Fische, p. 11, pl. 3 (Red Sea).
*Thalassoma umbrostigma,* J. and E., p. 300, fig. 129.

### Thalassoma lunare

*Labrus lunaris* Linnaeus, 1758, Systema Naturae, Ed. X, p. 283 (India).
*Thalassoma lunaris,* J. and E., p. 303.

### Thalassoma lutescens

*Julis lutescens* Lay and Bennett, 1839, Zool. Beechey's Voy., p. 65, pl. 19 (Riu Kius).

*Thalassoma aneitense,* J. and E., p. 304, pl. 41.
*Thalassoma neanis* Jordan and Evermann, 1907, Bull. Bur. Fish., vol. 26, p. 214, pl. 12. (This may prove to be a valid species.)

### Thalassoma duperreyi

*Julis duperrey* Quoy and Gaimard, 1824, Voy. "Uranie," Zool., p. 286, pl. 56.
*Julis clepsydralis* Smith and Swain, 1882, Proc. U. S. Nat. Mus., vol. 5, p. 136 (Johnston).
*Thalassoma pyrrovinctum* Jenkins, 1900, Bull. U. S. Fish Comm., vol. 19, p. 51, fig. 7.
*Thalassoma duperrey,* J. and E., p. 302, fig. 130 and col. pl. 35.

### Thalassoma purpureum

*Scarus purpureus* Forskål, 1775, Descript. Animal., p. 27 (Red Sea).
*Thalassoma berendti* Seale, 1901, Occ. Pap. B. P. Bishop Mus., vol. 1, no. 4, p. 15, fig. 7.
*Thalassoma purpureum,* J. and E., p. 295.

### Thalassoma ballieui

*Julis ballieui* Vaillant and Sauvage, 1875, Rev. Mag. Zool., vol. 3, p. 284.
*Julis obscura* Günther, 1880, Rept. Shore Fishes "Challenger," Zool., vol. 1, pt. 6, p. 61, pl. 26.
*Julis verticalis* Smith and Swain, 1882, Proc. U. S. Nat. Mus., vol. 5, p. 135 (Johnston).
*Thalassoma ballieui,* J. and E., p. 297, fig. 128.

### Thalassoma quinquevittata

*Scarus quinquevittatus* Lay and Bennett, 1839, Zool. Beechey's Voy., p. 66, pl. 19 (Riu Kius).

### Gomphosus varius

*Gomphosus varius* Lacépède, 1801, Hist. Nat. Poiss., vol. 3, p. 104, pl. 15 (Tahiti); J. and E., p. 289, fig. 125; Strasburg and Hiatt, 1957, Pacific Sci., vol. 11, p. 133 (Marshalls).
*Gomphosus tricolor* Quoy and Gaimard, 1824, Voy. "Uranie," Zool., p. 280, pl. 55; J. and E., p. 290, col. pl. 36.
*Gomphosus pectoralis* Quoy and Gaimard, 1824, Voy. "Uranie," Zool., p. 282.
*Gomphosus cepedianus* Cuvier and Valenciennes, 1839, Hist. Nat. Poiss., vol. 14, p. 18.
*Gomphosus fuscus* Cuvier and Valenciennes, 1839, Hist. Nat. Poiss., vol. 14, p. 25.
*Gomphosus sandwichensis* Günther, 1862, Cat. Fishes British Mus., vol. 4, p. 194.

### Coris flavovittata

*Julis flavovittatus* Bennett, 1829, Zool. Jour., London, vol. 4, p. 36; J. and E., p. 308, col. pl. 28.

*Julis eydouxi*, J. and E., p. 309, col. pl. 29.

### Coris lepomis

*Julis lepomis* Jenkins, 1900, Bull. U. S. Fish Comm., vol. 19, p. 48, fig. 4; J. and E., p. 306, fig. 131.

### Coris venusta

*Coris venusta* Vaillant and Sauvage, 1875, Rev. Mag. Zool., vol. 3, p. 285; J. and E., p. 312, fig. 133.

*Hemicoris remedius* Jenkins, 1900, Bull. U. S. Fish Comm., vol. 19, p. 49, fig. 5.

### Coris gaimardi

*Julis gaimard* Quoy and Gaimard, 1824, Voy. "Uranie," Zool., p. 265, pl. 54; J. and E., p. 305.

*Julis greenovii* Bennett, 1829, Zool. Jour., London, vol. 4, p. 37; J. and E., p. 308, col. pl. 30.

*Julis pulcherrima*, J. and E., p. 306, fig. 131.

### Coris ballieui

*Coris ballieui* Vaillant and Sauvage, 1875, Rev. Mag. Zool., vol. 3, p. 285; J. and E., p. 310, col. pl. 32.

### Coris rosea

*Coris rosea* Vaillant and Sauvage, 1875, Rev. Mag. Zool., vol. 3, p. 286; J. and E., p. 311, fig. 132.

*Coris argenteo-striata* Steindachner, 1900, Denkschr. K. Akad. Wiss. Wien, vol. 70, p. 507, pl. 3.

*Hemicoris keleipionis* Jenkins, 1900, Bull. U. S. Fish Comm., vol. 19, p. 51, fig. 6.

### Pseudojuloides cerasinus

*Pseudojulis cerasinus* Snyder, 1904, Bull. U. S. Fish Comm., vol. 22, p. 528; J. and E., p. 294.

*Pseudojuloides cerasinus*, Fowler, 1949, p. 119.

### Stethojulis axillaris

*Julis axillaris* Quoy and Gaimard, 1824, Voy. "Uranie," Zool., p. 272.

*Stethojulis axillaris*, J. and E., p. 284, fig. 121.

### Stethojulis albovittata

*Labrus albovittatus* Bonnaterre, 1788, Tableau Ichthyologique, p. 108, pl. 98 (no locality).

*Julis balteatus* Quoy and Gaimard, 1824, Voy. "Uranie," Zool., p. 267, pl. 56.

*Stethojulis albovittata*, J. and E., p. 284, pl. 26.

### Novaculichthys woodi

*Novaculichthys woodi* Jenkins, 1900, Bull. U. S. Fish Comm., vol. 19, p. 52, fig. 3; J. and E., p. 323, figs. 137, 138.

*Novaculichthys entargyreus* Jenkins, 1900, Bull. U. S. Fish Comm., vol. 19, p. 53, fig. 9.

*Novaculichthys tattoo* Seale, 1901, Occ. Pap. B. P. Bishop Mus., vol. 1, no. 4, p. 5, fig. 2.

### Novaculichthys taeniourus

*Labrus taeniourus* Lacépède, 1801, Hist. Nat. Poiss., vol. 3, pp. 448 and 518 (tropical Pacific).

*Novaculichthys taeniourus*, J. and E., p. 325, fig. 138.

### Novaculichthys bifer

*Julis bifer* Lay and Bennett, 1839, Zool. Beechey's Voy., p. 64.

*Novaculichthys kallosoma*, J. and E., p. 327, col. pl. 41.

### Macropharyngodon geoffroyi

*Julis geoffroy* Quoy and Gaimard, 1824, Voy. "Uranie," Zool., p. 270, pl. 56.

*Macropharyngodon aquilolo* Jenkins, 1900, Bull. U. S. Fish Comm., vol. 19, p. 46, fig. 1.

*Macropharyngodon geoffroy*, J. and E., p. 288, fig. 124.

### Anampses chrysocephalus

*Anampses chrysocephalus* Randall, 1958, Jour. Washington Acad. Sci., vol. 48, p. 100, fig. 3.

### Anampses rubrocaudatus

*Anampses rubrocaudatus* Randall, 1958, Jour. Washington Acad. Sci., vol. 48, p. 103, fig. 4.

### Anampses cuvieri

*Anampses cuvier* Quoy and Gaimard, 1824, Voy. "Uranie," Zool., p. 276; J. and E., p. 291, fig. 126.

### Anampses godeffroyi

*Anampses godeffroyi* Günther, 1881, Fische der Südsee, pt. 7, p. 252, pl. 140; J. and E., p. 294.

*Anampses evermanni* Jenkins, 1900, Bull. U. S. Fish Comm., vol. 19, p. 57, fig. 14; J. and E., p. 293, fig. 127.

### Halichoeres ornatissimus

*Julis ornatissimus* Garrett, 1863, Proc. California Acad. Sci., vol. 3, p. 63; J. and E., p. 287, fig. 123.

*Halichoeres iridescens* Jenkins, 1900, Bull. U. S. Fish Comm., vol. 19, p. 47, fig. 2.

*Halichoeres lao* Jenkins, 1900, Bull. U. S. Fish Comm., vol. 19, p. 48, fig. 3; J. and E., p. 285, fig. 122.

## SCARIDAE

The bibliographic references originally supplied here for the Scaridae have been outdated by Schultz's (1958) "Review of the Parrot Fishes Family Scaridae," U. S. Nat. Mus. Bull. 214, 143 pp., 27 pls., 31 text figs. (which appeared since this book went to press). The reader is therefore referred to that volume for synonymies of the Hawaiian parrot fishes.

## AMMODYTIDAE

### Bleekeria gillii

Bleekeria gillii T. H. Bean, 1894, Proc. U. S. Nat. Mus., vol. 17, p. 629 (no type locality); Fowler, 1928, p. 426, fig. 70; Duncker and Mohr, 1939, Mitt. Zool. Mus. Berlin, vol. 24, p. 14 (Hawaiian record in part).

## CHAMPSODONTIDAE

### Champsodon fimbriatus

Champsodon fimbriatus Gilbert, p. 648, pl. 88.

## PARAPERCIDAE

### Pteropsaron incisum

Pteropsaron incisum Gilbert, p. 647, pl. 87.

### Parapercis schauinslandi

Percis schauinslandi Steindachner, 1900, Anz. Akad. Wiss. Wien, No. 16, p. 175.

Parapercis pterostigma Jenkins, 1901, Bull. U. S. Fish Comm., vol. 19, p. 402, fig. 15.

Osurus schauinslandi, J. and E., p. 475, figs. 209 and 209a; Gilbert, p. 642.

### Neopercis roseoviridis

Neopercis roseoviridis Gilbert, p. 643, pl. 83.

## BEMBROPSIDAE

### Bembrops filifera

Bembrops filifera Gilbert, p. 643, pl. 84.

### Chrionema chryseres

Chrionema chryseres Gilbert, p. 645, pl. 85.

### Chrionema squamiceps

Chrionema squamiceps Gilbert, p. 646, pl. 86.

## TRICHONOTIDAE

### Crystallodytes cookei

Crystallodytes cookei Fowler, 1923, Occ. Pap. B. P. Bishop Mus., vol. 8, p. 391; Fowler, 1928, p. 426, fig. 69.

Crystallodytes cookei cookei, Schultz, 1943, U. S. Nat. Mus. Bull. 180, p. 266.

### Limnichthys donaldsoni

Limnichthys donaldsoni Schultz, 1959, U. S. Nat. Mus. Bull. 202, vol. 2, p. (?) (Marshalls).

## ZANCLIDAE

### Zanclus canescens

Chaetodon canescens Linnaeus, 1758, Systema Naturae, Ed. X, p. 272 (East Indies).

Zanclus canescens, J. and E., p. 382, col. pl. 57.

Zanclus ruthiae Bryan, 1906, Occ. Pap. B. P. Bishop Mus., vol. 2, no. 4, p. 22, fig. 2.

## ACANTHURIDAE

### Acanthurus sandvicensis

Acanthurus triostegus var. sandvicensis Streets, 1877, U. S. Nat. Mus. Bull. 7, p. 67 (Honolulu).

Hepatus sandvicensis, J. and E., p. 394, fig. 172.

Acanthurus sandvicensis, Gosline, 1955, Pacific Sci., vol. 9, p. 474.

Acanthurus triostegus sandvicensis, Randall, 1956, Pacific Sci., vol. 10, p. 175, fig. 4.

### Acanthurus guttatus

Acanthurus guttatus Bloch and Schneider, 1801, Syst. Ichth., pp. 38, 215 (Tahiti).

Hepatus guttatus, J. and E., p. 392, fig. 170.

### Acanthurus achilles

Acanthurus achilles Shaw, 1803, General Zoology, vol. 3, p. 383 (no locality).

Hepatus achilles, J. and E., p. 384, pl. 58.

### Acanthurus glaucopareius

Acanthurus glaucopareius Cuvier, 1829, Règne Animal, ed. 2, vol. 2, p. 224 (after Seba). (Günther gives type locality as Tahiti).

Acanthurus glaucopareius, Randall, 1956, Pacific Sci., vol. 10, p. 199, pl. 2 (various localities).

### Acanthurus leucopareius

Teuthis leucopareius Jenkins, 1903, U. S. Fish Comm. Bull. 22, p. 476, fig. 23 (Honolulu).

Teuthis umbra Jenkins, 1903, U. S. Fish Comm. Bull. 22, p. 477.

Hepatus leucopareius, J. and E., p. 386, fig. 167.

Hepatus umbra, J. and E., p. 387, pl. 47.

### Acanthurus nigrofuscus

Chaetodon nigrofuscus Forskål, 1775, Descript. Animal., pp. xiii, 64 (Red Sea).

Hepatus elongatus, J. and E., p. 389.

*Hepatus lucillae* Fowler, 1938, Acad. Nat. Sci. Philadelphia, Monograph 2, p. 231, fig. 23.
*Acanthurus nigrofuscus,* Randall, 1956, Pacific Sci., vol. 10, p. 190, pl. 1.

### Acanthurus nigroris

*Acanthurus nigroris* Cuvier and Valenciennes, 1835, Hist. Nat. Poiss., vol. 10, p. 208 (Hawaii).
*Teuthis atrimentatus* J. and E., 1903, U. S. Fish Comm. Bull. 22, p. 198.
*Hepatus atramentatus,* J. and E., p. 393, fig. 171.
*Acanthurus nigroris* Randall, 1956, Pacific Sci., vol. 10, p. 187, fig. 12.

### Acanthurus thompsoni

*Hepatus thompsoni* Fowler, 1923, Occ. Pap. B. P. Bishop Mus., vol. 8 (7), p. 386.
*Acanthurus thompsoni,* Randall, 1956, Pacific Sci., vol. 10, p. 182, fig. 8.

### Acanthurus olivaceus

*Acanthurus nigricans* var. *olivaceus* Bloch and Schneider, 1801, Syst. Ichth., pp. 213–214 (Tahiti).
*Hepatus olivaceus,* J. and E., p. 385, fig. 166.

### Acanthurus dussumieri

*Acanthurus dussumieri* Cuvier and Valenciennes, 1835, Hist. Nat. Poiss., vol. 10, p. 201 (Mauritius).
*Hepatus dussumieri,* J. and E., p. 390, fig. 169.
*Acanthurus dussumieri,* Randall, 1956, Pacific Sci., vol. 10, p. 213, pl. 3.

### Acanthurus xanthopterus

*Acanthurus xanthopterus* Cuvier and Valenciennes, 1835, Hist. Nat. Poiss., vol. 10, p. 215 (Seychelles).
*Teuthis güntheri* Jenkins, 1903, U. S. Fish Comm. Bull. 22, p. 477, fig. 29.
*Hepatus matoides,* J. and E., p. 387.
*Hepatus guntheri,* J. and E., p. 388, fig. 168.
*Hepatus xanthopterus,* J. and E., p. 389.
*Acanthurus xanthopterus,* Randall, 1956, Pacific Sci., vol. 10, p. 215, pl. 3.

### Acanthurus mata

*Chaetodon meta* Cuvier, 1829, Règne Animal, ed. 2, vol. 2, p. 224 (after Russell).
*Acanthurus mata,* Randall, 1956, Pacific Sci., vol. 10, p. 218, pl. 3.

### Ctenochaetus strigosus

*Acanthurus strigosus* Bennett, 1828, Zool. Jour., vol. 4, p. 41 (Hawaiian Islands).
*Ctenochaetus striatus,* J. and E., p. 398 (fig. 174 not *strigosus,* but the true *striatus*).

*Ctenochaetus strigosus,* Randall, 1955, Zoologica, vol. 40, p. 159, pl. 2 (various localities).

### Ctenochaetus hawaiiensis

*Ctenochaetus hawaiiensis* Randall, 1955, Zoologica, vol. 40, p. 161, pl. 2.

### Zebrasoma flavescens

*Acanthurus flavescens* Bennett, 1828, Zool. Jour., vol. 4, p. 41 (Oahu).
*Zebrasoma flavescens,* J. and E., p. 397, pl. 59.
*Zebrasoma flavescens,* Randall, 1955, Pacific Sci., vol. 9, p. 404, fig. 7.

### Zebrasoma veliferum

*Acanthurus velifer* Bloch, 1797, Ichthyologie, . . . p. 106, pl. 427, fig. 1 (seas of East Indies).
*Zebrasoma veliferum,* J. and E., p. 396, fig. 173.

### Naso lituratus

*Acanthurus lituratus* Bloch and Schneider, 1801, Syst. Ichth., p. 216 (no locality).
*Callicanthus lituratus,* J. and E., p. 404, fig. 177, pl. 60.

### Naso hexacanthus

*Priodon hexacanthus* Bleeker, 1855, Nat. Tijd. Ned. Ind., vol. 8, p. 421 (Ambon, East Indies).
*Callicanthus metoposophron* Jenkins, 1903, U. S. Fish Comm. Bull. 22, p. 481, fig. 31 (Honolulu).
*Callicanthus metoposophron,* J. and E., p. 405, fig. 178.

### Naso brevirostris

*Naseus brevirostris* Cuvier and Valenciennes, 1835, Hist. Nat. Poiss., vol. 10, p. 277 (Moluccas, Mauritius, and New Guinea).
*Acanthurus brevirostris,* J. and E., p. 401, fig. 176.

### Naso unicornis

*Chaetodon unicornis* Forskål, 1775, Descript. Animal., pp. xiii, 63 (Red Sea).
*Acanthurus unicornis,* J. and E., p. 402.

### Naso annulatus

*Priodon annulatus* Quoy and Gaimard, 1824, Voyage autour du monde . . . L'Uranie . . . , p. 337 (Timor).
*Acanthurus incipiens* Jenkins, 1903, U. S. Fish Comm. Bull. 22, p. 480, fig. 32.
*Acanthurus incipiens,* J. and E., p. 400, fig. 175.

## GEMPYLIDAE

### Ruvettus pretiosus

*Ruvettus pretiosus* Cocco, 1829, Giorn. di Scienze per la Sicilia, vol. 42, p. 21 (Mediterranean); J. and E., p. 177, fig. 67.

### Promethichthys prometheus

Gempylus prometheus Cuvier and Valenciennes, 1831, Hist. Nat. Poiss., vol. 8, p. 213 (St. Helena).
Promethichthys prometheus, J. and E., p. 178, pl. 29.

### Lepidocybium flavobrunneum

Cybium flavo-brunneum Smith, 1849, Illus. Zool. South Africa, vol. 4, pl. 20 (South Africa).
Nesogrammus thompsoni Fowler, 1923, Occ. Pap. B. P. Bishop Mus., vol. 8, p. 376.
Lepidocybium flavo-brunneum Munro, 1949, Proc. Roy. Soc. Queensland, vol. 60, pp. 31–41, pl. 1 (various localities).

### Gempylus serpens

Gempylus serpens Cuvier and Valenciennes, 1831, Hist. Nat. Poiss., vol. 8, p. 207 (Martinique).
Lemnisoma thyrsitoides, J. and E., p. 179.

### SCOMBRIDAE

### Acanthocybium solandri

Cybium solandri Cuvier, 1831, Hist. Nat. Poiss., vol. 8, p. 192 (no type locality).
Acanthocybium solandri, J. and E., p. 176; Kishinouye, 1923, Jour. Coll. Agr. Univ. Tokyo, vol. 8, p. 411 (Japan); Fraser-Brunner, 1950, Ann. Mag. Nat. Hist., ser. 12, vol. 3, p. 162, fig. 35 (various localities).

### Scomber japonicus

Scomber japonicus Houttouyn, 1782, Verhand. Holl. Maatsch. Haarl., vol. 20, p. 331 (Japan); J. and E., p. 169, fig. 62; Kishinouye, 1923, Jour. Coll. Agr. Univ. Tokyo, vol. 8, p. 403, figs. 1, 7, 16, 28–30 (Japan); Fraser-Brunner, 1950, Ann. Mag. Nat. Hist., ser. 12, vol. 3, p. 153, fig. 21 (various localities).

### Auxis thazard

Scomber thazard Lacépède, 1801, Hist. Nat. Poiss., vol. 3, p. 9 (New Guinea).
Auxis thazard, J. and E., p. 171, fig. 63; Fraser-Brunner, 1950, Ann. Mag. Nat. Hist., ser. 12, vol. 3, p. 152, fig. 20 (various localities).
Auxis maru Kishinouye, 1923, Jour. Coll. Agr. Univ. Tokyo, vol. 8, p. 463, figs. 2, 15, 27, 56, 60 (Japan).

### Auxis thynnoides

Auxis thynnoides Bleeker, 1855, Nat. Tijd. Ned. Ind., vol. 8, p. 301 (East Indies).

### Katsuwonus pelamis

Scomber pelamis Linnaeus, 1758, Systema Naturae, Ed. X, p. 297 (tropic seas).
Gymnosarda pelamis, J. and E., p. 172, fig. 64.
Katsuwonus pelamis, Kishinouye, 1923, Jour. Coll. Agr. Univ. Tokyo, vol. 8, p. 453 (Japan).
Euthynnus pelamis, Fraser-Brunner, 1950, Ann. Mag. Nat. Hist., ser. 12, vol. 3, p. 152, fig. 19 (Japan).

### Euthynnus yaito

Gymnosarda alletterata, J. and E., p. 173, fig. 65 (fig. of Atlantic Euthynnus alletterata).
Euthynnus yaito Kishinouye, 1915, Sui Gak. Ho, vol. 1, p. 22, pl. 1 (Japan); Kishinouye, 1923, Jour. Coll. Agr. Univ. Tokyo, vol. 8, p. 457, figs. 26, 54, 58 (Japan).
Euthynnus affinis, Fraser-Brunner, 1950, Ann. Mag. Nat. Hist., ser. 12, vol. 3, p. 150, fig. 17a (various localities).

### Sarda orientalis

Pelamys orientalis Schlegel, 1842, Fauna Japonica, Poiss., p. 99, pl. 52 (Japan).
Sarda chilensis, J. and E., p. 175.
Sarda orientalis, Kishinouye, 1923, Jour. Coll. Agr. Univ. Tokyo, vol. 8, p. 424, figs. 11, 17, 33, 42 (Japan); Fraser-Brunner, 1950, Ann. Mag. Nat. Hist., ser. 12, vol. 3, p. 147, fig. 12.

### Thunnus thynnus orientalis

Scomber thynnus Linnaeus, 1758, Systema Natural Ed. X, p. 297 (Tropical seas).
Thunnus orientalis Schlegel, 1842, Fauna Japonica, Poiss., p. 94 (Japan).
Thunnus orientalis, Kishinouye, 1923, Jour. Coll. Agr. Univ. Tokyo, vol. 8, p. 437, figs. 3, 21, 43, 44, 50 (Japan); Jordan and Evermann, 1926, Occ. Pap. California Acad. Sci., vol. 12, p. 14 (various localities).
Thunnus thynnus, Fraser-Brunner, 1950, Ann. Mag. Nat. Hist., ser. 12, vol. 3, p. 143, fig. 4 (various localities).
Thunnus thynnus orientalis Collette and Gibbs, 1963, F.A.O. Fish Rept., no. 6, vol. 1, p. 28 (Pacific Ocean).

### Thunnus alalunga

Scomber alalunga Gmelin, 1789, Systema Naturae, vol. 1, p. 1330 (Mediterranean).
Thunnus germo, Kishinouye, 1923, Jour. Coll. Agr. Univ. Tokyo, vol. 8, p. 434, figs. 20, 46, 52 (Japan).
Germo germo, Jordan and Evermann, 1926, Occ. Pap. California Acad. Sci., p. 16, pl. 3 (various localities).

*Thunnus alalunga,* Fraser-Brunner, 1950, Ann. Mag. Nat. Hist., ser. 12, vol. 3, p. 143, fig. 5 (various localities).

### Thunnus obesus

*Thunnus obesus* Lowe, 1949, Proc. Zool. Soc. London, III, pp. 1–20. (Madeira). *Thynnus sibi* Schlegel, 1842, Fauna Japonica, Poiss., p. 97, pl. 50 (Japan). *Parathunnus mebachi* Kishinouye, 1923, Jour. Coll. Agr. Univ. Tokyo, vol. 8, p. 442, figs. 4, 22, 47, 49 (Japan). *Parathunnus sibi,* Jordan and Evermann, 1926, Occ. Pap. California Acad. Sci., no. 12, p. 17, pl. 3. *Thunnus obesus* Fraser-Brunner, 1950, Ann. Mag. Nat. Hist., ser. 12, vol. 3, p. 144, fig. 6 (various localities); Collette and Gibbs, 1963, F.A.O. Fish Rept., no. 6, vol. 1, p. 28 (pantropical).

### Thunnus albacares

*Scomber albacares* Bonnaterre, Encycl. Meth. 140, 1788 (based on drawing of a tuna by Hans Sloane). *Thynnus macropterus* Schlegel, 1842, Fauna Japonica, Poiss., p. 98, pl. 51 (Japan). *Germo germo,* J. and E., p. 174, fig. 66. *Neothunnus macropterus,* Kishinouye, 1923, Jour. Coll. Agr. Univ. Tokyo, vol. 8, p. 446, figs. 13, 19, 23, 45, 51 (Japan); Jordan and Evermann, 1926, Occ. Pap. California Acad. Sci., vol. 12, p. 20 (various localities). *Neothunnus itisibi* Jordan and Evermann, 1926, Occ. Pap. California Acad. Sci., vol. 12, p. 22, pl. 6 (Hawaii–Japan). *Thunnus allisoni* Mowbray, 1920, Copeia, no. 78, p. 9, text fig. (east coast Florida). *Thunnus albacora,* Fraser-Brunner, 1950, Ann. Mag. Nat. Hist., ser. 12, vol. 3, p. 144, fig. 7 (various localities). *Thunnus albacares* Collette and Gibbs, 1963, F.A.O. Fish. Rept., no. 6, vol. 1, p. 28 (pantropical).

## ISTIOPHORIDAE

### Tetrapterus angustirostris

*Tetrapterus angustirostris* Tanaka, 1914, Figs. and Descrs. Fishes of Japan, vol. 18, pl. 88 (Japan); Royce, 1957, Fish. Bull. U. S. Fish Wildlife Serv., vol. 57, p. 520. *Tetrapterus illingworthi* Jordan and Evermann, 1926, Occ. Pap. California Acad. Sci. vol. 12, p. 32, pl. 18. *Tetrapterus kraussi* Jordan and Evermann, 1926, Occ. Pap. California Acad. Sci., vol. 12, p. 33, pl. 9.

### Istiophorus orientalis

*Histiophorus orientalis* Schlegel, 1842, Fauna Japonica, Poiss., p. 103, pl. 55 (Japan);

Royce, 1957, Fish. Bull. U. S. Fish Wildlife Serv., vol. 57, p. 522. *Istiophorus eriquius* Jordan and Ball, in Jordan and Evermann, 1926, Occ. Pap. California Acad. Sci., vol. 12, p. 48, pl. 15.

### Istiompax marlina

*Makaira marlina* Jordan and Hill, in Jordan and Evermann, 1926, Occ. Pap. California Acad. Sci., p. 59, pl. 17 (Lower California). *Makaira mazara,* LaMonte, 1955, Bull. Amer. Mus. Nat. Hist., vol. 107, p. 336, pl. 9. *Istiompax marlina,* Royce, 1957, Fish. Bull. U. S. Fish Wildlife Serv., vol. 57, p. 524.

### Makaira ampla

*Tetrapterus amplus,* Poey, 1860, Memorias, vol. 2, tab. 15, fig. 2 (Cuba). *Tetrapterus mazara* Jordan and Snyder, 1901, Jour. Coll. Sci. Imper. Univ. Tokyo, vol. 15, p. 304 (Japan). *Makaira mazara,* Jordan and Evermann, 1926, Occ. Pap. California Acad. Sci., vol. 12, p. 53, pl. 11 (various localities). *Makaira ampla,* Royce, 1957, Fish. Bull. U. S. Fish Wildlife Serv., vol. 57, p. 532.

### Makaira audax

*Histiophorus audax* Philippi, 1887, Anales Universidad Chile, vol. 71, pp. 35–38, pl. 8 (Chile). *Tetrapterus mitsukurii* Jordan and Snyder, 1901, Jour. Coll. Sci. Imper. Univ. Tokyo, vol. 15, p. 304, pl. 16 (Japan). *Makaira mitsukurii,* Jordan and Evermann, 1926, Occ. Pap. California Acad. Sci., p. 61, pl. 18 (various localities). *Makaira grammatica* Jordan and Evermann, 1926, Occ. Pap. California Acad. Sci., p. 55, pl. 16. *Tetrapterus ectenes* Jordan and Evermann, 1926, Occ. Pap. California Acad. Sci., p. 34, pl. 11. *Makaira audax* Royce, 1957, Fish Bull. U. S. Fish Wildlife Serv., vol. 57, p. 528.

## XIPHIIDAE

### Xiphias gladius

*Xiphias gladius* Linnaeus, 1758, Systema Naturae, Ed. X, p. 248 (Europe); J. and E., p. 168, fig. 61; Royce, 1957, Fish. Bull. U. S. Fish Wildlife Serv., vol. 57, p. 518.

## ELEOTRIDAE

### Eleotris sandwicensis

*Eleotris sandwicensis* Vaillant and Sauvage, 1875, Rev. Mag. Zool., ser. 3, vol. 3, p. 280; J. and E., p. 479, fig. 210.

### Eviota epiphanes

*Eviota epiphanes* Jenkins, 1903, Bull. U. S. Fish Comm., vol. 22, p. 501, fig. 42; J. and E., p. 481, fig. 211.

### Asterropteryx semipunctatus

*Asterropteryx semipunctatus* R ü p p e l l, 1821, Atlas Fische, p. 138, pl. 34 (Red Sea); J. and E., p. 480.
*Gobiomorphus hypselopteryx* Pietschmann, 1938, B. P. Bishop Mus. Bull. 156, p. 38, pl. 12.
*Gobiomorphus robustus* Pietschmann, 1938, B. P. Bishop Mus. Bull. 156, p. 39, pl. 12.
*Asterropterix eumeces* Pietschmann, 1938, B. P. Bishop Mus. Bull. 156, p. 39, pl. 11.

### GOBIIDAE

### Vitraria clarescens

*Vitraria clarescens* Jordan and Evermann, 1903, Bull. U. S. Fish Comm., vol. 22, p. 205; J. and E., p. 486, pl. 60.

### Oxyurichthys lonchotus

?*Sicydium albotaeniatum* Günther, 1877, Fische der Südsee, p. 183, pl. 110; J. and E., p. 490, fig. 217.
*Gobionellus lonchotus* Jenkins, 1903, Bull. U. S. Fish Comm., vol. 22, p. 503, fig. 44.
*Gobiichthys lonchotus,* J. and E., p. 485, fig. 213.

### Sicydium stimpsoni

*Sicydium stimpsoni* Gill, 1860, Proc. Acad. Nat. Sci. Philadelphia, p. 101; J. and E., p. 489, fig. 216.
*Sicydium nigrescens* Günther, 1880, "Challenger" Repts., Zoology, Shore Fishes, vol. 1, pt. 6, p. 60, pl. 26.

### Lentipes concolor

*Sicyogaster concolor* Gill, 1860, Proc. Acad. Nat. Sci. Philadelphia, p. 102.
*Lentipes concolor,* J. and E., p. 491.

### Lentipes seminudus

*Lentipes seminudus* Günther, 1880, "Challenger" Repts., Zoology, Shore Fishes, vol. 1, pt. 6, p. 61; J. and E., p. 491.

### Kelloggella oligolepis

*Enypnias oligolepis* Jenkins, 1903, Bull. U. S. Fish Comm., vol. 22, p. 504, fig. 45.
*Kelloggella oligolepis,* J. and E., p. 488, fig. 215.

### Chonophorus genivittatus

*Gobius genivittatus* Cuvier and Valenciennes, 1837, Hist. Nat. Poiss., vol. 12, p. 64 (Tahiti).

*Awaous genivittatus,* J. and E., p. 492, fig. 218.

### Chonophorus stamineus

*Gobius stamineus* Eydoux and Souleyet, 1841, Voy. "Bonite," Poiss., p. 179, pl. 5.
*Awaous stamineus,* J. and E., p. 493.

### Ctenogobius tongarevae

*Glossogobius tongarevae* Fowler, 1927, B. P. Bishop Mus. Bull. 38, p. 28, fig. 4 (Tongareva).

### Bathygobius cotticeps

*Gobius cotticeps* Steindachner, 1880, Sitz. Akad. Wiss. Wien, vol. 80, p. 137, pl. 1 (Society Islands).
*Chlamydes laticeps* Jenkins, 1903, Bull. U. S. Fish Comm., vol. 22, p. 503; J. and E., p. 486, fig. 214.

### Bathygobius fuscus

*Gobius fuscus* Rüppell, 1828, Atlas Reis. Nörd. Afrika, Fische, p. 137 (Red Sea).
*Gobius homocyanus* Vaillant and Sauvage, 1875, Rev. Mag. Zool., ser. 3, vol. 3, p. 280.
*Gobius sandvicensis* Günther, 1880, "Challenger" Repts., Zoology, Shore Fishes, vol. 1, pt. 6, p. 60.
*Mapo fuscus,* J. and E., p. 483, fig. 212.

### Zonogobius farcimen

*Gobiopterus farcimen* Jordan and Evermann, 1903, Bull. U. S. Fish Comm., vol. 22, p. 205; J. and E., p. 482, pl. 59.

### Quisquilius eugenius

*Quisquilius eugenius* Jordan and Evermann, 1903, Bull. U. S. Fish Comm., vol. 22, p. 203.
*Gobiomorphus eugenius,* J. and E., p. 483, pl. 57.

### Quisquilius limbatosquamis

*Quisquilius limbatosquamis* Gosline, 1959, Pacific Sci., vol. 13, p. 69, fig. 2.

### Quisquilius aureoviridis

*Quisquilius aureoviridis* Gosline, 1959, Pacific Sci., vol. 13, p. 68, fig. 1.

### Hazeus unisquamis

*Hazeus unisquamis* Gosline, 1959, Pacific Sci., vol. 13, p. 70, fig. 3.

### Opua nephodes

*Opua nephodes* E. K. Jordan, 1925, Proc. U. S. Nat. Mus., vol. 66, art. 33, p. 36, pl. 2.

### Gnatholepis anjerensis

*Gobius anjerensis* Bleeker, 1850, Nat. Tijd. Ned. Ind., vol. 1, p. 251, fig. 11 (East Indies).

Gnatholepis knighti Jordan and Evermann, 1903, Bull. U. S. Fish Comm., vol. 22, p. 204; J. and E., p. 487, pl. 58.

### Fusigobius neophytus
Fusigobius neophytus Günther, 1877, Jour. Mus. Godeffroy, vol. 6, pt. 11, p. 174, pl. 108 (Carolines).

## KRAEMERIIDAE
### Kraemeria bryani
Kraemeria bryani Schultz, 1941, Jour. Washington Acad. Sci., vol. 31, p. 271, fig. 1; Rofen, 1958, Nat. Hist. Rennell Is., British Solomon Is., vol. 1, p. 183, pl. 4.

## CALLIONYMIDAE
### Pogonymus pogognathus
Pogonymus pogognathus Gosline, 1959, Pacific Sci., vol. 13, p. 72, fig. 4.

### Synchiropus rubrovinctus
Callionymus rubrovinctus Gilbert, p. 650, fig. 251.

### Callionymus decoratus
Callionymus decoratus Gilbert, p. 651, pl. 90.
Callionymus corallinus Gilbert, p. 649, fig. 251.
Calliurichthys astrinius Jordan and Jordan, Mem. Carnegie Mus., vol. 10, p. 80, pl. 4.
Calliurichthys zanectes Jordan and Jordan, Mem. Carnegie Mus., vol. 10, p. 81, pl. 4.

### Callionymus caeruleonotatus
Callionymus caeruleonotatus Gilbert, p. 648, pl. 89.

## DRACONETTIDAE
### Draconetta hawaiiensis
Draconetta hawaiiensis Gilbert, p. 652, pl. 91.

## SCHINDLERIIDAE
### Schindleria praematurus
Hemiramphus praematurus Schindler, 1930, Anz. Akad. Wiss. Wien, No. 9, p. 13.
Schindleria praematurus, Bruun, 1940, Dana-Rept. No. 21, pp. 1–12, figs. 1–6 (Tahiti, Samoa); Gosline 1959, Pacific Sci., vol. 13, p. 73.

### Schindleria pietschmanni
Hemiramphus pietschmanni Schindler, 1931, Anz. Akad. Wiss. Wien, No. 1, p. 15.
Schindleria pietschmanni, Bruun, 1940, Dana-Rept. No. 21, pp. 3–12 (South Pacific).

## TRIPTERYGIIDAE
### Tripterygion atriceps
Tripterygion atriceps Jenkins, 1903, Bull. U. S. Fish Comm., vol. 22, p. 505, fig. 46; Strasburg, 1956, Pacific Sci., vol. 10, p. 245.
Enneapterygius atriceps, J. and E., p. 496, fig. 219.

## BLENNIIDAE
### Exallias brevis
Salarias brevis Kner, 1868, Sitz. Akad. Wiss. Wien, vol. 58, p. 334, pl. 6 (Samoa).
Exallias brevis, J. and E., p. 503, fig. 224; Strasburg, 1956, Pacific Sci., vol. 10, p. 246.
Leoblennius schultzi Reid, 1943, Jour. Washington Acad. Sci., vol. 33, p. 382, fig. 3.

### Cirripectus obscurus
Exallias obscurus Borodin, 1927, American Mus. Novitates, No. 281, p. 1, fig.
Cirripectus obscurus, Strasburg, Pacific Sci., vol. 10, p. 247.

### Cirripectus lineopunctatus
Cirripectus lineopunctatus Strasburg, 1956, Pacific Sci., vol. 10, p. 248, fig. 1.

### Cirripectus variolosus
Salarias variolosus Valenciennes in Cuvier and Valenciennes, 1836, Hist. Nat. Poiss., vol. 11, p. 317 (Guam).
Alticus variolosus, J. and E., p. 497.
Ophioblennius vanderbilti Fowler, 1938, Acad. Nat. Sci. Philadelphia, Monograph 2, pp. 242, 300, figs. 26, 27.
Ophioblennius capillus Reid, 1943, Jour. Washington Acad. Sci., vol. 33, p. 380.
Cirripectus variolosus, Strasburg, 1956, Pacific Sci., vol. 10, p. 250.

### Entomacrodus marmoratus
Blennius marmoratus Bennett, 1828, Zool. Jour., vol. 4, p. 35.
Alticus marmoratus, J. and E., p. 498 but not fig. 220.
Entomacrodus marmoratus, Strasburg, 1956, Pacific Sci., vol. 10, p. 251, fig. 2.

### Istiblennius zebra
Salarias zebra Vaillant and Sauvage, 1875, Rev. Mag. Zool., ser. 3, vol. 3, p. 281; J. and E., p. 501, figs. 223 and 223a.
Salarias cypho Jenkins, 1903, Bull. U. S. Fish Comm., vol. 22, p. 506, fig. 47.
Istiblennius zebra, Strasburg, 1956, Pacific Sci., vol. 10, p. 253.

### Istiblennius gibbifrons
Salarias gibbifrons Quoy and Gaimard, 1824, Voy. "Uranie," Zool., p. 253.

*Salarias saltans* Jenkins, 1903, Bull. U. S. Fish Comm., vol. 22, p. 508, fig. 48.
*Salarias rutilus* Jenkins, 1903, Bull. U. S. Fish Comm., vol. 22, p. 509, fig. 49.
*Alticus gibbifrons,* J. and E., p. 499, figs. 221, 221a.
*Blenniella rhessodon* Reid, 1943, Jour. Washington Acad. Sci., vol. 33, p. 383, fig. 4.
*Istiblennius gibbifrons,* Strasburg, 1956, Pacific Sci., vol. 10, p. 254.

### Ecsenius hawaiiensis

*Ecsenius hawaiiensis* Chapman and Schultz, 1952, Proc. U. S. Nat. Mus., vol. 102, p. 526; Strasburg, 1956, Pacific Sci., vol. 10, p. 255.

### Enchelyurus brunneolus

*Aspidontus brunneolus* Jenkins, 1903, Bull. U. S. Fish Comm., vol. 22, p. 510, fig. 50.
*Enchelyurus ater,* J. and E., p. 500, fig. 222.
*Enchelyurus edmondsoni* Fowler, 1923, Occ. Pap. B. P. Bishop Mus., vol. 10, p. 389.
*Enchelyurus brunneolus,* Strasburg, 1956, Pacific Sci., vol. 10, p. 256.

### Omobranchus elongatus

*Petroscirtes elongatus* Peters, 1855, Archiv für Naturges., 21 Jahrg., vol. 1, p. 249 (Mossambique).
*Omobranchus elongatus,* Strasburg, 1956, Pacific Sci., vol. 10, p. 257, fig. 3.

### Runula ewaensis

*Petroscirtes ewaensis* Brock, 1948, Pacific Sci., vol. 2, p. 125.
*Runula ewaensis,* Strasburg, 1956, Pacific Sci., vol. 10, p. 259.

### Runula goslinei

*Runula goslinei* Strasburg, 1956, Pacific Sci., vol. 10, p. 260, fig. 4.

### BROTULIDAE

### Brotula multibarbata

*Brotula multibarbata* Temminck and Schlegel, 1846, Fauna Japonica, Poiss., pp. 251–253, pl. 111 (Japan); Hubbs, 1944, Copeia, pp. 170–175 (various localities including Hawaii); Gosline, 1953, Copeia, p. 217, figs. 1a, 2a, 5a.
*Brotula multicirrata* Vaillant and Sauvage, 1875, Rev. Mag. Zool., ser. 3, vol. 3, p. 282; J. and E., p. 508.
*Brotula marginalis* Jenkins, 1901, Bull. U. S. Fish Comm., vol. 19, p. 403, fig. 16.

### Brotula townsendi

*Brotula townsendi* Fowler, 1900, Proc. Acad. Nat. Sci. Philadelphia, p. 518, fig. 20; Gosline, 1953, Copeia, p. 218, fig. 1b.

### Microbrotula nigra

*Microbrotula nigra* Gosline, 1953, Copeia, p. 220, fig. 1d.

### Microbrotula rubra

*Microbrotula rubra* Gosline, 1953, Copeia, p. 219, figs. 1c, 4, 5b.

### Cataetyx hawaiiensis

*Cataetyx hawaiiensis* Gosline, 1954, Pacific Sci., vol. 8, p. 76, figs. 1g, 2c, 3c.

### Volcanus lineatus

*Volcanus lineatus* Gosline, 1954, Pacific Sci., vol. 8, p. 79, figs. 2d, 3d.

### Pycnocraspedum armatum

*Pycnocraspedum armatum* Gosline, 1954, Pacific Sci., vol. 8, p. 80, figs. 2e, 3e.

### CARAPIDAE

### Snyderidia canina

*Snyderidia canina* Gilbert, p. 655, pl. 92.

### Encheliophis gracilis

*Oxybeles gracilis* Bleeker, 1856, Nat. Tijd. Ned. Ind., vol. 11, p. 105 (East Indies).
*Fierasfer umbratilis* Jordan and Evermann, 1903, Bull. U. S. Fish Comm., vol. 22, p. 206; J. and E., p. 505, pl. 61.
*Jordanicus umbratilis,* Gilbert, p. 656.
*Encheliophis (Jordanicus) gracilis,* Arnold, 1956, Bull. British Mus., Zool., vol. 4, p. 299, fig. 20 (various localities).

### Carapus margaritiferae

*Fierasfer margaritiferae* Rendahl, 1921, Kungl. Vet. Akad. Handl., vol. 61, no. 9, p. 5 (Australia).
*Carapus (Onuxodon) margaritiferae,* Arnold, 1956, Bull. British Mus., Zool., vol. 4, p. 285, fig. 15 (Australia, East Indies).

### Carapus homei

*Oxybeles homei* Richardson, 1844, Ichthyol., Voy. "Erebus" and "Terror," p. 73 (Timor?).
*Fierasfer microdon* Gilbert, p. 655, fig. 254.
*Carapus homei* Arnold, 1956, Bull. British Mus., Zool., vol. 4, p. 273, fig. 11 (various localities).

### NOMEIDAE

### Nomeus gronovii

*Gobius gronovii* Gmelin, 1789, Systema Naturae, p. 1205 (American seas).
*Nomeus gronovii,* Fowler, 1928, p. 138.

## Psenes arafurensis

*Psenes arafurensis* Günther, 1888, "Challenger" Repts., vol. 40, p. 13, pl. 2 (Arafura Sea); Fowler, 1928, p. 139, fig. 33.

## Ariomma evermanni

*Ariomma evermanni* Jordan and Snyder, 1907, Bull. Bur. Fish., vol. 26, p. 209, fig. 1.
*Cubiceps thompsoni* Fowler, 1923, Occ. Pap. B. P. Bishop Mus., vol. 8, p. 378; Fowler, 1928, p. 138, fig. 32.

## Ariomma lurida

*Ariomma lurida* Jordan and Snyder, 1904, Proc. U. S. Nat. Mus., vol. 27, p. 943; J. and E., p. 217, pl. 37.

## TETRAGONURIDAE

### Tetragonurus cuvieri

*Tetragonurus cuvieri* Risso, 1810, Ichthyol. Nice, p. 347, pl. 10, fig. 37 (Mediterranean); Fowler, 1928, p. 140; Grey, 1955, Dana-Rept. No. 41, p. 30 (various localities).

## SCORPAENIDAE

### Taenianotus triacanthus

*Taenianotus triacanthus* Lacépède, 1802, Hist. Nat. Poiss., vol. 4, pp. 303, 306 (no locality).
*Taenianotus garretti* Günther, 1874, Jour. Mus. Godeffroy, vols. 2–3, pts. 5–6, p. 83, pl. 57.
*Taenianotus citrinellus* Gilbert, p. 636, pl. 81.

### Pterois sphex

*Pterois sphex* Jordan and Evermann, 1903, Bull. U. S. Fish Comm., vol. 22, p. 201; J. and E., p. 464, fig. 203.

### Dendrochirus brachypterus

*Pterois brachyptera* Cuvier in Cuvier and Valenciennes, 1829, Hist. Nat. Poiss., vol. 4, p. 270 (no locality).
*Pterois barberi* Steindachner, 1901, Denkschr. Akad. Wiss. Wien, vol. 70, pl. 3.
*Dendrochirus hudsoni* Jordan and Evermann, 1903, Bull. U. S. Fish Comm., vol. 22, p. 202.
*Dendrochirus chloreus* Jenkins, 1903, Bull. U. S. Fish Comm., vol. 22, p. 498, fig. 41; J. and E., p. 465, fig. 204.
*Dendrochirus barberi,* J. and E., p. 465, col. pl. 73.

### Peloropsis xenops

*Peloropsis xenops* Gilbert, p. 630, fig. 245.

## Iracundus signifer

*Iracundus signifer* Jordan and Evermann, 1903, Bull. U. S. Fish Comm., vol. 22, p. 210; J. and E., p. 470, fig. 207.

### Scorpaenodes guamensis

*Scorpaena guamensis* Quoy and Gaimard, 1824, Voy. "Uranie," Zool., p. 326 (Guam).

### Scorpaenodes parvipinnis

*Scorpaena parvipinnis* Garrett, 1863, Proc. California Acad. Sci., p. 105.
*Sebastopsis kelloggi* Jenkins, 1903, Bull. U. S. Fish Comm., p. 492, fig. 37; J. and E., p. 462, fig. 202.
*Sebastopsis parvipinnis,* J. and E., p. 463.

### Scorpaenopsis gibbosa

*Scorpaena gibbosa* Bloch and Schneider, 1801, Syst. Ichthy., p. 192, pl. 44 ("America").
*Scorpaenopsis catocala* Jordan and Evermann, 1903, Bull. U. S. Fish Comm., vol. 22, p. 201.
*Scorpaenopsis gibbosa,* J. and E., p. 468, pl. 56 and fig. 206.

### Scorpaenopsis cacopsis

*Scorpaenopsis cacopsis* Jenkins, 1901, Bull. U. S. Fish Comm., vol. 19, p. 401, figs. 13, 14; J. and E., p. 467, col. pl. 71 and figs. 205, 205a.

### Setarches remiger

*Scorpaena remigera* Gilbert and Cramer, 1897, Proc. U. S. Nat. Mus., vol. 19, p. 418, pl. 11.
*Setarches remiger,* Gilbert, p. 634.

### Plectrogenium nanum

*Plectrogenium nanum* Gilbert, p. 634, fig. 248.

### Merinthe macrocephala

*Sebastes macrocephalus* Sauvage, 1882, Bull. Soc. Philos., ser. 7, vol. 6, p. 169.
*Merinthe macrocephala,* J. and E., p. 461, pl. 55.

### Scorpaena coniorta

*Sebastapistes coniorta* Jenkins, 1903, Bull. U. S. Fish Comm., vol. 22, p. 495, fig. 39; J. and E., p. 458, fig. 200.
*Scorpaena coniorta,* Gosline, 1955, Pacific Sci., vol. 9, p. 461.

### Scorpaena coloratus

*Sebastapistes coloratus* Gilbert, p. 627, fig. 243.

### Scorpaena ballieui

*Scorpaena ballieui* Sauvage, 1875, Rev. Mag. Zool., ser. 3, vol. 3, p. 278; Gosline, 1955, Pacific Sci., vol. 9, p. 461.

*Sebastapistes corallicola* Jenkins, 1903, Bull. U. S. Fish Comm., vol. 22, p. 493, fig. 38; J. and E., p. 456, fig. 199.
*Sebastapistes galactacma* Jenkins, 1903, Bull. U. S. Fish Comm., vol. 22, p. 496, fig. 40; J. and E., p. 459, fig. 201.
*Sebastapistes ballieui,* J. and E., p. 455, col. pl. 72.
?*Scorpaenodes fowleri* Pietschmann, 1938, B. P. Bishop Mus. Bull. 156, p. 30, pl. 9.

### Scorpaenopsis altirostris

*Scorpaenopsis altirostris* Gilbert, p. 628, fig. 244.

### Helicolenus rufescens

*Helicolenus rufescens* Gilbert, p. 631, fig. 246.

### Pontinus spilistius

*Pontinus spilistius* Gilbert, p. 633, fig. 247.

## PERISTEDIIDAE

### Peristedion hians

*Peristedion hians* Gilbert and Cramer, 1897, Proc. U. S. Nat. Mus., vol. 19, p. 419, pl. 41; Gilbert, p. 638.

### Peristedion engyceros

*Peristedion engyceros* Günther, 1871, Proc. Zool. Soc. London, p. 663; Gilbert, p. 639; Fowler, 1928, p. 302, pl. 36.
*Peristedion gilberti* Jordan, 1922, Proc. U. S. Nat. Mus., vol. 59, p. 655, fig. 8.

## CARACANTHIDAE

### Caracanthus maculatus

*Micropus maculatus* Gray, 1831, Zool. Miscell., p. 20 (Tuamotus).
*Caracanthus maculatus,* J. and E., p. 453, fig. 198.

### Caracanthus unipinna

*Micropus unipinna* Gray, 1831, Zool. Miscell., p. 20 (Pacific).
*Caracanthus unipinna,* J. and E., p. 454.

## PLATYCEPHALIDAE

### Bembradium roseum

*Bembradium roseum* Gilbert, p. 637, pl. 82.

## HOPLICHTHYIDAE

### Hoplichthys citrinus

*Hoplichthys citrinus* Gilbert, p. 640, fig. 249.

### Hoplichthys platophrys

*Hoplichthys platophrys* Gilbert, p. 642, fig. 250.

## DACTYLOPTERIDAE

### Dactyloptena orientalis

*Dactylopterus orientalis* Cuvier and Valenciennes, 1829, Hist. Nat. Poiss., vol. 4, p. 134, pl. 76 (Indian Ocean).
*Cephalacanthus orientalis,* J. and E., p. 473, fig. 208.

## PEGASIDAE

### Pegasus papilio

*Pegasus papilio* Gilbert, p. 614, fig. 239.

## ECHENEIDAE

### Remora remora

*Echeneis remora* Linnaeus, 1758, Systema Naturae, Ed. X, p. 261 (Indian archipelago); J. and E., p. 494.
*Echeneis albescens,* J. and E., p. 494.
*Remora remora,* Maul, 1956, Boletim do Museu Municipal do Funchal, No. 9, p. 45, fig. 2b (Madeira).

## BALISTIDAE

### Canthidermis maculatus

*Balistes maculatus* Bloch, 1786, Naturges. Ausl. Fische, pt. 2, p. 25, pl. 151 (American waters).
*Canthidermis angulosus* Quoy and Gaimard, 1824, Voy. "Uranie," Zoology, p. 210; J. and E., p. 415.
*Canthidermis aureolus,* J. and E., p. 415.
*Canthidermis maculatus,* Clark, 1949, American Mus. Novitates, No. 1397, pp. 3, 9, fig.

### Xanthichthys ringens

*Balistes ringens* Linnaeus, 1758, Systema Naturae, Ed. X, p. 329 (no locality).
*Xanthichthys lineopunctatus,* J. and E., p. 416, fig. 182.
*Xanthichthys ringens,* Clark, 1949, American Mus. Novitates, No. 1397, p. 10, fig.

### Rhinecanthus rectangulus

*Balistes rectangulus* Bloch and Schneider, 1801, Syst. Ichthy., p. 465 (Indian Ocean).
*Balistapus rectangulus,* J. and E., p. 413, col. pl. 43.
*Rhinecanthus rectangulus,* Fraser-Brunner, 1935, Ann. Mag. Nat. Hist., ser. 10, vol. 15, p. 662 (generic allocation).

### Rhinecanthus aculeatus

*Balistes aculeatus* Linnaeus, 1758, Systema Naturae, Ed. X, p. 328 (India).
*Balistapus aculeatus,* J. and E., p. 414, col. pl. 42.
*Rhinecanthus aculeatus,* Fraser-Brunner, 1935, Ann. Mag. Nat. Hist., ser. 10, vol. 15, p. 662 (generic allocation).

## Melichthys buniva

*Balistes buniva* Lacépède, 1803, Hist. Nat. Poiss., vol. 5, pp. 668, 669, pl. 21 (no locality).

*Balistes fuscolineatus* Seale, 1901, Occ. Pap. B. P. Bishop Mus., vol. 1, no. 4, p. 9, fig. 4; J. and E., p. 409.

*Melichthys radula,* J. and E., p. 417, col. pl. 44.

*Melichthys buniva,* Clark, 1949, American Mus. Novitates, No. 1397, p. 9, fig.

## Melichthys vidua

*Balistes vidua* Solander in Richardson, 1843, Voy. "Sulphur," Fishes, p. 128, pl. 59 (Tahiti); J. and E., p. 409, pl. 41.

*Melichthys vidua,* Fraser-Brunner, 1935, Ann. Mag. Nat. Hist., ser. 10, vol. 15, p. 662 (generic allocation).

## Balistes nycteris

*Pachynathus nycteris* Jordan and Evermann, 1903, Bull. U. S. Fish Comm., vol. 22, p. 199.

*Balistes nycteris,* J. and E., p. 408, fig. 179.

## Balistes fuscus

*Balistes fuscus* Bloch and Schneider, 1801, Syst. Ichthy., p. 471 (no locality); Fowler, 1928, p. 451, pl. 45.

## Balistes bursa

*Balistes bursa* Bloch and Schneider, 1801, Syst. Ichthy., p. 476 (Indian Ocean); J. and E., p. 10, fig. 180.

## Balistes capistratus

*Balistes capistratus* Shaw, 1804, General Zoology, vol. 5, p. 417 (no locality); J. and E., p. 411, fig. 181.

## MONACANTHIDAE

### Alutera monoceros

*Balistes monoceros* Osbeck in Linnaeus, 1758, Systema Naturae, Ed. X, p. 327 (China).

*Alutera monoceros,* J. and E., p. 423, fig. 185.

### Alutera scripta

*Balistes monoceros scriptus* Gmelin, 1788, Systema Naturae, p. 1463 (China).

*Osbeckia scripta,* J. and E., p. 422, fig. 184.

*Alutera scripta,* Fraser-Brunner, 1941, Ann. Mag. Nat. Hist., ser. 11, vol. 8, p. 187 (generic allocation).

### Pervagor spilosoma

*Monacanthus spilosoma* Lay and Bennett, 1839, Zool. Beechey's Voy., p. 70, pl. 22.

*Stephanolepis pricei* Snyder, 1904, Bull. U. S. Fish Comm., vol. 22, p. 534, pl. 12; J. and E., p. 421, pl. 48.

*Stephanolepis spilosomus,* J. and E., p. 420, col. pl. 40.

*Pervagor spilosoma,* Fraser-Brunner, 1941, Ann. Mag. Nat. Hist., ser. 11, vol. 8, p. 183 (generic allocation).

### Pervagor melanocephalus

*Monacanthus melanocephalus* Bleeker, 1853, Nat. Tijd. Ned. Ind., vol. 5, p. 95 (East Indies).

*Pervagor melanocephalus,* Fraser-Brunner, 1941, Ann. Mag. Nat. Hist., ser. 11, vol. 8, p. 183 (generic allocation).

### Amanses albopunctatus

*Monocanthus albopunctatus* Seale, 1901, Occ. Pap. B. P. Bishop Mus., vol. 1, no. 4, p. 13, fig. 6.

*Cantherines albopunctatus,* J. and E., p. 420.

### Amanses carolae

*Cantherines carolae* Jordan and McGregor, in Jordan and Evermann, 1898, Fishes North and Middle America, vol. 2, p. 1713 (Socorro Island).

*Cantherines sandwichiensis,* J. and E. (in part, not of Quoy and Gaimard), p. 418, fig. 183.

### Amanses sandwichiensis

*Balistes sandwichiensis* Quoy and Gaimard, 1824, Voy. "Uranie," Zool., p. 214.

*Cantherines sandwichiensis,* J. and E. (in part), p. 418.

### Amanses pardalis

*Monacanthus pardalis* Rüppell, 1855, Neue Wirbelthiere: Fische, p. 57, pl. 15 (Red Sea).

*Cantherines verecundus* E. K. Jordan, 1925, Proc. U. S. Nat. Mus., vol. 66, p.

## OSTRACIONTIDAE

### Aracana aculeata

*Ostracion aculeatus* Houttuyn, 1782, Holl. Maatsch. Wet. Haarl., Verh., vol. 20, p. 346 (Japan).

*Aracana spilonota* Gilbert, p. 626, fig. 242.

### Ostracion lentiginosus

*Ostracion lentiginosus* Bloch and Schneider, 1801, Syst. Ichthy., p. 501 (Ile de France); Fraser-Brunner, 1940, Ann. Mag. Nat. Hist., ser. 11, vol. 6, p. 392 (on sexual dimorphism); Brock, 1956, Copeia, p. 195 (on poisonous exudations).

*Ostracion camurum* Jenkins, 1901, Bull. U. S. Fish Comm., vol. 19, p. 396, fig. 9.

*Ostracion oahuensis* Jordan and Evermann, 1903, Bull. U. S. Fish Comm., vol. 22, p. 200; J. and E., p. 443, pl. 51.

*Ostracion sebae,* J. and E., p. 442, fig. 195.
*Ostracion lentiginosum,* J. and E., p. 443.

### Ostracion solorensis

*Ostracion solorensis* Bleeker, 1853, Nat. Tijd. Ned. Ind., vol. 5, p. 96 (East Indies); Fowler, 1928, p. 462.

### Lactoria fornasini

*Ostracion fornasini* Bianconi, 1846, Nuovi Ann. Soc. Nat. Bologna, ser. 2, vol. 5, p. 115 (Mozambique).
*Lactoria galeodon* Jenkins, 1903, Bull. U. S. Fish Comm., vol. 22, p. 487, fig. 34; J. and E., p. 445, fig. 196.

### Lactoria diaphanus

*Ostracion diaphanus* Bloch and Schneider, 1801, Syst. Ichthy., p. 501 (no locality).
*Lactoria schlemmeri* Jordan and Snyder, 1904, Proc. U. S. Nat. Mus., vol. 27, p. 945; J. and E., p. 444, pls. 52, 53.

### TETRAODONTIDAE

#### Sphoeroides cutaneus

*Tetrodon cutaneus* Günther, 1871, Cat. Fishes British Mus., vol. 8, p. 287 (St. Helena).
*Liosaccus cutaneus,* Fowler, 1928, p. 468.

#### Lagocephalus lagocephalus

*Tetraodon lagocephalus* Linnaeus, 1758, Systema Naturae, Ed. X, p. 332 (India).
*Tetraodon janthinus* Vaillant and Sauvage, 1875, Rev. Mag. Zool., ser. 3, vol. 3, p. 268.
*Lagocephalus oceanicus* Jordan and Evermann, 1903, Bull. U. S. Fish Comm., vol. 22, p. 199; J. and E., p. 425, pl. 49.
*Canthigaster janthinus,* J. and E., p. 434.

#### Lagocephalus hypselogeneion

*Tetraodon hypselogeneion* Bleeker, 1852, Nat. Tijd. Ned. Ind., vol. 3, p. 300 (East Indies).
*Tetrodon florealis* Cope, 1871, Trans. American Philos. Soc., vol. 14, p. 479.
*Spheroides florealis,* J. and E., p. 426.

#### Arothron meleagris

*Tetrodon meleagris* Bloch and Schneider, 1801, Syst. Ichthy., p. 507 (Asia).
*Tetrodon lacrymatus* Quoy and Gaimard, 1824, Voy. "Uranie," Zool., p. 204.
*Ovoides latifrons* Jenkins, 1901, Bull. U. S. Fish Comm., vol. 19, p. 398, fig. 10.
*Tetraodon lacrymatus,* J. and E., p. 429, fig. 186.

### Arothron hispidus

*Tetraodon hispidus* Linnaeus, 1758, Systema Naturae, Ed. X, p. 333 (India); J. and E., p. 427, pl. 46.

### CANTHIGASTERIDAE

#### Canthigaster cinctus

*Canthigaster cinctus* Solander in Richardson, 1850, Zool. Voy. "Samarang," pp. 19, 20 (Tahiti); J. and E., p. 433, fig. 189.

#### Canthigaster jactator

*Tropidichthys jactator* Jenkins, 1901, Bull. U. S. Fish Comm., vol. 19, p. 399, fig. 1.
*Canthigaster jactator,* J. and E., p. 430, fig. 187.

#### Canthigaster amboinensis

*Canthigaster amboinensis* Bleeker, 1865, Ned. Tijd. Dierk., vol. 2, p. 180 (East Indies).
*Tropidichthys psegma* Jordan and Evermann, 1903, Bull. U. S. Fish Comm., vol. 22, p. 209.
*Tropidichthys oahuensis* Jenkins, 1903, Bull. U. S. Fish Comm., vol. 22, p. 485, fig. 32.
*Canthigaster oahuensis,* J. and E., p. 432, fig. 188.
*Canthigaster psegma,* J. and E., p. 433, pl. 50.
*Canthigaster polyophthalmus* Pietschmann, 1938, B. P. Bishop Mus. Bull. 156, p. 51, pl. 1.

#### Canthigaster rivulatus

*Tetraodon rivulatus* Schlegel, 1850, Fauna Japonica, Poiss., p. 285, pl. 124 (Japan).
*Eumycterus bitaeniatus* Jenkins, 1901, Bull. U. S. Fish Comm., vol. 19, p. 400, fig. 12.
*Tropidichthys epilamprus* Jenkins, 1903, Bull. U. S. Fish Comm., vol. 22, p. 485, fig. 33.
*Canthigaster epilamprus,* J. and E., p. 434, fig. 190.
*Canthigaster bitaeniatus,* J. and E., p. 435, fig. 191.
*Canthigaster notospilus* Fowler, 1941, Proc. Acad. Nat. Sci. Philadelphia, vol. 93, p. 278, fig. 31.

### DIODONTIDAE

#### Chilomycterus affinis

*Chilomycterus affinis* Günther, 1870, Cat. Fishes British Mus., vol. 8, p. 314 (no locality); J. and E., p. 438.

## Diodon hystrix

*Diodon hystrix* Linnaeus, 1758, Systema Naturae, Ed. X, p. 335 (India); J. and E., p. 437, fig. 192.

*Diodon nudifrons* Jenkins, 1903, Bull. U. S. Fish Comm., vol. 22, p. 488, fig. 35; J. and E., p. 438, fig. 193.

## Diodon holocanthus

*Diodon holocanthus* Linnaeus, 1758, Systema Naturae, Ed. X, p. 335 (India); J. and E., p. 436.

## MOLIDAE

### Ranzania laevis

*Ostracion laevis* Pennant, 1776, British Zool., Ed. IV, vol. 3, p. 129, pl. 19 (England).

*Ranzania makua* Jenkins, 1895, Proc. California Acad. Sci., ser. 2, vol. 5, pp. 780, 784, col. pl.; J. and E., p. 440, fig. 194.

*Ranzania laevis,* Fraser-Brunner, 1951, Bull. British Mus. Nat. Hist., Zool., vol. 1, p. 95, figs. 3–5 (various localities).

### Masturus lanceolatus

*Orthagoriscus lanceolatus* Liénard, 1840, Rev. Zool., p. 291 (Mauritius).

*Masturus lanceolatus,* Fowler, 1928, p. 474, fig. 80 (adult); King, 1951, Pacific Sci., p. 108, fig. 1 (juveniles); Fraser-Brunner, 1951, Bull. British Mus. Nat. Hist., Zool., vol. 1, p. 107, fig. 10 (various localities).

### Mola mola

*Tetraodon mola* Linnaeus, 1758, Systema Naturae, Ed. X, p. 334 (Mediterranean).

*Mola mola,* Fraser-Brunner, 1951, Bull. British Mus. Nat. Hist., Zool., vol. 1, p. 113, figs. 15–18 (various localities).

## LOPHIIDAE

### Lophiomus miacanthus

*Lophiomus miacanthus* Gilbert, p. 691, fig. 273.

## ANTENNARIIDAE

### Abantennarius analis

*Abantennarius analis* Gosline, in Schultz, 1957, Proc. U. S. Nat. Mus., vol. 107, p. 67, fig. 2.

### Abantennarius duescus

*Antennarius duescus* Snyder, 1904, Bull. U. S. Fish Comm., vol. 22, p. 537, pl. 13; J. and E., p. 522, pl. 65.

*Abantennarius duescus,* Schultz, 1957, Proc. U. S. Nat. Mus., vol. 107, p. 66, pl. 2.

### Phrynelox cunninghami

*Antennarius cunninghami* Fowler, 1941, Proc. Acad. Nat. Sci. Philadelphia, vol. 93, p. 279, fig. 32.

*Phrynelox cunninghami,* Schultz, 1957, Proc. U. S. Nat. Mus., vol. 107, p. 74, pl. 5.

### Antennarius moluccensis

*Antennarius moluccensis* Bleeker, 1855, Nat. Tijd. Ned. Ind., vol. 8, p. 414 (Amboina); Schultz, 1957, Proc. U. S. Nat. Mus., vol. 107, p. 91, pl. 9.

### Antennarius chironectes

*Antennarius chironectes* Lacépède, 1798, Hist. Nat. Poiss., vol. 1, p. 325, pl. 14 (no locality); Schultz, 1957, Proc. U. S. Nat. Mus., vol. 107, p. 93, pl. 10.

*Lophius sandvicensis* Bennett, 1840, Narr. Whaling Voy., vol. 2, p. 258, fig.; J. and E., p. 518.

*Chironectes rubrofuscus* Garrett, 1864, Proc. California Acad. Sci., vol. 3, p. 64.

*Chironectes niger* Garrett, 1864, Proc. California Acad. Sci., vol. 3, p. 107.

*Antennarius laysanius* Jordan and Snyder, 1904, Proc. U. S. Nat. Mus., vol. 27, p. 947; J. and E., p. 520, pl. 63.

*Antennarius leprosus,* J. and E., p. 519, fig. 228.

*Antennarius commersonii,* J. and E., p. 518.

### Antennarius drombus

*Antennarius drombus* Jordan and Evermann, 1903, Bull. U. S. Fish Comm., vol. 22, p. 207; J. and E., p. 521, pl. 64.

*Antennarius nexilis* Snyder, 1904, Bull. U. S. Fish Comm., vol. 22, p. 537, pl. 13; J. and E., p. 523, pl. 65.

### Antennatus bigibbus

*Antennatus bigibbus* Lacépède, 1798, Hist. Nat. Poiss., vol. 1, p. 325, pl. 14 (no locality); J. and E., p. 520.

*Chironectes leprosus* Eydoux and Souleyet, 1842, Voy. "Bonite," Zool., vol. 1, p. 187, pl. 5.

*Antennatus bigibbus,* Schultz, 1957, Proc. U. S. Nat. Mus., vol. 107, p. 80 (various localities).

## CHAUNACIDAE

### Chaunax umbrinus

*Chaunax umbrinus* Gilbert, p. 693, fig. 274.

## OGCOCEPHALIDAE

### Malthopsis mitrigera

*Malthopsis mitrigera* Gilbert and Cramer, 1897, Proc. U. S. Nat. Mus., vol. 19,

p. 434, pl. 48; J. and E., p. 524, fig. 229; Gilbert, p. 695.

### Malthopsis jordani

Malthopsis jordani Gilbert, p. 695, pl. 100.

### Halieutaea retifera

Halieutaea retifera Gilbert, p. 696, pl. 101.

### Dibranchus erythrinus

Dibranchus erythrinus Gilbert, p. 697, fig. 275.

### Dibranchus stellulatus

Dibranchus stellulatus Gilbert, p. 698, fig. 276.

## CERATIIDAE

### Ceratias holboelli

Ceratias holboelli Kröyer, 1844, Naturh. Tidsskr., vol. 1, p. 639 (Greenland); Bertelsen, 1951, Dana-Rept. No. 39, p. 133, figs. 90–92 (various localities).

Myopsarus myops Gilbert, p. 694, pl. 99.

# *Index*

## A

**348**

**349**

**352**

**355**

**356**

potteri, Centropyge, 197, 329
  Holacanthus, 329
poweriae, Gonostomus, 311
  Vinciguerria, 311
praematurus, Hemiramphus, 339
  Schindleria, 273, 339
  Pranesus insularum, 153, 323
premaxillary, 29
preorbital, 29
preorbitalis, Paeudupeneus, 328
  Upeneus, 328
preopercle, 29
pretiosus, Ruvettus, 253, 335
Priacanthidae, 76, 159, 324
Priacanthus alalaua, 160, 325
  boops, 160, 324
  cruentatus, 160, 324
  helvolus, 325
  meeki, 161, 325
pricei, Stephanolepis, 343
Priodon annulatus, 335
  hexacanthus, 335
Priodonophis moluccensis, 315
Prionace glauca, 90, 309
pristilepis, Dasyscopelus, 313
Pristipomoides microlepis, 186, 327
  sieboldii, 185, 186, 327
proboscidea, Halosauropsis, 318
Prognichthys albimaculatus, 318
  gilberti, 131, 318
prometheus, Gempylus, 336
  Promethichthys, 253, 336
Promethichthys prometheus, 253, 336
Promyllantor alcocki, 120, 316
propinquus, Lionurus, 320
  Macrourus, 320
proridens, Chlorophthalmus, 312
prorigera, Chascanopsetta, 149, 322
psalion, Echidna, 315
psegma, Canthigaster, 344
  Tropidichthys, 344
Psenes arafurensis, 282, 341
Pseudamiops gracilicauda, 162, 325
Pseudanthias kelloggi, 157, 324
pseudobranch, 32
Pseudocheilinus evanidus, 221, 331
  octotaenia, 221, 331
  tetrataenia, 221, 331
Pseudochromidae, 71, 158, 324
Pseudochromis polyacanthus, 324
Pseudogramma polyacantha, 158, 324
Pseudojulis cerasinus, 333
Pseudojuloides cerasinus, 230, 333
Pseudupeneus bifasciatus, 328
  chryserydros, 328
  chrysonemus, 328
  crassilabrus, 328
  pleurostigma, 328
  multifasciatus, 328
  porphyreus, 328
  preorbitalis, 328
Ptenonotus melanogeneion, 318
Pteraclis velifer, 180, 327

Pteranthias longimanus, 156, 324
Pterois barberi, 341
  brachyptera, 341
  sphex, 285, 341
Pterolamiops longimanus, 90, 309
Pteropsaron incisum, 239, 334
pterostigma, Parapercis, 334
pualu, 249
puffer, sharpbacked, 300
  spiny, 302
puhi, 102
puhi-kauhila, 110
puhiki'i, 131
puhi-laumilo, 117
puhi-oa, 110
puhi-paka, 114
puhi-uha, 120
pulcherrima, Julis, 333
punctatissimus, Holocentrus, 321
punctatofasciatus, Chaetodon, 330
purpurascens, Seriola, 325
purpurescens, Chimaera, 310
  Hydrolagus, 310
purpureum, Thalassoma, 227, 332
purpureus, Scarus, 332
  Stolephorus, 96, 311
pu'u-ola'i, 301
Pycnocraspedum armatum, 340
pyrrovinctum, Thalassoma, 332

Q

quadrimaculatus, Chaetodon, 202, 329
quernus, Epinephelus, 157, 324
quinquevittata, Thalassoma, 227, 332
quinquevittatus, Scarus, 332
Quisquilius aureoviridis, 270, 338
  eugenius, 270, 338
  limbatosquamis, 270, 338

R

Rabula fuscomaculata, 107, 314
radula, Melichthys, 343
  Taeniopsetta, 149, 322
Raja narinari, 310
Ranzania laevis, 303, 345
  makua, 345
ray, eagle, 93
  manta, 93
rectangulus, Balistapus, 342
  Balistes, 342
  Rhinecanthus, 293, 342
regius, Lampris, 145, 322
  Zeus, 322
reinhardti, Hygophum, 312
  Lampanyctus, 313
  Nyctimaster, 313
Reinhardtii, Scopelus, 312
remedius, Hemicoris, 333
remiger, Setarches, 288, 341

**367**

woodi, *Novaculichthys*, 232, 333
wrasse, 213

## X

*xantherythrus, Holocentrus*, 143, 321
*Xanthichthys lineopunctatus*, 342
  *ringens*, 293, 342
*xanthopterus, Acanthurus*, 249, 335
  *Hepatus*, 335
*xanthostomus, Gymnothorax*, 315
*xenandrus, Engyprosopon*, 150, 323
Xenocongridae, 80, 117, 316
*xenodontus, Phyllophichthus*, 126, 317
*xenops, Peloropsis*, 286, 341
Xiphiidae, 85, 265, 337
*Xiphius gladius*, 265, 337
*Xyrichthys lecluse*, 331
  *microlepidotus*, 332
  *niveilatus*, 223, 332, 333
  *pavoninus*, 332

## Y

*yaito, Euthynnus*, 258, 336
yellowtail, 170

## Z

*zacalles, Thunnus*, 336
*Zalarges nimbarius*, 311
Zanclidae, 67, 241, 334
*Zanclus canescens*, 241, 334
  *ruthiae*, 334
*zanectes, Calliurichthys*, 339
zebra, 277
*zebra, Echidna*, 111, 314
  *Gymnothorax*, 314
  *Istiblennius*, 277, 339
  *Salarias*, 339
*Zebrasoma flavescens*, 250, 335
  *veliferum*, 250, 335
Zeidae, 54, 146, 322
*Zeus ciliaris*, 326
  *regius*, 322
*zonarcha, Scaridea*, 236
*zonata, Echidna*, 315
zonation, 9–16
*Zonogobius farcimen*, 270, 338
*zonophaea, Echidna*, 315
*zonurus, Cheilinus*, 331
*zoster, Chaetodon*, 329
  *Hemitaurichthys*, 198, 329
*Zygaena lewini*, 310
*zygaena, Sphyrna*, 310

**372**